About this book

In this, the first comprehensive study of the Sikh community in Britain, Gurharpal Singh and Darshan Singh Tatla look at how British-Sikh identity has developed from the nineteenth century to the present. At a time when much public debate centres on Muslim integration, this is a highly valuable alternative perspective on the challenges faced by another Asian community in becoming part of multicultural Britain.

Using a vast amount of new source material, the authors examine the complex Anglo-Sikh relationship that led to the initial Sikh settlement and the processes of community-building around Sikh institutions such as gurdwaras. They explore the nature of British Sikh society as reflected in the performance of Sikhs in the labour markets, the changing characteristics of the Sikh family and issues of cultural transmission to the young. The book also provides an original account of a community transformed from the site of radical immigrant class politics to a leader of the Sikh diaspora in its search for a separate Sikh state.

This is an indispensable guide for anyone interested in the evolution of contemporary British society.

About the authors

Gurharpal Singh is the Nadir Dinshaw Chair in Inter-Religious Relations in the Department of Theology and Religion at the University of Birmingham. He is also an editor of *Sikh Formations: Religion, Culture, Theory*.

Darshan Singh Tatla is a Research Associate in the Department of Theology and Religion at the University of Birmingham. His books include *The Sikh Diaspora: The Search for Statehood*.

Sikhs in Britain

The Making of a Community

Gurharpal Singh
&
Darshan Singh Tatla

Zed Books

LONDON & NEW YORK

501090426

Sikhs in Britain: The Making of a Community was first published in 2006 by
Zed Books Ltd, 7 Cynthia Street, London N1 9JF, UK and
Room 400, 175 Fifth Avenue, New York, NY 10010, USA.

www.zedbooks.co.uk

Cover designed by Andrew Corbett
Set in 10½/12 pt Bembo by Long House, Cumbria, UK
Printed and bound in Malta
by Gutenberg Press Ltd

Distributed in the USA exclusively by Palgrave Macmillan, a division of
St Martin's Press, LLC, 175 Fifth Avenue, New York, NY 10010.

A catalogue record for this book
is available from the British Library

US Cataloging-in-Publication Data
is available from the Library of Congress

ISBN 10: 1 84277 716 5 hb
ISBN 10: 1 84277 717 3 pb
ISBN 13: 978 1 84277 716 9 hb
ISBN 13: 978 1 84277 717 6 pb

Contents

List of Tables, Maps, Figures vi
Glossary and Abbreviations vii
Acknowledgements x
Preface xi

Introduction 1

One
The Sikhs of the Punjab 9

Two
Punjabi Society and Sikh Migration 26

Three
Settlement, Demography and Social Profile 43

Four
Gurdwaras and Community Building 69

Five
'Homeland Politics': Class, Identity and Party 94

Six
British Multiculturalism and Sikhs 126

Seven
Employment and Education 145

Eight
Family, Gender and Sexuality 165

Nine
Punjabi, *Bhangra* and Youth Identities 186

Conclusion 208

Notes 220
Bibliographical Note and Select Bibliography 255
Index 260

Tables, Maps & Figures

Tables

1.1	Punjab's Area and Population, 1941–2001	19
2.1	Global Sikh Population, 2005	32
3.1	Indian Immigration to the United Kingdom, 1956–66	51
3.2	Population of Great Britain by Religion, 2001	58
3.3	UK Sikhs by Country of Birth, 2001	58
3.4	Estimates of the Growth of the Sikh Population of Great Britain, 1951–2001	59
3.5	Sikh Population by Region, 2001	62
3.6	'Little Punjabs': Local Authorities with the Largest Sikh Concentrations, 2001	63
3.7	Social Profile of Sikhs in Britain, 2001	66
4.1	Gurdwaras in Britain, 1910–2001	76
4.2	Distribution of Gurdwaras in England and Wales by Region, 1997	76
4.3	Gurdwaras by Caste Identification, 2001	78
4.4	Sikh Sects' Places of Worship, 2003	79
4.5	Sants' Main Centres and Visiting Years	91
5.1	Sikhs in British Politics, 2005	123
7.1	League of Sikh Businesses in Britain, 2004	157
7.2	Sikhs' Educational Qualifications by Sex, 2003/4	158
7.3	Sikhs' Employment by Industry and Sex, 2003/4	161
9.1	Number of Students for Punjabi GCSE, AS and A Level Examinations, 1985–2004	188
9.2	British Punjabi Press, 1964–2005	191
9.3	Punjabi Magazines, 1962–2005	192
9.4	English-Language Periodicals on British Sikhs, 1960–2005	194

Maps

1.1	Pre-Independence Punjab, as Partitioned in 1947	16
1.2	Punjab after November 1966	22
3.1	Geographical Distribution of Sikhs in Britain, 2001	61

Figure

1.1	Modern Sikh Identity	18

Glossary & Abbreviations

Akal Takht	Sikhs' highest seat of temporal and religious authority
akhand path	The uninterrupted reading of *Guru Granth Sahib*
AKJ	Akhand Kirtan Jatha
amrit-dhari	A Sikh initiated into the Khalsa; a 'baptised' Sikh
ASR	Anandpur Sahib Resolution (1973) which calls for limiting the Indian Union's powers to defence, currency, communications and foreign affairs. It became the 'Magna Carter' of the Sikh autonomy campaign in Punjab in the 1980s.
barapind	Large village
behzti	Dishonour
bhangra	Traditional Punjabi folk music/popular music among Sikh and Asian youth
Bhatras	A Sikh sub-group; traditionally peddlers; among the earliest of British Sikh settlers
biradari	Extended kinship networks
BK	Babbar Khalsa
chamaras	Outcaste group traditionally associated with leather work; also know as Ravidasis and Dalits
CKD	Chief Khalsa Diwan
COK	Council of Khalistan
CPI	Communist Party of India
CPI(M)	Communist Party of India (Marxist). Formed in 1964 after the Sino-Soviet split
CPI(M-L)	Communist Party of India (Marxist-Leninist)
CRE	Commission for Racial Equality
CSGB	Council of Sikh Gurdwaras, Birmingham
Dalit	The 'oppressed' or 'broken'. Political movement of groups outside the traditional Hindu caste hierarchy. Formerly 'outcastes'/'untouchables'.
Darbar Sahib	The Golden Temple. Also referred to as the *Harimandir Sahib*.
DK	Dal Khalsa

dharma yud morcha	'The struggle for existence'. Political agitation started by SAD in Punjab in August 1982 for greater autonomy for Punjab
diwali	Festival of light
Doaba	A region of the central Punjab historically comprising the districts of Jalandhar, Kapurthala, Hoshiarpur (and now Nawashere)
GNPG	Guru Nanak Prakash Gurdwara, Coventry
GOI	Government of India
golak	'Money box'; offerings by the congregation
gurdwara	Sikh place of worship
gurpurabs	Birthdates of the Sikh Gurus
Guru Granth Sahib	Sikh holy scripture. Also referred to as *Adi Granth*.
GNNSJ	Guru Nanak Neshkam Sewak Jatha
illaqa	Locality
INC	Indian National Congress
IOC	Indian Overseas Congress
IWA	Indian Workers' Associations
ISYF	International Sikh Youth Federation
Jat	Sikh agriculturalists caste; comprises almost two-thirds of the community
kesh-dhari	A Sikh who keeps uncut hair
Khalsa	Collective Sikh society; especially *amrit-dhari* Sikhs
kirpan	A sword. One of the Five Ks
KJBI	Khalsa Jatha British Isles
khatri	Urban, mercantile Sikh caste
langar	Communal kitchen attached to a gurdwara
misl	Eighteenth-century Sikh organisation of armed warriors
mona-Sikh	Shaven Sikh
Namdahri	A Sikh sect whose members believe in a living guru
Narankari	A reformist sect which operates on the boundaries of mainstream Sikhism
panth	Literally the path; the Sikh community
pendus	Villagers. Often used derogatively to refer to fresh migrants from Punjab.
Radhaswami	A reformist sect which operates at the boundaries of mainstream Sikhism; has considerable appeal among Sikhs
rahit maryada	Sikh code of conduct
Ramgharia	Sikh caste traditionally engaged in woodwork and construction

Ravidasi	Formerly categorised as untouchables within the Hindu caste hierarchy; now also referred to as Adi–Dharmis, Scheduled Castes and Dalits.
SAD	Shiromani Akali Dal – the main Sikh political party in Punjab since 1925
sangat	Congregation
Sant	Spiritual and political leader
SBS	Southall Black Sisters
sahaj-dhari	'Slow learner'; non-*kesh-dhari* Sikh
SGPC	Shiromani Gurdwara Prabandak Committee. Committee for managing Sikh places of worship often referred to as the 'Sikh Parliament'
SGSSGS	Sri Guru Singh Sabha Gurdwara, Southall
SGSSS	Sri Guru Singh Sabha, Southall
SF (UK)	Sikh Federation (United Kingdom)
Valmiki	A Punjabi low-caste group that operates at the cultural and religious boundaries of mainstream Sikhism
vaisakhi	The Sikh new year celebrated around March/April

Acknowledgements

A substantial part of Chapter One was published in Gurharpal Singh, *Ethnic Conflict in India: a Case Study of Punjab* (Basingstoke: Macmillan, 2000). It is reproduced with the permission of Palgrave Macmillan.

Chapter Three is forthcoming in *Contemporary South Asia* 15: 2 (June 2006) as 'Gurdwaras and Community-Building among Sikhs'. It is reproduced with the permission of Routledge.

Sections of Chapter Five were published in Darshan Singh Tatla, *The Sikh Diaspora: the Search for Statehood* (London: UCL Press, 1990). Pages 103–6, 109-10, 137–8, 140–53 and 158–65 of that volume are reproduced with the permission of Taylor and Francis Books (UK).

Chapter Six was published in *Sikh Formations: Religion, Culture and Theory*, 1: 2 (December 2005), 157–73. It is reproduced with the permission of Routledge.
http://tandf.co.uk/titles/17448727

Map 3.1 is reproduced by kind permission of Ordnance Survey © Crown copyright 100054291.

We are grateful to institutions and individuals for allowing us to reproduce the photographs. The sources are listed with the photographs.

Preface

The list of people and organisations to whom we became indebted in the production of this volume is too long to do justice to them all. We thank the British Academy for a Small Grant in 2001 that enabled some of the research to be completed. We also thank our former colleagues at the Punjab Research Group and the *International Journal of Punjab Studies* with whom we embarked on Punjab and Sikh Studies in Britain in 1984. In particular we would like to acknowledge the significant contribution of Ian Talbot for his enduring support and encouragement through the years. The Centre for Research in Ethnic Relations at the University of Warwick for a very long time functioned as our surrogate home as we co-ordinated this research and our work on Punjab Studies. In recognition of this support we thank John Rex, Robin Cohen, Zig Leyton-Henry and Harry Goulbourne who provided such a warm and encouraging environment.

We acknowledge the support and assistance of staff at the following libraries and collections who helped us with our research: British Library, the Public Record Office, the University of Leicester, the Modern Record Centre, University of Warwick, University of Birmingham, the Birmingham City Archives, Central Library Birmingham, Record Office for Leicester and Rutland, Wigston Magna, British Library of Political and Economic Science, London School of Economics and the School of Oriental and African Studies. In addition to these institutions we have appreciated the support of the office of *Des Pardes* and its founding editor, the late Tarsem Singh Purewal, who gave us unlimited access to past copies of the paper and diligently answered our every query. His successor, Gurbax Singh Virk, has continued this tradition of generosity and support. We are indebted to him for allowing us to reproduce some of the photographs from the paper's collection. Also deserving of special mention is Nick Carter, editor of the *Leicester Mercury*, who allowed us to reproduce photographs from the paper's library.

The list of Sikhs and Sikh organisations that helped us in our endeavour is also far too long to mention. However we would like to recognise the particular contribution of Avtar Singh Johal, whose name has been synonymous with the Indian Workers' Association in the West Midlands since the mid-1960s. Members and former members of the International Sikh Youth Federation also gave freely of their time as well as assisting us in helping to map the complex history of that organisation. We further acknowledge the support and suggestions of Indarjit Singh of the Network of Sikh Organisations, Jasdev Singh Rai of the Sikh Human Rights Group, Bhai Mohinder Singh of the Guru Nanak Nishkam Sewak Jatha, Birmingham, Resham Singh Sandhu of the Leicester Council of Faiths, and Sujinder Singh Sangha, former editor of the *Punjabi Guardian*. The list of those interviewed would be inordinately long; where relevant they have been referenced in the text.

Over the years, directly or indirectly, many colleagues and friends have contributed to discussions that helped us to clarify our own ideas. Among these the following deserve a special mention: Arvind-pal Singh Mandair, Christopher Shackle, Pal Aluwalia, Varinder S. Kalra, Navtej Kaur Purewal, Navdeep Singh Mandair, Surinder Singh Jodhka, David Cheetham, Martin Stringer, Verne Dusenbery, Giorgio Shani, Brian Keith Axel, Nikky Guninder-Kaur Singh, Iftikhar Malik, John Martin, David Clark, Yunus Samad, Mohammed Waseem, Jeevon Singh Deol, Uday S. Mehta, Noel O'Sullivan, Harjot Oberoi, Paul R. Brass, N. G. Barrier, Joyce Pettigrew, Harish K. Puri, Steve Vertovec, Ceri Peach and Judith M. Brown.

Our main debt, however, is to our families, who have suffered unnecessarily because this work took far longer than we ever anticipated. A part of the motivation for writing this volume was that our children would find it useful in making sense of their lives. We hope our labour has not been in vain.

Finally, this work is entirely our own responsibility and none of the individuals mentioned above are in any way accountable for errors of fact or interpretation.

Gurharpal Singh
Birmingham
Darshan Singh Tatla
Jalandhar

For
Harman, Harjeet, Rajwant and Sukhmani
– all British-born Sikhs

Introduction

In the aftermath of the 7 July 2005 (7/7) bombings in central London British public opinion appeared to agree on one thing: that multiculturalism was dead and that militant Islam had killed it off. Such an outlook was perhaps to be expected in the light of such unprecedented violence, but it came almost a year after Sir Trevor Phillips, head of the Commission for Racial Equality (CRE), the premier state body charged with combating racial and ethnic discrimination in Britain, had pronounced that British multiculturalism had failed.[1] Phillips's declaration was a major turning point in a process that began before 9/11 with urban riots in northern British towns in 2001 and climaxed in early August 2005 when, in outlining a new policy response to the London bombings, Prime Minister Tony Blair made it clear that the 'rules of the game have changed and are changing'.[2]

In terms of ethnicity and religion, Britain is a diverse society. In the 2001 census nearly 8 per cent of the total population consisted of minority ethnic communities, with a significant representation of Muslims, Hindus, Sikhs, Jews and Buddhists.[3] However the translation of this ethnic and religious diversity into ideological multiculturalism[4] has been an uphill task – and one which, as the Commission on the Future of Multi-Ethnic Britain recognised, has failed to touch most of the country and 'many significant power centres'.[5] In Britain and most of Western Europe today ideological multiculturalism is increasingly viewed as the national equivalent of what Samuel Huntington has called the 'clash of civilisations'.[6] The movement towards the further cultural democratisation of public space that began in the 1960s has come to a firm halt – at least for the time being.

While the attention of policy makers in the West today is focused on the 'Muslim question', it is important also to study other religious and ethnic minorities for a more nuanced understanding of how communities with similar histories and ethnicities have developed. Most British Muslims are from South Asia, and most share with Hindus, Sikhs and other religious and ethnic communities common social histories that have 'separated' only in recent times. Sikhs in particular provide an exceptionally interesting comparative case study as a community that shares with many British Muslims common histories, cultural traditions and ethnic associations, as well as a distinctive religious identity that combines the sacred and the temporal. British Sikhs, moreover, have recent experience of being a 'stigmatised' transnational community which, in the 1980s and 1990s, became involved in separatist homeland politics and was infamously associated with terrorism throughout the globe. In the 1960s, 1970s and 1980s British Sikhs also campaigned tenaciously for the right to observe the Sikh dress code, thereby 'pioneering' British multiculturalism. And, as the furore over the closure of the play *Behzti* in December 2004 illustrated, British Sikhs are not reluctant forcibly to assert their right to defend religious sensibilities in a secular liberal democracy when the occasion demands it.

The 336,000 Sikhs who live in Britain today constitute one of the largest and most identifiable segments of the minority ethnic population. Sikh settlement dates from the middle of the nineteenth century, when the arrival of the last Sikh ruler, Maharaja Duleep Singh, followed the annexation of Punjab by the East India Company in 1849. It developed most notably after the Second World War, with mass immigration from Punjab, East Africa and, later, the Far East. In the century and a half of Sikh presence in Britain the community has emerged as leader of the growing Sikh diaspora, established firm institutions in the new homeland, and received public recognition across the institutions of the state and civil society. Sikhs today are to be found as broadcasters, judges, academics, MPs, councillors, leading businessmen, medics, journalists, fashion designers, service personnel and industrial workers. Localities in west London and the West Midlands, and to a lesser extent elsewhere, have been transformed into 'Little Punjabs' where new cultural and social industries thrive. *Bhangra*, a global music industry, emerged from the inner-city areas of initial Sikh settlement. Sikh gurdwaras – along with mosques and temples – have changed the urban landscape by rising as the 'new cathedrals of Britain': they are now indispensable components of faith in the inner city of the twenty-first century. Sikh political organisations have perfected single-issue politics. They remain the leading exponents of the 'messy', transnational politics that so perplexed the British political establishment in the 1980s and 1990s and helped to modernise its outlook before 9/11 and 7/7.

The making of a British Sikh community has its roots in the complex Anglo-Sikh relationship that evolved after the conquest of Punjab in the middle of the nineteenth century. During colonial rule in India, Sikhs became the ideal subaltern community, their loyalty rewarded by mass recruitment into the Indian Army and recognition as the 'favoured sons of the Empire'. As such they spread throughout the globe. But colonial modernity also significantly influenced the development of a modern Sikh identity that shared the experience of other religious identities (Hindu and Muslim) in giving rise to the twentieth-century religious nationalism that produced the partition of India in 1947. After decolonisation some Sikhs relocated in Britain and began the process of mass emigration that was encouraged by the post-war reconstruction boom. In just over sixty years the British Sikh community has grown from fewer than 2,000 to 336,000.

Although the colonial encounter between the *raj* and Sikhs has produced a rich body of scholarship that has been renewed in recent times by fresh interest in colonial modernity,[7] surprisingly there is no comprehensive study of the British Sikh experience. The dominance of the race relations and ethnic studies paradigm in which Sikhs, along with other post-war immigrants, were viewed as part of the 'race problem', has produced much disparate research that is neither integrated nor woven into a meaningful narrative of the community's development.[8] A number of scholars have produced local, city-based case studies with national titles, but these are either seriously dated or suffer from an extremely narrow focus on aspects of Sikh settlement.[9] There is clearly a major gap in the histories of British minority ethnic communities.

The aim of this volume is to provide the first systematic and comprehensive national study of the British Sikh experience since the Second World War. Its general focus is on Sikh institution building and the transmission of Sikh values and norms to successive generations in a modern, developed liberal society which, until recently, has been characterised by overt racial hostility to non-white migrants. It does so by drawing on many elements of discrete research on Sikhs undertaken by specialists within race and ethnic studies over the past forty years, as well as contextualising this research much more extensively than hitherto by using the community's own narratives as recorded in the British Punjabi press, oral histories, personal papers and interviews with key participants.[10] This body of evidence is further enriched by our extensive use of the 2001 census, which for the first time provides a comprehensive profile of the British Sikhs – a profile that has eluded previous researchers who have had to rely on approximate data. The range and extent of the new data sources, we believe, not only enable us to reassess traditional narratives of Sikhs in Britain, but also to understand better the trajectory of the community's future development in what is an increasingly socially plural and globalised society.

A work of this nature is necessarily interdisciplinary. It has evolved at the intersection of several disciplines – political science, history, sociology, religious studies and race and ethnic studies – that reflect our own disciplinary backgrounds and the unusual location of the subject matter that is common to studies of religious minorities of South Asian origin in the West.[11] We recognise some of the contributions of recent constructivist methodologies in providing new points of departure for the study of identities. These methodologies may be especially relevant for a community such as the Sikhs that has been the focus of intense intellectual debate about the nature of its identity,[12] but our concern here is primarily to provide a community history that is firmly grounded in a body of empirical evidence – even though we are only too acutely aware, as subsequent chapters will illustrate, of the contested nature of Sikh 'community'. As Margaret Thatcher once famously declared, there is 'no such thing as society'. In these late-modern times, some may find the idea of a 'community', and a religious one at that, even harder to stomach. Where relevant, we have attempted to recognise the force of some of these arguments.

Chapter 1 provides a brief overview of Sikh history from the time of the gurus with special emphasis on the impact of colonial rule which ended with partition of Punjab, the Sikhs' homeland. It locates the growth of modern Sikh institutions that have their roots in colonial history and have shaped the dominant discourse of Sikhism and Sikh identity today. An outline is also provided of the Sikhs' ambiguous relationship with post-independence India, where the search for political autonomy led first, in the 1950s and 1960s, to the demand for a Punjabi-speaking province, and then, in the 1980s and 1990s, to a bloody campaign for an independent Sikh state of Khalistan. The vexed relationship between British Sikhs and India is one of the key factors in understanding the community's development.

In Chapter 2 we discuss at some length the nature of Punjabi society, from which most British Sikhs originated, and the underlying factors responsible for Sikh emigration. The typical characteristics of British Sikh society – its norms, values, rituals, and enduring patterns of behaviour – have their roots in the mainly rural social structure of mid-twentieth-century Punjab, the 'imagined village' that most migrants left behind: these traits are examined with special reference to social cleavages that have remained indelible. One such trait is the cultural compulsion to migrate that dates from the late nineteenth century. We explore in some detail the highly localised nature of British Sikh emigration from the Doaba region and its significance for the evolution of British Sikh society.

Chapter 3 provides a highly condensed synthesis of the history of Sikh settlement in Britain. A detailed history of settlement would probably have required a volume in itself: we have focused instead on the crucial divide made by the Second World War between colonialism and elite settlement, on one side, and decolonisation and mass immigration on the other. While we have certainly failed to do justice to the complex nature of post-war settlement – the extraordinary range of moving personal stories that make up the Sikh experience – we have sought nonetheless to identify key signposts as well as persistent patterns within the flow of Sikh migration to Britain. These patterns are then discussed with reference to the demographic growth of the community and its areas of settlement, especially the emergent 'Little Punjabs' in Sikh strongholds. The chapter concludes by drawing on recent data to provide a contemporary social profile of the community in relation to the British national norms, as a prelude to more systematic discussion of these aspects in subsequent chapters.

Chapter 4 reviews at length the process of community building by analysing the history of the British Sikh gurdwara movement – a movement to create Sikh sacred institutions. Remarkably, the role of gurdwaras in community development has received little academic attention. In this chapter we highlight how the growth of these institutions corresponds with the growth of the community, but also increasingly reflects its religious and social diversity; and because the gurdwaras are the Sikhs' main communal resource, we examine the competition for their control that defines leadership. The changing role of gurdwaras in British Sikh society is explored through the challenges posed by the searches for new 'spirituality', the place of faith in the inner city, and, increasingly, the regulation of minority religious institutions since 9/11 and 7/7.

Along with gurdwaras the other major institutions of British Sikhs are political and social organisations. Chapter 5 traces their history from before the Second World War to present times and identifies a shift in outlook from class to identity politics, a change that was hastened by the rise of the Khalistan movement in Britain after the Indian Army's entry into the Golden Temple complex in 1984, the 'critical event' that propelled British Sikhs to the leadership of the Sikh diaspora. The chapter traces the rise and fall of the British Khalistan movement and its subsequent transmutation into *groupscules* and identity politics. The chapter also reflects on Sikh engagement in mainstream politics.

It is likely that the impact of Sikhs on British society has been more pervasive than is often recognised, but one area where it is clearly evident is in contests over the neutrality of public space. In Chapter 6 we evaluate the Sikh contribution to British multiculturalism which began with the initial campaign for wearing turbans, *kirpans* (swords/small daggers) and beards but achieved global notoriety with the forceful closure of the play *Behzti* at the Birmingham Repertory theatre. The Sikhs, it is argued, offer an unusual case of a community that can always – perhaps because of the Anglo-Sikh heritage – negotiate an opt-out from general rule making. This proposition is critically assessed with reference to the Sikh dress-code campaigns, *Behzti* and the rise of local multiculturalism.

Chapter 7 provides an overview of the community's employment and education profile. It reviews the initial patterns of employment which were determined essentially by areas of settlement and the educational background of the immigrants, then considers the changes that have taken place by concentrating on the rise of self-employment and Sikhs' performance in school and post-school education. The chapter discusses at length the current employment profile of the community, which reveals the Sikhs as 'middle-level' achievers rather than 'high flyers'. On the basis of the evidence available we also attempt to identify the class hierarchy within today's British Sikh society.

Perhaps the most important changes in the nature of that society since the 1950s are to be found in the role of the family. These are examined in Chapter 8 where we also review the community's discourses about gender and sexuality. While the Sikh community appears to be exhibiting trends similar to broader British society – high divorce rates, family breakdowns, lone-parenthood – its responses to these issues highlight the underlying tension between the dominant discourse of Sikhism as articulated by established Sikh institutions in Britain (and Punjab) and the challenges posed by new social formations emerging among young Sikhs in the West. This tension has come to the fore in a number of highly publicised cases and also appears to be far more pervasive than has been recognised.

Most of these new social formations are to be found among the young.

Chapter 9 examines in some depth the failure of efforts to institutionalise the teaching of Punjabi and the broader use of the mother tongue in the British Sikh media. This failure is set against the background of the rise of *bhangra,* which is often seen as the site of new Punjabi and Sikh identities among the younger generations. This argument is assessed with reference to available evidence on contemporary youth identities among British Sikhs.

In a work such as this it is inevitable that there will be many omissions and oversights, more so because it is the first exercise of its kind. We are very conscious of some of the areas that we have neglected – such as British Sikh culture, the community's complex relationship with Punjab, and developments within British Sikhism. We plead lack of space and the absence of rigorous primary research on which we could draw. Nevertheless, we hope that this work will provide a stimulus to more systematic and broad-ranging research on a community that so far has been seriously neglected by academics.

Looking back, the writing of this volume might itself be considered a part of the history of British Sikhs. The work began in the early 1980s when we established the Punjab Research Group (1984)[13] and published the first paper on the British Punjabi press (1987). This was followed by Tatla and Nesbitt's bibliography on Sikhs in Britain. The Punjab Research Group later gave birth to the *International Journal of Punjab Studies* (1994);[14] as its editors, our mission was to create a new forum for academic scholarship on Punjab that included the Punjabi diaspora. In the 1990s, changes in employment and new priorities led us along different paths (Singh, to Indian politics; Tatla, to the Sikh diaspora); although these were considerable digressions, they involved us in seminal projects on the Sikh diaspora[15] and new approaches to Sikh Studies.[16] One result of these endeavours has been the launch of a new journal, *Sikh Formations: Religion, Culture and Theory* (2005),[17] of which Singh is one of the editors.

The first mapping exercise for this volume was undertaken in the 1990s but it proved to be inadequate, unbalanced and badly dated. Only Chapter 5 survives substantially in its current form. As a result we decided to rethink the whole project in the light of two major developments: 9/11 and the gradual release of 2001 census data that provided hard evidence for what had been mere conjecture or speculation. The result, we believe, is a work that is far more balanced, reflective and rich in data; as such, it is more likely to stand the test of time. This is very much a joint effort arising out of a collaborative partnership dating from the early 1980s. Inevitably, however, there was a proportional division of labour. Thus one of us (Singh) was mainly responsible for the overall design and writing of the volume while the other (Tatla) focused his energies on research. It is a testimony to our partnership that the work was completed despite Tatla's premature retirement to Punjab due to ill-health.

One

The Sikhs of the Punjab

Of the major world religious communities the Sikhs are probably among the most distinctive: clearly distinguished by their familiar dress code of unshorn hair and a turban (for males) and covered head (for females), as their gurus intended they stand out from the crowd, more especially so in the diaspora where today about a million Sikhs are settled. This distinctiveness is only too evident in the popular images of Sikhs in the West over the past century, in which they have been regularly portrayed as a noble military race, as victims of racial abuse, as troublemakers deeply committed to their faith, as an exceptionally talented business community – or, more recently since the 1980s and 1990s, as terrorists committed to the politics of homeland. From North America to Europe, from Africa to the Far East, wherever they have settled Sikhs have made their presence felt, if only by constantly raising uncomfortable issues for public policy. Sikhs, in short, are the archetypal transnational community of the early-twenty-first century and have been at the forefront of framing multicultural policies in the West.

The Sikh diaspora is of relatively recent origin, having developed gradually from the late nineteenth century through successive waves of migration.[1] For most Sikhs, however, Punjab remains the homeland, the province where the faith was founded and the home of their most sacred institutions. This intimate association between Punjab and the Sikhs remains critical for understanding the fortunes of the community in India and overseas. In this chapter we explore the historical evolution of the Sikh community from the time of its birth to the present, and show how history has shaped the development of Sikh identity. The chapter also identifies key landmarks in Sikh history that continue to cast their powerful shadows over the future of the Sikh diaspora.

9

The Age of the Gurus

Punjab was one of the most distinctive provinces of modern India. Historically it has formed a transitional zone between the Muslim and Hindu worlds of north-east South Asia, covering a vast area extending from Delhi in the south-east to the borders of Afghanistan in the north-east. In the east it was bounded by the Himalayas and the river Jamuna; in the west the river Indus marked the province's extreme limits. The point where the provincial rivers flowed into the Indus also represented the province's natural southern boundary. These boundaries created a fertile plain criss-crossed by five rivers that give the province its name: *Pun-jab*, the 'land of five rivers'.

Three factors marked Punjab off from the rest of the Indian sub-continent. As the premier land gate to India the province witnessed the continual flow of foreign armies – Greeks, Turks, Persians, Moguls and Afghans. Political stability was rare for there was never 'a period of peace long enough to allow a forgetfulness of the contingent'.[2] Uncertainty and violence bred a suspicion of, and hostility towards, the unfamiliar, a respect for physical vigour, and a reluctance to submit to political authority. Regularly occupied, the Punjab became a 'home and grave for the careerism of collaborators and the bravery of [its] heroes'.[3]

A related feature of this geographical position was the evolution of a social structure that was in many ways atypical of the traditional Indian pattern based on caste. Although all the four *varnas* (caste groups) were present – Brahmins (priest), Kashatriaya (warrior), Visyya (trader), Sudra (service) – caste was a compound of irregular classical pattern and tribal adaptation.[4] There were very few pure castes: Brahmins as such constituted a smaller proportion of the population than anywhere else in north India and did not enjoy an especially favoured social status. The social structure was dominated by the Jats (agriculturalists), whose outlook was closely identified with the frontier-agrarian features of Punjabi life.

Modern Punjab's identity was also reflected in Punjabi, a mixture of Arabic, Persian, Pushtu, Pahari, Western Hindi and Sanskrit which captured in full the rugged raucousness of its rural speakers. Folklore, the culture of Punjabis, was glorified in epics like Waris Shah's *Heer*, Pilu's *Sabhan* and Hashim's *Sassi Pannu,* as well as the more common forms

Plate 1 (opposite)   Maharajah Duleep Singh, aged sixteen,
by Franz Xaver Winterhalter, 1854
(© *The Royal Collection, 2006, Her Majesty Queen Elizabeth II*)

like *lookgeets* (folksongs) or village festivals.[5] The violent and romantic emotions familiar to the 'land of five rivers' also found powerful expression in the popular and common idiom of poetry; and though the development of modern nationalisms in the province was to result in the marginalisation of Punjabi – the Muslim League-led Pakistan movement opting for Urdu and the Indian National Congress championing Hindi, with only the Sikhs appropriating Punjabi as their 'national' language – it nevertheless remains the common spoken language of both East and West Punjab.

The Punjab of Guru Nanak (1469–1539), the founder of Sikhism, had been influenced by religious reform movements in north India which coincided with the establishment of Mogul rule in India. These movements contested the orthodoxy of Islam and Hinduism in the name of regional tradition, devotional practice and folk heritage. Guru Nanak, who was aware of these movements, is sometimes described as a reformer within the Sant tradition familiar to north India at the time.[6] Sikh tradition, in contrast, argues that Guru Nanak drew on the influences of the reformers in order to transcend Islam and Hinduism by creating a new religion for a new age. 'There is', he proclaimed, 'neither Hindu nor Muslim.' Instead Guru Nanak's message focused on the devotional formless Creator who 'graciously bestows, through the spiritual True Guru, who is the manifestation of His message to humanity'.[7] The essence of Guru Nanak's message is to be found in the opening hymn of the *Guru Granth Sahib* (the Sikhs' sacred text):

> There is one supreme eternal reality; the truth; immanent in all things; creator of all things; immanent in creation. Without fear and without hatred; not subject to time; beyond birth and death; self-revealing. Known by the Guru's grace.[8]

Sikhs believe that God (*waheguru*), who created the universe and everything in it, is omnipresent, immanent as well as transcendent, and omnipotent. Because God is formless and beyond the reach of human intellect, a relationship with the Creator can be established only by recognising divine self-expression and truth. This relationship is possible through meditation on God's Name (*nam*) and Word *(shabad)* which are the revelations of the divine instructor (the Guru). Without the Guru's grace an individual is doomed to the perpetual cycle of death and rebirth.

Most Sikhs accept that Guru Nanak's message went beyond mere personal reflection and meditation to incorporate a new social vision. This emphasis, it is argued, was all too evident in his insistence on social equality, the rejection of all forms of caste distinction and the centrality of the concept of *seva* (community service). Moreover for Guru Nanak the present and the divine are linked together in three simple injunctions to his followers: to adore the divine name, to work hard and to share the rewards of one's labour with others.[9]

Guru Nanak's message soon attracted many followers. He was succeeded by nine other gurus who guided the development of the community and by the time of Guru Arjan (1581–1606), the fifth guru, Sikhism had established a strong foothold in Punjab's central districts, where Jats converted to the faith in large numbers.[10] With the founding of the Golden Temple (Harmandir Sahib) in 1604 in Amritsar and the compilation of the *Guru Granth Sahib* (also known as the *Adi Granth*) moves were made to further institutionalise the expanding community. But this growth did not go unnoticed. Emperor Jahangir's efforts to check the spread of the new faith led to the execution of Guru Arjan in 1606. His martyrdom marked the beginnings of the transformation of Sikhism from pacifist reformers to a militant creed.

This transformation began with Guru Hargobind (1606–44), the sixth guru, who responded to the death of his father by constructing a fortress at Amritsar and the Akal Takhat (seat of temporal authority) opposite the Golden Temple (seat of spiritual authority). It was further consolidated by Guru Hargobind's decision to wear two swords that symbolised the union of spiritual and temporal authority, a process that culminated with Guru Gobind (1658–1707), the last guru, who introduced two major innovations that were to lay the foundations of modern Sikh identity. First, on Vaisakhi (Sikh new year) 1699 he baptised the Khalsa (the pure), the elite saint-soldiers of the fledgling community who were to be distinguished by external symbols of identity, the five Ks – *kesh* (unshorn hair and beards), *kacha* (short drawers), *kirpan* (sword/steel dagger), *kara* (iron bangle) and *kanga* (comb) – and were renamed as Singh (male) or Kaur (female). Second, before his death Guru Gobind invested the guruship in the *Guru Granth Sahib*, thereby terminating the line of personal guruship. In due course these two changes were to draw the boundary around Sikh identity much more clearly than hitherto: whereas the end to personal guruship set a limit on schismatic pluralism, the Singhs (and Kaurs) of Guru Gobind were destined to assume a pre-eminent position within the *panth* (Sikh community).[11]

In the eighteenth century the collapse of the Mogul empire and the decline of Afghan influence in Punjab were accompanied by the rise of Sikhs to political power. This century is often described by Sikhs as the 'heroic age' when the institutions and teachings bequeathed by Guru Gobind inspired his followers to establish political rule in Punjab. As centralised Mogul rule imploded, and parts of Punjab were ceded to the Afghan rulers, the latter and their vassals became engaged in a continuous campaign to contain the growing power of Sikhs in central Punjab. By 1765 Sikhs had occupied Lahore and extended their influence throughout most of Punjab. This remarkable rise, however, was due as much to the demise of Mogul rule as to Sikh state formation. Institutions such as *rakhi* (protection), *misls* (armed militias), and *Dal Khalsa* (combined militias) encouraged the 'revolt of common people' against landlords, the local state and centralised authority. But if the revolt of 'peasant tribes' fuelled this 'revolution', it was sustained by the collective vision of Gobind's Khalsa which proclaimed 'the right of every Singh to fight, to conquer and to rule'.[12]

The 'heroic age' climaxed with the proclamation of Ranjit Singh's 'Kingdom of Lahore' in 1801. In the next forty years Ranjit Singh was able to establish a powerful state that subjugated Afghan territories to the west, included Kashmir, and extended as far as Lahsa and Tibet. This expansion was sustained, above all, by the creation of a military meritocracy led by Sikhs, a period of tranquillity which encouraged economic development, and the weakness of rival states, especially when British influence was limited to cis-Satluj states by the treaty of 1809. Ranjit Singh's kingdom, which flourished under these conditions, was described by one contemporary as 'the most wonderful object in the world', constructed by a skilful architect from essentially 'unpromising fragments'.[13]

However Ranjit Singh's kingdom was shaped in the image of its founder. Upon the maharaja's death it imploded as a result of royal rivalry and British intrigue. Gradually the army took over the state, engaging in encounters with steadily expanding British power. The Treaty of Lahore (1846), and the subsequent annexation of Punjab by the East India Company (1849), marked the final end to Sikh sovereignty: it had lasted less than fifty years. Duleep Singh (see p. 11), Ranjit Singh's successor, was made a ward of court and compelled to surrender the famous Koh-i-Noor diamond to Queen Victoria as a 'gift'. Duleep Singh, as we shall see (Chapter 3), was to become 'Queen Victoria's Maharaja', the symbol of an enduring link between the British monarchy and Sikhs.

Ranjit Singh's kingdom led to a major change in the fortunes of the Sikh community as a whole. From being primarily peasant cultivators, Sikhs came to represent over 50 per cent of the ruling class and constituted more than half of the army. State patronage was also liberally bestowed upon Sikh cultural and religious institutions, with the latter enjoying 60 per cent of all revenues alienated to such bodies.[14] Moreover, within the *panth* the position of Singhs, who led the Khalsa army, was strengthened at the expense of non-Singh Sikhs who often retained the pre-Khalsa identities that had blurred the boundaries between Sikhism and Hinduism. In many ways the doctrine of the Khalsa was better suited to the social and political conditions of the eighteenth and nineteenth centuries because of the ideas of equality, the need for mobility, and the requirements of guerrilla warfare. And though a wide gulf separated the Khalsa nobility and the ordinary Sikhs, nonetheless there was a consciousness of the community's political power, a shared feeling that 'the rulers of their land were their own people'.[15]

The Colonial Period

The annexation of Punjab by the East India Company introduced colonial rule that lasted a century. During this period the Punjab underwent dramatic changes that were to leave a permanent imprint on the successor provinces after the partition of 1947. For the Sikhs the century witnessed a dramatic decline from a ruling community to one of minor status reflecting its numerical strength as the smallest of Punjab's three religious traditions after Muslims and Hindus.

In the aftermath of the British takeover, Sikhs were viewed with suspicion by the colonial authorities. However their fortunes were quickly revived after Sikh soldiers provided invaluable support in the defeat of the Indian Mutiny (1857–8). This timely assistance was reciprocated with the designation of Punjab as the 'land of the martial race', a designation which led the province to become the principal recruiting ground for the Indian Army. By the end of the century the Punjab provided almost 50 per cent of the Indian Army's strength, and of this component Sikhs constituted about 25 per cent. The high-water mark of Sikh military participation was reached during the First World War, when their representation increased from 35,000 at the outbreak of hostilities to over 100,000 by the end of the war.[16] This recruitment was also accompanied by the promotion of Singh identity by the army which, according to some scholars, deliberately nurtured 'an orthodox, separatist and martial Singh identity' in preference to the pacifist, non-martial orientation of non-Singh Sikhs.[17]

Mass military recruitment and the rewards that it generated – income, grants, pensions and patronage – was followed by other forms of colonial social engineering which benefited the Punjab agriculturalists from

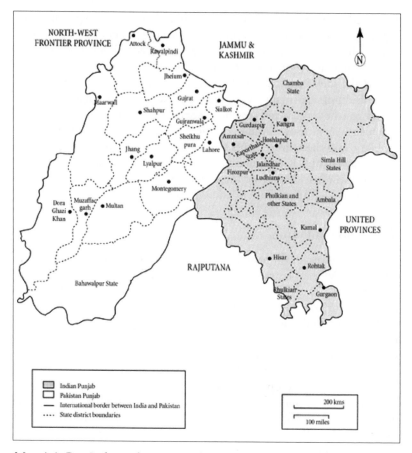

Map 1.1 Pre-Independence Punjab, as Partitioned in 1947

Source: G. Singh, *Ethnic Conflict in India*, 84.

whom most of the Sikhs were drawn. The Land Alienation Act (1901), for example, enabled the Punjab government to protect the owner cultivators from the vagaries of agricultural commercialisation and usury. The construction of new Canal Colonies – in the barren lands of West Punjab – provided a valuable resource with which the colonial state could reward 'patriotic' and 'loyal' cultivators. From the late nineteenth century onwards, new settlements of Hindu, Muslim and Sikh 'loyal colonists' were established in western Punjab, creating one of the most agriculturally productive regions in the colonial world.[18]

Religious Revivalism and the Singh Sabhas

Equally profound were the social consequences unleashed by colonialism. Social reformers unnerved by the colonial encounter attempted to revive, reform and rejuvenate traditional religious identities in the face of the potential Christian missionary threat. The Arya Samaj movement, for instance, attempted to deritualise Hinduism and absorb what were seen as lapsed groups, including the Sikhs. Aggressive and proselytising, the Arya Samaj gave rise to the Singh Sabhas (1880s), which sought to reassert the distinctiveness of Sikhism. It is now generally accepted that the efforts of the Singh Sabhas to translate Sikhism culturally in order to withstand the colonial encounter introduced new hermeneutics into the understanding of the tradition and its historiography, consciously re-shaping the dominant discourse of Sikhism around the Khalsa identity.[19] Their message was epitomised, above all, in the popular tract *Ham Hindu Nai* (We Are Not Hindus), the establishment of distinctive Sikh rituals, and the defence of Sikh institutions (gurdwaras). Singh Sabhas did much to mark out the modern Sikh identity as well as the distinctive Sikh rituals that have subsequently become enshrined in the *Rahit Maryada* (Sikh code of conduct).[20]

The Singh Sabhas' project was completed by the Akali Movement (1920–5). It began as a movement for the liberation of gurdwaras from the control of *mehants* (traditional custodians), but soon turned into the 'third Sikh war', a full-scale confrontation between the Sikhs and the colonial administration in which 4,000 suffered death, 2,000 were wounded, and 30,000 men and women were jailed.[21] In the event the demands of the movement were conceded: the upshot was the passing of the Gurdwara Act (1925), which created the Shiromani Gurdwara Parbandhak Committee (SGPC) as the legal authority to manage and control Sikh gurdwaras. The Act established a 175-member SGPC that was to be elected democratically by all Sikhs on a tenure of five years. The Shiromani Akali Dal (SAD), which had led the movement, was recognised as the political wing of the SGPC. The SGPC and the SAD combined to provide the institutional framework for what has been termed the 'Sikh political system',[22] a self-governing religious community. Religion and politics, which had been inextricably linked in the development of Sikhism, were henceforth formally entwined in a new legal arrangement.

Both the Singh Sabha and Akali movements made significant contributions to the evolution of the modern Sikh identity. Figure 1.1 represents the significant *religious* sub-identities. Positions of importance within Sikhdom are occupied by the baptised Singhs and Kaurs (*amritdhari Khalsa*) who, though proportionately few in number, nonetheless

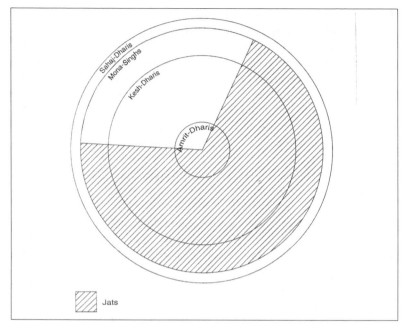

Figure 1.1 Modern Sikh Identity

Source: G. Singh, *Ethnic Conflict in India*, 86.

represent the 'orthodoxy'. *Amrit-dhari Khalsa,* as the name applies, have taken the ritual initiation into the Khalsa and wear the five Ks. Non-baptised Singhs and Kaurs (*kesh-dhari Khalsa*), on the other hand, represent the vast majority of Sikhs and are distinguished by their commitment to some of the five Ks, especially unshorn hair. Tradition-ally in Punjab the *amrit-dhari* Khalsa and *kesh-dhari* Khalsa Singhs and Kaurs have accounted for between two-thirds and three-quarters of the total Sikh population. In a third category, numerically small but of increasing importance, are the clean-shaven Sikhs of the diaspora. This group has evolved with migration to Western and non-Western countries since the end of the nineteenth century, but is also increasing in Punjab and India under the influence of globalisation. This category, in the main, originates from and is reproduced culturally among the baptised and non-baptised Singhs and Kaurs. Accordingly the designation *mona*-Singhs (shaven Sikhs) seems appropriate, particularly as many often revert to keeping unshorn hair or take the *amrit* (initiation) in old age. On the outer boundary are the non-Singh Sikhs (*sahaj-dharis*), who still adhere to pre-Khalsa pluralism. Today they are few in number and their distinctiveness seems to be in 'rapid decline'.[23] Since 1947 many non-Singh and non-Kaur Sikhs have succumbed to the assimilationist appeal of Hindu sects or encouraged the proliferation of Sikh heterodoxy through such movements as the Radhaswami, Ad-Dharm, or Sant Nirankar.

Sikhs and the Partition of Punjab

Before the partition of the historic province of Punjab in 1947, Sikhs comprised only 15 per cent of the total population (see below), a figure that was equally distributed between West and East Punjab and nowhere constituted a significant majority. In the drive towards independent nationhood by the Congress and the Muslim League the Punjab became the battleground, with the Sikhs unable to argue the case for a separate state or prevent the division of Punjab.

Table 1.1 Punjab's Area and Population, 1941–2001

Year	Area (sq. km.)	Population (millions)	Muslim (%)	Hindu (%)	Sikh (%)	Other (%)
1941	256,000	28.4	53	31	15	1
1951+	122,500	16.1	2	62	35	1
1961	122,500	20.3	2	64	33	1
1966★	50,260	13.2	–	38	60	2
1971	50,260	13.5	–	38	60	2
1981	50,260	16.7	–	36	62	2
1991	50,362	20.3	1.2	35	63	1
2001	50,362	24.3	1.7	37	60	2

Source: G.Singh, *Ethnic Conflict in India*, 88 and *Census of India, 1991 and 2001*.
+ After partition. ★ After linguistic reorganisation.

In March 1940 the Muslim League passed the Pakistan resolution calling for numerically majority Muslim states in north-east and north-west India to be constituted as 'independent states'. The Sikh leadership's response to this resolution was pragmatic, reflecting the community's dispersed (and minority) status. Hence when the Cripps mission (1942) appeared to concede Pakistan, the Akalis floated an 'Azad Punjab' (an independent Punjab). During the Gandhi–Jinnah talks (1944), the demand for 'Sikhistan' was advanced lest the two leaders should accept a formula that made the 'Sikhs the slaves of Pakistan [or] Hindustan'.[24] The Simla Conference (1945) and the Cabinet Mission (1946), which followed the breakdown of these talks, were presented with equally ambiguous proposals: the SAD favoured an undivided India with constitutional guarantees and electoral weighting for the Sikhs, but demanded an independent Sikh state should Pakistan be conceded.

Throughout these rounds of discussion the idea of a Sikh state was deployed as a counterweight to Pakistan. Even the Communist Party of India (CPI), in its ingenious solution, envisaged a 'transfer of populations' to create a 'Sikh homeland' that would command only 33 per cent of the total population in such a region.[25] The Sikh leadership's strategy thus consisted of sabotaging the Pakistan demand while seeking assurances for favoured status in post-partition India. Nehru's declaration (July 1946) that the 'Sikhs of Punjab were entitled to special consideration' in north India where they could 'also experience the glow of freedom',[26] shifted negotiations in the Congress's favour. When Master Tara Singh, the SAD leader, rejected the Muslim League offer of Sikh accession to a Muslim-majority Punjab, the prospect of partition was grudgingly accepted. In the tragedy that subsequently unfolded, 'East Punjab became a gift of the Akalis to the Indian Union'.[27]

Post-Colonial India and the Sikhs

On 15 August 1947 the partition of India became a reality. The creation of a Muslim state of Pakistan, commanding most of the united Punjab, was accompanied by communal disorder on an unprecedented scale. Almost the entire Hindu and Sikh populations of West Punjab migrated to East Punjab, while the Muslim population in the latter region followed their example in the opposite direction. In all about 8.6 million people were uprooted in the ethnic cleansing and over 300,000 died. East Punjab was reduced to two divisions of Jullundur and Ambala, and some of the Himalayan region was reorganised as a new state, Himachal Pradesh. The former princely states were grouped as the Patiala and East Punjab States Union (PEPSU), which merged with Punjab in 1956.

In post-colonial India the Sikh community's quest for political and cultural autonomy has led to an almost permanent state of mobilisation against the central governments in New Delhi. In the 1950s and 1960s a bitter campaign was conducted for a Punjabi-speaking state; in the 1980s and 1990s, a regional autonomy movement following the India Army's Operation Blue Star in the Golden Temple (1984) led to a violent search for an independent Sikh homeland of Khalistan. Since 1947 Sikh nationalism has struggled to find a harmonious *modus operandi* with Indian nation and state building.

Punjabi Suba

Partition transformed Punjab into a bi-ethnic state with Hindus and Sikhs accounting for 62 and 35 per cent of the population respectively. Pre-independence fears of Hindu domination had led Sikh leaders to seek constitutional assurances of the kind promised by Nehru; when the Constituent Assembly rejected any idea of such 'special' status, the Sikh representatives responded by refusing to sign the draft constitution of India. Thereafter the process of social differentiation between Sikhs and Hindus became regularised in the demand for, and opposition to, a *Punjabi Suba* (a Punjabi-speaking province).

The resettlement of refugees from West Punjab for the first time created a Sikh majority area in the central districts. This development was seized upon soon after 1947 by the Sikh political leadership to demand a Punjabi Suba, a 'homeland for the Sikhs' as the 'principled' fulfilment of the Congress's pledge to reorganise Indian states along linguistic lines. For Punjabi Hindus, on the other hand, this demand was seen as a mere ruse for the pursuit of 'Sikhistan'; their leadership therefore encouraged them to thwart the demand by declaring Hindi rather than Punjabi as their mother tongue in the 1951 and 1961 census returns. This opposition was also supported by the provincial and national leadership of the Congress, which viewed the demand for a Punjabi Suba on India's sensitive border with Pakistan as a form of 'linguistic communalism'.

In the 1950s and early 1960s there were a number of sustained campaigns by the SAD to force the central government to concede a Punjabi Suba. Nehru and his regional leader, Kairon, remained implacably opposed, viewing any concession as a charter for separatism and the further division of the province. The deaths of Nehru (1964) and Kairon (1965), however, removed the demand's main political opponents. Thus when Sant Fateh Singh, the SAD leader, suspended his fast-unto-death at the outbreak of the Indo-Pakistan war (1965), this recognition of 'patriotism' in the 'national interest' was rewarded with a parliamentary committee that duly recommended the creation of a Punjabi Suba and a separate state of Haryana.

Under the Punjab Reorganisation Act (1966) the new province had a 60 per cent Sikh population. A form of 'Sikh homeland' was realised but it was an extremely truncated province which excluded many Punjabi-speaking areas and had to share the Le Corbusier capital, Chandigarh, and the flow of waters with the new state of Haryana. This legacy of incomplete reorganisation would eventually provide the justification for the new round of mobilisation in the early 1980s.

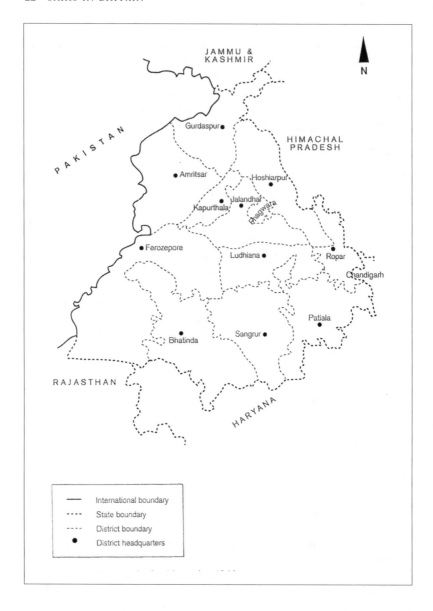

Map 1.2 Punjab after November 1966

Source: G.Singh, *Ethnic Conflict in India*, 92.

Punjabi Suba and After

If the aims of a Punjabi Suba were to consolidate Sikh political and cultural power then Sikh leadership was only partially successful. In the first elections to the new province the SAD formed a non-Congress coalition, and subsequently led several short-term administrations. There were also a number of mobilisations over the disputed elements of the reorganisation process, but these soon petered out due to factional rivalries.

A more serious confrontation over the unresolved legacies of linguistic reorganisation in the late 1960s and early 1970s was avoided by the unprecedented prosperity produced by the 'Green Revolution' – the most radical transformation of the province's agrarian economy since the Canal Colonies. The 'Green Revolution', through the intensive use of high-yielding varieties of cereals (especially wheat and rice), chemical fertilisers and mechanised agricultural machinery, multiplied outputs and incomes. Agricultural production rose by leaps and bounds. From a food-deficit state Punjab became the 'granary of India', contributing 72.1 per cent of wheat and 53.3 per cent of rice to the all-India central pool of food production in 1988–9.[28] All sectors of the economy felt the systemic consequences of this change as Punjab became the most prosperous state within the Indian Union.

By the early 1980s, however, the shortcomings of a development strategy based on the Green Revolution were becoming increasingly apparent. Punjab's economy became lopsided, with agriculture's contribution to the gross domestic product persisting above 50 per cent. Outlets for industrial diversification were few or firmly controlled by the 'permit licence *raj*' of centralised planning; in 1988 manufacturing accounted for only 11.4 per cent of the state's income.[29] The centre's reluctance to encourage industrial development, and the rising input costs of agricultural production, led some Sikh leaders to make the argument that Union governments were practising 'internal colonialism' in the state.

Socially the Green Revolution, in unleashing the catalytic forces of an emergent modern society, also had dramatic consequences, especially in the rural areas where almost 80 per cent of Sikhs lived.[30] Commercial agriculture heightened the differentiation between 'capitalist' Sikh farmers and agricultural labourers, on the one hand, and traditional Hindu mercantile capital on the other. The historical cleavage between the towns and the villages, between Hindus and Sikhs, and between traders and cultivators became enmeshed in the modernisation process and class antagonisms. Some have suggested that these conflicts provided the main driving force behind the set of events that were to climax in Operation Blue Star.[31]

Against this backdrop Sikh grievances against the Indian state became formalised in the campaign for the Anandpur Sahib Resolution (ASR), passed in 1973, which sought to limit the Union government's powers over defence, foreign affairs, currency and communications – a status not unlike that enjoyed by pre-1953 Kashmir. Such a political framework, the resolution suggested, would provide an appropriate environment 'where the voice of the Khalsa Sikhs can be pre-eminent'. The resolution also demanded the integration into the state of excluded Punjabi-speaking areas, economic reforms in favour of the agricultural sector, and central assistance for the construction of power generation projects. Although the resolution was to become the 'Magna Carta of the Sikhs', at the time of its passing it attracted little attention.[32]

Following the dismissal of the SAD government in 1980, the ASR became the focus of an autonomy movement led by moderate Akalis. In August 1982 the SAD launched the *dharma yud morcha* (religious war) to press for the implementation of the ASR. When this campaign failed to achieve a political settlement with the centre, a militant faction led by Sant Jarnail Singh Bhindranwale called for direct action and this led to the gradual breakdown of law and order in Punjab. On 5 June 1984 the Indian Army, in Operation Blue Star, entered the Golden Temple in order to evict Sant Jarnail Singh Bhindranwale and his followers, who had taken refuge in the precinct. The clash resulted in the deaths of 1,000 security personnel and Sikh militants.

In the aftermath of Operation Blue Star Prime Minister Indira Gandhi was killed by her Sikh bodyguards. Her death was followed immediately by pogroms against Sikhs in Delhi in which approximately 3,000 people were killed in the full glare of the global media. In 1985 Rajiv Gandhi attempted to restore the political process through the Rajiv–Longowal Accord, but his reluctance to make concessions on the main Sikh demands undermined the moderate Akalis and led to the rise of militant groups campaigning for a separate Sikh state of Khalistan. Between 1984 and 1993, almost 30,000 people were killed in Punjab as a result of militant violence and counter-insurgency operations conducted by the security forces. During these years Punjab became an 'area of darkness' where people lived in constant fear of violence by Sikh militants and the security forces. By the end of 1993 the army's use of overwhelming force, including nearly 250,000 military and paramilitary personnel, succeeded in eliminating most of the militant groups operating in Punjab.[33]

In February 1997, in the first free and fair elections held in the province since 1985, the SAD won a landslide victory in the provincial elections. It ruled the state until 2002 in coalition with the national partner, the Bharatiya Janata Party (BJP). Despite the fact that the SAD remains committed to the ASR, it did little during its tenure in office to seek any realisation of the demands that had brought such chaos to the province. Indeed, the desire of the SAD leadership to return to mainstream politics has led to its political decline, with the success of the Congress administration in the provincial assembly elections of 2002. Nevertheless, the SAD remains a significant political force, if only by virtue of its control of the 'Sikh political system'. In opposition it is again reverting to a mobilisation strategy by drawing on the widespread discontent generated by the collapse in agricultural incomes, but whether this will rekindle the agitation for the successful realisation of the ASR remains to be seen.

Conclusion

Almost five centuries of modern history have made the Sikhs relatively unusual among religious communities. Sikhism has been heavily influenced by the environment around it – adapting, changing and firmly institutionalising itself. As Brass notes, Sikhs today have 'succeeded in acquiring a high degree of internal social and political cohesion and subjective self-awareness'.[34] The formation of this consciousness as a distinct religious community has been a long, drawn-out process that has built on the foundations established by Sikh gurus but reached its climax under the impact of colonial modernity. It could be argued that the development of a more homogeneous Sikh identity has been thwarted by the failure to achieve national statehood – in contrast to Pakistan or India. But such a reading overlooks the fact that the failure of the Sikh national project, especially with the Khalistan movement, has opened the tradition and the community to alternative conceptions of modernity that are perhaps less prone to ethnocidal outcomes. If in the recent past the Sikh diaspora has been the main driver of the Sikh nationalism and homeland project, today it is also the site of creative alternatives. The history of the British Sikhs underscores this development. Before we turn to a consideration of this subject in more detail, it is necessary to provide a detailed account of the Punjabi society from which most of the British Sikhs migrated.

Two
Punjabi Society
and Sikh Migration

Out migration has been a permanent feature of Punjabi society since time immemorial: the tradition of wandering is so embedded that it can be traced in the earliest literature on the Punjabis. From the eighteenth century onwards there is evidence of Punjabi settlements across India and beyond, and it appears that the growth of mass migration was not only the product of colonial modernity but also deeply rooted as a cultural tradition. Colonial and post-colonial modernity no doubt accelerated the process, especially to the West, but it would be seriously misleading to suggest that Punjabi migration is essentially a modern phenomenon.

In this chapter we examine the nature of Punjabi society: the values and institutions that influenced – and continue to influence – the outlook of British Sikhs. We then explore the patterns of Sikh migration with particular reference to the areas of origin, identifying those geographical, economic and social characteristics that have contributed to the distinctive development of British Sikh society.

Sikhs and Punjabi Society

Sikhism as a faith tradition, as we have noted in the previous chapter, was greatly influenced by the nature of Punjabi society. While many aspects of Punjabi social structure and culture were receptive to Sikhism's teachings, the new faith took root in an agrarian society that was very much part of the broader Indic tradition. Sikh values with their special emphasis on equality, community and service have always nestled uncomfortably within broader Punjabi values. Ethnicity and cultural tradition have often overshadowed them; sometimes, misleadingly, religion and culture have been conflated.[1]

Caste

Caste is one cleavage that cuts across all Sikh formations as an inerasable distinction, whether in India or overseas (see Figure 1.1, p. 18). Notwithstanding Sikhism's egalitarian message or the fact that the more outward manifestations of caste distinctions such as 'pollution' are clearly less visible in Punjab society, caste nonetheless provides the justification for a social hierarchy that is sustained by endogamy. Interestingly, the distinctive social pluralism that pervades Sikh society is to be found not along the familiar cleavages of region, language, ethnicity or class, but in caste distinctions.[2]

Most British Sikhs, whether they arrived via East Africa or other regions such as the Far East, can trace their origins to the ancestral family village. Urban Sikhs, who traditionally provided the leadership of the community in India, were relatively few in number or emphasised their social distance from their more rustic brethren. It is within rural village society, therefore, where agriculture was the only culture, that we can identify some of the enduring characteristics of Punjabi society. As in most agrarian societies, the social structure of Punjab was determined by access to landholding; but, unlike most other societies, landownership was also reinforced by caste.

Punjabi villages in the mid-twentieth-century – when the mass migration to Britain began – were organised along the lines of caste hierarchy. Although Brahmins, and below them the urban castes, exercised considerably less influence than elsewhere in India, rural life was dominated and shaped in the image of its leading landowning caste: the Jats. Traditionally a low-caste group, the Jats over successive centuries had risen to power, most notably during Sikh rule, by capturing the agrarian economy of the province. As the leading cultivators, their landholdings could range from a few to several hundred acres, though the more common pattern was that of a middle or poor peasant, idealised by the British colonialists as the 'yeoman farmers'. Typically, Jats commanded the largest and most productive village land resources, lived in the most desirable part, and, if they were Sikh, managed and controlled the local religious and political institutions. Jats were inclined to assert their superiority *vis-à-vis* inferior castes, many of whom were economically dependent on them in patron–client relationships. They were also fiercely egalitarian in their outlook, a quality that bred, and continues to breed, internecine factionalism wherever they are to be found.[3] Because Jats made up almost two-thirds of Sikh society, it was not uncommon to view them as interchangeable with Sikhism. 'In fact', as Helweg observes, 'when Sikh Jat culture is studied, it is impossible to separate the Sikh from the Jat, as their goals and values are tightly inter-woven.'[4]

Below Jats were skilled artisan castes: *Tarkhans-Ramgarhias* (carpenters), *Lohars* (blacksmiths), *Chhimbas* (tailors), *Julahas* (weavers), *Nais* (barbers), *Jhinwars* (water carriers) and *Ghumars* (potters) provided essential services for the village economy and beyond. While in many ways dependent on the Jats, these castes had significant relative autonomy, both religious and financial, because their skills were normally in high demand within the village and immediate locality. Many of these castes traced their lineage to the evolution of the Sikh *panth* in which members of these caste groups played a leading role in the life and times of the Sikh gurus, or authored compositions to be found in the *Guru Granth Sahib*, or played a major leadership role in subsequent Sikh history. The Ramgarhias, for instance, emphasise the role of Jassa Singh Ramgarhia, a distinguished leader of a Sikh *misl* that waged an unrelenting guerrilla campaign against the Mogul and Afghan authorities in the eighteenth century. Ramgarhias, like some of the other caste groups, have successfully constructed a narrative of identity that combines caste and the Sikh tradition while marking both aspects as equidistant from Jat-Sikhdom. This process has been further reinforced by the migration of a large number of Ramgarhias to East Africa from the end of the nineteenth century onwards, facilitating their upward social mobility from skilled artisans to model globalised professionals.[5]

At the bottom of the village caste hierarchy were the outcastes, the labouring and service castes, many of whom were tied to landowners through systems of hereditary dependence or were engaged in tasks that others considered too degrading – leather workers/landless *Chamars* (labourers), for example, *Mazbis* (sweepers) or *Bhangi* (cleaners). These groups are often referred to as Scheduled Castes (because of affirmative action policies designed for them after the 1950s), *Adi-Dharmis*, *Ravidasis*, or, most recently and in line with the rise of lower-caste parties in India, as *Dalits* ('the oppressed').These groups lived in segregated areas of the villages and because of their vulnerable positions were most prone to economic, political and sexual exploitation by the Jat Sikhs. These social antagonisms were congealed in the caste hierarchies; they were rarely, if at all, mediated by Sikhism or other local religions. The harsh realities of the village economy, with its insatiable demand for agricultural labour, regularly brought to the surface these underlying tensions and conflicts. Consequently the non-Jat Sikh castes, like the Ramgarhias, were inclined to assert their cultural as well as religious autonomy. But whereas the Ramgarhias did this by strict adherence to Sikh customs in which they emphasised their own caste tradition, other castes did so by engaging in and emphasising heterodox practices which combined many elements of the Sikh tradition with reverence for Sants (religious leaders) like Ravidas, who historically had championed the cause of the lower castes. It was among these groups that the boundaries of Sikhism began to blur, where alternative visions of religion as social emancipation were fostered, and where the bitter contestations about Sikh, Hindu and other world faith identities would take place.[6]

Social Norms
As in most agrarian societies life within a Punjabi village was set within a complex system of norms and customs which regulated almost all aspects of everyday existence. The family was the primary unit of social organisation and, in the absence of class or other permanent institutions, commanded intense loyalty. Like most traditional and patriarchal societies, a family's esteem was measured by its prestige and honour (*izzat*) and capacity to limit dishonour (*behzti*).[7] Families acquired high social status through wealth, principally landholdings, which determined their ability to forge future marital alliances for their children. Fear or prospects of loss of honour (*behzti*), often through continuous sub-division of landholdings, was a powerful factor driving Sikh peasants of the central districts of Punjab to seek livelihoods beyond Punjab and overseas.

In the 1950s a typical Sikh family in rural Punjab consisted of a joint household in which several generations of kindred lived together under the same roof, most likely a large farmhouse with several living quarters. Such a household would have been distinguished by the common ownership of land and the leadership of a patriarch, though matriarchs were not uncommon. Within the family relationships were based on hierarchy, dependences and mutual obligation: the elders were respected and sons and daughters (until they were married) and their children knew their place. Given the Sikh tradition of marrying outside the village, such a family would have developed an extensive state-wide network of *biradari* (kinship) connections. Like the family, the relationships within the *biradari* would have been determined by mutual respect, obligation and patterns of regular exchange relating to the life cycle, religious ceremonies and social functions. A family's social standing was determined by its ability to maintain its *izzat*, a concept intimately bound up with a family's social status, wealth and power, with women's purity and with notions of equivalence in reciprocations. *Izzat* provided the psychological *leitmotiv* for the community, a moral code liable to visit revenge or complete social rejection on the transgressor. Unsurprisingly, women's chastity was central to *izzat*, and this was seen in the necessary requirement of modest behaviour and dress and a strict taboo on adultery. In a rigidly patriarchal society women's place was defined primarily within the home – as the mothers and carers of children, a status further reinforced by the social taboo against divorce and non-existent property rights.[8]

Although *izzat* and *behzti* were the key codes of normative behaviour, they were also deeply ingrained in the related concepts of communal behaviour. These are far too numerous to enumerate except to note that they defined the patterns of friendship, loyalty and hospitality, the idea of service to others, and the need for respect for power and wealth. In Punjabi village society Sikhs valued power and wealth in itself but also as a form of protection for the family. The exercise of power over others was greatly admired as well as deeply resented as a mark of inferior social status.[9]

Forms of Organisation: Factions

The main organisation of Sikhs in Punjabi village society was the faction (or *paarti*). Unlike some Mediterranean societies or other regions in India, Punjabi villages were not hermetically sealed units organised along patron–client networks. For one thing, the Sikh tradition of marrying outside the village encouraged the development of broad kinship connections and political and social alignment outside the family village. For another, especially among Jat Sikhs, the normative requirements of independence and equality encouraged widespread linkages within the community across the province. The loss of independence was often identified as an 'insult' to one's status, a condition which fostered the search for interdependence as a safeguard. 'The refusal to submit' as Pettigrew has noted was:

> a sign of independence, and also an indication that ties of interdependence in the form of a faction exist. Factions ... exist[ed] to provide a collective protection to each individual family in friendship and enmities, and thereby to protect their honour and their reputation and hence their parity of standing with all other families.[10]

The existence of a faction organised around a 'leader' pervaded all forms of Sikh organisation – political, social, economic, religious and cultural. Factions were so systemic that the history of Sikh institutions is probably best understood as the history of internecine factional conflict. Even the most ideological of such organisational groups, the CPI, throughout its history was divided less by ideology than by factional disputes.[11] Factionalism therefore, regardless of caste background, is endemic in Sikh organisations, a permanent 'state of nature' that has neither diminished nor lost its significance after several generations of British Sikh society and major economic change in Punjab. What *has* changed, however, are the kinds of resources that factions are able to mobilise to further their interests, and in Britain factions rely not only on the traditional loyalties of village society but on the new resources of the state and non-state actors.[12]

Punjabi society in the middle of the twentieth century shared many of the characteristics of the homeland societies of the New Common-wealth migrants to Britain after the Second World War. It was a traditional, hierarchical and patriarchal society in which the norms and values of the Sikh faith coexisted with other faith traditions, most notably Hinduism and Islam (until the partition), as well as local folk and heterodox traditions. The relative homogeneity of Sikh identity as represented by Jat Sikhs, who made up almost two-thirds of the com-munity, had its significant counterpoints in caste divisions, intense faction-alism, and the everyday conflicts over wealth, power and status. The 'remembered' village of British Sikh migrants was to exercise a powerful hold over the imagination of subsequent Sikh generations in Britain, but, in narrating the tales of the village, Sikh parents often overlooked its remarkable diversity and social dynamism.[13] While these narratives have been much influenced by the conditions of settlement in Britain, it must be recognised that the Punjabi village was a remarkably socially diverse institution. If this diversity has now been magnified in Britain among Sikhs, most Punjabis at the time were also susceptible to the allure of the *phoren* (foreign).

Patterns of Sikh Migration

Before 1945

Among Sikhs the tradition of migration is in danger of becoming a culture. Beginning with internal migration in the eighteenth century and expanding through mass movements in the nineteenth and twentieth centuries, the tradition has developed a lore and economy of its own, becoming ingrained as part of the modern Sikh psyche. Sikhs, it seems, are permanently on the move, for ever in search of better pastures, restlessly seeking out different countries. The pattern of going abroad to better oneself might well be the natural outgrowth of Punjab's highly competitive frontier society; it might also have deeper psychological

Table 2:1 Global Sikh Population, 2005

Country	Population	Main Areas/Characteristics
Europe		
UK	336,179	London, West Midlands
Germany	25,000	Frankfurt, Heidelberg
Italy	20,000	South
Belgium	20,000	Luxemburg
Ukraine	8,000	
Cyprus	7,000	
Greece	5,000	
France	4,000	Paris
Spain	3,000	Barcelona
Denmark	2,000	Copenhagen
Sweden	2,000	Lund
Switzerland	2,000	
Americas		
Canada	278,415	BC & Ontario
United States	250,000	California, Mid-West, New York
Mexico	5,000	
Argentina	1,000	
Far East		
Australia	40,000	Woolagoogla, Sydney
Malaysia	36,000	Kuala Lumpur, Penang
Singapore	32,000	City
Philippines	20,000	Manila and suburbs
Thailand	12,000	Major cities
New Zealand	8,000	Auckland
Indonesia	5,000	
Middle East		
Gulf states	60,000–175,000★	Bahrain, Oman, Dubai
South Asia		
Afghanistan	7,000	Kabul
Pakistan	5,000	Nankana Sahib, Lahore
Sri Lanka	1,000	Colombo
Burma	1.000	Rangoon
Punjab and India		
India	19,923,000	
Punjab	14,592,387	Mainly rural
Rest of India	5,331,000	Delhi, Haryana, Uttar Pradesh, Maharashtra, Rajasthan

Sources: For Canada and the UK figures are derived from Census 2001. For European countries, estimated numbers are calculated from national statistics. For Far Eastern countries, data is derived from Census reports using reasonable interpolation.
★ The number of Sikh migrants in the Middle East has varied dramatically due to wars and other factors.

roots that go beyond conventional social science explanations. 'Each time a Sikh ... leaves his homeland', as the popular saying goes, 'it is a return to his most permanent tradition – that of roaming.'[14] Punjab's folklore mingles this sense of rupture with the pain of separation brought about by migration and its attendant loss, and with the longing to be reunited.[15] Sometimes migration has been an adventure, sometimes a necessity; always it has been the mark of an open community with few physical or spiritual barriers restraining a readiness to explore the modern world. Thus migration often has no end; instead it becomes a staging post for further movements and explorations.

Estimates of the Sikh diaspora suggest that today nearly 1 million, or about 5 per cent of the total Sikh population of about 20 million, live outside India and Punjab. By far the largest community is settled in Britain, with significant historic settlements in Canada, the United States, Australia and the Far East.

The first wave of migration began between the 1860s and 1890s when the favoured position of Sikhs in the Indian Army attracted them to foreign lands. Many had served in Central Asia, Africa, and the Far East or had acted as security auxiliaries for British firms. Some Sikhs accompanied their fellow officers on tour and were recruited by British companies in the rubber plantations of Malaysia. From South East Asia these individuals then explored the Far East or made their way to the Pacific Coast, Australia, New Zealand and Fiji.[16] The first contingent reached the Pacific Coast in 1905, and from there some ventured into Mexico, Panama and Argentina.

The second phase of migration began in the 1880s and lasted beyond the Second World War. This period is characterised by incorporation into the system of indentured labour and then free labour. Most migration from India in the mid-nineteenth century was in the form of indentured labour to colonies in Mauritius, British Guyana, Natal, Trinidad, Fiji, East Africa, the Transvaal, Cape Province, Ceylon, Malaya and Jamaica. Because of Punjab's late incorporation into colonial rule, few Punjabis went abroad as indentured labourers.[17] In 1895, 350 Punjabi workmen were contracted to work on Ugandan railways, a figure which rose to 31,895 six years later.[18] After the rail project some 6,000 men decided to stay on in East Africa. Some Sikhs went as indentured labourers to Fiji and the West Indies but they often rebelled against the appalling conditions, prompting the authorities to ban further recruitment.[19]

By the 1920s Indians could enter most British colonies but access into the White Dominions was restricted. Entry into Britain could be secured on the production of a passport, and the British Nationality Act of 1914 greatly extended the scope of British citizenship by conferring common citizenship on all subjects of the Crown. Despite this legislation, admission into the Dominions remained difficult, especially after the first wave of migration to Canada by 1910 triggered the imposition of strict controls. The United States soon followed suit by limiting Asian migration, and many Sikhs who had acquired citizenship were deprived of the status.[20] Although these entry barriers successfully limited any further mass migration during the inter-war years, by the end of the Second World War Sikh colonies had been established throughout the globe to become magnets for future migrants.

After 1945

Following the end of colonial rule a different set of conditions began to determine the patterns of Sikh migration. Among the pull factors were the growing demand for labour in the Western economies, more liberal migration policies, and the development of the Gulf states. Among the push factors were the impact of the partition, regular political instability in Punjab, the collapse of the rural economy from the 1990s onwards, and indigenisation policies in countries such as Fiji, Kenya, Uganda and China (Hong Kong). These sets of factors have operated in mutually reinforcing ways, a process hastened by the emergence of globalised networks within the Sikh diaspora.

The post-war reconstruction boom in Western economies fuelled by Keynesian economic policies created an insatiable demand for labour as shortages developed and governments increasingly turned to the former colonies to secure new recruits. In Britain this recruitment from the New Commonwealth countries of India, Pakistan and the Caribbean region was officially encouraged, with particular emphasis on public sector workers but also on general unskilled labour. In the early 1950s British government policy was aimed at overcoming labour shortages.[21] In these conditions Sikhs were easily able to secure employment and the new workers quickly communicated this message to kith and kin at home, triggering large-scale chain migration.[22]

The post-war demand for labour was also accompanied by liberal immigration policies. In Britain the Nationality Act of 1948 theoretically gave every citizen of the Commonwealth the right to settle, but in practice this right was circumscribed by informal restrictions such as the control over the issuing of passports and informal diplomatic pressures. Nonetheless, migrants from India proved particularly resourceful in circumventing some of these restrictions. For instance, in the 1950s when the Government of India was pressured into limiting the issue of passports, many Sikhs crossed the border and secured passports from Pakistan with Islamic names. It was not until the Commonwealth Immigrants Act of 1962 that the 'liberal regime' came to an end.

Liberal immigration policies were also adopted by Canada and the United States. In Canada the push towards a multicultural society was accompanied by a policy that opened the door wider to non-white settlers. Over the last four decades this has encouraged significant primary emigration from Punjab, with Canada's Sikh population increasing from 7,000 in 1960 to nearly 278,415 in 2001. Similarly, in the US the 1960s saw the repeal of much of the restrictive immigration legislation that had been put into force in the 1920s to curtail Asian immigration. While the bias of US immigration policies has been towards attracting professionals, the 1990s witnessed a significant influx of Sikh non-professionals who gained access as asylum seekers or through illegal means. This change is also reflected in the size and social composition of the Sikh US population.[23]

The oil boom of the early and mid-1970s provided the next major demand-led Sikh migration. Awash with petro-dollars, the Gulf states launched major infrastructure and building programmes that attracted millions of Indian workers on the pattern of 'neo-indentured' labourers who worked on fixed-term contracts without any rights. Precise figures for Sikh migration are unavailable but it is estimated that currently there are 60,000 to 175,000 Sikhs in the Gulf states. The number of those who have been in the Gulf states at any time since the 1970s is considerably higher, for the average period of the contract varies from several months to a few years. This migration has created a substantial remittance economy and contributed further pressures for migration, as the returnees have often sought more permanent locations once their contracts have expired. The Middle East has often constituted the transition zone between India and further migration to the West or the Far East.[24]

In the 1970s and the 1980s the onset of recession together with the rise of anti-immigration policies seriously curtailed the flows of Sikhs to the West. In Britain Thatcherism destroyed the manufacturing economy, the mainstay of Sikh employment, while imposing strict controls that all but curtailed primary immigration. As a result Sikh migrants from Punjab increasingly made North America and other countries their main destination. But as the economy in Britain in the 1990s revived, fuelled by the dot.com boom, Sikh migration also witnessed something of a revival, though this was not professional-led but allied to supporting labour shortages on the back of asylum and refugee settlement. Recent measures to allow for more flexible and temporary workers from South Asia to meet skill shortages in key areas have added significantly to the temporary Sikh population as a whole. These changes in policy suggest that Sikh migrants are highly knowledgeable about migration opportunities and are always primed to exploit them as they arise (see Chapter 3).

Push Factors

Of all the factors that have contributed to Sikh (and Punjabi) migration the partition of India in 1947 was perhaps the single most dramatic act. As we saw in Chapter 1, the division of the historic province of Punjab led to unprecedented ethnic cleansing with the accompanying transfers of population that made West Punjab a homogeneous Muslim territory and East Punjab a province of mainly Sikhs and Hindus. For Sikhs and Hindus of the former Canal Colonies, resettlement in East Punjab was a traumatic event: the settlement process dragged on and in many cases inferior and inadequate landholdings were allocated in exchange for those they had relinquished. In fact, the partition threw the whole economy of East Punjab into turmoil, generating excessive demographic pressure on agriculture and the need to accommodate and resettle several million refugees who were often compelled to eke out an existence for several years. Many of these refugees, particularly the urban Sikhs, moved to Delhi or other states within the Indian Union. Many more saw the despair of the partition as an opportunity to build lives abroad on the back of post-war reconstruction. The 'Third Punjab', or the 'diaspora Punjab', it has been argued, arose directly from the 'ashes of the partition'. For some of the migrants, even Delhi seemed an impermanent, insecure place to construct the 'new home'.[25]

Since 1947 political instability in Punjab has also played a major part in Sikh emigration to Britain and other countries. Operation Blue Star in 1984 probably triggered the largest wave of Sikh migration to the West since the 1950s and 1960s. Young Sikh men, either to avoid persecution in Punjab or to exploit the opportunities for migration, sought political asylum in Western states in their thousands. The exact figures for the post-1984 refugee outflow will probably never be available but the numbers were not insignificant. From 1984 to 1992, 5,900 Indian citizens, excluding dependants, applied for political asylum in Britain and most of these were Sikhs.[26] European countries with recognised asylum policies also received large numbers: Germany, France, the Netherlands, Norway, Denmark, Italy and Switzerland now have sizeable Sikh settlements that date from the post-1984 overspill as the 'Punjab problem' became internationalised. The European influx was extended to Canada and the United States, where large numbers of asylum applications were reluctantly granted. Immigration authorities in these states had to tread a fine line between granting asylum and maintaining controls. Several actually sent out their own missions to India to check the veracity of the asylum seekers' claims that brutal repression had driven them overseas.[27] Asylum applications tailed off only with the rising asylum population in Western countries in the late 1990s. The end of the militancy in Punjab has effectively undermined the legitimacy of any further claims for asylum, though it would be premature to suggest that this mode of migration has now been closed permanently.

Sikhs, like other Indians, have also been the victims of indigenisation policies in some decolonised states. In East Africa, the Far East, Hong Kong, South Africa, the Caribbean and, most recently, Afghanistan, small and large Sikh populations, often resident in these countries for several centuries, have increasingly relocated themselves to Western states because of such policies. This relocation has obeyed a natural bias towards places where the largest Sikh populations are centred, thereby invoking the immigration obligations of former imperial rulers. Interestingly, it follows the overall pattern of movement of the Indian diaspora, from the traditionally low-income economies of the South to the North.

Of all the push factors, it is economic circumstances that have received most scrutiny from scholars.[28] As most of the migration to Britain has taken place from the three districts of Hoshiarpur, Jalandhar and Kapurthala, all located in the Doaba region (see Map 1.2, p. 22), studies have sought to identify particular reasons for this outflow. Today the Doaba is one of the most economically developed regions in India, but in the 1950s and 1960s it was characterised by small, uneconomic landholdings, high population density and few sources of employment outside agriculture. Partition had a particularly unsettling impact on agriculturalists in this region because the resettlement of refugees from West Punjab required a substantial reduction in the average landholding to accommodate the displaced population. Historically the average landholding in the region had been small (in 1951 average landholdings in Jalandhar and Hoshiarpur were 2.5 and 4 acres respectively, compared with the Punjab average of 7.5 acres) and partition thus created further demographic pressure for outward migration.[29]

However some of these pressures were mediated by the onset in the 1960s of the Green Revolution, which modernised agriculture through the use of new, high-yielding seeds and technologies. Rich and poor fortunes alike were transformed. As well as multiplying agricultural incomes, the new methods also created a powerful lobby of Sikh agriculturalists, led by the SAD, that pressed for the further economic development of the state. It was these demands that precipitated the autonomy movement of the early 1980s for more provincial control of Punjab's economic development. But tragically this movement, and the violence which ensued afterwards in the 1980s and 1990s, substantially undermined the province's potential for economic development at a juncture when India's economic liberalisation programme and globalisation further eroded the central government's capacity to support agriculture. Since the early 1990s the collapse of the rural economy in Punjab has created a vicious cycle of low growth, falling agricultural incomes and declining employment opportunities. Once again the local state is facilitating migration as a safety valve against the pressures created by the new circumstances, although increasingly this is articulated in the language of diaspora-led economic development.[30] Today, as in the past, those most affected by the new squeeze are the marginal and poor farmers, the majority of whom tend to be concentrated in the Doaba.

While economic factors have undoubtedly played a major part in Sikh migration, we also need to acknowledge the role of cultural factors. Migration from Punjab today is not only determined by the migrant's economic status: even well-established families have felt the need for 'foreign connections', more so in the last decade as the pressures of globalisation undermined agriculture while introducing Punjabis to global markets. The modernisation of Punjab society over the last half century, moreover, has created a large graduate population who prefer migration to commercial or agricultural employment, even though this often means taking up low-status employment in developed economies. One commentator has noted the famous 'PhD taxi rank' in Sydney, run by alumni of Punjab Agricultural University.[31] These alumni also proliferate in New York, Seattle and Vancouver. But, paradoxically, while status compulsions lead Sikhs to outward migration, Punjab's Green Revolution has witnessed the large-scale immigration of almost 3 million agricultural labourers from other Indian states, most notably Bihar. For many Sikhs migration in modern Punjab has become a compulsion to maintain the status differential, not least from India's own immigrants.

This culture of migration has been fuelled further by the development of probably the most sophisticated migration industry in India, if not the whole of Asia. This industry initially began by enticing would-be migrants with information on the rich prospects in the West; it has now blossomed into a multi-billion-dollar enterprise that is singularly responsible for creating the current size of the Sikh diaspora. The Doaba has more travel agents per square mile than any other region in the world, and since the early 1950s this industry has established elaborate connections both within the provincial and national state bureaucracy in India that have enabled it to develop complex networks of people-trafficking that extend to all regions of the globe. There is, indeed, nowhere in the world where the travel agents of Jalandhar cannot deliver a migrant: the only constraint is the ability of the would-be migrant to raise the requisite funding. Over the years several agents have developed reputations for delivering migrants that have been woven into the cultural folklore of the region.[32] A recent visit to travel agents in Jalandhar highlighted the easy access a potential migrant has to details of the immigration and welfare policies of most Western states.[33] The lobbying from this industry, with its networks in Punjab and overseas, especially Britain and Canada, has led to pressure for immigration procedures and airline travel to be made more accessible to its needs. In view of further plans to expand cheap airline travel to Punjab by most Western airliners, the size of this industry is likely to increase substantially in the near future.[34]

Doabian Migration: Some Distinct Features

Doabians have been stereotyped by non-Doabian Punjabis as land-starved, shrewd, untrustworthy, enterprising and relatively better-educated – people who are unusually resourceful because of the misfortunes of geography. There is more than a grain of truth in this as in most stereotypes. Doabians have been (and remain) exceptionally adept at developing survival strategies over generations to replenish the family capital, whether this has involved migration (initially to the Canal Colonies in West Punjab and then overseas), recruitment into the Indian Army, or investing heavily in education to secure government appointments. Constantly threatened by the spectre of subdivision of landholding, Doabians have faced unremittingly overwhelming pressures to achieve. It was these pressures that led to the first patterns of chain migration overseas at the end of the nineteenth century.[35] It was also these pressures that gave rise in the 1920s to the Doabian leadership of the fledgling CPI. Today, these same pressures have been further compounded by the emergence of the Doaba as the globalised 'Midlands' heartland of the new Punjabi economy.

Within the Doaba the pattern of migration is highly localised. Several villages, known as *barapinds* (large villages), have been transplanted overseas *en bloc*. Of particular note are villages in the subdistricts of Jalandhar (Nakodar), Kapurthala (Phagwara and Nawanshahar) and Hoshiarpur (Garhshankar). These villages were central to the construction of many overseas Sikh communities as waves of chain migration followed the early settlers: they created bridgeheads for future arrivals, as well as staging posts for further movement and dispersal. Gravesend has been noted as a leading UK example of a bridgehead where Jalandhians provided the core founding community.[36] Similar examples can be found in many other British Sikh localities of the 1950s and 1960s, such as Leicester, Derby, Coventry, Leamington Spa, Smethwick, Bedford, Walsall, Glasgow, East Ham and Erith. Big-village chain migration has been so successful that today many of these villages are populated only by the elderly or migrant labourers from other states of India. Some of the elderly are retired people who have returned after a lifetime of work overseas.

In an interesting development that aims to sustain the link with the ancestral village, Sikhs in Britain and elsewhere have founded village associations as vehicles for re-establishing links among new generations and sustaining contact with villagers in Punjab. These associations have sought to re-establish transnational networks for mobilising resources for developing social and religious institutions such as schools, hospitals and gurdwaras. In many notable instances they have displaced the role of the local state as a provider of services.[37] While the supply of migrants fuelling chain migration from the big villages has now been exhausted in many cases, the importance of this phenomenon for understanding British Sikh society probably lies, amongst other things, in the key it provides for unravelling the myriad factional disputes that bedevil Sikh organisations and that often have their roots in the ancestral village. The village in the global Sikh imagination is never far away. As Le Brack has noted, 'the Punjab village remains the psychological "homebase", even if "home" is England, Canada or the United States'.[38]

Last, it needs to be emphasised that the Doaba as a region has always had a high proportion of the former outcastes or Dalits in its population. In Punjab as a whole this percentage was 28.3 per cent in 1991 and 30 per cent in 2001. In the four districts of the Doaba the equivalent figure was 35.6 per cent, with Nawashare district recording the highest with 40.5 per cent.[39] The strength of the Dalit population in this region is reflected in its political, religious and cultural organisations, some of which have produced the main leadership of the lower-caste political parties in India today. Naturally this population also exploited the avenues for migration, more especially so as they provided an opportunity to escape from conditions of social oppression. To be sure, Dalit migration had always mirrored, though to a lesser degree, the pattern of broader Sikh migration, but in the 1950s and 1960s it developed a dynamic of its own. Often the earlier settlers were the sons of well-educated Dalits who sought to escape the stigmatisation of a society dominated by caste. Many of them also replicated the patterns of the *barapinds* in localities like Bradford, Bedford, Walsall and Handsworth; and as with *barapinds* strong ties have evolved with the sending villages and localities, sustaining elaborate transnational exchanges that involve marriages, business and return migration. But the principal importance of Punjabi Dalit migration to Britain was that it was rural and provided a caste-based frame of reference to counter the ambiguous boundaries of the Sikh faith dominated by Jats. The fraught caste relations of the Punjabi village were thus transferred to the British foundry, the pub and even the school playground. In the development of British Sikh society over the decades these tensions were to play a not inconsiderable part in the struggle for the control of Sikh institutions such as gurdwaras, trade unions and political parties.

Conclusion

Since the mid-nineteenth century almost a million Sikhs have settled overseas, creating a visible, dynamic and at times troublesome diaspora. Nearly a third of this diaspora is now based in Britain, an association that dates from the colonial encounter that dispersed the Sikhs across the globe in search of new opportunities opened up by travel and military service in the Indian Army. These early pioneers contributed significantly to the development of a cultural tradition of migration that became much more pervasive throughout Punjabi society with the rise in demand for labour in the post-war boom and the liberalisation of immigration controls. For Sikhs the global migration needs of Western and Middle Eastern economies have now supplanted the migratory mechanism provided by the Indian Army during colonial times. Sikhs are, in many ways, the premier migrants of South Asia.

At the same time we need to recognise that there were very specific reasons for some of the Sikh migration. Political dislocation – whether the partition or the 'Punjab problem' of the 1980s and 1990s – has always played a major role in the movement of Punjabi and Sikh populations; economic pressures also have their own momentum, especially in the central districts of the Doaba. As political instability over the last few decades has undermined economic development, the Punjab, once the most prosperous province in India, has found itself reeling from an agricultural depression at a time when India's non-agricultural economy is making global waves. In these circumstances it is more than likely that the culture of migration will become Punjabis' *only* culture – at least for the foreseeable future.

Finally, we need to note that Sikh migrants in the main were drawn from an agrarian society that was overwhelmingly traditional, patri-archal, conservative and hierarchically structured by caste rules – at least for the non-Jat Sikhs. For most of these migrants Sikhism as a faith defined their outlook and behaviour but it was also mediated by the everyday experience of living in broader Punjabi society, of which the village constituted the main social unit. In due course the *pendus* (villagers) would be supplemented by Sikh professionals from India, East Africa, the Far East and other parts of the Sikh diaspora, but it was the former group who were at the forefront in the pioneering organisations of British Sikhs. In the traditions and culture of today's British Sikhs, the 'remembered' village still occupies a pre-eminent position, and this recognition must underlie any serious understanding of British Sikh society.

Three
Settlement, Demography and Social Profile

Britain's landscape today is littered with unfamiliar structures which symbolise the presence of New Commonwealth immigrants and their descendants: gurdwaras, mosques and temples are a familiar sight in the inner cities that have been transformed by the permanent establishment of ethnic enclaves resembling what the anthropologist Roger Ballard has called 'colonisation from below'.[1] Sikh presence in these landscapes is a distinctive feature of contemporary British life, marked as it is by religious buildings and 'Little Punjabs' that have emerged over the past half century. In this chapter we examine the pattern of Sikh settlement in Britain from the mid-nineteenth century onwards. We review the history of settlement before and after the Second World War, consider the demographic changes that have occurred within the Sikh community over the past half-century, and provide an overview of the community's profile by drawing on some of the data produced by the 2001 census – all this as a prelude to a more detailed study of the development of Sikhs in Britain in the subsequent chapters.

Settlement in Britain

The historiography of ethnic minorities in Britain recognises the Second World War as the watershed which marked the onset of mass migration. Before 1945 the South Asian population of the UK consisted mainly of 'ayahs, lascars and princes', who were often transient visitors.[2] The Sikh element of this population was founded by a prince whose presence contributed significantly to the 'ornamentalisation' of the empire during the Victorian era. At the top of this hierarchy were the maharajas (Punjab's princes), followed by students, sojourners, soldiers and workers.

Duleep Singh – the Sikhs' Last Maharaja

There appears to be no record of Sikhs in Britain before the arrival in 1854 of Duleep Singh, who, as the son of the last adult ruler of Punjab, ascended the throne at the age of five in 1843. Following the annexation of Punjab by the East India Company in 1849, Duleep Singh was forced to renounce all his claims to the 'Kingdom of Lahore' while much of the Lahore treasury and state property was shipped to London – including the famous Koh-i-noor diamond, a 'gift' from the 'loyal subjects of Punjab' to Her Majesty Queen Victoria.[3] At the age of ten Duleep Singh was made a ward of court, separated from his mother, Rani Jindan Kaur, and exiled from Punjab to Futtaghar, where his education was entrusted to Dr Login, a doctor and devout Christian from Stromness in Orkney, Scotland.[4]

Under Login's influence Duleep Singh had converted to Christianity before his arrival in London in May 1854. The young Duleep soon made a favourable impression on Queen Victoria and quickly became her favourite, being invited regularly to stay at Osborne House.[5] He was given the rank of a European 'prince' with an allowance of £25,000 per year drawn on the East India Company, and, guided by his mentors, first settled in Scotland at Castle Menzies in Perthshire, where he gained popularity among Scottish gentry by dressing up in a kilt and displayed a keen interest in hawking and shooting. In 1860 Duleep Singh visited India to see his ailing mother, who returned with him to Britain in 1861 only to die in the summer of 1863. In the same year, following another visit to India to perform the last rites for his mother, he married Bamba Muller, a Eurasian of Coptic faith, in Aden on his return journey.

In 1863 Duleep Singh purchased Elveden Hall, a 17,000-acre estate on the borders of Norfolk and Suffolk, for £105,000; there he settled down to family life as a country squire and became known as a 'black prince' who socialised lavishly and hosted the royalty and the aristocracy. In 1873, with the support of the Duke of Richmond and Lords Walsingham and Colville, he was elected to the Carlton Club and considered standing for Parliament until dissuaded by Queen Victoria.

In the mid-1880s Duleep Singh's extravagant lifestyle, combined with an agricultural depression, led him into an acrimonious dispute with the India Office over his annual allowance, a dispute that was conducted publicly in letters to the *Times*.[6] Increasingly isolated, he left for India in 1886 with his family, with the intention of recovering his 'lost kingdom', but was detained at Aden where he renounced Christianity and re-embraced Sikhism.

While his family eventually returned to Britain, Duleep Singh decamped to Paris to become a self-declared exile who became embroiled in elaborate intrigues with Russia and other European powers to reclaim his kingdom. Under the pressure of exile and constant surveillance by British intelligence, Duleep Singh's health collapsed. He died in 1893 at the age of 55 in a Paris hotel, leaving behind two more daughters from a second marriage to an 'actress'. The official narrative has it that Duleep Singh reconverted to Christianity on his deathbed, thereby enabling his 'royal reappropriation' through burial at Elveden Hall with floral tributes from the Queen.[7]

Duleep Singh was survived by three sons and three daughters: Victor (1866–1918), Frederick (1868–1926) and Edward (1879–93); and Bamba (1869–1957), Catherine (1871–1942) and Sophia (1876–1948). Victor and Frederick were educated at Eton and Cambridge, and Victor became a Captain in the Royal Dragoons after attending Sandhurst: he resigned in 1898. Frederick attained the rank of Major in the army but retired to live the life of a squire at Blo Norton in Norfolk. Bamba and Catherine were educated at Somerville College, Oxford. Bamba subsequently married a Dr Sutherland and settled in Lahore, where she died in 1957. Both Sophia and Catherine took part in the Suffragette movement. Duleep Singh also left behind two other daughters – Ada Pauline (1887–?) and Irene (1889–1926) from his second marriage to Ada Wetherill.[8] Despite his large issue, Duleep Singh's line did not extend to modern times: it ended with the death of Bamba in Lahore.

In 1997 Duleep Singh's legacy was subjected to a dramatic twist when the Swiss banks, under pressure from Holocaust survivors, opened about 5,000 accounts unclaimed since the Second World War. One such account was discovered to be in the name of Catherine Hilda Duleep Singh and her governess, Linda Schaefer. The Claims Commission, after being deluged by several persons contesting their lineage from Punjab and Pakistan, decided in favour of a family from Lahore.[9]

A century after his death Duleep Singh continues to excite the Sikh imagination. Today he has become an icon for new generation of British Sikhs, a tangible link with royalty for 'reimagining' the British Sikh experience. In the summer of 1999 Prince Charles opened a permanent statue of Duleep Singh in Thetford, built by the Maharaja Duleep Singh Centenary Trust to promote the Anglo-Sikh heritage. As the British Sikh community seeks to establish a new identity, one which transcends the familiar image of racialised migrants, Duleep Singh's legacy provides an enduring symbol of Sikhs' British attachment as well as the potential for dissonance and ultimate rebellion.[10]

Transients: Princes, Soldiers and Students

Duleep Singh was not the only Sikh prince who made an impression on the British public. After the annexation of Punjab, several Sikh princely states – historically outside the Kingdom of Lahore – retained their statehoods. The Maharaja of Patiala, Bhupendra Singh, was a regular visitor to Britain who often stayed at the Savoy, arriving theatrically in a cavalcade of Rolls-Royces. He was the patron of the first Sikh gurdwara at Shepherd's Bush (see Chapter 4) and toured as captain of the Indian cricket team in 1911. A colourful character, Bhupendra Singh also chaired the Indian Chamber of Princes, a role which involved participation in the Roundtable Conferences of the early 1930s. Another Sikh prince, the Maharaja of Nabha, was a contemporary of Nehru at Harrow, although he did not distinguish himself academically there. The Maharaja of Kapurthala, who in India and France had a reputation for salaciousness, was entertained at court, much to the disdain of Lord Curzon, the Viceroy of India (1899–1905), who considered him a 'third rate chief'.[11]

The earliest visitors from Punjab were Sikh soldiers in the Indian Army. From the 1880s detachments of Sikh soldiers were brought to London almost annually for various parades and displays.[12] The *Illustrated London News* and other magazines depicted soldiers on parade in London during 1882; in a painting by Hall at the National Portrait Gallery, they are seen being presented to the Duke and Duchess of Kent. Sikh regiments paraded for Queen Victoria's Golden Jubilee (1885) and Diamond Jubilee (1897), and for the coronations of King George VI (1902), George V (1911) and George VI (1937).

Apart from state occasions it was the First World War that gave Sikh soldiers glimpses of British life. Almost 100,000 Sikhs served in France, Belgium, Greece, Turkey, Palestine, Egypt, Sudan and East Africa.[13] While most were from the Indian Army based in India, there were a few, like Hardit Singh Malik,[14] ex-public school and Balliol undergraduate, who enlisted in the Royal Flying Corps. The wounded were often brought to Britain for recuperation. Letters sent home by the Sikh soldiers give their impressions of Western life, the despair of trench warfare, and the awe induced by modern industrial life.[15] At Brighton the Pavilion was adapted as a hospital for Indian soldiers, with provision for religious service.[16] Sophia, Duleep Singh's daughter, visited wounded Indian soldiers and especially entertained them at her house in Hampton Court, despite strict restriction on access. Today the Chattri Memorial in Brighton commemorates Indian soldiers' contribution to the First World War.

During the Second World War Sikh soldiers were engaged mainly in the South East Asia theatre, though some regiments saw action in the Middle East, North Africa and Italy and some Sikhs based in Britain, like Shivdev Singh, Manmohan Singh and Mohinder Singh Pujji, saw distinguished service in the Royal Air Force.[17] Kip's experience in the novel and film *The English Patient* was not untypical, however, of many Sikhs for whom faith in British imperialism was ultimately undermined – resulting first in resentment and frustration, and later, near the end of the war, in the attempt to lead the Indian National Army towards the objective of liberating India from British rule.

With the opening of the civil service to Indians in the early twentieth century there was also a steady stream of travellers, writers and students. More affluent Punjabis started sending their young sons (and in a few cases daughters) to Britain for education. Umaro Singh, the elder brother of Sir Sundar Singh Majithia, visited Britain but soon left for Paris, where he married a Polish woman.[18] Kahan Singh, a distinguished Sikh scholar at the court of the Maharaja of Nabha, visited London in 1907, 1908 and 1910 on a tour of Europe with Prince Ripduman Singh, while also assisting Macauliffe in his seminal study of the Sikhs.[19] Teja Singh was among the first batch of Sikh students to arrive in London in 1907.[20] More followed in the 1920s and 1930s, many heading for Oxbridge, or for the Inns of Court to train for the Indian Civil Service or the legal profession. Among these were Kapur Singh, Patwant Singh, Balwant Singh Anand, Satinder Singh, Giani Sher Singh, Khushwant Singh, Chatur Kaur, Tarlok Singh, Mulk Raj Anand, E. N. Mangat Rai and G. B. Singh – most of whom were to pursue distinguished careers in administration, arts and business in India. Some of these students were no doubt involved in the activities of the India League, but it is unclear to what extent they had contacts with fellow Sikhs beyond the educational institutions. Very few left any lasting impressions of their life at the heart of the empire.[21] Khushwant Singh, for one, who subsequently became a distinguished writer, describes the social milieu of the Sikh elite, where there was intense rivalry and eager pursuit of educated Sikh females. He also recalls that he and another colleague from King's College, London, Basant Singh, were sent to Wiesbaden as part of a joint English Universities Indian hockey team just to give the team an 'authentic look'.[22]

Early Settlers: Bhatras and Doabians
Whereas most of the princes, soldiers and students returned to India, the first steps towards a permanent Sikh settlement in Britain were taken

almost anonymously, beyond the imperial gaze. Bhatras who came from the West Punjab district of Sialkot, mainly from Daska Tahsil, were among the first to start the process. It is unclear what triggered this migration but some suggest the Bhatras first moved to Sri Lanka before arrival in Britain. In any case in the early 1920s a colony of Punjabi Muslims had been established in Glasgow's Anderton and Port Dundas districts, where they were soon followed by the Bhatras.[23] By the mid-1930s a few hundred Bhatra Sikhs had spread to Wales, northern England and Scotland, where they came to specialise in peddling clothes. Soon a cycle was established of regular visits to India followed by the arrival of more migrants. In 1939–40 there were 37 Sikhs registered as peddlers with the Glasgow Council.[24] This small community was self-supporting. As the daughter of a Manchester Bhatra recalls:

> my father had settled in Britain in the 1930s; he would assist anyone new to England, at one time there was a stage when anyone coming over from India would stop first in Manchester and stay for twenty-one days which is what it took to make a peddler's licence. Father would supply them with food and accommodation and set them up in the business in which they wanted to go about. He was a salesman in clothes, drapery, ladies underwear, perfumes from France and various other items of that nature.[25]

Although their main areas of settlement were the coastal towns of Wales, North England and Scotland, Bhatra colonies gradually extended to Manchester (especially Moss Side), Birmingham and Peterborough.[26]

The inter-wars years also saw, as well as the Bhatras, the first signs of migration from the Doaba region, which was to become the base of most of Sikh migration after 1945. This trickle began when one Nathoo Mohammed of the village Kot Badal Khan in Nakodar subdistrict sent for Fateh Mohammed in 1924, and the latter then asked his relatives and friends to migrate. Because this locality had a large Sikh population it is likely that the news also percolated to local Sikhs. Indeed, Thakur Singh of Haripur village, who arrived in 1926 and went to settle in Scotland, is probably the first Sikh settler from the Doaba in Britain. Others like Narain Singh of Paban and Mansa Ram of Talwan followed him, beginning a pattern of chain migration from the *barapinds* around Nakodar that included Bilga, Sidhwan, Rurka Kalan, Bundala, Shankar, Pandori Khas, Malsian, Nangal, Mehatpur, Talwandi, Kiri, Bhaini, Salimpura, Sadarpura, Tihara and Pindori.[27] While some of these men followed the Bhatras' route to the north and Scotland, others settled in the industrial towns of the Midlands.[28]

Plate 2 A Sikh gathering at the Shepherd's Bush gurdwara, West London, 1937, to celebrate the birth of Guru Nanak. It includes Udham Singh (capped, back row) who was later hanged for the murder of Sir Michael Dwyer (1940), a former Governor of Punjab. (© Greater Manchester Council Record Office)

Coventry was the first midlands city to have a number of Punjabis living in its northern districts. According to one of the earlier settlers, these newcomers felt the need for an association and founded the Indian Workers' Association (IWA) in 1938. Its membership consisted of Punjabis (Sikhs, Muslims and Hindus) from the Doaba villages, though the Sikhs were in the majority, and as an organisation it ran in parallel with the more illustrious India League led by Krishna Menon.[29] At the time the Coventry IWA was mainly a social organisation, but it was active in supporting the case of Udham Singh, who shot Sir Michael Dwyer, a former Governor of Punjab, at Caxton Hall in March 1940 in revenge for the Jallianwala Bagh massacre (1920).[30]

During the war years some of the Sikh settlers enlisted in the services or worked on the domestic front. By the end of the war the number of permanent Sikh settlers was probably around 1,000 but certainly no more than 2,000. The majority lived isolated lives with little semblance of communal organisation, apart from special religious gatherings at the Shepherd's Bush gurdwara.

Towards Mass Migration: from 1945 to the Commonwealth Immigrants Act (1962)

Soon after the war there was little indication that Britain would become a magnet for Sikh migration. Historically immigration had been strictly controlled, with the colour distinction deeply seared into British immigration policy. Initially Britain's post-war labour needs were met by European migrants, many of whom were recruited as European Volunteer Workers to meet specific shortages.[31] But as the post-war boom took off and simultaneously the Iron Curtain came down across Eastern Europe, New Commonwealth migrants readily filled the gap.

It is most likely that after the war Sikh residents in Britain began communicating knowledge of opportunities for work to kith and kin in Punjab. Letters home often described in vivid detail the modern way of life the migrants were leading, with abundant opportunities to earn easy money.[32] These links were instrumental in inspiring many Sikhs to leave Punjab, which at the time suffered serious dislocation following partition. There was no symbolic mass arrival of Sikhs during these years, in the style of the docking of the *Empire Windrush* with its passenger list of settlers from the Caribbean, but the British Nationality Act of 1948, passed in response to India's independence, gave the citizens of the Commonwealth the right to settle and work in Britain and provided the impetus for regular migration. Unofficial controls, however, such as the pressure on governments from South Asia not to issue passports, or the requirement of an endorsement to travel to the UK, created practical difficulties. Between 1947 and 1950 very few passports were issued in Punjab, as the main passport office was moved to Delhi. Nevertheless, many Sikhs circumvented these regulations by travelling to Ceylon, Pakistan or the Far East, changing their names and assuming a new nationality. Some estimates suggest that as many as 5,000–10,000 arrived through these countries.[33]

It was in the early 1950s that the demand for labour increased dramatically. In the industrial towns of the Midlands and the north, jobs in foundries and textile mills were difficult to fill. Migrant labour readily met the need, setting in train further stimulus for inward migration. As Table 3.1 indicates, the 1950s saw the regular arrival of migrants from India, many of whom were Sikhs.

Until 1962 most of this immigration was of single, young men, seeking employment to make their fortunes abroad with the intention of returning to the 'homeland'. Few if any thought of laying down permanent roots; some, already disillusioned with the rigours of industrial life, returned home with what savings they had, though they were in a minority.[34]

Table 3.1 Indian Immigration to the United Kingdom, 1955-66

Year	Number
1955	5,800
1956	5,600
1957	6,600
1958	6,200
1959	2,950
1960	5,900
1961	23,750
1962	22,100
1963	17,498
1964	15,513
1965	18,815
1966	18,402

Source: E. J. B. Rose *et al.*, *Colour and Citizenship*, 4.

Where the new migrants settled upon arrival in Britain was deter-mined by two considerations: the location of kith and kin and the availability of work. Relatives, kinsmen or friends sponsored almost all migrants, except those who managed to secure their passage illegally. These sponsors, many of whom became famed for sponsoring whole villages, had established foothold in the cities of settlement before 1945 – Coventry, Birmingham, Leicester, Gravesend and Glasgow. Soon chain migration accelerated, with favoured locations being the West Midlands (Birmingham, Walsall, Wolverhampton), West (Southall, Slough, Ealing) and East (East Ham, Barking, Forest Gate) London, Gravesend, Bedford, Derby, Bradford, Leeds, Nottingham, Glasgow, Manchester, Scunthorpe and Huddersfield. In these cities unskilled industrial employment was not too difficult to find, with some employers having established a reputation for recruiting Sikhs because of their known ability for enduring hard work or because of prior connections with Punjab, often through the armed forces (see Chapter 7).

Family, kin or friends helped to settle in new arrivals. A familiar ritual was the cutting of hair as the migrants shed the turban for their new identity as industrial workers. Sometimes they were taken to work immediately upon arrival. Colonies soon formed around foundries of the West Midlands or the industrial belts of West and East London. For most migrants early social life in Britain was like a commune in which relatives supported each other and villagers pooled their resources in the first steps towards community building. The ties of tradition and social reciprocation ensured the harmonious integration of new arrivals. For most young men these were the golden years of 'bachelorhood' when they were away from the pressures of family norms and duties. Typically they lived as singles in one house, with occupancy ranging from 5 to 25, or sometimes more. Overcrowding in inner-city slums was the norm. As one Sikh later recalled:

> You cannot imagine how barbarously we lived in those days. The front room had three beds, two of them double. The back room had a similar number of beds. The large front room on the same floor had four beds. The two other bedrooms on the same floor had five beds. The number of people living there fluctuated between twenty and twenty-five. Some of the beds were used during the day by the night shift workers and at night by the day workers. The lavatory was blocked half of the time.... God knows how things have changed.[35]

Cases of overcrowding were regularly brought to the attention of local authorities in West London and the West Midlands.

Domestic economy in the overcrowded slum dwellings often consisted of a communal kitchen. Only the weekend was reserved for a proper meal and that after a regular visit to the local pub or the local cinema that now began to show Bollywood films to the newcomers.[36] Heavy drinking soon became the norm of the new macho culture, especially among foundry workers, with illicit liaisons with local women a regular occurrence, often facilitated by local publicans who responded to the changing clientele by introducing cabaret acts. Occasionally tales of moral waywardness would be communicated to the ancestral village by kith and kin, frequently spiced with the prospects of a marriage to a local white (*gori*) female unless a family reunion was sponsored soon.[37]

By the end of the 1950s immigration had become a major political issue, highlighted, amongst other things, by the Notting Hill riots of 1958. As the pressure on the Conservative government increased to impose strict controls, the number of migrants arriving from Punjab rose sharply in anticipation of more rigorous immigration controls in the offing. In 1961 and 1962 almost 46,000 migrants arrived from India. The Commonwealth Immigrants Act (1962) in effect curtailed the rights of Commonwealth citizens to enter Britain by introducing the selective voucher system: henceforth the general right of entry was limited to the reunion of dependants.

*Family Reunions: from the Commonwealth Immigrants Act (1962) to the
Expulsion of Ugandan Asians (1972)*
The 1960s and the 1970s witnessed a mainstream backlash against
coloured immigration with the rise of Powellism and, subsequently, the
extremist National Front. Both the Labour and Conservative parties
responded to this threat and the powerful resentment within their own
ranks by tightening immigration controls further. Sikh migration during
this period was restricted to family reunions and East African British
passport holders who arrived under the threat of expulsion. There was
also a small category of illegal migrants.

After 1962 the fear that immigration controls were likely to become
even more prohibitive led most British Sikhs to sponsor their families.
For the married men this involved the sponsorship of wife and children.
At this time it was not uncommon for male Sikhs to claim more direct
dependants than they actually supported. Some used this to defer tax
payments; others to broaden the possibility of relatives being eligible to
enter Britain. As the dependants joined their relatives the figures for
settlement rose sharply (see Table 3.1 above). Between 1961 and 1966,
the number of immigrants in Southall increased from 7,743 to 16,770,
and it is safe to assume that the majority of these were Sikhs.[38] The new
arrivals created additional pressure on housing as families were not
prepared to live in rented accommodation for any length of time. Cheap
inner-city slum dwellings, often scheduled for demolition or clearance,
became the new starter homes. In general, family reunions did not result
in any significant variations in the patterns of settlement: in fact, for a
whole host of reasons new arrivals were attracted to existing Sikh
locations, thereby strengthening the presence of earlier settlers.

'Twice Migrants': Sikhs from East Africa and Far East
Whereas the family reunions brought together Sikhs mainly from rural
Punjab, though migration from cities such as Jalandhar, Ludhiana and
Delhi was not unknown, East African Sikhs, who began to arrive in
Britain in large numbers from the mid-1960s, were 'twice migrants',
having previously emigrated to East Africa. Holders of British passports,
they were entitled to settle in Britain, despite the Commonwealth
Immigrants Act (1962). As Africanisation was implemented in states like
Kenya, Tanzania and Uganda, many British passport holders of Indian
origin decided to move to Britain. The mass influx of Kenyan Asians
between 1965 and 1968 further fuelled the anti-immigration backlash,
resulting in the Commonwealth Immigrants Act (1968), which made
the holders of such passports subject to immigration controls 'unless they

or at least one parent or grandparent was born, adapted, naturalised or registered as a citizen of the United Kingdom and the colonies.[39] The Immigration Act (1971) passed by the Conservative government further tightened controls by drawing a distinction between 'patrials' who were entitled to settle in Britain and non-patrials who would be subject to normal controls. This legislation, however, was unable to pre-empt the expulsion of about 60,000 Ugandan Asians in 1972, the majority of whom settled in Britain.

Sikhs from East Africa were generally better educated than their Punjabi brethren, urban, and previously either self-employed or in non-manual jobs. Although precise figures for those who arrived in Britain are unavailable, a substantial segment consisted of Ramgarhia Sikhs whose ancestors had migrated from Punjab at the end of the nineteenth century. Many were attracted to areas like Southall and other parts of London such as the south-east, Leeds and Leicester, where opportunities for business start-ups or professional work were plentiful. Nor were East African Sikhs encumbered by the complex problems of family reunions: the majority arrived as family units and soon acquired dwellings, often in desirable suburban locations. With marketable skills and close-knit families, frequently with established social and economic networks, East African Sikhs had a distinct advantage over the Punjabi Sikhs, a distinction that has strengthened over time to reinforce the separate identities of the two groups.[40]

During the 1960s and 1970s Punjabi and East African Sikhs in Britain were joined by settlers from other settlements of the Sikh diaspora – Malaysia, Singapore, Hong Kong, Fiji, the West Indies and other parts of Africa, like Nigeria, South Africa and Zambia. Like East African Sikhs, they were 'twice' or 'thrice' migrants, with significant skills and broad social networks. Again many gravitated towards existing areas of Sikh settlement, particularly in London and the South-East. The majority of these diaspora Sikhs were of varied caste backgrounds, often culturally assimilated with their former country, possessing neither the distinctive identity of Ramgarhia nor the strong links with Punjab of the Punjabi Sikhs. In many ways, because of this background they have become the most ardent exponents of a new ideological Sikhism that has sought to transcend the narrow peculiarities of Sikh ethnicities located in South Asia.[41]

Sikh Immigration since 1972

In the 1970s and the 1980s the rise of the New Right in British politics, symbolised by the premiership of Margaret Thatcher, was accompanied by further restrictions on the ability of migrants to settle in Britain. The British Nationality Act (1981) created three categories of citizen – British, dependent territories and overseas – and effectively excluded the latter, most of whom were Asian, from the right of abode in Britain. Thereafter immigration controls were applied much more rigorously through the introduction of the 'primary purpose rule', which was intended to exclude brides or bridegrooms from South Asia whose main aim was seen as settlement in Britain.

During these years Sikh migration to Britain has consisted of family reunions, asylum seekers, and illegals. Although family reunions involving immigrants of the 1950s and 1960s were by and large complete by the early 1970s, the tradition of marrying brides and bridegrooms in Punjab has continued to create new avenues for migration. The majority of these arranged marriages are with Punjabi Sikh partners, often with the direct intention of sponsoring a bride or a bridegroom. It is common to come across village *biradaris* transplanted by this route, despite the strict rules of endogamy that Sikhs are enjoined to practise. It is not possible to estimate the size of new arrivals through this route over the last three decades: suffice it to say that the link has not been eroded entirely, even though the third- and fourth-generation Sikhs are increasingly marrying partners from Britain or elsewhere in the Sikh diaspora.

Refugees, Economic Migrants and 'Illegals'

As immigration controls have become more strict, Sikhs have found more ingenious ways to circumvent them. Following Operation Blue Star in 1984, several thousand Sikh youths sought political asylum in Britain and elsewhere as Punjab became a battleground for insurgency and counter-insurgency in which almost 30,000 lives were lost over a decade. Many of the asylum seekers were essentially economic refugees who became ensnared in the ingenious plans of travel agents in Punjab. By the end of the 1980s only a small number of Sikhs had been granted asylum status in Britain, and the prospects of others were greatly diminished by the signing of the Indo-British Extradition treaty in 1992.[42]

Asylum seekers who arrived in European countries like Germany, Belgium, the Netherlands and France sometimes fared better. Often they have been able to forge marriage alliances with British partners; frequently they have made their passage illegally. As the asylum regime in Britain has become tougher, the number of Sikhs who arrive through illegal channels has increased. Ever since the 1960s and 1970s there has been a rich folklore among Punjabi Sikhs of endeavours by 'illegals' or *kabootars* (pigeons) – that is, those who have arrived in Britain through informal channels such as lorries or boats, via Ireland or Pakistan, or, as in the much-publicised case of two brothers, in the undercarriage of an aeroplane.[43] To these we need to add the overstayers who come on holidays, to attend family functions like marriages, or as students. Again it is difficult to estimate the number who have arrived and continue to arrive through illegal networks, but what is certain is that most of them are from Punjab, that they service the local black economy, and that they endeavour to become permanent or else migrate to other countries such as Canada and the USA where the immigration regimes are less daunting. They, like the recent arrivals via marriages, continue to replenish the Sikh community in Britain with traditional Punjabi values, and often were at the forefront of the community's social and political affairs in the 1980s and 1990s. According to some community leaders, a figure of 40,000–50,000 'illegals' would not be unreasonable.[44]

Out-Migration and Return

Alongside Sikh immigration there has been a steady increase in Sikh out-migration from Britain since the mid-1970s. Many Sikhs with professional qualifications who have felt frustrated in Britain have sought employment in North America, Australia and Europe. Doctors, information technology specialists, engineers and accountants have been at the forefront of this out-migration, the community's own 'brain drain'. With globalisation the Sikh diaspora has become increasingly integrated: transnational links are a common feature of contemporary Sikh life, whether in business, politics, marriage or cultural activities. This integration has brought with it regular exchanges of information and flows of interaction that have engaged the whole Sikh community in often very complex patterns of relations throughout the globe. Movements within the Sikh diaspora are now a constant feature of contemporary Sikh life, whether it is the incessant shuttling between Punjab and the host country or the unending search for new opportunities across the globe. Globalisation, in short, chimes with the Sikh ethos of mobility and constant movement, and it would be premature in the future to rule out the possibility of major movements in the Sikh population – either to or from Britain.

Finally, there is some element of 'return migration'; that is of permanent or quasi-permanent resettlement in Punjab. Conventionally this tended to consist of pensioners who, after a working life in Britain, sought to enjoy their wealth and status in a low-income environment. The proportion of Sikh pensioners in the total UK Sikh population (see

Table 3.7) is significantly low and it reasonable to assume that some do return or spend a considerable part of their retirement life in Punjab. This group, who are beginning to organise in Punjab, are also supplemented by a significant business and non-business segment, especially since the economic liberalisation of the Indian economy and the onset of cheap airline travel that has sharply reduced travel and bureaucratic delays. As with other minority ethnic communities (Afro-Caribbean, for example) this trend is likely to increase in the future.

Demography

Until the 2001 census, which included a category for religious identification, it was difficult to get an estimate of the Sikh population in Britain. Historically, census data have not required respondents to stipulate their religion. The inclusion of such a question in the 2001 census has given us a more comprehensive picture of the Sikh population today. In the absence of these figures in the past, social scientists relied on estimates based on assumptions about the size of the ethnic group of respondents classifying themselves as Indian. It was commonly assumed, perhaps mistakenly, that up to half or 40 per cent of those who have migrated from India were Sikhs. This figure is derived from the fact that most migration from India was from Punjab and Gujarat. Thus Brown, in the Population Services International (PSI) survey published in 1984, suggested that 'two-fifths of the Indian ethnic population are Sikhs, whilst a little less than a third are Hindus, with Muslims accounting for a third of this population group'.[45] As the 1981 census figure for people of Indian ethnic origin was 671,000, it was assumed that Sikhs accounted for about 268,400 of the total. The latter figure was at the lower end of some estimates, which put the total at 500,000 or in the broad range between 350,000 and 500,000.[46] The higher estimates, however, were confounded by the 2001 census, which enumerated the Sikh population of Britain at 336,179 or 0.59 per cent of the total (see Table 3.2).

This total was not only much smaller than many community activists had anticipated, it was also significantly less than the Hindu population with which traditionally it had been compared. Suggestions that the Sikh population had been under-enumerated, perhaps by a significant proportion, because of the exclusion of groups who did not state a religion or state no religion, were undermined by the high proportion (96 per cent) identification rate with the religious question by minority ethnic communities of South Asian origin.[47]

Table 3.2 Population of Great Britain by Religion, 2001

Religion	Number	Percentage
Christian	41,014,811	71.82
Muslim	1,588,890	2.78
Hindu	558,342	0.98
Sikh	336,179	0.59
Jewish	267,373	0.47
Buddhist	149,157	0.26
Other religion	159,167	0.28
No religion	8,596,488	15.05
Religion not stated	4,433,520	7.76
Total	57,103,927	100.00

Source: 2001 Census, Office of National Statistics.

Table 3.3 UK Sikhs by Country of Birth, 2001

Country	Numbers	Percentage
UK	188,906	56.19
Rest of Europe	785	0.23
Kenya	13,747	4.09
Other Africa	6,399	1.90
India	117,366	34.91
Other Asia	6,784	2.02
North America	547	0.16
Other	1,645	0.49
Total	336,179	100.00

Source: 2001 Census, Office of National Statistics.

The census also, for the first time, identified the community's composition by country of birth. The majority of UK Sikhs are now born in Britain. The proportion of those born in India, on the other hand, is roughly one-third. There is also notable representation from Africa, reflecting the migration from East African countries in the 1960s and 1970s, though this is much smaller than is sometimes suggested. The integration of British Sikhs into the global Sikh diaspora is further reflected in those born in Asia and in Europe and North America. As there are very few white European converts to Sikhism, it is safe to

Table 3.4 Estimates of the Growth of the Sikh Population of Great Britain,
1951–2001

Year	Sikhs	% Increase
1951	7,000	
1961	16,000	128.57
1971	72,000	350.00
1981	144,000	100.00
1991	206,000	43.05
2001	336,179	38.72

Source: Ceri Peach and Richard Gale, 'Muslims, Hindus, and Sikhs in the New Religious
Landscape of England', *The Geographical Review* 93:2, 469–90.

assume that most of this figure consists of Sikhs of Indian parentage.
Based on the 2001 census figure, the geographer Ceri Peach has compiled a retrospective estimate of the growth of the Sikh population since
1951.

These figures appear far more realistic historically. First, they capture
the first wave of migration and family reunions in the 1960s and 1970s.
Second, the growth in the Sikh population in the 1980s and the 1990s,
when immigration controls were strictest, suggests this occurred as a
result of the emergence of a second and third generation who were born
here to parents of Indian or East African origin. Third, because rural
Punjabi Sikhs who settled in the 1950s and 1960s tended to have large
families, with three to four children being the norm, this multiplier is
reflected in the size of the community – which almost doubled between
1971 and 1981, increased by 43 per cent between 1981 and 1991, and
increased by a further 38.7 per cent between 1991 and 2001.

Today 56.1 per cent of the Sikh population in Britain is British-born,
and although it has a demographical profile that is skewed towards
youth, with 59.4 per cent of the total population aged below 34
(compared with the national average of 45.2 per cent), the percentage
of Sikhs in the critical 0–15 age group is *only* 4.4 per cent higher than
the national average (see Table 3.7). In short, it is reasonable to argue
that the Sikh population's growth rate is now beginning to reach a
plateau, and that barring a major influx of new migrants in the future, it
will increasingly follow the pattern of other minorities such as the
Hindus and Jews which mirrors the national trends in terms of both
growth and age distribution.

Notwithstanding this evidence, some community leaders continue to insist that this figure of 336,179 is a substantial *under-representation* of Sikhs in Britain, and that the exact figure is around 500,000. The difference, it is argued, can be accounted for by a number of factors. First, one-third of Sikhs, as we have seen, traditionally belonged to the Dalit category. It is suggested that they have become increasing reluctant to classify themselves as Sikhs because the Khalistani movement of the 1980s and 1990s reopened old wounds between Jat and non-Jat Sikhs. While this may, indeed, have occurred, it is difficult to get a measure of the extent of the development, the degree of conscious *collective* organisation not to identify as Sikhs, or, alternatively, to identify as belonging to other categories – Hindu, Buddhist, Christian, Muslim, 'Other', or non-religious. There is no doubt that some of the Punjabi Dalit communities have classified themselves among the latter groups, but at the same time there is a strong component among Ravidasis and Mazbis that remains reluctant to disassociate from Sikhism, notwith-standing the strong divisions of caste.[48] Given these qualifications and the fact that Dalits made up almost one-third of Sikh migrants from Punjab, if we assume that almost half did *not* register as Sikhs, that would leave about 56,000 on the boundaries of the Sikh community – people, no doubt, that the dominant discourse of the Sikh community regards as part of the *panth,* but who no longer subjectively identify themselves as such.

Second, alongside the Dalit population we also need to take account of some estimates of the illegal Sikh migrants. It is just as difficult to get a measure of this total, but anecdotal evidence suggests that a large number of Sikh migrants now live in Britain and work within the informal ethnic economy sector. The 'Little Punjabs' (see below) have increasingly been transformed into processing zones for illegal and temporary visitors from Punjab as the original inhabitants have moved out to the suburbs. Although these groups are excluded from formal citizenship rights, they nonetheless participate fully in the community's economic and religious life. Guesstimates suggest that there are 40,000–50,000 illegal Sikh migrants, whose numbers have been swelled by extensive internal migration within the European Union. This total consists of overstayers, illegal entrants and asylum seekers who have 'disappeared'.[49]

Finally, some recognition also needs to be given to the Sikh population in transit. Although it is perfectly reasonable to assume most of these would have been included in census returns, there are no doubt some who missed out or were omitted when the census was taken. A figure of about 10,000 would not be unreasonable given the travelling

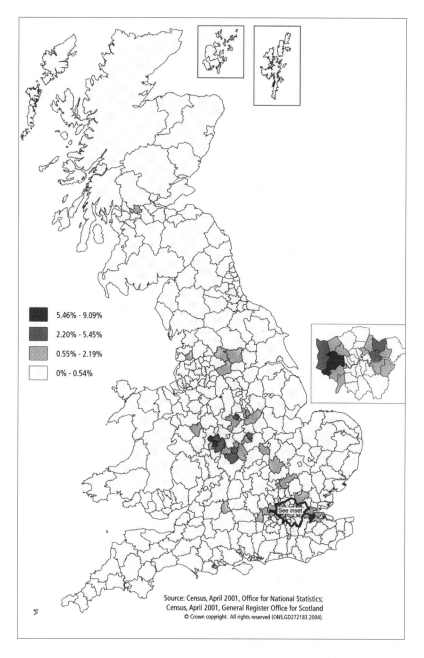

5.46% - 9.09%

2.20% - 5.45%

0.55% - 2.19%

0% - 0.54%

Map 3.1 Geographical Distribution of Sikhs in Britain by area, 2001

Table 3.5 Sikh Population by Region, 2001

Region	Total population	Sikh population	% of Total
London	7,172,091	104,250	1.45
West Midlands	5,267,308	103,870	1.97
South East	8,000,645	37,735	0.47
East Midlands	4,172,174	33,351	0.80
Yorkshire and Humberside	4,964,833	18,711	0.38
East	5,388,140	13,365	0.25
North West	6,729,764	6,478	0.10
North East	2,515,442	4,780	0.19
South West	4,928,434	4,614	0.09
Scotland	5,062,011	6,821	0.13
Wales	2,903,085	2,015	0.07
Northern Ireland	1,685, 367	219	0.01

Source: 2001 Census Office of National Statistics.

itinerary of Sikhs, both to Punjab and to other destinations within the Sikh diaspora.

If these three categories are taken into account, then we have two possible projections of the Sikh population in Britain today: a baseline figure of 336,179 provided by the 2001 census, and a more substantial and flexible figure of around 450,000 that accords with the estimates of the community's leaders. The higher total is not to be explained by under-enumeration; it reflects groups and categories that *cannot* be included or have chosen to *exclude* themselves. Until these residual categories receive official recognition, it is the baseline figure that provides a more accurate reflection of the community's strength today.

Geographical Distribution
The geographical distribution of the Sikh population can be seen in Map 3.1. Most of this population, 73.1 per cent, is concentrated within Greater London, the South East and the West Midlands. There is, of course, Sikh presence throughout Britain, but for most of the country it rarely exceeds 2.20–5.45 per cent; in large swathes of the country it is as low as 0-0.54 per cent. Beyond the areas of traditional settlement we need to take note of Sikh presence in the East Midlands cities of Leicester, Derby and Nottingham, and the Yorkshire and Humberside

Table 3.6 'Little Punjabs': Local Authorities with the Largest Sikh
Concentrations, 2001

Local authority	No. of Sikhs	% of total population
1. Slough	10,820	9.09
2. Hounslow	18,265	8.60
3. Ealing (Southall)	25,625	8.51
4. Wolverhampton	17,944	7.85
5. Sandwell	19,429	6.87
6. Gravesham (Gravesend)	6,379	6.66
7. Redbridge	13,022	5.46
8. Coventry	13,960	4.64
9. Hillingdon	11,058	4.55
10. Leicester	11,796	4.21
11. Birmingham	28,592	2.93

Source: 2001 Census Office of National Statistics.

towns of Bradford, Leeds and Huddersfield. The only significant settlement outside of England is in Glasgow, Scotland, though nominal presence can also be found in Cardiff, Wales and Belfast and Londonderry, Northern Ireland.

The regional concentration of the Sikh population is further highlighted by Table 3.5. Within these regions there is even greater concentration within particular local authorities and wards. Since the 1960s it has been common to talk of areas of such settlement as 'Little Punjabs' – the Sikh enclaves that dot the country but are integrated by Sikh commercial, social and political networks. Interestingly, some of the more obvious signs of this integration are community-based bus services which link Punjabi internal travel between these localities. The concentration of the Sikh population in these localities is listed in Table 3.6.

The 11 localities listed in this table account for 47 per cent of the total Sikh population, and – like Southall, Slough and Sandwell's Handsworth and Smethwick – are ethnic enclaves that over the last fifty years have changed from inner-city backwaters to dynamic economies of goods and culture that are thoroughly commercialised and at the forefront of popular British Asian identity, as represented in well-known TV series such as *Goodness Gracious Me!* or popularised in films such as *Bend It Like Beckham* and *Bhaji on the Beach*. Of all these localities it is Southall, especially since the riots of 1979, that has become the premier symbol of Sikh settlement in Britain, a fact recently illustrated by the inauguration of the new Sri Guru Singh Sabha Gurdwara (see photograph on p. 70), which has won international accolades for architectural design. Southall, moreover, figures prominently in the imagination of travellers from overseas as the place where 'Southalli', a strange dialect of Punjabi and English, is the operative vernacular, where the Punjabis have evolved their own hybrid of the English pub (the 'Glassi Junction') and where it is possible 'buy a pint in Indian rupees'. But it would be grossly misleading to suggest that the 'Little Punjabs' are overwhelmingly Sikh. Today their social composition is in transition; as the ethnic economies have developed, their success has also attracted other South Asians, notably new Hindu and Muslim groups.

However the main segment of the Sikh population is still located in the traditional areas of settlement in the inner city where access to work, business and gurdwaras remains a key consideration. Even as the inner-city economies have revived, with shops and businesses replacing the familiar manufacturing sector, better-off Sikhs continue to retain commercial and residential footholds. Notwithstanding this continued attachment, there is also a noticeable drift of the Sikh population to the traditionally fashionable 'leafy suburbs' and 'golf course' belts like Oadby and Wigston (4.16 per cent of the total population in 2001) on the edge of Leicester, Edgbaston, Mosley and Solihull in Birmingham, Stychill in Coventry, Kingston in west London, and Redbridge in east London. As some of the traditionally white suburbs become wealthy ethnic neighbourhoods, for Sikhs the availability of large, fashionable houses in these areas has become the new status symbol of professional families and the *nouveau-riche* businessmen eager to flaunt their wealth while seeking to retain firm control over extended joint-family households. New buildings and makeovers have created some garish Punjabiesque architectural temples to British Sikh success where, for example, the peacock motif in the pane glass has now become *de rigeur*.

Social Profile

Given the nature of migration from Punjab and elsewhere in the 1950s and 1960s, a clear social profile of the migrants, with a baseline measure of their background and skills, did not exist. Today, thanks to the 2001 census and other surveys, we have a range of data that provide such a profile. Some of this data will, of course, be discussed in more detail in the subsequent chapters, but at this stage we draw on the key findings to provide a preliminary overview of the community.

For the majority of British Sikhs religion remains a key marker of self-identity. In a Home Office survey in 2001, 64.3 per cent of the non-UK-born Sikhs highlighted religion as the key variable of self-identity, while the figure for the UK-born was slightly lower at 55.9 per cent. Sikhs, however, are not Britain's most religious community in terms of self-identification. This distinction is held by Jews (80.3 per cent), followed by Muslims (66.6 per cent) and then Sikhs (61.3 per cent).[50]

While religion remains an important determinant of self- and collective identity, British Sikh attitudes towards the broader issue of 'British identity' are divided by country of birth and age group. Those born in the UK showed a 90.4 per cent identification with 'British identity' while for those born outside the UK the comparable figure was only 54.4 per cent. The strength of this identification varies considerably over generations: among the 16–24 age group it is as high as 80.0 per cent while for those 75 or over it plummets to only 45.6 per cent.[51] Clearly one possible inference from the above findings is that the younger generation of Sikhs are both *less* religious and *more* likely to identify with 'British identity'.

These findings are also reflected in the nature of Sikh ethnicity in Britain today (see Table 3.7). Ethnically in 2001 an overwhelming majority of Sikhs (91.48 per cent) classified themselves as 'Indian', with only 4.37 per cent opting for the designation 'Asian or British Asian'. At the time of the census the campaign to declare Sikhs as a separate (non-Indian) ethnic category had not begun (see Chapter 5); such a campaign has the potential to dilute the 'Indian' ethnic category in a future census, though it might also be overtaken by the self-selection of other categories. However, though the ethnic identification is almost homogeneous there are interesting developments at the margins: 2.09 per cent of Sikhs returned themselves as 'White', 0.84 per cent as 'Mixed' and 0.35 as 'Black or Black British'. In addition nearly 1 per cent identified themselves as Chinese or Other ethnic group. Although the latter probably refers to new arrivals from the Sikh diaspora, the former is certainly an indication of increasing mixed heritage or parenthood within the community.

The changes in religious identification and ethnicity are clearly related to the fact that the majority of Sikhs (56.1 per cent) are now British-born. To some extent this was inevitable given the age profile of the early migrants, but they still retain a significant representation (at 43.8 per cent), though the proportion of these who came from India is now only about a third (34.9 per cent).

Table 3.7 Social Profile of Sikhs in Britain, 2001

	% of the Sikh population	% of the national average	%+/-
1. Ethnic group			
White	2.09	91.31	NA
Mixed	0.84	1.27	-0.43
Asian or Asian British	96.18	4.37	NA
Black or Black British	0.19	2.19	-2.00
Chinese or other ethnic group	0.71	0.86	-0.15
2. Sex			
Male	50.20	48.61	+1.59
Female	49.48	51.39	-1.49
3. Age structure			
0–15	24.53	20.07	+4.46
16–34	34.91	25.15	+9.76
35–64	34.39	38.81	-4.42
Over 65	6.17	15.97	-9.80
4. Households with dependent children			
No dependent children	45.07	70.62	-25.55
1 dependent child	19.46	12.40	+7.06
2 dependent children	21.97	11.21	+10.76
3 or more dependent children	13.51	5.21	+8.30
5. Household tenure			
Social rented	8.00	19.92	-11.92
Private rented	8.24	9.59	-1.35
Owned	81.97	68.29	+13.68
Rent free	1.80	2.19	-0.39
6. Employment (2004)			
Public admin., education, health	19.5	27.3	-7.80
Banking, finance and industry	11.7	15.6	-3.90
Transport and communications	12.9	6.9	+6.00
Distribution, hotels and restaurants	26.4	20.0	+6.40
Construction	6.4	7.7	-1.30
Manufacturing	18.7	14.1	+4.60
Energy and water	1.6	1.0	+0.60
Agriculture and fishing	0.0	1.2	-1.20
Other	3.0	6.2	-3.20

Source: Census 2001, and Labour Force Survey 2003/4, Office of National Statistics.

Given the community's age structure and the effectiveness of immigration policies in the 1980s and early 1990s, it is likely that, other things being equal, the proportion of British-born Sikhs will continue to increase. One of the likely long-term trends is the decline of Indian-born Sikhs; as we shall see in subsequent chapters, this trend would have profound implications for the development of the British Sikh community.

Sikh household size remains large compared with the national average, but that is because the national average has declined remarkably at a time when the Sikh household size has also been coming down. The one significant anomaly, however, is the number of households with three or more children. As we review this issue in Chapter 8, it needs to be recognised that there might well be particular reasons for this variation – such as the preference for male children or the recent arrival of the household from developing countries.

One of the striking social statistics that distinguishes the Sikh community in Britain is the high rate of private home ownership. In 2001 it was recorded at 82 per cent, higher than Jews (77 per cent) or Hindus (74 per cent).[52] This may well be due to the rural background of the community, where ownership of land was highly prized both as a mark of status and for productive reasons, to avoid the stigma of tenancy. Certainly there is a marked reluctance among Sikhs to rent property or be in the social rented sector, though Sikh presence in the latter is probably increasing for some of the ageing population.

The employment profile of Sikhs remains uneven, owing perhaps to the very low baseline (unskilled wage labour) at which the early migrants entered the employment market. As noted above, there is significant under-representation in particular industries and over-representation in others (manufacturing, distribution, hotels and restaurants, and transport and communications) as well as in self-employment. These variations are important to understand and explain, as we attempt to do in Chapter 7. Nonetheless, the overall profile represents significant progress for what at the time of migration was essentially a community of peasants.

If we were to capture a snapshot image of the Sikh community's social profile today, what would it be? British Sikhs continue to self-identify through religion, but are comfortable with this self-designation as compatible with British identity, however that is understood. They are ethnically homogeneous ('Indian') but recognise the realities of diversity that flourishes at their margins. A majority are British-born, have a lower age profile and a higher birth rate than the national average, are distinguished by high rates of private home ownership, and increasingly resemble, with some major qualifications, the national profile for employment. Of course, as we shall discover in subsequent chapters, there are significant variations in this picture – between Sikh males and females, between the British-born and those born overseas, and between the young and the old. But then such variations, to a greater or lesser extent, are to be found in all communities.

Conclusion

Sikh settlement in Britain now spans almost three centuries. It began with a royal embrace for the 'model' colonised community at the zenith of Victorian Britain; it exists comfortably now in the age of 'cool Britannia', where social diversity and multiculturalism are the official creeds and 'colonisation from below' is apparent throughout the country. The journey from the mid-nineteenth to the early twenty-first century has been a difficult one, marked as it has been by romantic fascination with the leading 'ornaments' of the empire, overt hostility to mass immigration after the Second World War, and, now, a reluctant acceptance of the *fait accompli* of permanent settlement amidst broader diversity in an era of globalisation. As with other minorities before them, the settlement of Sikhs has produced its own accretions as well as divisions between the early and late arrivals, accentuating existing cleavages while also creating new ones. Sikh enclaves remain primarily within the areas of traditional settlement, though rising incomes and prosperity have begun to disperse the population to new suburbs and made Sikhs venture into almost all the major localities of Britain. After almost three decades of growth, the Sikh population has begun to stabilise and reproduce along the pattern of the host community and there are few indications that it is likely to witness any dramatic growth in the future unless immigration controls are relaxed. Yet because of its size and influence the Sikh community in Britain will remain a magnet for Sikhs all over the world.

Four

Gurdwaras
and Community Building

On 30 March 2003 the largest Sikh gurdwara outside India, Sri Guru Singh Sabha Gurdwara, Southall (SGSSGS), was officially opened amid a gathering of 40,000 Sikhs and an opening ceremony at which Sant Mann Singh was especially flown in from Punjab to officiate. Designed by Architect Co-Partnership, the gurdwara cost £17 million to build, has a capacity of 3,000 people and can serve up to 20,000 meals during weekends. This imposing mogul-style building was described as 'one of the largest regeneration projects in Southall', befitting the ambition of the local Sikh community to 'create a temple second only to the Golden Temple in Amritsar'.[1] Such is the significance of the new gurdwara that its official opening was followed by a visit by Prince Charles in June. Situated in the heart of one of the largest Sikh communities, the SGSSGS has quickly become the premier symbol of Sikh presence in Britain, one of the new emerging 'cathedrals' of multicultural Britain.[2]

Gurdwaras are the Sikhs' principal religious institutions. First and foremost, as places of worship they are the foundations of community building, act as guardians of its core values, and provide a forum for collective worship by the *sangat* (congregation). Yet as institutions gurdwaras are much more. As we noted in Chapter 1, the emergence from the late nineteenth century onwards of a modern Sikh identity was also accompanied by the demarcation of a distinctive sacred space as symbolised by the Akali Movement (1920–5), which brought the main gurdwaras under the community's control in Punjab and gave birth to a committee for managing gurdwaras, the SGPC, and its political wing, the SAD. These two bodies are sometimes referred to as the Sikh 'political system'.[3] Community leadership, in short, can emerge only

Plate 3 Sri Guru Singh Sabha Gurdwara, Southall, the main icon of the Sikh presence in Britain today. It was opened in March 2003. (Reproduced with the permission of SGSSGS)

from *within* gurdwaras, and, as the popular adage goes, 'those who control the gurdwaras control the Sikh community'.

In this chapter we examine the history of the gurdwara movement in Britain from the early twentieth century onwards, with particular reference to its growth and diversity. We review the complex – and often fraught – processes relating to the management of these institutions that now involves an interface with a variety of British institutions. The chapter concludes by assessing the gurdwaras' contemporary role and their position as pillars of faith in the inner city, and reflects on the broader issue of Sikh religiosity today.

The Gurdwara Movement in Britain

Before the Second World War

In the early twentieth century London emerged as the main centre of education for Indians. The first Sikh association, Khalsa Jatha of the British Isles (KJBI), was established in 1908 at the instigation of Teja Singh, then a student at Cambridge. Teja Singh had been sent abroad by his religious sponsors to become 'familiar with challenges to the Sikh faith'. He arrived in London accompanied by his wife and three other students in 1907, but

Plate 4   Prince Charles during a visit to the Sri Guru Singh Sabha Gurdwara, Southall, June 2003. (Reproduced with the permission of SGSSGS)

after a brief spell in London enrolled at Downing College where, with a few other like-minded students, he established the KJBI as an affiliate of the Chief Khalsa Divan (CKD) in Amritsar – then the principal Sikh organisation in Punjab. The KJBI met annually to celebrate Guru Nanak's birth and other key dates in the Sikh calendar: students would hire a small hall or visit India House for religious celebrations. In January 1910 there was a gathering at the Westminster Palace Hotel for the anniversary of Guru Gobind Singh's birth. In 1911 Teja Singh, who had earlier left for the United States, returned from Canada to become the moving spirit behind the proposal that a property should be acquired in London to serve as a gurdwara. In the first instance a house was rented in Putney for two years. The proposal for a London gurdwara was greeted with much enthusiasm in Punjab, with an appeal launched for funds in the *Khalsa Samachar*.[4] The Maharaja of Patiala, who was in London at the time, donated £1,000. As a result of these sustained efforts, a house at 79 Sinclair Road, Shepherd's Bush, was leased for 63 years and, after essential repairs, the property became the first British gurdwara in an opening ceremony performed by the Maharaja of Patiala.[5]

The Shepherd's Bush gurdwara quickly became the focal point of the small community in Britain: on special occasions such as *Vaisakhi*, Sikhs settled as far away as Scotland would make the long journey to London. Many students were helped and supported by the gurdwara and its congregation in enabling them to adjust to life in Britain, and for most Sikh visitors from India the gurdwara was their first port of call. In 1967 the Shepherd's Bush gurdwara was sold and relocated at Queensdale Road in Kensington and Chelsea. The first gurdwara, like the first Sikh, had princely origins: for almost fifty years it remained the only recognised communal centre.

Apart from Shepherd's Bush there appear to be no references to other gurdwaras before the 1950s. During the First World War, wounded Sikh soldiers who were hospitalised in Brighton were provided with a temporary facility within the Pavilion lawns.[6] It is more than likely, however, that the small pockets of Sikhs throughout Britain, especially the Bhatras, improvised services by meeting in private residences or hiring public accommodation. In the 1950s the Bhatras eventually pioneered the gurdwaras movement, but the marginal nature of their sub-identity within broader Sikh society (see below) ensured that this initiative was unable to establish a leadership advantage.

Gurdwaras after the Second World War

In the early 1950s, as the number of Sikh immigrants began to rise sharply in the West Midlands, east and west London, the East Midlands and the North, pressure grew to create gurdwaras. Since then the gurdwaras movement has followed a common trajectory: initially the renting of a house or a hall for communal gatherings (1950s/1960s); the purchase of larger, inner-city premises (1960s/1970s); the construction or modification of existing premises for all-purpose gurdwaras and the creation of *separate* institutions by disgruntled factions within the original founding body or by castes (1980s); and, more recently, at the turn of the millennium (1990s/2000s), the emergence of imposing grand 'new cathedrals'. The tremendous increase in the size and number not only reflects the denominational diversity among British Sikhs, but is also the by-product of internecine factional rivalries that have driven competing projects within same locality. A few examples will illustrate the phenomenon.

As a major destination for Sikh settlers Southall became the focus of early Sikh endeavour to have a place of worship. The Singh Sabha Southall was established in the late 1950s, to be superseded by the Southall Cultural Society in 1960. Among its founder organisers were Sohan Singh Akali, Surjit Singh Bilga, Karam Singh Kailay, Pritam Singh Dhadi and Avtar Singh Sewak. Initially they rented Shackleton Hall for

Sunday service and then moved to 11 Beaconsfield Road. But with the arrival of Malaysian and Singaporean Sikhs in the early 1960s, a rival association, Sri Guru Nanak Singh Sabha, came into existence led by Balwant Singh Gill, Kesar Singh Mand and Bibi Gurdial Kaur. This new association started another congregation by hiring a hall at the Green. As the Malaysian and Singaporean Sikhs were mainly from the Malwa or Majaha regions of Punjab – whereas the early arrivals were Doabians – regional rivalries between the two associations soon came to the surface. In 1964 the Guru Nanak Singh Sabha purchased the Green for £6,000, but when it was faced with the cost of servicing the property, it sought the help of the Sikh Cultural Society, with which it merged to form the Sri Guru Singh Sabha, Southall (SGSSS, 1964).[7]

When in 1965 Yadvinder Singh, the Maharaja of Patiala, visited the newly purchased site, he exhorted the *sangat* to 'let the gurdwara's Nishan Sahib (flag) be visible from London's Heathrow Airport'. The Green was soon found wanting, and when a dairy at Havelock Road was put on the market for £26,000, it was quickly purchased to be redeveloped for the 300th anniversary of Guru Gobind Singh's birth (1966). In 1984 the SGSSS bought a new site on Park Avenue to enable redevelopment of the Havelock Road site, where the current gurdwara, the SGSSGS, 'second only to the Golden Temple', is located.

Meanwhile by the early 1950s Smethwick in the West Midlands, with its foundries, had become a magnet for Sikh migrants. During 1955–6 some of the new arrivals began hiring a local school hall near the West Bromwich Albion football ground, to which Lachman Singh would bring a copy of *Guru Granth Sahib*. As this proved unsatisfactory, several other halls were tried before the decision was taken to buy a disused church hall on High Street, Smethwick. Buta Singh and his associates, with village kinship ties among local Sikh workers, spearheaded the fund collection. 'We dictated the amount they would donate,' one of the fundraisers recalled.[8] A church building was eventually purchased for £11,600 in May 1958 and formally opened as Guru Nanak Gurdwara, Smethwick in October 1958, with Durga Dutt Shukla as its treasurer.

Birmingham also illustrates well the trend that over time diversity within the Sikh *panth* has emerged as castes and sects that were initially together in the founding gurdwara have gone on to establish their own institutions, either because of discrimination or because of a desire to preserve a distinctive sub-identity. The Bhatra community in south Birmingham, for example, was able to establish its own gurdwara in 1957 in Balsall Heath. As the building was in a highly congested residential area, local people raised many objections and the management fought a case against the City Council which served a notice to close it. An alternative site was found in Mary Street until 1989, from where it was relocated to High Gate at the cost of £300,000.[9] Likewise, the Ramgarhia Sikhs established two gurdwaras;[10] the Ravidasi Sikhs, who had earlier worshipped at Guru Nanak Gurdwara, Smethwick High Street, purchased a building in Grove Lane in 1971 that was eventually converted into Sri Guru Ravidass Bhawan. Similarly, Ghumar Sikhs (potters), led by a successful businessman, established the Sri Guru Dasmesh Gurdwara in Lozells in 1972, with further expansion in 1985.[11] By 2001 Birmingham had 12 gurdwaras for the Sikh population of nearly 29,000; in the neighbouring borough of Sandwell, which now contains Smethwick, formerly part of Birmingham, the corresponding figure was seven for 20,000.

More typical than either Southall or Birmingham is the history of the gurdwara movement in Leicester, which further underlines the historical evolution of both denominational and caste pluralism and factional rivalries. The first congregations of early settlers were held in a school hall in Highfields in the 1960s, when Sikhs constituted the largest ethnic minority in the city. This was followed by the purchase of a double-storey building in New Walk where the first Guru Nanak Gurdwara was established in 1968. A faction within the management committee, which was divided along political (SAD and CPI (M)) and *illaqa* (locality) lines, broke away to form the Guru Tegh Bahadur Gurdwara on East Park Road in 1976. As a large number of Ramgarhias from East Africa began to arrive in the city from the late 1960s onwards, the Ramgarhia Board Gurdwara on Maynell Road was established in 1978. In the 1980s the Guru Nanak and Guru Tegh Bahadur gurdwaras purchased a large, vacant industrial building that has since been converted to all-purpose use. In August 2002 the Guru Nanak Gurdwara at Holy Bones hosted Her Majesty's visit during her Golden Jubilee year (see cover photograph). But the competition between the two main gurdwaras has spawned further growth: in 1997, a faction defeated in the elections within the Guru Tegh Bahadur Gurdwara broke away to establish the Guru Amar Das Gurdwara, adding to another new Sri Dasmesh Gurdwara which was established a year earlier on the site of a former pub in the north of the city. The Ravidasi population of the city, which formerly had frequented the main gurdwaras of the city, established its own building, Sri Ravidas Gurdwara, on Harrison Road in 1985. With a population of fewer than 12,000 Sikhs in 2001, Leicester has six main gurdwaras and several 'unofficial' private makeshift buildings which serve such a purpose for occasional gatherings by sects and denominations.[12]

In addition to the above we also need to note the contribution of sants (traditional Sikh preachers) in establishing gurdwaras.[13] The role of sants within Sikhism, as we shall see later, is a highly controversial topic, but at this juncture we need to note that sants have been prolific galvanising forces for the foundation of gurdwaras throughout Britain. The Nanaksar sants, especially Sant Amar Singh followed by Mihan Singh, have been particularly enterprising in building gurdwaras in Wolverhampton, Coventry, Birmingham and Leicester to complement their extensive transnational portfolio in Singapore, Vancouver, Toronto and Punjab. Another sant, Puran Singh, who arrived from Kericho, Kenya in the 1970s and established the Guru Nanak Nishkam Sewak Jatha (GNNSJ), founded gurdwaras in Handsworth, Hounslow and Leeds; the GNNSJ also has many gurdwaras in Punjab, East Africa and North America.[14] While a few of the sants have become permanent residents (Domeliwale in West Bromwich, Sant Puran Singh Karicho-wale and his successors in Handsworth), others (Nanaksarias and Rare-walas) have made their visits routine, an almost annual event among their diaspora Sikh followers.

Growth and Diversity

More than anything else the increase in gurdwaras mirrors the changing profile of the British Sikh community itself. As such it is necessary to develop an overall picture of the number, denominational character and geographic distribution of these institutions.

Actual numbers have increased remarkably since the 1950s; the total figure in Britain today is about 250 gurdwaras. In 1961 only three gurdwaras were recognised by the Office of Register of Places in England and Wales. This figure increased to 33 in 1971, 69 in 1981, 138 in 1991 and 193 in 2001.[15] In contrast, *Religion in the UK: a Multi-faith Directory* gives a total of 213 for 2001, of which the overwhelming majority are in England and Wales. Tables 4.1 and 4.2 give a more detailed picture of the growth and geographical distribution of these institutions.[16]

To understand the tremendous increase in the number of gurdwaras in the 1980s and 1990s it is important to recognise that the increase is both concentrated in areas of established settlement, where the community has grown and diversified, and also reflects *new localities* where the Sikhs, though still small in number, now feel confident enough to construct permanent structures. Underlying these two developments are a complex array of interlocking factors – the arrival, over time, of *different* waves of

Table 4.1 Gurdwaras in Britain, 1910–2001

	1910–51	1972	1975	1980	1985	1990	1995	1999	2001
England & Wales	1	40	59	90	129	149	174	180	202*
Scotland	–	2	3	5	9	11	11	11	11
N. Ireland	–	–	–	–	–	–	–	1	1
Total	1	42	62	95	138	160	185	192	214

*Includes 5 for Wales.
Source: Paul Weller, ed., *Religions in the UK: a Multi-faith Directory* (2001).

Table 4.2 Distribution of Gurdwaras in England and Wales by Region, 1997

North East	5
York & Humbs.	25
North West	10
East Midlands	15
West Midlands	49
East	12
London	31
South East	23
South West	7
Wales	3
Total	180

Source: Recorded and certified places of worship by region in England and Wales on 30 June 1999, General Registrar and Paul Weller, ed., *Religions in the UK: a Multi-faith Directory* (1997).

Sikh migrants from Punjab and the diaspora, persistent factionalism in the founding body, the increasing responsiveness of local authorities to the planning demands of ethnic communities for new places of worship,[17] the role of transnational sant-based organisations that have been *outsourcing* operations to the West since the 1960s and, above all, the desire of denominations and sects to establish a *distinctive* identity overshadowed during the initial period of settlement. This rate of growth, moreover, has not decelerated; if anything it is yet to reach its peak, let alone a plateau. Given a current ratio of one gurdwara to every 1,664 Sikhs, there is every indication that the *supply* will continue to increase, especially in the inner city where there is now *intense* competition between gurdwaras in creating more 'Golden Temple'-like structures.

Caste

The existing literature on Sikhs in Britain rightly draws attention to the diversity within the Sikh tradition.[18] However, though this diversity clearly exists, has increased and continues to increase, very little substantive evidence has been provided of its extent, size and proportionality, or of its reflection in gurdwaras or other places of worship. Drawing on a variety of sources of self-identification – directories, official reports, websites and other forms of listing – we have attempted to construct a more comprehensive contemporary picture along the axis of Sikh sub-identities described previously (Chapter 1 and 2).[19] As previously noted, caste determines the major cleavage within Sikhism at the sub-identity level, and as gurdwaras have multiplied, this has increasingly come to the fore.

From the data in Table 4.3 (see below) a number of observations need to be made. First, the overwhelming majority of gurdwaras in Britain, 83.3 per cent, belong to what might be called the Sikh 'mainstream'; that is, they do not identify along caste lines. Since the 'mainstream' is commonly associated with Jats, who make up most of the community, it might reasonably be argued that these are in fact *de facto* Jat caste gurdwaras. Such an interpretation would be misleading, however, because these institutions do not restrict membership or participation in the management committee to particular caste groups and their *sangat* can be, and often is, caste-plural.[20] Interestingly, Sikh urban castes (Khatris, Aroras) in Britain have eschewed the model of the former rural non-Jat castes in setting up their own separate establishments. One reason for this could be that they identify most strongly with the dominant Khalsa discourse of Sikh identity; another that their numbers in Britain do not warrant such endeavours. In any case, 'mainstream' gurdwaras are anything but uniform: they range from sant-managed institutions that often resemble franchised transnational off-shore operations to locally run institutions that would be more appropriately described as religious cooperatives. Nonetheless, what separates these bodies from the rest is precisely the *explicit distinction* of caste.

Beyond the 'mainstream', the second major cluster of gurdwaras is provided by Ramgarhias who combine a *social identity* that draws on a *caste heritage* with a narrative of Sikh history that underscores their distinctive contribution to the development of the *panth* (see Chapter 1). This consciousness of a separate identity has been further consolidated by migration to East Africa in the nineteenth century and, following Africanisation, settlement in Britain as 'twice migrants'. Occupationally upwardly mobile with significant skills, the Ramgarhia migrants soon

Table 4.3 Gurdwaras by Caste Identification, 2001

	Total	No caste identified	Ramgarhias	Bhatras*
North East	5	4	–	1
Yorkshire	16	14	2	–
North West	10	10	–	–
East Midlands	19	15	3	1
West Midlands	43	34	7	2
East England	13	10	2	1
London	40	36	4	–
South East	19	16	3	–
South West	16	14	1	1
England total	181	153	22	6
Scotland	6	4	–	2
Wales	4	2	–	2
Northern Ireland	1	1		
Total	192	160	22	10

* Bhatras are not a caste group as such, of course, but a sub-identity; in the literature on British Sikhs, however, they are normally identified with caste divisions.
Sources: Drawn from Paul Weller, ed., *Religions in the UK: a Multi-faith Directory* (2001) websites, interviews and personal communications.

began to establish their own places of worship both as a mark of separate identity and as a way of distancing themselves from what many saw as lapsed Punjabi 'rustics'. In many ways this drive was underpinned by a perception that Ramgarhias were more committed Sikhs than the early settlers by virtue of their adherence to the male mark of identity, the turban and unshorn hair. Bhachu asserts that in the late 1960s the Ramgarhias led the return to the familiar Sikh dress code that triggered a religious revival within the community in locations like Southall, Birmingham and Leeds.[21] While indeed this is generally recognised to have been the case, Ballard points out that the process is better understood 'as pursuing a Sikh version of Sankritisation' – a form of upward mobility by a social lower caste based on promoting religious virtue.[22] And precisely because of this attachment to the Sikh tradition, the main divide between 'mainstream' Sikhs and Ramgarhias occurs along the faultlines not of doctrine or theology, but of caste/social class.[23]

Bhatras, one of the oldest Sikh sub-communities in Britain, are not strictly part of the rural Punjabi caste hierarchy out of which most of the migration has emerged. Originating from Sialkot, West Punjab, they are generally viewed by other Sikhs as a low-caste group, but despite this have remained steadfastly loyal towards Khalsa ideals, preserving a form of religious and social conservatism that is atypical of 'mainstream' British Sikhs.[24] Outwardly sharing the symbols of the Sikh tradition, Bhatras nonetheless remain aloof from broader British Sikh society, preferring to maintain their autonomy from fellow brethren as well as from British society. Most migration among this community occurred between the 1920s and the 1940s, with settlement in the port cities of Bristol, Cardiff, Liverpool, Glasgow and Edinburgh and subsequent growth in Manchester, Peterborough and Birmingham, where gurdwaras were founded from the 1950s onwards.

Sikh 'Lower-Caste' Groups and Sects[25]

Whereas Ramgarhias (and Bhatras), despite their caste distinction, share the common dominant Khalsa discourse familiar in the 'mainstream', the same cannot be said of sects and movements at the boundaries of Sikhism. Among those represented in Britain are Ravidasis, Valmikis, Namdharis, Nirankaris and Radhasoamis. All five have established centres in Britain and beyond, asserting their distinction through institutions, lifestyles and ritual practices. Table 4.4 presents a count of their places of worship.

Of these groups the largest is the Ravidasis, who are sometimes viewed as Sikhs.[26] Although such a designation might be justified with reference to ritual practices, there is also sufficient evidence to argue that

Table 4.4 Sikh Sects' Places of Worship, 2003

Region	Ravidasis	Namdharis	Nirankaris	Radhasoamis	Valmikis
England	13	6	12	4	9
Scotland	1	1	–	–	–
Wales	–	–	–	–	–
N. Ireland	–	–	–	–	–
Total	14	7	12	4	9

Source: BBC website; Paul Weller, *Religions in the UK: a Multi-faith Directory*, websites (1997 and 2001), interviews and personal communications. For Nirankaris, Namdharis and Valmikis the numbers include all listed associations that generally make arrangements for congregations at hired halls or private dwellings.

Ravidasi identity is far more heterodox and reflective of their emerging desire to be at some distance from conventional Sikhism even if they remain 'within the Sikh universe'.[27] As former untouchables outside the caste hierarchy, Ravidasis suffered the double indignity of caste and religious discrimination in rural Punjab, though most had been influenced to some degree by Sikhism. In the 1920s this community's leadership began a movement to establish an alternative social vision for itself in response to the general mobilisation led by the Indian National Congress (INC). This movement received a further momentum with the independence of India, followed by affirmative action in government employment for the former untouchables groups (designated as Scheduled Castes) and the rise of the Dalit movement. In contrast, in Britain the assertion of Ravidasi identity has taken the form of separate Ravidasi gurdwaras and bhavans (centres), the innovation of new practices and rituals, and a desire to be recognised as equals in a new society where egalitarianism is valued. Hence, although the community retains a superficial adherence to gurdwara rituals and Punjabi identity, in terms of its self-identification it seems to have settled at some distance from the Sikh faith.[28]

The position of Valmikis, also of former untouchable/Scheduled Caste/Dalit background and the next largest group, is far more ambiguous. Smaller in number, they straddle several Punjabi folk traditions that also combine elements of Sikhism and Hinduism. As Nesbitt has observed, 'Valmiki religious identity has largely been forged as a means of resistance to higher-caste Sikh and Hindu exclusionism, so it is hardly surprising that contemporary Valmiki practice draws freely on both those traditions, while adding something distinctive of its own.' While the behavioural conventions in the Valmiki temple in Coventry were found to be 'indistinguible from the gurdwara', the dominant idiom was 'reinterpreted to create their own distinctive variations'.[29] The largest concentrations of Valmikis are in Birmingham, Bedford, Bradford, Southall, Coventry, Oxford, Wolverhampton, Glasgow, Derby, Gravesend, Huddersfield and Hounslow – all areas of main Sikh settlement.

If Ravidasis and Valmikis can be understood as caste-based sects, then the Namdharis, Nirankaris and Radhasoamis are distinguished by their veneration for the 'living guru', which fundamentally challenges the basic tenets of Sikh orthodoxy. The Namdharis, however, have evolved a relatively benign image within the *panth* through their intense religiosity that draws on a historical narrative emphasising the tradition of revolt against colonial rule.[30] They have seven gurdwaras and are currently trying to develop a resource centre and a library in order to build a 'worthy' historical lineage.[31]

This benign image of the Namdharis within Sikh society generally is not associated with the other two sects – Nirankaris and Radhasoamis. Nirankaris had been ignored by radical Sikhdom until 1978, but then a clash between Nirankaris and orthodox Sikhs in Amritsar resulted in 13 deaths. Two years later the Nirankari chief, Gurbachan Singh, was murdered by Ranjit Singh, who later became the Jathedar of Akal Takht. These events symbolically triggered the turmoil that eventually engulfed Punjab in the 1980s and 1990s and naturally resulted in an overspill in Britain, with clashes and confrontations between militant Sikhs and Nirankaris.[32]

Finally, the Radhasoami sect has considerable appeal among Sikhs of all castes. The movement emerged in the early twentieth century but now thrives in Punjab by promoting orthopraxy and the veneration of a living guru.[33] Radhaswami is among the fastest-growing sects in contemporary Punjab, with an extensive social network system that has all the attributes of a comprehensive social welfare system. Many of its opponents have accused the movement of emulating the worst methods of modern franchising, where all its bhavans in Punjab's major towns are planned uniformly with whitewashed exteriors. In Britain Radhasoamis, like Nirankaris, tend to keep a low public profile but have an extensive network of support and collaboration.

Managing Gurdwaras

By conservative estimates the real estate values of gurdwaras in Britain today range from £125–£250 million; their actual value is probably much higher.[34] Located as the religious, social and political hubs in Sikh enclaves, they are a major resource for nurturing and developing the community, and as such an essential institution for legitimate leadership. Religion, politics, business and social concerns come together in a heady mixture to provide the dynamism for growth as well as the sources of conflict. And because gurdwaras, like most ethnic minority religious institutions in the contemporary inner city, have increasingly assumed an adjunct role to the local state and welfare service, the competition to control them has further intensified.

Structure of Factional Conflicts
The basic organising structure of Sikh society is the faction (see Chapter 2) centred on an individual leader. Although factions are constantly

restructured in line with the success or failure of leaders, for understanding the conflicts over control of gurdwaras in Britain – and the
roots of leadership struggles within the community – the regularity of
certain patterns needs to be identified.

First there is a perennial conflict between 'old timers' and new
'arrivals'. Whereas the 'old timers' tend to be of the older generation or
the original founder members of the management committee of
gurdwaras, the 'new arrivals' are invariably recent migrants from Punjab
or elsewhere. As such the latter rely initially on the gurdwara resources,
eagerly seek patronage, are hyperactive in kinship networks, and are
distinguished by their high rates of membership and participation. This
cleavage had always been there but was accentuated, for example,
following the arrival of East African Sikhs in the 1960s and, after 1984,
with the rise of the Khalistan movement and refugees.[35]

Second, as the Sikh community has developed, 'new arrivals' have
tended to accentuate the divisions between the 'orthodox' (*amrit-dharis*)
and 'modernisers' (*kesh-dharis,* and *mona*-Sikhs). Traditionally the
'orthodox' have tended to occupy the controlling positions as heads of
gurdwaras and allied political institutions in the Punjab, especially the
SGPC and the SAD, but in the initial waves of settlement most Sikhs
were *mona* (clean-shaven), and only subsequently became *kesh-dari*
(wearing a turban and unshorn hair). These individuals were the main
founders of gurdwaras and Sikh associations. However since the mid-
1970s, but more especially since 1984, the 'orthodox' have been able to
dislodge 'modernisers' by moving amendments to gurdwara constitutions
that limit the membership of management committees to *amrit-dharis*
only.[36] The emphasis on 'orthodoxy' is a regular manoeuvre to outflank
opponents.

Third, factional conflicts are allied to political and social organisations
that operate within gurdwaras and broader Sikh society. As we shall see
(Chapter 5), historically all political organisations have sought to control
and influence gurdwaras, either directly or indirectly. For most of the
twentieth century these bodies were the overseas chapters of the parent
organisation in Punjab and India – the Communist parties (CPI, CPI
(M)), SADs, Congress and Khalistani organisations. These organisations,
by and large, are unable to function unless they control the resources and
the followers of gurdwaras, because control enables Sikh political
organisations to promote integration – whether class- or identity-based –
with Punjabi 'homeland' politics. In sum, the strength of Sikh political
organisations in Britain is directly proportionate to the number and size
of the gurdwaras they control.[37]

Fourth, *illaqa* (local) rivalries often constitute an important element of gurdwara conflicts. Disputes in ancestral villages are amplified; vendettas that appear meaningless are resurrected with passion and intensity that defy belief, often to a point where the defeat or humiliation of the opponents becomes a matter of *izzat* (honour). For instance, the history of the conflict at Guru Nanak Gurdwara, Smethwick, is inextricable from the history of the broader village rivalry between Jandialvis and Moranwalians, two sets of villagers in the Doaba. Similarly, in Leicester the factional dispute between the main gurdwaras was initially rooted in village and kinship loyalties, spiced by political rivalry between the Communists and Akalis. But, as we noted in the case of Southall, these rivalries can extend beyond the village to a whole area: while the Doabians have uniquely imported their own quarrelsome village culture into the style of management of many gurdwaras in Britain, they are also not averse to differentiating themselves from migrants loyal to the Malwa and Majaha regions when such differentiation proves advantageous.[38]

Finally, some scholars have highlighted the role of caste in gurdwara politics.[39] This was clearly the case when gurdwaras were first established and the congregation tended to be inclusive, but as Sikh denominations and sects have established their own institutions, the salience of caste as a source of factional disputes has greatly diminished. Nonetheless it needs to be recognised as an important axis, for most gurdwaras remain potentially open to charges of caste discrimination.

Management Structures

There is no standardised pattern of gurdwara organisation in Britain, with variations in practice and management being the norm. Broadly speaking, there are two modes of organisation: individual or group ownership, or a trust structure. In practice, most gurdwaras are trusts, with a management committee that oversees the day-to-functioning of the institution. Since most gurdwaras are registered with the Charity Commission, there is a legal requirement to provide a written constitution according to which the institution is governed.[40]

Most large gurdwaras are administered by a management committee that is directly elected through ballot of the membership, usually resident around the locality of the gurdwara. As their importance has increased, the prestige and honour attaching to service on the management committees have risen correspondingly. Thus elections to become a president or secretary often involve intense political campaigns, with the main gurdwaras in Southall and Smethwick often occupying centre stage. Once elected the management committee normally serves for two years. In addition to a president, a secretary and a treasurer, with their deputies, there is usually a 21-member team. The representation of women remains negligible; most committees elect or co-opt one or two. Besides appointing *granthis* (readers of scriptures), the management committee is responsible for keeping financial accounts. Many gurdwaras have written constitutions with rules and functions specified and daily routines displayed on noticeboards. Recently there has been a trend to post some details on websites. Procedural changes are often made to debar potential rivals, however, or unnaturally to extend the life of management committees. Thus SGSSS witnessed a fierce debate to bar Sikh shopkeepers engaged in selling cigarettes from seeking management posts. In Smethwick, in the post-1984 turmoil, the gurdwara's constitution was amended to include only members who were committed to Khalistan.[41]

Elections, moreover, are elaborate affairs and there is frequent vote rigging or gerrymandering. Once elected, the office bearers tend to ensure their opponents are kept at bay and elections postponed for as long as possible. The elections of the SGSSS held in April 1977, for instance, came after a lapse of nine years. In this campaign the candidates sought the support of all Punjabi organisations, including the Communists.[42] Violent disputes over the control of gurdwaras are common. As one local newspaper reported:

> An argument between warring factions at a Sikh temple in Coventry erupted into violence and mayhem yesterday. One man was taken to hospital and two others were treated at the scene by paramedics after trouble flared at the Guru Hargobind Sahib Gurdwara. Police wearing protective vests recovered 40 weapons from inside the building, including ceremonial swords and daggers. Twenty people, both men and women, were arrested in or outside the temple (gurdwara).[43]

In another case two factions that had shared the same coach to travel to a High Court hearing in London ended up in 'a bloody pitched battle at a motorway service area, [where] knives were drawn as rival groups battled on the car park'.[44] In yet another dispute worshippers described how

> a meeting at the Sikh temple descended into chaos when swords were waved around the congregation. More than 15 police cars, a dog unit, two police vans and four armoured response teams were called to the Guru Nanak Gurdwara, Holy Bones.[45]

Probably no gurdwara in the country has remained immune to such conflicts. Case after case can be cited where management committees were involved in disputes, engaged in unseemly fights, went to court or sought the help of the Charity Commissioners to obtain redress.[46] The case of Guru Nanak Parkash Gurdwara (GNPG), Coventry, is typical, with a history of disputes including irregularities in its use of funds and election procedures since the 1980s. In 1993 the Charity Commissioners imposed a Scheme (a framework) for regular elections, including a qualification that no GNPG 'member (was) permitted to stand for election to the Executive Committee until a period of two years had elapsed since the person was last a member of the Committee'. Despite this ruling – and the opposition of the Charity Commissioners – the GNPG proceeded to hold an election in December 2000 in which it accepted the nominations of candidates who were barred by the two-year ruling. The defeated faction sought legal proceedings but on the advice of the Charity Commissioners accepted the latter's intervention. In taking this action the Commission observed:

> elections held on 10 December 2000 were unconstitutional and unlawful and, as a consequence, the funds and property of the GNPG were not under the control of properly authorised persons. The Commission invoked powers under section 18 of the Act (Charities Act 1993) to freeze the charity's (GNPG) bank and building society accounts.

The Commission under section 26 of the Act directed fresh elections to take place within a specified timescale and a procedural framework accompanying it. While concluding the investigation, it gave a salutary warning:

> When the constitution of a body of charity trustees is to be achieved by elections, the Commission recommends that this should be through a process which is *open and transparent and in strict accordance with procedures set out in the governing document.*[47]

Sometimes in circumstances of intense conflict the management committee is taken over by women. For example, in three gurdwaras – in Coventry, Leicester, and Birmingham – when rival factions, all men, came to blows within the premises, local women seized control.[48] Guru Nanak Gurdwara, Smethwick, was managed by local women during 1981–2; Guru Tegh Bahadur Gurdwara, Leicester, which had no elections for nine years, was also taken over by women. The Shepherd's Bush Gurdwara, when faced with a crisis as a result of rivalry between two factions, delegated charge to an all-women's committee in March 1983; another dispute in 2003 required the Charity Commission's arbitration.[49]

Income

One reason why factional disputes appear highly animated is the income and expenditure gurdwaras now generate. Most medium-to-large gurdwaras have an annual income of anything from about £100,000 to £300,000, giving a total of £25–£75 million as annual cash donations. Over the last two decades the income revenue streams have multiplied to include: *golak* (contributions by the congregation), contributions to the building fund, special campaigns, contributions in kind, income from *akhand paths* (dedicated readings of the scriptures, normally three days), local, national and European Union development grants, fees from educational or other classes, fees for officiation at birth, death and marriage ceremonies (many leading gurdwaras issue marriage licences), and the hire of halls and allied premises for ceremonies and official functions. Some gurdwaras have branched out into other activities, becoming learning nodal points or local welfare centres for the Sikh elderly, disabled or mentally handicapped. In addition, they also provide a new range of services that includes such things as matchmaking between prospective brides and grooms. No area of contemporary social life is excluded; with the gradual decline of *biradari* connections and the extended joint family, gurdwaras are seeking to fill this vacuum as the authentic venues for community *seva* (service). Increasingly these services aspire to compete with the professionalised levels provided by private entrepreneurs.[50]

Of course there are significant variations in gurdwara income. The weekly cash takings at the larger ones can average several thousand pounds, while in smaller ones it can be as low as a few hundred. For instance, the Guru Nanak Gurdwara, Smethwick, in April 2000, just a week before Vaisakhi, received *golak* donations of £2,716 and a further £3,560 through receipts.[51] If these contributions were consistent throughout the year they would give an annual income of £326,352. The largest gurdwara in Birmingham, managed by GNNSJ, claimed an income of £2.27 million a year, with total funds valued at £4.42 million.[52] Elsewhere gurdwara incomes have also been rising: Guru Nanak Gurdwara, Bedford had an annual income of £111,781 (2002–3),[53] the Ramgarhia Sikh Gurdwara, Slough £221,191 (2002),[54] and the Guru Nanak Gurdwara, Leicester £196,388 (2002).[55] Indeed, the construction of the SGSSGS at a cost of £17 million suggests that income flows, especially cash flows, are more than proportionate to meet the total outlay. If anything, there is probably some substantial under-reporting of income for official purposes, particularly given that most of the income is generated by cash donations.

Faith in the Inner City: Gurdwaras' Changing Role

In the last two decades the gurdwaras' role has changed dramatically. From fledgling institutions of the faithful, they have become – along with the mandirs and mosques – the new pillars of faith in the inner city. These changes have taken place against the backdrop of seismic changes in British politics and society over this period – the rise of ideological multiculturalism, the gradual erosion of the welfare state, the transformation of local 'government' to 'governance', the 'return of religion' in public life, and the emergence of the community cohesion agenda.[56] Against these profound changes gurdwaras have shown a remarkable capacity for adaptation and survival.

Most important, the gurdwaras have come to resemble other organisations of the welfare state. Local multicultural policies in the 1980s and 1990s created an intimate nexus between the Labour Party and minority ethnic community religious institutions, enabling the former to reap considerable political rewards while the latter gained access to public goods and other forms of patronage as well as an institutional representation in the local and sometimes national structures of power.[57] This relationship has led to an exponential growth in gurdwara services: they now provide advice centres, learning centres, care for the elderly, 'one stop shops' for local agencies, and centres of learning and community development. In some cases staff assigned to these tasks are funded by local government or have been relocated from traditional local departments; and the range of funding available through urban grants, lottery projects, European Union support and voluntary aided agencies has created a highly professionalised lobby among young Sikhs that seeks to further concentrate resources and functions among gurdwaras by placing them at the centre of community cohesion and urban renewal programmes currently under way.[58]

Local and National Coordination

It was against this background that the Council of Sikh Gurdwaras in Birmingham (CSGB) was formed in 1989 under the sponsorship of the Birmingham City Council, then controlled by the Labour Party. The CSGB exists to provides a 'two-way communication to empower the community', enabling it to integrate within the mainstream society. In 2001 it secured a £181,503 grant from the National Lottery Charities Board for a three-year project on community building with the aim

> to build the capacity of the community to enable gurdwaras in Birmingham to become effective community organisations, directly providing

services, and to become partners in local regeneration, development and service delivery.[59]

This stress on gurdwaras as *co-partners* in service delivery has also been accompanied by pressure that local authorities recognise the distinctive needs of local Sikhs by instituting a method of service monitoring that recognises Sikhs as an 'ethnic' category.

The Birmingham model has also been followed by the authorities such as Sandwell, Coventry and Leicester which have all formed umbrella organisations for local gurdwaras. As well as coordinating routine functions such as the annual celebrations, marches and festivals that fall in the Sikh calendar, these bodies act as important representative intermediaries between the gurdwaras and the local state on a whole range of everyday issues in a context where the idiom of 'ethnicity' has now been supplanted by 'religion'. For most local and statutory bodies today, especially following the recent legislation on racial and religious discrimination, local gurdwara federations have become the first contact point. The growth in inter-faith dialogue since 9/11 and 7/7 has also given these bodies additional importance that often extends beyond the local to international fora.

The CSBG and other such bodies in the Midlands, however, also illustrate the limits of organic growth. Although the gurdwaras partici-pating in them are willing to cooperate as part of 'federations', they are zealous – especially the sant-run bodies – in protecting their autonomy. In many ways the local federation model reflects the Sikh *misl* pattern and it is precisely for this reason that despite calls for a national organi-sation in Britain since the 1960s, *à la* SGPC, nothing tangible has emerged, nor is anything likely to do so in the foreseeable future. At the time of writing the British government, notwithstanding the strong pressures post-9/11 and post-7/7 to have a national organisation of Sikhs, is reluctant to facilitate such a process, preferring to consult *ad hoc* with organisations like the CSGB, sants, the Network of Sikh Organisa-tions, the Sikh Human Rights Group, the Sikh Federation (UK) and the British Sikh Consultative Form.[60] While the latter was initially identified with the Sikh Federation, which adopted aggressive lobby practices on Sikh homeland issues, the other organisations, especially the Network of Sikh Organisations led by Indarjit Singh and the Sikh Human Rights group led by Jasdev Rai, aim to project a less overt political stance, often seeking legitimation for their action on spiritual and temporal issues on behalf of British Sikhs from the Akal Takht in Amritsar. The former in particular has, through patient work since the 1970s, gained an enviable reputation within the British establishment, enhanced significantly by Indarjit Singh's popular contributions to BBC Radio Four's 'Thought for the Day'. His access to state and royal channels is deeply resented by heads of other rival organisations, yet, in comparison to these groups, Indarjit Singh's cultivated approach appears to be more effective, as attested by his ability regularly to secure royal attendance at Sikh events – for example, the 400th anniversary of the installation of the Guru Granth Sahib at the Royal Albert Hall (26 September 2004), at which the Prince of Wales was the chief guest.

In the absence of a recognised national religious organisation of Sikhs that has genuine legitimacy, questions of doctrine or authority within British Sikhism remain ambiguous, resolved *ad hoc* where necessary with reference to the Akal Takht, the SGPC in Amritsar, or, still, the courts, Charity Commissioners and other executive or judicial bodies. Para-doxically, most Sikh leaders recognise the need for such a body; in reality, however, they work to ensure that such a goal is never realised.[61] Consequently, the absence of structured leadership often produces a multivocal response to issues of doctrine or policy that is regularly displayed as unseemly competition between recognised and self-appointed leaders, gurdwaras, sants and transnational (cyber-group) interlopers.[62]

Nurturing the Faithful: Contemporary Challenges
Surprisingly, there is no systematic research into the nature of Sikh religious congregations. Although attendances remain remarkably high, with one survey recording that 39 per cent of all Sikhs attend once a week, and most visit on *gurpurbs* (births of the gurus),[63] this figure conceals some deep concern. Many of the young, it is often claimed, are failing to observe the five Ks, are poor attenders and shun the learning of Punjabi, traditionally taught within the gurdwara premises. This trend was somewhat arrested by 1984, but re-emerged in the 1990s. Because Punjabi is the main way of accessing the tradition, this high threshold is a powerful disincentive. Some gurdwaras, recognising this, have adopted innovative approaches to respond to the dilemma: in Leicester, Birmingham and Southall on special occasions plasma screens are provided for simultaneous translation into English.[64] It is quite possible that in the future the key prayers will be provided in the Romanic script (as in some mandirs) or some efforts will be made to use an English version of *Guru Granth Sahib*, though this is likely to be fiercely resisted by traditionalists.[65] Many gurdwaras organise youth camps that are increasingly developing a transnational character, with coordination in

North America, Europe and India. The strong ideological content of most of these camps, however, has proved unattractive to most Sikh youth and remote from their everyday concerns in the Western diaspora.[66] In this void many are increasingly turning to 'cyber gurdwaras' to access the tradition – and certainly the liveliness with which key issues are debated on Sikh websites by youngsters contrasts remarkably with the conservative liturgy of most gurdwaras in Britain today and their familiar routine of Punjabi and local factional politics.[67]

Youth disenchantment is also reflected in the disengagement of a substantial section of the emerging professional classes who are alienated by gurdwara politics or imported functionaries, often with low levels of education. Professional Sikh gurdwara attenders regularly complain about these functionaries, who are prone to regale the congregation with parables of 'cats, jackals and lions' in idioms that have little relevance even to rural Punjab, let alone twenty-first-century Britain. The more subliminal, majestic and spiritual dimensions of Sikhism, it is often argued, are marginalised in regular services. This disjunction is more than an idiomatic difference: poorly trained, inarticulate functionaries add to the existing dissonance between transmitters and receivers of the tradition, resulting in an extreme polarisation between the 'star' performers from Punjab or elsewhere, who are able to attract sizeable audiences on the gurdwara circuit, and everyday functionaries with minimal or no qualifications. A move to professionalise religious training post-9/11 and -7/7 is probably inevitable.[68] However it is likely to be strongly resisted by gurdwara management committees, not least because of the considerable patronage attached to managing and sponsoring functionaries, many of whom have a tendency to 'disappear' into the informal economy.[69]

It is partly in response to these developments that the religious revivalism within British Sikhdom has been led by sants. The sant tradition has sought to provide a personal dimension to the faith: this clearly has a strong psychological appeal, despite the fact that the Sikhs are a textual community for whom the line of living gurus ended with the tenth master. The importance of an active human agency interceding between the followers and the faith is reflective of the broader Indic tradition that is familiar to most rural Punjabis. For followers, on the other hand, the larger sant organisations can provide a totally integrated network of support that sometimes embraces the family, marriage and business across the Sikh diaspora and for several generations – a powerful attraction in the highly risk-prone contemporary world. Yet perhaps more important in Britain, the sant-led gurdwaras, because

Table 4.5 Sants' Main Centres and Visiting Years

Sant	British Centre	Punjab Centre	Years
Teja Singh	London	Mastuana [Faridkot]	1908–10
Jagjit Singh [Namdhari]	East London	Bhaini Sahib [Ludhiana]	1967–77
Gurbachan Singh [Nirankari]	Smethwick	Delhi	1967–78
Khem Singh	Leeds	Ghunachaur [Hoshiarpur]	1967
Hardev Singh [Nirankari]	London	Delhi	1979
Darbari Das	Wolverhampton	Lopon [Faridkot]	1968–74
Amar Singh Burundi	Wolverhampton	Nanaksar [Ludhiana]	1969
Harbans Singh Domeliwale	West Bromwich	Domeli [Jalandhar]	1970–90
Ishar Singh Rarewala	Wolverhampton	Rara Sahib [Ludhiana]	1970–5
Sadhu Singh	Smethwick	Nanaksar [Ludhiana]	1970
Charan Singh	Leeds	Bhikhowal [Hoshiarpur]	1970
Gurmel Singh Baghapurana	Wolverhampton	[Baghapurana] Ferozepore	1971–4
Mihan Singh Siarhwale	Coventry	Siarh [Ludhiana]	1972–95
Gurdev Singh	Smethwick	Nanaksar [Ludhiana]	1975
Puran Singh Karichowale	Birmingham	Karicho, Kenya	1977–83
Gian Singh	Bradford/Oldbury	Kutya Johlan [Jalandhar]	1974–6
Garib Das	Birmingham	Balan [Jalandhar]	1976
Kirpal Singh [Radhaswami]	Midlands	Beas [Jalandhar]	1979
Gurbachan Singh Kambliwale	Southall	Jalandhar	1980–2000
Mann Singh	Leeds	Nanglan [Hoshiarpur]	1982
Naurang Singh	Birmingham	Jalandhar	1983–5
Nihal Singh Harian Velan	Southall	G. Hakimpur [Jalandhar]	1985
Jagjit Singh	Birmingham	Harkhowal [Hoshiarpur]	1987
Nahar Singh	Stratford	Nanaksar [Ludhiana]	1989
Mann Singh Rarewale	London	Pehowa [Ludhiana]	1990
Harnek Singh	Coventry	Edmonton [Canada]	1995
Mohinder Singh	Birmingham	Zambia	1995
Bhag Singh Lamme	Birmingham	Lamme [Ludhiana]	2003
Sarup Singh	London	Chandigarh	2005
Ranjit Singh Daddriwale	Manchester	Daddriwala	2005
Niranjan Singh	Wolverhampton	Jawaddi [Ludhiana]	2005

they are unencumbered with elected management committees, have been better able to cater for the spiritual needs of their followers. The Guru Nanak Nishkam Sewa Jatha (GNNSJ) gurdwaras, for example, are generally viewed as models of 'good practice' with a strong emphasis on Sikh spirituality, an emphasis that is underlined by the popularity of their support in the locality and beyond.[70]

Not all sants, however, have an institutionalised presence in Britain and their increasing influence is deeply resented by some elements of the community on the grounds that their stress on spirituality is often at the neglect of *temporal* concerns.[71] Nor are all sants seen as equally benign; some in the past have been accused of dividing the community's outlook over homeland issues, particularly the campaign for Khalistan.[72] In fact, in contrast to some militant Islamic traditions from South Asia, in the main the role of Sikh sants has been to *undercut* rather than *fuel* militancy. The one militant sant tradition – that of Bhindranwale, which led the Sikh agitation in Punjab in the 1980s and 1990s – has singularly failed to establish an institutionalised presence in Britain, though one of its leaders, Baba Thakur Singh, has toured British gurdwaras.[73]

Lastly, gurdwaras perform badly on two key indicators: transparency and democratisation. Management committees continue to be male-dominated and undemocratic, their functioning shrouded in mystery. Women's representation within the governing structures of the gurdwaras remains negligible, a fact made all the more obvious because they tend to constitute the largest section of the congregation and provide the most labour power, particularly for the *langar*. Women's role in gurdwaras still remains that of the default option; that is, they are brought to exercise authority when 'things go wrong'. Efforts to exercise independent authority by women continue to be frustrated or discouraged.[74]

Conclusion

Almost a century divides the establishment of the Shepherd's Bush gurdwara and the SGSSGS's 'Golden Temple'-like structure in Southall. In this period, more especially since the Second World War, a distinctive British gurdwara movement has emerged, creating nearly 250 buildings throughout Britain that have clearly demarcated Sikh sacred spaces, most notably in the inner cities. At the same time, because of the backgrounds of the migrants from Punjab and elsewhere in the Sikh diaspora, this movement has been marked by a diversity and complexity that have frustrated the emergence of Punjab-like national structures such as the

SGPC. Today as hubs of the community the gurdwaras have become the focal points of its anxieties and aspirations in a post-9/11, post-7/7 world where minority religious institutions are under the microscope as never before in a climate in which Eastern religious traditions are now easily conflated with transnational terrorism or 'rotten multiculturalism' that is viewed as a threat to Western values. How successfully gurdwaras respond to this challenge will be determined as much by the future trajectory of Sikh 'homeland' politics as by their capacity to meet the changing needs of *all* generations of British Sikhs, the majority of whom are now British-born.

Five

'Homeland Politics':
Class, Identity and Party

Associations of immigrants in Britain have generally served two functions: to facilitate the integration of the new arrivals and as conduits of homeland politics, and these functions have further strengthened with the onset of globalisation, which has underpinned the rise of trans-nationalism and diaspora movements.[1] Indeed, since 1984 British Sikhs have become the premier example of a 'constructed disapora'.[2] Although these studies mark a significant new theoretical departure, they have tended to overlook the continuities in Sikh organisation *before* and *after* 1984. In the last 60 years the outlook of these organisations has shifted from the politics of class (IWAs up to the early 1980s) to the politics of identity (Khalistan 1984–97) and is now marked by an emphasis on political organisation (Sikh Political Party (UK)). Yet, whatever the label, ethnicity and class have remained conjoined. The communist-led IWAs were essentially *ethnic* organisations; the Sikh Political Party (UK), though aggressively promoting the politics of Sikh identity, is a party with *distributionist* aims. Ethnicity and class are therefore difficult to distinguish in the politics of immigrant organisations, and this is especially so in the case of Sikh organisations, where formal ideological outlooks and organisational structures provide few clues to their actual behaviour.

To further highlight these continuities it is appropriate to make some preliminary observations. First, nearly all the leading Sikh political organisations in Britain have had their *raison d'être* in Punjab or Indian politics. Whether one considers the IWAs, the SADs, the Indian Overseas Congress (IOC), or the post-1984 Khalistan groups, the clear objective has been to create chapters in Britain while providing clientistic support for parent organisations in Punjab and India. Regardless of ideological considerations, access to homeland patronage systems has been the main driver for old and new organisations alike; and as the fortunes of the parent bodies have changed, correspondingly these changes have been reflected in the British chapters.

Second, the familiar method of organisation in Punjab is reproduced among British Sikh bodies. Because in rural Punjab horizontal associations based on class or interest have traditionally been very weak, the main method of organisation has been a structure based on a leader who controls a faction with access to resources and patronage (see Chapter 2). Organisations are only as strong as the ability of the leader to deliver to his faction. Factionalism therefore is endemic, a permanent 'state of nature' among all Sikh organisations. It flourishes because of cultural norms in which Sikh political activity is embedded and the easy access to alternative forms of legitimacy – rival parent bodies in Punjab and India, recourse to litigation, and the ability to generate new resources.

Third, factionalism ensures that most Sikh organisations have a short shelf-life, regularly undergo multiple reincarnations or reinvent themselves with grandiose titles. The history of the IWAs, SADs, IOC, Khalistan organisations and, most recently, Internet-based organisations is replete with bodies that are little more than a postal address, operated by a single individual. Internet technology has further intensified this process by short-circuiting the need for labour-intensive work. Some of these organisations are clearly opportunistic, responding to local or national and international developments, but their constant proliferation and demise represent a more permanent trait that distinguishes Sikh society: its enduring failure to build institutions.

Finally, because British Sikhs have failed to evolve national and local institutions that command legitimacy, collective action has been possible mainly on single-issue movements such as anti-racism, immigration policies, turban and *kirpan* campaigns, or, after 1984, pro-Khalistan, or, post-Khalistan, the politics of victimhood. Single-issue movements are popular as a mode of mobilisation because they are more likely to reward a leader and a faction by offering the potential for leadership, as well as simultaneously undermining opponents, especially opposing gurdwara management committees. This is why the popularity of single-issue causes greatly transcends routine efforts at institution building.

In the rest of this chapter we will examine the nature of Sikh organisations up to the early 1980s, when the politics of class appeared to predominate. We then explore the impact of Operation Blue Star (1984) on British Sikhs, with the rise of the Khalistan movement. In the late 1990s, as this movement waned in Punjab, there was a distinct change in the politics of identity; this was highlighted by 9/11, 7/7 and the war on terror. We conclude by reflecting on the broader issue of Sikh participation in British politics.

Politics of Class before the 1980s

Although, as we noted in Chapter 4, the KJBI (1908) was the first organisation of Sikhs in Britain, formed by Teja Singh who was then a student at Cambridge, this body – after participating in the move to establish the Shepherd's Bush gurdwara – soon collapsed upon Teja Singh's return to Punjab. Thereafter there is no mention of a similar body until the formation in Coventry in 1938 of the first IWA. This organisation was founded at the initiative of local Punjabi workers, whose leadership was overwhelmingly *mona*-Sikh, as a club for socialising with no political overtones. However, when in 1940 Udham Singh killed the ex-governor of Punjab in Caxton Hall, the IWA organised financial support for his legal defence. The IWAs remained active during the Second World War, with particular emphasis on organisation in a few localities in the Midlands.[3] The Coventry IWA appears to have become inactive in the late 1940s, when it dissolved after the resignation of Muslim members, and was only revived by the arrival of fresh migrants from India in the early 1950s.[4]

Indian Workers' Associations (IWAs)
The first major post-war IWA was set up in Southall in 1957 by Sikhs and Punjabi Hindus of Doabian communist background.[5] These migrants came from the young and articulate sections of Punjabi society who were heavily influenced by the leadership of the Communist Party of India (CPI).[6] Many, like Vishun Dutt Sharma, were former party members who found the Communist Party of Great Britain unreceptive to the new arrivals. With encouragement from the CPI, new IWAs were soon established in the main cities of Sikh settlement.

The Southall IWA initially had a membership of about 100,[7] and its leading activists included Vishnu Dutt Sharma, Ajit Singh Rai and Sardul Singh Gill. During the 1950s the organisation provided an essential community service for many Punjabi immigrants: form filling, 'regularising' documents (of illegal migrants) and helping to secure employment. Soon branches were established in the West and East Midlands, the North, Glasgow and in east and south London. By the mid-1960s most Punjabi Sikhs and Hindus were members of the local IWA: in 1965 the Southall branch had a membership of 3,900, Coventry of 1,000.[8] The growth of the IWA, however, was closely monitored by the CPI – and following the Sino-Soviet split this was also to be its undoing.

After the Indo-China war (1962), the pro-Chinese faction within the CPI broke away to form the Communist Party of India (Marxist), CPI (M). This split in India was reproduced in Britain when the IWA Southall branch, which dominated the organisation, stayed loyal to the CPI while most of the Midlands and northern branches allied with the new CPI (M). A further split occurred in late 1967 with a schism in the Indian CPI (M) and the formation of the CPI (M-L) (Marxist-Leninist). Popularly known as the Naxalites, these radical communists advocated armed rebellion through the physical elimination of class enemies and had a significant following among Punjabi youth. The ruthless suppression of the Naxalite movement in Punjab by police action provided another burning cause for the more militant communists. The Midlands IWA, led by Avtar Johal and Jagmohan Joshi, backed the Naxalite movement, leading to their expulsion from the CPI (M) on 7 January 1968.[9] In the same month Joshi and Johal founded the IWA (MLGB) with its monthly organ *Lalkar*.

The 1970s were the high-water mark of IWA influence. However, the local IWA branches were only as strong as the individuals who ran them. Thus while Bradford was well organised, Leeds with a similar Sikh population had no branch. The Midlands emerged as the hub of IWA activities, with branches in Derby, Coventry, Leicester, Nottingham and Birmingham enjoying considerable support among Sikh workers. Soon Avtar Johal, Prem Singh, Avtar Sadiq and Niranjan Singh Noor became well-known figures in the Midlands who dedicated themselves to the anti-racist class struggle by attempting to build broad alliances with organisations like the Campaign Against Racial Discrimination (CARD).[10] In 1976, when immigration laws were the major concern of the Indian population, a procession attracted more than 7,000 demonstrators. Even the IWA Southall, a reluctant fellow traveller, decided to participate in the march.[11] The case of a virginity test at Heathrow on Vijay Lakshmi in 1979 also led to a furore in the Asian community. The IWAs organised several protest marches, stressing an anti-racist strategy.

IWA activists further established their reputations within the community by regularly contributing to weekly Punjabi papers. Vishnu Dutt Sharma, Raghbir Dhand, N. S. Noor and Makhan Johal used their pens to become popular among the readers. Exposing racism was a recurring theme in their journalism and creative writing, which included poems.

Gurnam Singh Sanghera, an activist in Bradford, wrote on the history of racial riots in October 1972, followed by a series on how colour discrimination started.[12] Some local IWAs organised Asian games and festivals that were funded by local gurdwaras.[13]

But the growth of the IWAs was not without its problems. Elections of officers became a source of regular factional disputes. Entrenched leaders became reluctant to relinquish power. Often those elected used all means at their disposal to prolong their rule, while opposition groups employed similar means to enforce their exit. Elections to IWA Southall were always problematic with litigation common, usually invoked against the ruling group whose tactic was to delay elections as long as possible. In 1972, for example, the IWA election results were challenged in court, with a ruling in favour of a faction led by Ajit Rai.[14]

By the mid-1970s, differences between IWA Southall and those in the Midlands became unbridgeable. The IWA Southall changed its constitution in April 1976, renaming itself as IWA (UK). On several occasions its elections were decided by court intervention. In 1977, again prompted by the High Court, elections were held. These elections were far more significant as the leading activist, Vishnu Dutt Sharma, supported the State of Emergency (1975–7) imposed by India's Prime Minister Indira Gandhi.[15] When Mrs Gandhi visited Southall to address a gathering at the Dominion Cinema, angry protests by IWA (MLGB) and IWA (CPI (M)) and Akalis greeted her and the Indian flag was burnt. Matters did not rest there: some physical clashes took place between supporters of Congress and IWA (MLGB). Passions ran high as the IWA Southall was accused of hobnobbing with the Congress Party.[16]

Another event which particularly affected the influence of IWA Southall was the murder by racists of a Sikh youth, Gurdip Chaggar, on 4 June 1976.[17] The IWA leaders were blamed for failing to register a proper response as some 400 angry young men joined in the funeral procession. The youths subsequently formed a separate organisation, Southall Youth Movement (SYM), with Balraj Purewal as its leader.[18] For several years the SYM competed with IWA Southall, denting the latter's reputation. When Southall was again the scene of violence following the clash between the National Front and Punjabi youth in 1979, resulting in serious disturbances that resulted in the death of the student Blair Peach, the IWA undertook to fight Asian youths' cases. The action committee, led by Vishnu Dutt Sharma, appealed for a fund of £100,000, and a commemoration service for Peach was held on 1 July 1979 at a local gurdwara.

By the 1980s the influence of the IWAs had been seriously eroded. When the various IWAs celebrated the fiftieth anniversary of the first IWA in 1988, most of their branches were almost dormant. By then the IWA Southall had become an advisory agency; its old cinema building, once a lively place, had been converted into a civic centre. Piara Singh Khabra, one of its many activists, was elected a Labour MP in 1992, a seat he has held since then. Although some IWA factions attempted to forge a semblance of unity in 1989, by then most of their membership had gone over to new organisations.[19] While internal fissures exhausted its leaders, the issues of mobilisation no longer attracted support from Sikh workers as immigration became almost a non-issue, and cases of racial discrimination did not arouse previous levels of indignation. The rise of the Akalis and pro-Khalistani organisation after 1984 placed the IWAs on the defensive and in the 1990s they were almost wound up, with the old hands retired or dead and the youth showing little enthusiasm for class politics.

Shiromani Akali Dals (SADs)
By the end of the 1970s the predominance of the communist IWAs within the British Sikh community was beginning to be challenged by the rise of the SAD – the main political party of the Sikhs in Punjab (see Chapter 1). The creation of a majority Sikh-speaking Punjabi state in 1966, the increasing growth of gurdwaras in Britain, the turban campaigns, and the launch by the SAD in Punjab of an autonomy movement in 1982 – all these developments were a fillip towards the establishment of SAD chapters in Britain.

The first major Akali leader to visit Britain was Master Tara Singh in 1953.[20] The inspiration for the establishment of a SAD (UK) came with Sant Fateh Singh's visit in 1966, after he had campaigned successfully for a Punjabi-speaking state. Sant Fateh Singh was accompanied by Mohan Singh Tur and Arjan Singh Budhiraja. On his arrival at Heathrow Airport he was greeted by 5,000 Sikhs and the authorities took pains to announce his arrival in Punjabi.[21] During his stay he was received by the Archbishop of Canterbury and had talks with Maurice Foley, then minister responsible for immigration at the Home Office, raising the matter of job discrimination.[22] After his short visit several other Sikh leaders came from Punjab to streamline the fledgling organisation.

In the mid-1960s a number of developments further consolidated the ground for the organisational presence of the SAD. At the end of January 1967 British Sikhs celebrated the 300th anniversary of Guru Gobind Singh (the tenth guru) with a gathering of 6,000 at the Royal Albert

Hall. This was followed a year later by the 500th anniversary of the birth of the founder of Sikhism, Guru Nanak. At this time a number of major disputes about the right to wear a turban had mobilised sections of the local community (see Chapter 6), with the Manchester and Wolver-hampton municipal transport committees finally relenting after several years of controversy. Simultaneously, two Punjabi weeklies (*Des Pardes* and *Punjabi Times*) were established in 1965 and 1966 respectively, to exploit the new market. But perhaps more significantly, in 1967, for the first time in post-independence Punjab, a SAD-led coalition adminis-tration came to power, under a Sikh Chief Minister.

In response to these developments, in February 1968 Joginder S. Sandhu announced the establishment of an executive committee and office bearers of Shiromani Akali Dal of UK (SADUK).[23] The first annual meeting of the SADUK was held in Ealing Town Hall on 8 September 1968, with David Ennals MP, Sir Edward Boyle MP and Stephen Jacob present. It was soon followed by a new rival called the Shiromani Khalsa Dal UK. Despite this factionalism, in the 1970s there were SAD activists in most Sikh localities, and though most were new to politics, they had had strong kinship connections with IWA com-munists. Sometimes they allied to establish control of gurdwaras or join in anti-immigration campaigns; sometimes they were at odds, as for example over the anti-Naxalite campaign, because of the policies of the SAD governments in Punjab. From the late 1960s the SAD in Britain subscribed closely to the pattern of Akali politics in Punjab: activists owed allegiance to particular leaders in the Punjab and assiduously followed their fortunes and patronage.

A dramatic change in Akali politics occurred with the assumption of power in Punjab of a SAD government in 1977. Akalis in Britain became more visible in the gurdwaras. When in 1980 this government was dis-missed by Indira Gandhi through the imposition of President's Rule, the SAD in Punjab launched the *dharma yud morcha* (1982), a protest move-ment for greater constitutional autonomy from the central government. This agitation, as in Punjab, divided the Akalis into 'moderates' and 'militants' and assumed an increasingly violent form, culminating in the assault on the Golden Temple in June 1984 by the Indian Army.

Indian Overseas Congress (IOC)
In addition to the communists and the Akali, the other main political force in Punjab that has commanded the loyalties of Sikhs is the Indian National Congress (INC). Congress has ruled in Punjab for most of the post-independence period and, unlike the Akalis, and to some extent the

Plate 5 June 1984: Sikhs protest in Hyde Park at the storming of the Golden Temple by the Indian Army. Over 25,000 Sikhs (unofficial estimates put the figure at 50–60,000) demonstrated their anger against the action. (Reproduced with the permission of Des Pardes)

communists, has had a broad constituency, appealing to Sikhs, Hindus and, in particular, the lower castes, especially lower-caste Sikhs, who have always been more heterodox in their religious practice. Like the communists, the Congress historically has been strong in the Doaba region, which has the highest concentration of Scheduled Castes in Punjab. These localities have been the naturally constituency of the IOC, which, amongst other things, had direct access to patronage and power, both nationally in New Delhi and in Punjab.

The need for the IOC arose partly from the discomfort experienced by India's national leaders on their visits to Britain, when they often encountered hostile protests from the newly arrived Indians. Nehru during his regular visits was frequently lobbied by the IWAs in connection with migration matters. Prime Minister Lal Bahadur Shastri, (1964–5), was heckled by the IWAs outside Marlborough House, London in 1964. This opposition was condemned by some, who submitted a memorandum to the High Commission against the protest march. Among the signatories was Bakhshish S. Karnana of the National Front. As a result of the Shastri visit there were proposals to set up an organisation sympathetic to the Congress.

An Indian Overseas Congress (IOC) was first organised in Britain in the 1970s and attracted many Sikh members. The IOC's fortunes, however, remain tied to those of the governments in both the Punjab and New Delhi, where Sikhs have held major positions in the Party – with Dr Manmohan Singh currently the serving Prime Minister. Because of this institutionalised support the IOC, like Akalis and communists, has competed for control of the British gurdwaras. After 1984 the IOC, in conjunction with the High Commission of India, was to play an active role in attempts to frustrate the activities of Sikh militants. Since the return of a Congress government in Punjab in 2002, the IOC has again become active within the Sikh community, though its influence is not as strong as it used to be.

Khalistan Phase: 1984–97

Before 1984 the Sikh nationalist cause had only a few activists, who were involved in 'right to wear the turban' campaigns (see Chapter 6). Some of these activists had sought the help of the Indian High Commission, but, according to Charan Singh Panchi (afterwards the Khalistan Movement), despite repeated appeals, it was reluctant to intervene in this 'delicate matter'. In 1972 these disgruntled individuals formed the Sikh Homeland Front – a breakaway faction of the SAD.

The moving spirit behind the Sikh Homeland Front was Dr Jagjit Singh Chohan, who arrived in Britain in 1971. Chohan, an ex-minister in a short-lived SAD government (1967–9), voiced the Sikh Homeland issue at a Hyde Park meeting in September 1971. He placed a half-page advertisement in the *New York Times*, claiming that:

> At the time of partition of the Indian subcontinent in 1947 it was agreed that the Sikhs shall have an area in which they will have complete freedom to shape their lives according to their beliefs. On the basis of the assurances received, the Sikhs agreed to throw their lot with India, hoping for the fulfilment of their dream of an independent, sovereign Sikh homeland, the Punjab.[24]

In the 1970s Chohan dramatised his case by unfurling a Khalistan flag in Birmingham before several hundred Sikhs. However he soon came up against firm opposition.[25] A gurdwara in Leeds took the initiative to condemn Chohan in December 1971, provoking angry protests at another gurdwara in Wolverhampton. Dr A. K. S. Aujala, the new president of the SAD (UK), called him a 'traitor' in a full-page advertisement in the Punjabi media. Several management committees barred Chohan's entry to local gurdwaras. To discourage ideas of Sikh separatism gaining further momentum, the Indian authorities also arrested Chohan's supporter, Giani Bakhshish Singh, during his visit to Punjab in 1972, detaining him for a year without trial before releasing him following an intervention by the British High Commission. Frustrated by such strong opposition, the Sikh Homeland proponents then targeted their appeals to the Punjabi media. In a letter to *Des Pardes*, Charan Singh Panchi argued:

> Sikhs have to realise that there is no future in India dominated by Hindus. The honour and prestige of the community cannot be maintained without state power. Sooner we realise this challenge better it will be for us to set our objective of establishing a sovereign Sikh state in the Punjab. We cannot keep ourselves in bondage for ever. Our leaders act like beggars in New Delhi....[26]

This response was countered by Akalis, communists and ordinary Sikhs. Once generated, however, the debate continued for several years. Denounced by community leaders and denied entry into major gurdwaras, Chohan maintained his solitary campaign. He visited Canada and set up a small circle dedicated to the idea of a homeland. In Britain his efforts were temporarily boosted by the unexpected election of Zorawar Singh Rai, an activist of the Sikh Homeland Front, as president of the SAD (UK) in June 1972.[27] Rai claimed that the Indian High Commissioner could not enter any gurdwara in Britain, and though this was hardly the case, it underlined the fact that Akalis were now split into two competing factions: a group led by Joginder Singh Sandhu that launched *Shere-Punjab* (a Punjabi weekly) and sought the Indian High Commission's patronage, and Sikh homelanders led by Rai.[28]

In 1975 the Sikh Homeland Front also split into rival factions because of differences between Chohan and Panchi. To keep the issue in the limelight, Chohan travelled extensively, and on a visit to Punjab in August 1977 he proposed that it be renamed Khalistan. Two years later he attempted to install a radio transmitter in the Golden Temple.[29] For this cause, support came from several British Sikhs who formed an International Golden Temple Corporation and held several meetings at the Shepherd's Bush gurdwara during 1979–82.[30] Besides extending an invitation to Sant Jarnail Singh Bhindranwale to visit Britain, the

Corporation arranged a 'World Sikh Festival' in July 1982 with a seminar on 'Sikhs are a nation'. This event ran parallel to Ganga Singh Dhillon's address to the Sikh Educational Conference in Chandigarh emphasising the theme of 'Sikhs as a nation'.[31] This series of events rekindled the debate on whether Sikhs constituted a nation and on the need for an independent Sikh homeland.[32]

By the late 1970s the Sikh homeland cause had begun to assume renewed vigour. In 1978 a violent clash in Amritsar between a group of orthodox Sikhs and Nirankaris left 13 people dead. This provoked much anger among some British Sikh associations, who criticised the Indian government's role in encouraging the Nirankari sect. This event led to a partial rapport between Sikh Homeland protagonists and other community activists, and Bhindranwale wrote to Chohan 'appreciating his services to the *panth*'.[33]

Punjab Autonomy Campaign

In August 1982 the SAD in Punjab launched the *dharma yud morcha*. While some communists offered qualified support, most Sikh associations soon became thoroughly engrossed in the campaign. Aware of the Sikh diaspora's considerable resources, Sant Harchand Singh Longowal, President of the SAD, wrote a general letter to overseas Sikhs:

> I am sending this special letter to all of you because you ought to know what is happening to the *Panth*. It is now 144 days into the *dharma yud morcha*. Some 17,557 Sikhs have courted arrest. You should take a deputation to the Indian High Commission office on 17 October, with a letter stating how Sikhs are being repressed in India. You should make the world aware how India is treating the Sikh *Panth* and to show that Sikhs, wherever they are, share the anguish of the *Panth*. I am stating with firm conviction that the *dharma yud* will continue until the tyrant Indian government agrees to our just demands.[34]

The Akali leader's appeal received enthusiastic endorsement from British Sikh organisations. Major gurdwaras passed resolutions of support and plans were drawn for active support. To coordinate this growing campaign a Dharm Yud Morcha Action Committee was formed, with leading representatives across the gurdwaras. Earlier a rally was organised which attracted some five thousand people in London on 7 February 1982, and as the Indian Prime Minister Indira Gandhi arrived at the Royal Festival Hall to inaugurate a 'Festival of India' in March 1982, she faced angry Akali protesters, who were joined by the radical Marxists, IWA supporters, and members of the Hind Mazdoor Lahir.

At this stage the Akalis were unwilling to raise the demand for sovereignty. From 1982 onwards there were weekly collections in all leading gurdwaras to fund the autonomy campaign. These funds were forwarded to Amritsar with the receipts displayed on noticeboards. A number of gurdwara managers made visits to Amritsar offering their support for the campaign.[35] Rallies and marches were also planned. Sant Puran Singh Karichowale from Birmingham led a rally of eight thousand Sikhs in London on 10 May 1984. While the Indian Prime Minister warned that 'donations to extremists' were fuelling terrorism in Punjab, funds continued to flow from Britain and North America.[36] On instructions from Amritsar the Akalis also burnt copies of the Indian Constitution and began a process of reorganisation to better coordinate the increasing momentum of support. However, these plans were abruptly interrupted by Operation Blue Star.

British Khalistani Organisations
Operation Blue Star (June 1984), conducted in the glare of world-wide publicity, created a deep sense of outrage among British Sikhs. Dramatic pictures of the entry of the Indian Army into the Golden Temple and the destruction of the Akal Takht, where the militants led by Sant Jarnail Singh Bhindranwale made their last stand, galvanised the Sikh diaspora. In the condemnation of the Indian government's actions, British Sikh leaders, like other overseas Sikhs, reacted with extreme anger and sadness. They turned out for a mammoth protest on 10 June 1984. Over 25,000 Sikhs (unofficial estimates placed this at 50–60,000) from all walks of life joined in the march from Hyde Park (see p. 101) to the office of the Indian High Commission in Aldwych, denouncing the Indian government and shouting *'Khalistan Zindabad!'* (Long live a Sikh state).[37] The marchers were joined by leaders of the Kashmiri Liberation Front and the Nagas, the other main disaffected minorities of India. In addition, several gurdwaras organised local demonstrations in Birmingham, Bristol, Coventry and other cities. The anger of ordinary Sikhs over the army action found expression in other ways, too.[38] Responding to a call in the Punjabi media, several volunteered to liberate the Golden Temple complex, but the idea was soon dropped as the Indian government introduced strict visa regulations. Punjabi newspapers carried angry letters from Sikhs and the English media also saw extensive correspondence and editorials.[39] Indian banks and other official organisations were boycotted. A Sikh journalist wrote to the Indian High Commission to condemn the Indian army's characterisation of *amrit-dhari* Sikhs.[40] Photographs of Sant Bhindranwale along with Shahbeg Singh,

Amrik Singh and other Sikhs killed in the army action quickly appeared in major gurdwaras up and down the country. Videotapes and books explaining the army's action, distributed by the Indian High Commission, were sometimes publicly burnt.[41]

This bitter resentment was further reinforced a few months later by the aftermath of the killing of Indira Gandhi by her two Sikh bodyguards on 31 October 1984. The news was followed by media reports of Sikhs celebrating by appearing to drink champagne in Southall, Birmingham and other places.[42] When this coverage was telecast in India it further inflamed a volatile situation in which anti-Sikh riots had broken out. These pogroms claimed almost 3,000 lives while displacing several thousand people.[43] For several days Delhi became a smouldering cauldron where organised violence against Sikhs compounded British Sikhs' sense of alienation and anger. Subsequently there was some contrition among British Sikhs at their incautious acts and many gurdwaras organised financial support for the victims of the riots.[44]

Reflecting developments in Punjab politics, Sikh militants assumed the leadership of the British Sikh community, a power shift which lasted until the mid-1990s when the moderate SAD returned to power in Punjab in the elections of 1997. From 1984 until the mid-1990s Punjab became the site of a bitter struggle between Sikh militants campaigning for a separate state of Khalistan and the security services waging an anti-insurgency campaign, resulting in the deaths of almost 30,000 people.[45] For British Sikh political organisations, the return to normalcy has, in some measure, restored the *status quo* that prevailed before the early 1980s. Nonetheless, because this period was so turbulent and dramatic for British Sikh political organisations, we need to mention four bodies that held particular sway among the community: the Council of Khalistan (COK), the International Sikh Youth Federation (ISYF), Babbar Khalsa (BK) and Dal Khalsa (DK).

The COK was elected immediately after Operation Blue Star at a stormy meeting of over five thousand Sikhs on 23 June 1984 in Southall.[46] SAD leaders Giani Amolak Singh and his associates, who had supported and mobilised for the Punjab autonomy campaign from 1982 onwards, were severely reprimanded. Chohan, long ostracised for his idea of a separate Sikh homeland, was given overwhelming support and elected president of the Council. COK elected four other members from major organisations: Gurmej Singh of the BK, Sewa Singh of the Akhand Kirtani Jatha, Karamjit Singh representing the youth, and Harmander Singh from the reorganised SAD. A businessman offered a free office in central London, soon known as Khalistan House, where several volunteers undertook the campaign amid furious meetings and enquiries. COK's appeal for funds received a generous response from the community, which raised £100,000 within two months. Its leaders mobilised support by arranging meetings at gurdwaras where Khalistan was eagerly discussed by congregations. Several media ventures were also launched, including the radio programme 'Voice of Sikhs' (May 1985). This ceased broadcasting after a few months under pressure from the Indian government.[47] COK attempted to contact other governments but the 'exiled government of Khalistan' failed to win any recognition, despite some mild interest by an Ecuadorian diplomat who spoke at a rally in Birmingham.[48]

COK had been beset by factionalism from its inception. In 1986 the BK representative, Gurmej Singh, effectively parted company by forming his own 'government in exile' in Birmingham. Karamjit Singh was among other leadership casualties. These dissensions were merely compounded over time because COK lacked a strong foothold in the main gurdwaras. Its active supporters quickly dwindled to a small band of Chohan admirers. Chohan maintained his stand through speeches, often mixing wry humour with ideological advocacy of Khalistan, but he was unable to transform the COK into the premier organisation it set out to be, despite presenting a consistent case for sovereignty. He regularly cautioned about the existence of an extensive network of agent provocateurs bent on maligning a legitimate independence movement, but his opponents often levelled similar charges against him. COK was effectively wound up in the mid-1990s and in June 2001 Chohan, surprisingly, returned to Punjab – still committed to the cause of Khalistan 'by peaceful means'.[49]

Whereas the COK represented a somewhat older and moderate leadership, a more youthful organisation was inspired by Jasbir Singh Rode – a nephew of Sant Bhindranwale who had died defending the Akal Takht. Rode arrived in Britain in July 1984 from Libya, where he was a small contractor. At a meeting on 23 September in Walsall, Harpal Singh and Jasbir Singh announced the formation of the ISYF, with a 51-member panel headed by Dr Pargat Singh. According to its constitution the organisation's objectives were to 'establish a sovereign Sikh state' by, amongst other things, making Sikhs aware of their 'religion, the past struggle for independence, unique identity, and status as a separate nation'.[50] Within months of its formation the ISYF had established 21 branches with an estimated membership of 16,000 in 1985. The Birmingham and Southall branches quickly recruited over 1,000 members each. However, Rode, following a short visit to Pakistan, was detained in December 1984 and deported under pressure from the Indian government.[51] ISYF mounted a strong protest, alleging that Rode's emphasis on baptism had unnerved the Indian authorities.

The ISYF campaigned for Khalistan by holding regular meetings in gurdwaras where its leaders rallied supporters and collected funds. It made common cause with its sister organisation in Canada. At its annual convention foreign delegates regularly participated as it sought to establish a transnational network for supporting the Sikh militants' campaign in Punjab. The ISYF, in common with its Canadian sister organisation, gave support to Bhindranwale's family in Punjab, entering into a political alliance with United Akali Dal (UAD), led first by Baba Joginder Singh and then by Rode, who was 'rehabilitated' by the Indian authorities after a period in detention. Rode's later stand, which sought 'Sikh rights within the Indian national framework', disappointed many radical members, who broke away to form the ISYF (DT). By the mid-1980s the ISYF had atomised into militant factional *groupscules* operating in Punjab. Although these developments gradually eroded the ISYF's support by localising it to particular gurdwaras, the ISYF – along with the BK – remained a key militant group regularly cited by Indian authorities.

The BK was well known for its members' strict adherence to orthodox traditions. Before 1984 the majority of its members belonged to the Akhand Kirtani Jatha, a group that was content to recite scriptures through night-long hymn singing sessions. A leading member of the BK, Gurmej Singh, was nominated to the COK. When he applied for British citizenship a diplomatic row erupted between the British and Indian governments.[52] The BK was committed to a militant strategy and its posters and declarations called for revenge. As the death toll rose, especially during the 1990–2 period, its monthly *Wangar* headlined such news as signs of victory.[53] With an occasional caution about the ethics of violent strategy, some of its leaders seemed to be basking in the glory of murderous exploits.[54] In July 1992, one of its leaders, Gurdeep Singh, who had gone to Punjab to participate in the movement, bared his soul in a highly publicised surrender. His confession was seen as a betrayal and amounted to a major setback for the organisation.[55] The BK partially controls three gurdwaras (two in the Midlands and one in the North).

Finally, mention needs to be made of DK, a small group consisting of Jaswant Singh Thekedar, Manmohan Singh, Mohinder Singh Rathore, Ranjit Singh Rana and a few others. They all came from the Punjab in the early 1980s as refugees. The DK rose to prominence after an Indian Airlines plane was hijacked to Lahore by Gajinder Singh and four others, who were jailed.[56] Jaswant Singh Thekedar arrived in Britain in 1982, wrote a short book and produced a map of Khalistan. His activities were limited to a small circle of friends in Southall.[57] Ranjit Singh Rana has also been prominent in literary activities and floated a scheme to offer awards for Punjabi writers.[58] The DK leaders have also split into rival factions.

Methods of Mobilisation

The COK, ISYF, BK and DK were the main organisations that spear-headed the campaign for Khalistan. They did so by mobilising resources, staging demonstrations, establishing broader linkages with other groups and seeking to influence British government policies towards India.

Unlike COK, which established an office in London, the ISYF and BK operated from gurdwaras, which provided funds. Between 1984 and 1997 the ISYF members replaced many gurdwara governing committees, which traditionally had consisted of coalitions of Akalis, Congress and IWAs: elections were forced at leading gurdwaras in Derby, Nottingham and Leicester and control gained; in Southall the SGSSGS was brought under ISYF control; in Smethwick, a communist–Congress stronghold, the existing governing committee was ousted; and in Luton there was a bitter struggle between the ISYF and the Congress committee members. A similar situation also developed in Huddersfield and Coventry. However, at the Guru Nanak Parkash Gurdwara, Coventry, the ISYF crossed swords with the BK, leading to police intervention amidst ugly scenes that were widely reported (see Chapter 4). For a few years afterwards, its management was taken over by a women's committee.[59] At a gurdwara in Kent open violence erupted between the ISYF and other groups.[60] In some cases the struggle to control gurdwaras led to lengthy litigation involving the Charity Commissioners.[61] A few gurdwaras controlled by sants also faced diffi-culties.[62] By 1986 the ISYF had established a strong presence in all the major British gurdwaras, which gave the organisation access to consider-able funds, resources and manpower. In addition to the control of these resources, direct appeals were made to congregations, businesses and sympathetic supporters.

Although the COK, ISYF, BK and DK attempted to establish a broad-based appeal within the community, their constituency remained limited to Jat Sikhs. A Ramgarhia Panthic Convention held in Birmingham initially gave 'full support for the Khalsa Panth of which Ramgarhia is an integral part',[63] but in due course this position became more complex as the body divided into two factions: one group supported Khalistan while another took strong exception to abuses hurled at Zail Singh, a Ramgarhia and then the President of India.[64] Nonetheless Ramgarhia gurdwaras contributed generously to support funds for Delhi riot victims.[65] The Bhatras also showed enthusiasm for the homeland cause, but the Namdharis and Ravidasis exhibited little enthusiasm, though few dared to oppose the campaign through alliance with the anti-Khalistani groups led by the communists and Congress.[66]

All four organisations quickly established media outlets. The COK launched *Khalistan News* and published pamphlets and a major report on Punjab's troubles. Chohan became a prolific columnist; his contributions frequently appeared in the Punjabi media and he often offered advice through 'open letters'.[67] The ISYF launched its own Punjabi weekly, *Awaz-e-Quam,* consistently advocating the Sikh state.[68] Its editor, Raghbir Singh, was arrested in early 1995 and threatened with deportation for 'reasons of national security'.[69] The ISYF also published pamphlets, recorded popular songs and videos. The BK ran a monthly, *Wangar,* from 1987 to 1994. Similarly, DK leader Ranjit Singh Rana edited a monthly for several years.

The ideological work of disseminating Sikh nationalism was undertaken not only through publications, but also by popularising the message through traditional idioms. At major gurdwaras, *dhadis* (traditional folk singers) regularly narrated martyrs' tales combining the contemporary heroes with those from the past. Gian Singh Surjeet, the group Khiali's Dhadi Jatha and Jago Wale composed many songs in memory of the martyrs of Khalistan.[70] Several Punjabi writers published creative works that celebrated Sikh 'martyrs' sacrifices' and echoed the tragic conditions facing the community.[71] Much more broadly, these organisations sought to influence academics and intellectuals to reflect critically as well as sympathetically on the fortunes of Sikh nationalism.

Demonstrations, conventions and rallies were the main method of sustaining the campaign for Khalistan. These events were regularly attended by some parliamentarians as well as foreign delegates from North America and elsewhere, and frequently included India's other estranged minorities such as the Kashmiris and the Nagas. Often such gatherings would conclude with fulsome resolutions such as the following:

> On 26 April 1986, that Panthic committee [in Amritsar] made public the resolve of the Sikh nation to constitute itself in a sovereign state that shall bear the name Khalistan. This convention, on the fourth anniversary of that historic occasion, pledges its full support to the ideal of that sovereign state and urges all individuals, parties and organisations that oppose the

said ideal shall be given no recognition nor cooperation of any kind. This convention urges Sikhs all over the world to abide by the law of the country they are settled in and be good citizens wherever they are but be aware of the agents of the Indian government who roam around provoking strife in various gurdwaras for the very specific purpose of discrediting the Sikh settlers in the eyes of the host society. ... [T]his Convention urges ... to take new hope from the events of East Europe and other parts of the world which herald the dawn of the era of freedom of peoples.... This convention urges all national governments to link their aid and trade programme with India to its human rights record.[72]

Visiting Indian politicians and administrators became the targets of Khalistani frustration. In October 1985 the Indian Prime Minister Rajiv Gandhi was confronted by two thousand protesters.[73] His visit was preceded by the arrest of four ISYF members from Leicester, who were put on trial for conspiracy to kill the Indian premier.[74] Another protest confronted Prime Minister Narsimha Rao in 1994 when he concluded the Indo–British agreement on protection of investments and held talks on non-proliferation of nuclear weapons. An angrier band greeted the Punjab police chief, K. P. S. Gill, during his short visit to London in 1994.[75] Celebrations of India's fiftieth anniversary of independence in 1997 were marred by strong protests in Leicester, Birmingham and London.[76] Throughout the 1980s and 1990s, India's Independence Day was greeted with regular demonstrations outside the High Commission in Aldwych.

At the same time Akali leaders from Punjab were either shunned or abused. Darshan Singh and Manjit Singh, both Jathedars of Akal Takht, encountered embarrassing interrogations while visiting some gurd-waras.[77] Only with the election of a SAD government in the Punjab in early 1997 did some gurdwara committees start welcoming Akali leaders. In August 1997 an Akali minister spoke at the Southall gurdwara, although at the same time two BK activists were arrested for allegedly plotting to kill the Deputy Inspector-General of the Punjab police, also on a visit to London.[78] In contrast, the relatives of victims of counter-insurgency in Punjab were honoured and celebrated. When Basant Kaur, the wife of the late Beant Singh, hanged for killing Indira Gandhi, visited Britain, she was warmly welcomed by several gurdwaras.[79]

British political parties were compelled to respond to the new mode of mobilisation. The Labour Party, which traditionally has had fraternal links with the Congress, limited its response to human rights abuses, dismissing the idea of self-determination for Sikhs.[80] The Green Party, though an insignificant force in British politics, formulated a lengthy solution to the Punjab issue, supporting Sikhs' right of self-determination.[81] The Scottish National Party also endorsed this position:

> All nations of the world have a right to self-determination. In that context, both the Sikhs and Scots are still struggling to seek what is rightfully theirs. We are therefore united in our love for liberty.... The SNP, of course, rejects every means other than the democratic one to regain our independence.... At the same time, we do acknowledge that in many other parts of the world minorities suffer from oppressive imperialism. Those are obviously different conditions, and require different responses.[82]

The concentration of Sikhs in some inner-city areas prompted a few MPs to voice in Parliament their concern about the Sikhs' plight. While there is no record of the Conservative Party's collective stand on the Sikh homeland, in 1986 a dispute arose within the Anglo-Asian Conservative Association of West London that led to the dissolution of the association by Conservative Central Office in response to 'Sikh domination'.[83]

In the late 1980s and the early 1990s, as the Punjab became a battleground for protracted confrontation between Sikh militants and security forces with an average annual death toll of around of around 5,000, there were many cases of highly publicised human right abuses.[84] The COK and the ISYF spearheaded a new initiative based on the human rights agenda. Dr Jasdev Singh Rai, an ex-president of the ISYF, set up the Sikh Human Rights Group in Southall. In 1992 the ISYF established the Khalsa Human Rights group with an office in a Leicester gurdwara. Both groups held exhibitions to expose human rights abuses in India, but particularly in Punjab. These organisations supported the cases of Karamjit Singh Chahal and Raghbir Singh – two activists detained under the National Security Act and subsequently released upon appeal to the European Court.[85] Cases of relatives in Punjab who had been tortured or killed by the security forces were also highlighted in the international media.[86] Representatives of the Punjab Human Rights Organisation were brought over to brief MPs at the House of Commons,[87] where subsequently over the course of several meetings Sikh lobbyists were able to highlight cases of human rights abuses.[88]

A common feature of all the organisations was their close but shifting alliances with groups and leaders in the Punjab. Through such linkages considerable financial help was provided to the Khalistan movement and to families of 'martyrs' killed or tortured by the security forces.[89] While the ISYF has followed the fortunes of the Jasbir Singh and Bhindranwale families, the COK has allied itself with the Panthic Committee, formed in 1986 (and fated to endure four schisms by 1990). These fluid alliances with militant groups in Punjab led to bitter controversies and feuds among British activists who sought or contested legitimation from the parent bodies. The relationship between the COK and the ISYF became especially acrimonious following the murder of Harmander Singh Sandhu in January 1989.[90]

Opposition to Khalistanis

Opposition to Khalistanis took some time to organise. In the aftermath of 1984, members of the IOC were confronted in several gurdwaras and Indian Independence Day celebrations were postponed in several localities. Congress members were also expelled from gurdwara committees. In 1985 the IOC president, Sohan Singh Lidder, was wounded in Luton by an ISYF activist, Sulakhan Singh Rai. Tarsem Singh Toor, a businessman and IOC activist of Southall, was shot dead by unknown assailants.[91] Swaran Singh, a prominent Sikh and former Foreign Secretary, arrived in London in 1985 and set up the Punjab Unity Forum (later known as the Sikh Forum), but without much effect.[92]

Sandesh International, a minor Punjabi weekly that had endorsed the Indian government's Punjab policy, started a major campaign against Khalistanis.[93] It was supported in this effort by Darshan Das, a new sect leader of Sachkhand Nanak Dham who was preaching Hindu–Sikh reconciliation. Amid the allegation that he was an Indian government plant, Darshan Das, a Punjabi Hindu, established a centre in Handsworth and soon acquired a popular following. At the height of the 1984 tensions the newly established sant startled many Sikhs by promising to send a gold-wrapped copy of the *Guru Granth Sahib* to the Golden Temple to replace the original one destroyed during the fighting. He also announced that Sachkhand Nanak Dham was carrying out repairs to the damaged Akal Takht and that Sikhs should refuse donations to other organisations.[94] In a subsequent call the sant challenged anyone to burn the Indian flag, and when this was duly done the Das's supporters clashed with Sikh militants, who also attempted to set the sect's headquarters alight. This hostility reached its finale when Darshan Das was shot dead during a prayer meeting in Southall in November 1987.[95]

Opposition from communists was far more significant. Some IWA leaders branded the demand for a Sikh state as sectarianism and a foreign conspiracy, though this was mixed with criticism of the Congress government for mishandling the agitation.[96] In the post-1984 aftermath many Sikhs abandoned the IWAs: in Leicester and Derby there were resignations *en masse*. In Birmingham, IWA workers who tried to distribute a pamphlet in front of a gurdwara were severely beaten. This was the first of a series of fights that continued for several years in the Midlands.[97] As the number of communists murdered in the Punjab increased, relations between Khalistanis and IWAs became increasingly fraught.[98] Police had to intervene regularly in fights between ISYF and IWA supporters. Vishnu Dutt Sharma, the veteran leader of the IWA in Southall, launched *Charcha*, a monthly, to woo 'the patriotic section of Sikhs and the Punjabi population', and encourage 'unity' among Indians. But despite these efforts the IWAs remained on the defensive and were unable to re-establish their 1970s hegemony.

Khalistanis and Indo-British Relations

The most sustained opposition to Khalistan groups, not unnaturally, came from the Indian government. In a White Paper published soon after Operation Blue Star, it listed the organisations operating from Britain that were allegedly funding secessionist activities in Punjab.[99] Accordingly, steps were taken to restrict their activities by imposing strict visa controls for British visitors to India, surveillance of overseas Sikh groups, and the use of diplomatic pressure on host states to curtail Khalistani activism.[100] The Indian government was assisted in this move by acts of random terrorism throughout the 1980s and 1990s, and in particular the downing of the Air India flight over Ireland that was attributed to Canadian Sikh militants.[101]

Khalistanis' activities placed a special strain on Indo–British relations until the early 1990s.[102] In the aftermath of Operation Blue Star, Indian diplomats reacted with anger to the BBC's broadcast of Chohan's statement about the consequences of sacrilege at the Golden Temple.[103] British explanations about the episode fell far short of Indian expectations. The Indian High Commission alleged that 'Sikh extremists here are not only being allowed to break the laws of this land', but were also 'inciting communal passions'.[104] The Indian government's displeasure over Britain's lax attitude was conveyed through the cancellation of a British Aerospace Exhibition planned in New Delhi and the visit of Michael Heseltine, Minister for Defence (December 1984).[105] It also cancelled a £65 million order for Westland helicopters; another order for British Sea Harrier jets and Sea Eagle missiles, worth £175 million, became the subject of lengthy negotiations. During her visit to India in April 1985, the British premier, Margaret Thatcher, tried unsuccessfully to salvage Britain's export of aircraft missiles to India.[106] Even the threat of a reduction in foreign aid if the helicopter deal did not materialise was reported to have been ineffective. Perhaps in response to these rebuffs, a distinct change of tone occurred when Rajiv Gandhi visited Britain in September 1985. Several Sikh activists in Leicester were rounded up and the police foiled a 'conspiracy' to murder him.

In the mid-1980s the activities of Khalistanis became a major issue for the Indian government, which demanded an extradition treaty and a ban on fundraising. In April 1986 a formal request was submitted to the British Foreign Secretary, Sir Geoffrey Howe, who offered to amend certain sections of the Fugitive Offenders Act governing the extradition rules between the United Kingdom and Commonwealth countries. In an obvious reference to India's increasing pressure, the Minister of State for Foreign and Commonwealth Affairs, William Waldegrave, outlined the government's position in November 1988:

> We have been closely in touch with the Indian government during the past few days to find ways of strengthening our cooperation to combat the activities of extremists within the framework of our laws. That cooperation is something to which the Indian government understandably attaches great importance, and it has assumed a central place in the political relations between the two countries.... The extremists number perhaps a few hundred at most.... [B]ut organisations are active in the Sikh community whose main purpose is to offer help and support to the extremists in India. Those organisations have been able to draw on the moral and financial support of many Sikhs in Britain who do not share that objective. I call on all decent Sikhs in Britain to ensure, before they give their support to an organisation, that they are clear about its intention.[107]

In the event the Extradition Treaty was signed in September 1992 and it covered the tracing, freezing and confiscation of terrorist funds and the proceeds of serious crime, including drug trafficking. The treaty was presented to Parliament in July 1993.[108] During the debate several members questioned its need and the existence of safeguards for Sikh and Kashmiri citizens. Many MPs expressed serious reservations, with Terry Dicks and Max Madden lodging strong objections.[109] Others argued that the treaty was a convenient ploy to secure the arms trade at the expense of human rights, as one-third of British exports to India related to arms. The treaty was approved by 123 votes, with 38 MPs voting against. Significantly, Piara Singh Khabra, a Sikh and Labour MP from Southall, supported the treaty. L. M. Singhvi, the Indian High Commissioner, hailed the passing of the measure as 'probably the most significant' event between India and Britain.[110]

The Sikh Question in Parliament

In the 1980s and 1990s pro-Khalistan and other Sikh organisations developed an effective lobby system. MPs with significant Sikh constituents regularly tabled parliamentary questions or interceded in relevant discussions. Terry Dicks, a Conservative MP from Hayes and Harlington, emerged as a consistent campaigner, often attending annual meetings of the COK. On several occasions he spoke on the Punjab situation. In November 1988 he underlined the historic Anglo-Sikh connections, the 'contribution that Sikhs have made in two world wars' and the 'list of decorations won by Sikh soldiers' as proof of their 'loyalty and devotion to our country'.[111] He also alleged that 'Indian security services' were operating within the Indian community. Waldegrave responded by narrating cases of Sikh violence in Britain:

> The activities of the terrorists are not confined to India. In October 1985 a plot was uncovered to assassinate Prime Minister Rajiv Gandhi during his visit to the United Kingdom. A moderate Sikh leader Tarsem Singh Toor was murdered in January 1986. Another, Darshan Das Vasdev, was shot dead in November 1987 and three other attempts were made on the lives of leading Sikh moderates. In all those cases, those responsible have been tried and convicted.[112]

Max Madden MP (Bradford West, Labour) visited Punjab in 1990 with a team of British and European parliamentarians and reported to Parliament on human rights abuses.[113] Madden tabled many questions, including some on the Indian government's response to human rights violations and the use of gurdwara funds by militants in the Punjab.[114] In a major debate on human rights abuses in the Punjab in November 1991, Terry Dicks commented:

> I want to mention yet again in the House the persecution of Sikhs in the Punjab. Members of the Sikh community living in my constituency and Sikhs throughout the world have been concerned for the safety of family and friends living in the Punjab. The rape of young women, the beating of old men and the murder of young boys, to say nothing of the imprisonment without trial of many thousands of innocent people, has been going on since 1984 and continues unabated. Indian security forces are killing hundreds of innocent Sikhs in encounters and there is evidence that those forces have swept through villages in the Punjab intent on nothing less than widespread slaughter.[115]

Replying to the debate, Tristan Garel-Jones, Minister of State, Foreign and Commonwealth Office, offered this advice to British Sikhs:

We urge all decent, law-abiding Sikhs in this country to deny moral and financial support to those organisations that contribute to the misery and suffering brought to the Punjab and India by extremist violence.... The Sikhs have the right and will receive a sympathetic hearing from my Hon. Friends and me, but the Sikhs must also recognise that the cause they seek to serve will not be helped unless their condemnation of violence and extremism is wholehearted.... That is how they can best contribute to the cause in which they believe.[116]

Other MPs like Jeff Rooker (Birmingham-Perry Barr) questioned the use of British aid for projects in Kashmir and Punjab. John Spellar (Warley West) raised the human rights question in 1994, especially India's special law, the Terrorist and Disruptive Act, as it took away 'the basic right of free speech and political opinion'.[117] In 1995 the issue of 'unclaimed bodies' in Amritsar was highlighted by Terry Dicks, while Jacques Arnold (Grevesham) reminded members of British responsibility in the matter.[118]

Outside Parliament the Sikh question also became embroiled in a serious diplomatic discord involving Her Majesty during the royal visit to India in 1997 to commemorate the fiftieth anniversary of India's independence. Just before the visit the Prime Minister of India, Inder Kumar Gujral, advised the Queen not to visit Amritsar for fear that it might rekindle Sikh militancy;[119] and relations between the two governments deteriorated further when Foreign Secretary Cook suggested British mediation over the Kashmir dispute.[120] Sensing an opportunity, many British Sikh leaders campaigned to welcome the royal tour. While the ISYF president, Amrik Singh, wrote a supporting letter, a delegation headed by Bachittar Singh left for Amritsar to welcome the Queen 'on behalf of British Sikhs'.[121] The Queen laid a wreath at the Jallianwala Bagh and visited the Golden Temple where, it was reported, the Sikhs gave her an enthusiastic welcome.[122] Against calls in the Indian press for an apology for the Amritsar massacre of 1919, some Sikh leaders replied that the imperial crime paled into insignificance compared to the Indian government's own 'Amritsar massacre' in 1984.[123] Significantly at the Heads of Commonwealth meeting in Edinburgh a fortnight later, Sikhs and Kashmiris united to protest against the visit of Gujral.

Post-Khalistan: Transnationalism, Communal Cohesion and Political Party

In the early 1990s the campaign for a separate Sikh state of Khalistan in India was crushed by the overwhelming force deployed by the Indian security services. This was followed by a return to normalcy in Punjab politics, signalled by the election of a SAD regional government in 1997.[124] This turnabout inevitably had repercussions for British Sikh politics: the SAD, IWA and IOC camps, which had been overshadowed by the Khalistanis, began to regain support, to contest gurdwara elections, and to challenge the hegemony of the Khalistan campaign. If the latter were to survive it had be reinvented as an idea. This reinvention since has been marked by the aggressive politics of Sikh transnationalism, an agenda for ethnic cohesion, and after 9/11, the establishment of a Sikh political party around the politics of 'victimhood'.

Sikh Transnationalism
As the militancy in Punjab has waned, increasingly the sophisticated lobbying machine developed by British Sikh groups during the 1980s and 1990s has begun to focus on the politics of Sikh transnationalism: global issues affecting the Sikh diaspora where British Sikhs seek to spearhead the community's causes. At one level this development is a conscious effort to define a global Sikh interest; at another it is no more than the perpetuation of 'messy politics' between states, with the particular aim of embarrassing India by seeking to leverage the support of transnational organisations like the United Nations.[125] The areas of focus include the abuse of human rights in India, the project to establish UNESCO heritage status for the Golden Temple, and the recognition of the right to self-determination.[126] Most recently, British Sikh groups have been at the forefront of the campaign to pressure the French government to withdraw the ban on wearing turbans in public institutions. Although much of this activity thus far has yielded only a small measure of success, a significant breakthrough was made at the United Nations world conference against racism, racial discrimination, xenophobia and related intolerance at Durban in 2001, when Sikh groups succeed in challenging the narrow definition of racism. As result of this lobbying Article 67 of the final conference declaration recognised

> that members of certain groups with a distinct cultural identity [like the Sikhs] face barriers from the complex interplay of ethnic, religious, and other factors as well as their traditions and customs and call upon states to ensure that measures, policies and programmes aimed at eradicating racism, racial discrimination and xenophobia and related intolerance address the barriers to these factors.[127]

The practical implications of this article if it were adopted by the signatory states, it was subsequently pointed out, would require European Union legislation and, perhaps more important, a mechanism to monitor Sikh 'employment, appointments to public bodies, the practices and policies of public bodies towards Sikhism and an understanding of Sikhism by public bodies in the interpretation of policies'.[128]

Communal Cohesion

The desire of British Sikh groups to push for the incorporation of Article 67 into European Union legislation needs to be seen in a wider context, one in which it is underpinned by the drive towards communal cohesion among British Sikhs. This campaign – which has been led by the Sikh Human Rights Group, the British Sikh Federation, Sikhs in England and the Sikh Federation (UK) – ostensibly aims to highlight the unusual forms of racism that Sikhs suffer in Britain, where religion and ethnicity combine to produce a double-bind. Its underlying implications, on the other hand, are clearly to redefine Sikh ethnicity, which is overwhelmingly Indian (91.4 per cent in the UK 2001 census, see Chapter 3), in *religious* terms, to recognise Sikhs as a *distinct* and *separate* group in British law (as per the *Mandla v Dowell Lee* judgement) and to incorporate this category into the monitoring mechanism of local and national government. Systematic pressure has been brought to bear on MPs and the Office of National Statistics, as well as on central and local governments, to recognise this claim. Interestingly this drive is also underlaced by claims of *proportionality*. In a memorandum submitted by the Sikh Federation to the Select Committee on Work and Pensions, Kashmir Singh claimed that:

> Our [Sikh] fair share of central government departments' expenditure alone would be £4,000 million per year based on March 2001 budget. Our fair share of the total economy would be £10,000 million per year, based on GDP figures for 2000. If we are not monitored, then we do not count, and we will not get our fair share.[129]

This campaign has also benefited from the extensive monitoring mechanism now built into the new equalities legislation, notably the Race Relations Amendment Act (2000) and the new definition of institutional racism. Despite these pressures, however, the response of central government has been to resist the demand for systemic monitoring for Sikhs on the grounds that a voluntary *option* for such monitoring already exists, especially of local authorities, and to offer consultations with the Office of National Statistics so that 'national and religious identity questions [are] asked in addition to the standard ethnic group questions'.[130]

11 September 2001 and the Sikh Federation (UK)

Communal cohesion has been further aided by 9/11. In 2001 the ISYF and BK were proscribed by the Home Secretary under the Terrorism Act (2000), along with several militant Muslim organizations.[131] However the rise of hate crimes against Sikhs after 9/11 gave the Sikh nationalist organisations a new, if somewhat unexpected, lease of life. Front organisations such as Sikh Agenda and Sikh Secretariat were established to lobby against the restrictions on carrying *kirpans* and the increase in violent attacks on Sikhs who were mistaken for Muslims, and to articulate the discourse of Sikhism in public life. These developments triggered another hectic round of lobbying that included a representation by Joginder Singh Vedanti, the Akal Takht Jathedar, to Prime Minister Tony Blair. It was against this backdrop that a Punjabi All-Party Parliamentary Group was established in the House of Commons by John McDonnell, MP for Hayes and Harlington. This group initially met to raise issues of concern about the Punjabi community but in its successive debates after March 2000 it is evident that the primary driving force behind the body was Sikh lobbying and Sikh concerns.[132] Indeed, following particularly intensive lobbying by the Sikh Federation (UK) throughout 2004–5, a new *Sikh* All-Party Parliamentary Group was officially launched on 12 July 2005, with five vice-chairs from the Labour Party, Conservative Party, Liberal Democrats, Scottish Nationalists and Plaid Cymru.[133] Ironically, the first scheduled meeting of this group had to be postponed because of the 7/7 suicide bombings in central London.

This emphasis on parliamentary lobbying has also arisen from the reincarnation of the banned ISYF as the Sikh Federation (UK) (SF (UK)), a political party registered with the Election Commission. The SF (UK) was established as a national party of the Sikhs in September 2003, following a conference in Wolverhampton.[134] Heavily influenced by the professional lobbying tactics of British Muslims, who have sought to undercut established community leadership, the SF (UK) has attempted to steal a march on its rivals by reinventing the Khalistan agenda around issues of victimhood, underrepresentation, discrimination and the need for Sikh self-determination. The party's programme claims that its aims include 'giving Sikhs a stronger political voice by taking an increasing interest in mainstream politics in the UK', but this objective is soon qualified by the need to 'argue the case for the Sikhs' right to self-determination and lobbying politicians, the UK government, official representatives of foreign governments in the UK, the European Parliament and at the United Nations for the establishment of an independent sovereign Sikh State of Khalistan'.[135] The SF (UK) is, and views itself as, a campaigning party, a fact underlined by a decision not to contest seats but to act as the organising 'broker' for delivering the national Sikh vote to parties that are most responsive to Sikh interests. Perhaps more appropriately, one of the party's main objectives is to ensure that it secures *the* representation for the Sikh community in dealings with government – instead of the current state of affairs in which, it claims, such representation is exercised by a 'handful of individuals'.[136]

Sikhs and Mainstream Politics

As well as campaigning on homeland issues Sikh organisations have also played a crucial part in socialising the community into mainstream politics. This process, as we have seen, was led by the IWAs, but the extreme politics of class propagated by some of the communists drew individuals like Piara Singh Khabra into the Labour Party. From the 1960s onwards in the major areas of Sikh settlement such as west London and the West Midlands, the growth of the community has led to participation in local politics in an effort to secure representation within the Labour Party. But this process was an uphill struggle. During the 1960s and 1970s few Sikhs succeeded in moving up within a party hierarchy that was dominated by 'Old Labour' and institutionalised racialism. It was only with the emergence of radical black sections in the late 1970s that a profound change began, particularly at the municipal level. Building on successful years of community work within local Community Relations Councils, trade unions, welfare organisations and the local voluntary organisations, many Sikhs became councillors in the London area. Recently several have become Lord Mayors in councils like Ealing, Gravesham, Greenwich, Coventry, Leicester and Sandwell. These 'Little Punjabs' have also provided the foundations for the successful parliamentary candidatures of former local politicians like Piara Singh Khabra from Southall and Marsha Singh from Bradford, and the elevation into the House of Lords of the former Sandwell Council leader Tarsem King. The emergence of the new generation of 'New Labour' professional politicians is reflected in the success of Parmjit Dhanda (MP for Gloucester), whose career began as a local politician in west London and progressed rapidly through the Labour Party machine.

Nina Gill, an MEP for the West Midlands since 2000, is similarly a former Labour functionary with a highly mobile career in public sector housing. None of these national and EU representatives is a *kesh-dhari* Sikh – a fact that irks organisations like the SF (UK) but also shows the

Plate 6 Indarjit Singh, editor of the Sikh Messenger, *with Prime Minister Tony Blair in Downing Street, September 2004, on the occasion of the 400th anniversary of the first installation of the* Adi Granth (Guru Granth Sahib) *in the Golden Temple. (Reproduced with the permission of Indarjit Singh.)*

difficulties of building a monoreligious constituency in Britain. Not unexpectedly, the elected national politicians of Sikh background have been at pains to distance themselves from the politics of homeland.

Sikhs, like other ethnic minorities, have tended overwhelmingly to vote for the Labour Party. This relationship has persisted since the 1950s, though in more recent times there is some indication of increasing support for Liberal Democrats and the Conservative Party. The leftward turn of the Liberal Democrats, most notably over the second Gulf War, led to the spectacular success of Parmjit Singh Gill for the party in the Leicester East by-election in 2004, a seat he lost in the 2005 national elections. At the same time there has been increasing support for the Conservative Party among professional and business groups, though the party's anti-immigration stance has limited its appeal among ordinary Sikhs, despite successive appeals by various party leaders directed specifically at the community.

Apart from the three main parties, Sikhs have also sought representation within the smaller parties. In the 2001 elections Pritam Singh, a lecturer at Oxford Brooks University with a background in radical left-wing politics in Punjab, unsuccessfully stood as a Green Party candidate

Table 5.1 Sikhs in British Politics, 2005

Locality	Councillors		MPs	House of Lords	MEPs
Slough	7	(L)			
Hounslow	13	(L)			
Ealing	10	(L)	1		
Wolverhampton	4	(L)			
Sandwell	5	(L)		2**	
Birmingham	3	(L)			1
Hillingdon	4	(L)			
Leicester	3	(1 LD)			
Redbridge	3	(L)			
Coventry	2	(L)			
Others			2*		
Total	54		3	2	1

Source: Council websites.* These include Marsha Singh for Bradford West (since 1997) and Parmjit Dhanda for Gloucester (2001).** Includes Dilip Singh Rana, a cross-bencher from Northern Ireland who was made a peer in 2004. L = Labour; LD = Liberal Democrat

in Oxford East, securing 1,051 votes. In the same elections the Socialist Labour Party founded by Arthur Scargill (1996) had significant representation from the IWA *groupscule* led by Harpal Brar and centred on *Lalkar*. The party put up a number of candidates of Sikh background, including Harpal Brar, who stood against Piara Singh Khabra in Ealing Southall – but, notwithstanding his local background, Brar could secure only 921 votes. In 2004 Brar's faction was expelled from the Socialist Labour Party, but *Lalkar* continues online with its unique brand of Punjabi Stalinism.

Sikh representation in British politics at the national and local levels has been further underscored by an increasing recognition of Sikhs in public life – as broadcasters, judges, entertainers, businessmen, Justices of the Peace, journalists, senior administrators, academics, medical practitioners and trade union activists. The 'democratisation' of the public appointment and honours system in the 1990s has thrust many into the limelight – such as Gurbax Singh, who became the head of the Commission for Racial Equality in 2001 but was ignomiously dismissed following a brawl at a cricket match at Lords. Karamjit Singh, another lifelong Labour Party member, was appointed to the newly established

Election Commission in 2000. Quangos at national and local levels have provided significant opportunities for Sikhs to engage in public life, giving them the necessary experience for a much richer participation in public affairs.

While greater engagement in public life has professionalised Sikh political activity, it has singularly failed to produce an effective and legitimate articulation of *the* Sikh political interest in British politics. Even today such an articulation remains grounded in the mode of single-issue mobilisation because the structures of British elections necessitate plural coalition building and, given that Sikhs nowhere command more than 10 per cent of the total population in any local authority, the current emphasis by organisations like the SF (UK) on *community* seems destined to repeat the historic failures of the IWAs to build organisations of *class*. The quest for another form of ideological politics, this time centred on religious identity, sits uncomfortably with the harsh realities of political life and bitter rivalries among British Sikh leaders themselves.

Conclusion

Sikh organisations in Britain since the Second World War – whether communist IWAs, SADs, pro-Khalistan or, more recently, political parties like SF (UK) with the aim of 'bringing the Sikhs into mainstream politics' – have been driven mainly by the homeland issues. The politics of homeland was further accentuated by Operation Blue Star in 1984, which acted as a 'critical event' in galvanising the Sikh diaspora based in Britain, redirecting its energies into transnational identity and homeland issues. Although this shift from *class-* to *identity*-based organisations reflects a broader sociological trend, among Sikhs the bitter drama of the struggle in Punjab after 1984 has had the effect of institutionalising the Khalistan movement, which in some measure has reinvented itself post-9/11 in terms of 'victimhood' based on issues of religious discrimination.

Yet this success is more symbolic than real. For one thing, neo-Khalistanis are but one voice within British Sikh society and they no longer control, as they once did, most of the gurdwaras, the community's major resource. For another, British Sikh politics are becoming increasingly plural, with marginal shifts from the traditional loyalty to the Labour Party and leftist politics. And as more and more Sikhs, especially of the third and the fourth generation, establish successful careers within British political parties, a sharp disjunction is emerging between them and the neo-Khalistanis' agenda of *permanent mobilisation* on homeland politics. In due course this agenda, like the communist long march to revolution, might reach a dead end, especially as the number of Indian-born Sikhs, who have been the main drivers of this campaign, continues to decline rapidly. In the light of the community's recent tragic past, however, one needs to be wary of the potential of critical events – like 1984, 9/11 and 7/7 – to seriously reverse, if not completely undermine, this natural process.

$\mathcal{Six}$

British Multiculturalism
and Sikhs

In the history of multiculturalism as a public policy in Britain, the Sikhs occupy a distinctive position. According to Brian Barry, Sikhs have become the paradigm case of a special-interest group that can always negotiate an opt-out from general rule making. As Barry argues, 'Sikhs, whose relatively small overall numbers in Britain are offset by their concentration in a small number of parliamentary constituencies, have been remarkably successful at playing this game.'[1] Barry's trenchant critique of multiculturalism has evoked equally interesting responses. Drawing on the dilemmas for public authorities raised by the Sikh dress code that requires the wearing of turbans, *kirpans* (swords/small daggers) and beards, multiculturalists have been at pains to argue for a broader vision of liberal democracy, one which is capable of accommodating religious and cultural diversity.[2] These two contrasting analyses are testimony to the degree to which the development of the Sikh community in Britain over the last fifty years has telescoped the debates about multiculturalism. Equally significant, however, is the process of mobilisation over issues of religious dress for community building itself: the struggle for recognition of cultural and religious diversity by British Sikhs has also very much been a struggle for leadership *within* the community over single-issue mobilisation.

This chapter examines the British Sikhs' mobilisations over turbans, *kirpans* and beards and how they have shaped the formation of public policy in this area. It also discusses in some detail the emerging Sikh contribution to what might be called 'deep multiculturalism' – that is, the efforts to redefine public space beyond mere recognition – by examining the debate around the withdrawal of the play *Behzti* following protests by Sikhs in 2004. The chapter concludes by reflecting on Sikhs' place in the localised nature of contemporary multiculturalism and the limits of British statecraft in managing diversity.

Turbans, *Kirpans* and Beards

Wherever Sikhs have settled in large numbers, sooner or later one demand has always comes to the fore: the right to wear a turban.[3] Usually this demand develops gradually, as the early settlers, like most migrants, try sedulously to avoid overt symbols of difference. In Britain the early Sikh settlers tended to discard exterior symbols of the faith. Most opted for a clean-shaven appearance and only wore a turban either for ceremonial purposes or for the Sunday visits to the local gurdwara. However, as the numbers increased there was greater self-confidence among the *kesh-dhari* members of the community about wearing turbans and keeping beards, a trend reinforced by the arrival of East African Sikhs, who had always shown a marked reluctance to cut their hair. This development, noticeably in localities such as Southall, increased communal pressures for the familiar mode of dress in which, among men, the turban held pride of place; and though the turban is not one of the five Ks of *amrit-dhari* (baptised) Sikhs, historically it has become an inextricable part of Sikh identity. In fact, for most non-Sikhs the turban is synonymous with Sikhs and because of this association the turban has become the premier symbol of communal identity and its honour, whereas an inability to wear it is a sign of collective dishonour. As the recent global mobilisation over the banning of religious symbols in schools in France has demonstrated, the right to wear the turban is viewed as a core identity issue. Asserting this right in post-war Britain was not without its difficulties.

The First Turban Campaigns – Manchester 1959–66 and Wolverhampton, 1967–9
The first turban campaign arose when a Manchester Sikh, G. S. S. Sagar, a bus-garage worker, applied for the post of conductor with the Manchester City Council's transport department in 1959. His application was turned down on the grounds that his turban violated the company's uniform rules. Sagar's offer to wear a blue turban with a badge was considered by the transport committee, which, after 'considerable research and discussion', refused to countenance an exception to the rules.[4] Sagar then launched a campaign, involving the local gurdwara in his struggle. It took almost seven years to reverse the decision. After four full council debates it was finally resolved only on 5

October 1966, when the Council decided, by 71 votes to 23, to allow the wearing of turbans.[5] By then Sagar had passed the recruitment age for busmen, but his 'victory' succeeded in establishing an important precedent for others to follow.[6]

In a similar case in August 1967, Tarsem Singh Sandhu, a bus driver with Wolverhampton Council, who had secured employment as a clean-shaven Sikh, returned to work wearing a turban following a period of sick leave. On resuming his duties he was sacked for violating the company dress code.[7] Sandhu, like Sagar, launched a campaign that soon became embroiled in local, national and transnational politics, divided vertically between supporters of Enoch Powell and Labour, on the one hand, and the IWAs and the emerging SAD on the other.[8] The local IWA approached Enoch Powell for his support, just before the notorious 'rivers of blood' speech in which he warned against the dangers of coloured immigration to Britain, but he dismissed it as an industrial dispute, a foretaste of 'things to come'. Even the intervention of David Ennals, then a central government minister, was unable to persuade the local transport committee.[9] In frustration, Sikh leaders resorted to a public demonstration through Wolverhampton, which attracted a crowd of five thousand. However, the position of the local authority was backed by strong (white) local opinion, with one letter to a local newspaper claiming 'it is time they [the Sikhs] realised this is England, not India'.[10] After two further protest marches, Sohan Singh Jolly, a 65-year-old local leader, declared he would immolate himself on 13 April 1969 if the transport committee failed to change its policy.[11] This threat further inflamed an already volatile situation, leading to the involvement of the Indian High Commissioner, Shanti Sarup Dhawan, who met the transport committee on 29 January 1969 and appealed to the Department of Transport in Whitehall, warning of the serious consequences of a possible suicide, with wider ramifications in India.[12] In the event, despite the Mayor of Wolverhampton's description of the Sikh threat as 'blackmail', the council changed the rules on 9 April 1969 because it was 'forced to have regard to wider implications'.[13] The Wolverhampton case, as we saw in Chapter 5, became the first example of the transnational mode of mobilisation by British Sikhs and was also the genesis of the Khalistani movement.[14]

Second Turban Campaign: Motorcycle Helmets

The turban campaigns of the 1960s were the first mobilisations around markers of Sikh identity and as such provided the impetus for institution building within the community. By securing the right to wear turbans at the place of employment, albeit on buses, the community's organisations had achieved a notable success against the rising tide of racism fuelled by new waves of migration following the arrival of Kenyan Asians. But this victory appeared to be short-lived, for the Sikhs' ability to ensure rule exemption in the public sphere was threatened by a new regulation – the compulsory requirement for all motorcyclists to wear a helmet.

Section 32 of the Road Traffic Act 1972 made it compulsory for motorcyclists to wear protective headgear. The regulations making this act effective came into force on 1 June 1973, and despite representations by Sikh groups to the Ministry of Transport, the Minister refused to make an exception. Following this legislation, some Sikhs deliberately flouted the law by riding motorcycles without helmets. In the February 1974 general elections, MPs with significant numbers of Sikh constituents were lobbied to support a general exemption for turban-wearing Sikh motorcyclists. Baldev Singh Chahal, a leading activist in the campaign, even stood as a candidate for Ealing, Southall on this single issue. Earlier, following a conviction, Chahal had appealed to the High Court against the new regulation on three grounds: that the Ministry of Transport had failed to consult adequately with Sikh groups; that the Minister had been remiss in not taking into account the public policy implications of the Race Relations Acts of 1965 and 1968; and that the Act was in contravention of 'of the guarantee of freedom of religion enshrined in the European Conventions on Human Rights'.[15] This appeal was crisply dismissed by Lord Widgery, who declared:

> No one is bound to ride a motorcycle. All that the law prescribes is that if you do ride a motorcycle you must wear a crash helmet. The effects of the Regulations no doubt bear on the Sikh community in this respect because it means that they will be often prevented from riding a motorcycle, not because of the English law but the requirements of their religion.[16]

Lord Widgery's argument was further supported by a subsequent ruling of the European Commission on Human Rights:

> The Commission considers that the compulsory wearing of crash helmets is a necessary safety measure for motorcyclists. The Commission is of the opinion therefore that any interference there may have been with the applicant's freedom of religion was justified for the protection of health in accordance with article 9(2).[17]

Subsequently the reasoning behind these arguments was to lead to an animated debate between multiculturalists and anti-multiculturalists: that is, between those for whom the law struck an appropriate balance between considerations of safety and the freedom of religion, on the one hand, and those for whom equality of opportunity is *subject dependent*, on the other.[18] At the time, however, the public debate in Britain was conducted primarily between hardliners opposed to any exemption for Sikhs – citing the questionable religious status of the turban – and its proponents, for whom Sikh religious practice, the needs of religious tolerance, and the weight of Anglo-Sikh tradition provided an over-whelming case for granting the exemption.[19] The exemption was event-ually conceded when the Labour government decided to support a Private Members' Bill introduced by Sidney Bidwell, the MP for Southall. The Motor-Cycle Crash Helmets (Religious Exemption) Act (1976) modified section 32 of the Road Traffic Act (1972) by declaring that it 'shall not apply to a follower of the Sikh religion while he is wearing a turban',[20] and was reconfirmed in the Road Traffic Act (1988). In giving support to this measure, the government was quite clear that it was moved by considerations of religious tolerance. As Kenneth Marks, Under-Secretary of State for the Environment, observed during the debate on the bill:

> The Bill is based on religious tolerance and that, too, is an important and vital part of our society.... There is no possibility of a compromise on this difficult issue ... if Parliament concludes that in this case religious tolerance outweighs road safety and equality, the Government will accept the decision.[21]

Despite government backing for the measure, the host community's response to the new legislation brought forth some amusing episodes. Two persons felt enraged enough to put on a turban before driving a motorcycle. One subsequently apologised, saying he respected the Sikh community and appreciated its religious traditions.[22] Another, Brian Nicholas, was given a two years' conditional discharge after he attempted to ride a motorcycle wearing a turban. Nicholas maintained that helmet law discriminated against non-Sikhs and he even wore his turban in the court, claiming that a Sikh had actually wound it for him.[23]

Third Turban Campaign: Mandla v Dowell Lee
If the crash helmet campaign was largely symbolic because few Sikhs rode motorcycles, then the *Mandla v Dowell Lee* (1983) case marked a major landmark in the development of the community and anti-discrimination legislation in Britain. Interestingly, the case coincided with the willingness of minority ethnic communities to test the effectiveness

Plate 7 Ajmer Singh Matharu 1970, having completed the twelve-week initial training course for the police at Ryton-upon-Dunsmore near Coventry. He was a superintendent of police from 1956 to 1969 in Uganda. He served with the Leicester Constabulary until 1989. (Reproduced with permission of Ajmer Singh Matharu)

of the newly enacted Race Relations Act (1976) which had outlawed forms of direct and indirect discrimination and a parallel campaign in Punjab by radical Sikhs, with a significant lobby in Britain, for greater autonomy for Punjab (see Chapter 5). These two developments intersected in a fatal way to 'produce a translation of the dominant discourse [of Sikh identity] into British law'.[24]

The case arose in 1978 when a Sikh student, Gurinder Singh Mandla, sought admission to Park Grove School in Edgbaston, Birmingham. The headmaster of the school, A. G. Dowell Lee, refused to admit the student on the grounds that his desire to wear a turban was against the school dress code. The father of Mandla then lodged a complaint with the Commission for Racial Equality (CRE), the newly created executive authority established under the Race Relations Act (1976), on the grounds that his son had been discriminated against on racial grounds. Recognising the importance of the issue as a test case for *indirect discrimination,* the CRE then decided to support the legal challenge. Initially the County Court dismissed the complaint on the grounds that Sikhs did not constitute a 'racial group' under the meaning of the Act because they were indistinguishable from other Punjabis. The court refused to entertain an extended meaning of the word 'ethnic', limiting its construction to 'pertaining to race', and held that the wearing of a turban was a religious practice and as such was not covered under the Race Relations Act. This decision was also upheld by the Court of Appeal where the Master of the Rolls, Lord Denning, reprimanded the CRE for taking up the appeal as well as harassing Mr Dowell Lee 'like an inquisition'. In fact, LJ Kerr went further by arguing that:

> the right not to be discriminated against must give way to the beliefs and free will of others. If persons wish to insist on wearing bathing suits, then they cannot reasonably insist on admission to a nudist colony; similarly people who passionately believe in nudism cannot complain if they are not accepted on ordinary bathing beaches.[25]

This decision brought forth a predicable response.[26] Geoffrey Bindman, for one, took Lord Denning to task for not 'reassuring the ethnic minorities that the Race Relations Act would be enforced for their protection'. Instead, according to Bindman, Lord Denning's 'decision and insensitive comments aroused fury in every Sikh home and temple in the land'.[27] This general condemnation was not shared in New Delhi where Indira Gandhi's government, which was then waging its own struggle against militant Sikhs, viewed the appeal as a dangerous signpost on the road to Sikh separatism.[28]

In the autumn of 1982 the SAD launched a campaign for greater autonomy in Punjab that was supported by its chapters in Britain. For these groups *Mandla v Dowell Lee* became a *cause célèbre* encapsulating the demand for the distinctiveness of Sikh identity, and throughout 1982 demonstrations were held in London and the Midlands. On 10 October 1982 a major procession of over 40,000 Sikhs was organised in London, led by the charismatic religious leader Sant Puran Singh Karichowale of the GNNSJ, Birmingham. Before marching down Hyde Park, the demonstrators were addressed by Roy Hattersley and Neville Sanderson.[29]

Given the implications of the Court of Appeal's ruling the CRE and the appellants sought leave to appeal to the House of Lords, and this was granted. The Law Lords, in their verdict delivered on 23 March 1983, overturned the decision of the lower court and upheld the appeal. This about-turn was achieved by adopting a broader, sociological definition of an 'ethnic group' than its narrow 'racial' or 'biological' construction by the lower courts. In this new construction the Sikhs resembled an ethnic group because they filled two conditions:

(1) a long shared history, of which the group is conscious as distinguishing it from other groups, and the memory of which keeps it alive;

(2) a cultural tradition of its own, including family and social customs and manners, often but not necessarily associated with religious observance.[30]

Lord Templeman went even further, noting that the Sikhs 'are more than a religious sect, they are almost a race and almost a nation … they fail to qualify as a separate nation … because their kingdom never achieved a sufficient degree of recognition or permanence'.[31]

The Law Lords' ruling gave a formal stamp of approval to the dominant discourse of Sikh identity, and by designating their community as an 'ethnic group', Sikhs were brought, like Jews, within the protection of the Race Relations Act – a protection which continues to elude other religious groups. But perhaps more profoundly, the ruling established the importance of the principle that Sikhs could challenge *indirect discrimination* in the fields of employment, education and other sectors on the basis of dress, especially the right to wear a turban. In more ways than one, the *Mandla v Dowell Lee* judgement proved a turning point for Sikhs both in Britain and Punjab, a throw-back to the colonial encounter when Sikh separate identity was substantially strengthened.

Fourth Turban Campaign: Safety Helmets for Construction Workers
No sooner had the dust settled on the *Mandla v Dowell Lee* case than the community leadership was once more galvanised by a new legislative

proposal. In 1979 the Health and Safety Commission had mooted the idea of safety helmets for workers in the construction industry. Its efforts to establish the practice on a voluntary basis had proved ineffective, leading the Commission to propose that the requirement should have statutory force. As the proposal became a distinct possibility, Sikhs in the construction industry lobbied the Commission to secure an exemption alongside the motorcycle legislation. As the threat of legislation loomed, the issue assumed a particular urgency because it was claimed that 40,000 Sikhs worked in the construction industry, with an especially strong representation of the Ramgarhias, who specialised in trades associated with carpentry, bricklaying and blacksmithing. To further the case of these workers, the British Sikh Federation conducted an extensive campaign within gurdwaras and the Punjabi print media.[32] In the event, the government acceded to this pressure from the Sikh lobby by inserting an amendment to the Employment Bill during the Committee stage in the House of Lords. Section 11 of the Employment Act (1989) recognised the Sikh exemption by noting that

> Any attempt to wear a safety helmet ... [which] would, by virtue of any statutory provision or rule of law, be imposed on a Sikh who is on a construction site shall not apply to him at any time when he is wearing a turban.[33]

This exemption was secured by rehearsing some of the familiar arguments used in the preceding cases. Arrayed against the measure were those for whom it smacked of special privilege, positive discrimination, and a charter for ethnic separatism. For the supporters, in contrast, it was justified not only because of previous precedents, the weight of Anglo-Sikh tradition and the needs of 'religious freedom and tolerance', but also because of the balance-of-interests argument – namely, the potentially serious consequence for social and economic integration of the sudden termination of sizeable Sikh employment in the construction industry.[34] In fact, it was with these considerations in mind that Lord Strathclyde conceded that the measure was necessary because 'the wider issues of religious freedom and relations with the Sikh community must take precedence'.[35]

The value of this legislation appeared to have been compromised almost immediately when the Council of European Communities issued a new directive in June 1989 on measures to improve the health and safety of workers, including the requirement to wear safety helmets. This directive came into force at the end of 1992 in the guise of the Personal Protective Equipment at Work Regulations and allowed for no exemptions. The implementation of the directive created an anomaly because Sikhs were exempt from wearing safety helmets in the construction industry, but no such general exclusion could be maintained in other sectors. The existence of this anomaly was raised by Jim Marshall MP in a question to the Secretary of State for Employment, with a call to amend the legislation.[36] In his reply the Minister noted that no such 'universal exemption' had been sought because of the 'risk of challenge'.[37]

Kirpans

Apart from the turban, the other most important religious symbol of the Sikh which has regularly caused controversy in public life is the injunction for *amrit-dhari* Sikhs to carry the *kirpan*. Interestingly, while scholars and legal authorities have contested the religious legitimacy of the injunction to wear a turban, there is no such doubt about the *kirpan* because it is a necessary requirement for *amrit-dhari* Sikhs. Yet because the latter have always been in a minority within the community, the right to wear a *kirpan* has failed to attract the degree of mobilisation associated with campaigns on the more universally worn turbans – that is, until recently.

In the decades of initial settlement the wearing of *kirpans* and the use of ceremonial swords caused little controversy, apart from the occasional reference to their misuse in family or gurdwara disputes.[38] On the back of the motorcycle-helmet victory, a Sikh Religious Symbols Action Committee was formed in 1978 with the aim of extending the recognition of Sikh religious symbols in the statutory sector. In 1979 this committee, with the support of Margaret Thatcher, held a meeting with Timothy Raison, then a minister at the Home Office, at which it was agreed that Sikhs would be allowed to wear the *kirpan* on British Airways flights. But this concession was immediately withdrawn when in 1982 Sikh militants hijacked an Indian Airlines plane by using *kirpans* on a scheduled flight from Srinagar to Lahore.[39] In the aftermath of the Air India disaster (1985) – attributed to Sikh militants based in Canada and the United Kingdom and the rise of militancy following Operation Blue Star – there was little enthusiasm within government for the demands of Sikh groups, though an agreement was reached in 1985 between the British Airport Authority, Sikh groups and the unions at Heathrow to allow Sikhs to carry a *kirpan* no longer than 3 inches. However, in the late 1980s, in the face of growing public concern about law and order, the government proposed a ban on the carrying of knives and other sharp-pointed instruments in public places. After further hard lobbying by Sikh organisations the Criminal Justice Act (1988) granted an exemption for 'religious reasons', though it was made clear to Sikh organisations that this did not provide a licence to use *kirpans* or ceremonial swords for unlawful purposes.

Since the late 1980s the right to wear a *kirpan* has been gradually recognised in an increasing range of public places, such as schools, prisons and government institutions, though a significant degree of voluntarism and ambiguity prevails about the size of the *kirpan* that is allowed.[40] Cases of serious misunderstanding persist. In 1999 Lord Irvine, the Attorney-General, issued a formal apology to a Sikh solicitor whose *kirpan* was confiscated as he entered the High Court, an incident resulting in a formal direction that allowed *kirpans* in courts as long as they were less than six inches.[41] The greatest challenge, however, has come in the wake of 9/11.

Following the attack on the Twin Towers in New York on 11 September 2001, the Department of Transport in a security review ruled that *kirpans* could no longer be worn at airports by travellers and airport workers. This decision was taken against the charged background of the attacks that also triggered physical assaults on turban-wearing Sikhs, notably in the United States, where they were often mistaken for Arabs.[42] Sikh groups – at first overwhelmed by the developments, which appeared at a stroke to have reversed the exemption on *kirpans*, and had profound repercussions for the sizeable workforce employed at Heathrow airport – began a process of mobilisation culminating in the lobbying of MPs on 21 November 2001. Once again the issue became the point of focus for *competitive* mobilisation by groups such as gurdwara representatives from Southall and Hounslow, the Sikh Human Rights Group, the Network of Sikh Organisations and the Sikh Secretariat. This lobbying resulted in a meeting between Joginder Singh Vedanti, the Akal Takht Jathedar, and Tony Blair, with a promise by the latter to look into Sikh demands.[43] As a consequence of this pressure the British Airport Authority at Heathrow issued new guidelines that restored the exemption for wearing the *kirpan*, provided 'the blade is less than three inches in length, worn discreetly under clothing and can't be snatched'. This regulation led to strong opposition from the British Airline Pilots' Association.[44] The new regulation, however, applied to Sikh staff working at airports only; it did not include the public. The current situation remains that most Sikh travellers, if wearing a *kirpan*, are asked to hand it over to the attending staff, to be returned at the end of the journey. There have been cases where some Sikhs, if they have insisted, have been allowed to wear a *kirpan*, but this generally excludes travellers to the United States. The 'war on terror' will continue to raise issues of security, and the right to carry a *kirpan* is unlikely to be treated with such sensitivity in the United States as it is in Great Britain.

Turbans, Kirpans *and Beards: the Limit of Exemptions*
The argument that whenever vital Sikh interests are threatened they can always negotiate an exemption from British legislation is one that is popular among opponents of multiculturalism and, paradoxically, among some Sikh groups themselves that like to present a linear narrative of 'success' and community building. In reality, as we have seen, the exemptions are very much hedged about with qualifications that require constant monitoring for violation or are easily transgressed. Sikhs themselves are regularly 'surprised' by the reluctance of public authorities, courts and employment tribunals to accord the recognition that they feel is legally merited.

Take, for example, the case of *Dhanjal v British Steel* (1993) in which Dhanjal had brought a case of unlawful discrimination on the grounds that he had been made redundant because of his refusal to wear a hard hat. As an *amrit-dhari* Sikh, Dhanjal held that the company rule to wear a hard hat contravened the Race Relations Act. The industrial tribunal, in contrast, concluded that the British Steel condition was justified and its no-turban policy was in line with the Health and Safety Act 1974, and in the absence of a specific exemption for steel workers in the act, 'similar to one granted to Sikh workers on constructions sites in the building industry, the requirement guaranteeing safety and health must prevail over non-discrimination requirements of the Race Relations Act (1976)'.[45] Similarly in *Kuldip Singh v British Rail* (1985) the issue of hard hat headgear for safety reasons overrode considerations of religion or charges of indirect discrimination, even though the barrister for the appellant went to great lengths to highlight the exemption of Sikhs from wearing helmets during the Second World War, on motor-cycles and in the police.[46] In this case Kuldip Singh was obliged to take a less-well-paid job because he refused to wear the protective headgear provided by employers.

The courts have also been reluctant to accept the claims of religious custom when it has come to beards. When Panesar applied to Nestlé for a position at Hayes, he was told at the interview that he could not be employed unless he cut his beard, because the company's rules forbid long hair in the interests of public health. On being refused employment, Panesar appealed to an industrial tribunal, which found the company had not discriminated unlawfully against him in violation of the Race Relations Act. Thereafter Panesar took the case to the court, where the company called a series of experts to show how important it was that beards should not be worn at their factories where chocolate was produced. The decision of the industrial tribunal was upheld by Lord Denning, despite Panesar's counsel pointing out that moustaches were permitted in the factory. When the counsel for the complainant drew attention to the guarantee of freedom of religion in Article 9 of the European Commission on Human Rights, Lord Denning pointed out that there is an express reservation placed upon it – namely, that freedom-of-religion laws had to be balanced with the necessity for the protection of public health in a 'democratic society'.[47]

It has been suggested that one of the reasons for these continuing anomalies is that by ensuring recognition as an ethnic group under the *Mandla v Dowell Lee* judgement, Sikhs were able to secure only indirect protection for their religious practices. As a consequence 'the law concerning Sikhs and requirements to remove beards and turbans or to shorten hair', as one leading authority has concluded, 'has erred in adapting the wrong criteria in deciding whether employers have been guilty of indirect discrimination for the purposes of Section 1 of the Race Relations Act (1976)'.[48]

Recent British and European Union legislation – the Human Rights Act (1998), the Race Relations (Amendment) Act (2000), the Anti-Terrorism, Crime and Security Act (2001), the Race Relations (Amendments) Regulation (2003) and the Employment Equality (Religion or Belief) Regulation, (2003) – is certainly likely to provide more enhanced protection for religious beliefs and practices, but given the experience of Sikhs with the Race Relations Act since 1976 it would be surprising if Sikh dress code and religious customs did not throw up new test cases for this legislation.

Behzti

Whereas most of the mobilisations by Sikhs so far have been driven by the demand for *equality* and the recognition of *difference* in public life, most notably in terms of access to public services, the furore created over the withdrawal of the play *Behzti* in December 2004 marked a new shift, one which appeared to threaten the very premise of free speech in a liberal democratic society. Coming as it did against the backdrop of 9/11 and the heightened debate about the role of religion in public life, the 'outrage' attributed to sections of the Sikh community had all the makings of the 'Sikh Rushdie Affair'.[49]

The play *Behzti* (dishonour) was written by Gurpreet Kaur Bhatti,[50] a Sikh actress turned playwright who has been described as a 'fresh, original and provocative voice in British theatre'.[51] Set within the precincts of a gurdwara against the backdrop of daily rituals and prayers, its lead characters are a widowed mother and her daughter for whom she is eager to find a match. The play's plot revolves around their rare visit to the gurdwara, when it transpires that the mother's late husband had a homosexual affair with one of the gurdwara's functionaries before killing himself. It also comes to light that the functionary had sexually abused women in the temple; during the visit he rapes the daughter in his office. The play climaxes in a bloodbath when the functionary is killed with a *kirpan* by the mother and another of the functionary's abused victims. Bhatti's intention in writing the play, as she explained, was to expose 'the hypocrisy of (the) Sikh way of life'. In its publicity material, the Birmingham Repertory Theatre described the play as 'a black comedy that reveals just how many secrets can be hidden in a Sikh temple (gurdwara)'.[52]

Before the play opened at the Birmingham Rep on 9 December, Sewa Singh Mandla, of the *Mandla v Dowell Lee* case and chairman of the Birmingham Council of Sikh Gurdwaras, approached the Rep to express the community's concerns. The community leaders were invited to a reading of the play, after which they recommended that the setting be moved from a gurdwara to a community centre. Although the theatre directors recognised the need to incorporate minor changes in the text and decided to communicate the Sikh community's views to the audience before the performance, they refused to move the setting of the play, describing this as an attempt at overt censorship. Following the breakdown of these talks, peaceful protests were conducted outside the theatre during the week of 9 December. On Saturday 19 December, however, a large crowd of about 400 Sikhs gathered outside the theatre. A section of this crowd then stormed in, interrupting the play, which led to the evacuation of 800 people, most of them families and children who had come to see the Christmas show *The Witches*. Following these events, the theatre decided to cancel further performances of the play on the grounds that Sikh community leaders were unable to provide guarantees of future safe conduct. A local Sikh councillor, who acted as the spokesperson for the protesters, congratulated the theatre for its decision, describing it as a victory for 'common sense'.[53]

Not unexpectedly, these events caused a national uproar.[54] *Bezhti* became a global event and Bhatti went into hiding following threats of abduction and murder. The prospect of a threat to the freedom of expression from 'Sikh mob rule' led to a heated debate in the national dailies, which ranged from general attacks on multiculturalism and liberty to the *Daily Mail's* unexpected support for Sikh actions as an inspiration to 'Christian Britain'.[55] Several hundred actors, playwrights and leading personalities wrote an open letter to the *Guardian* in defence of freedom of expression. Salman Rushdie expressed his 'outrage' at the cancellation of the play, and in particular criticised Fiona MacTaggart, the Home Office minister and MP for Slough – which has a large Sikh population – who refused to condemn the violence and told BBC's Radio Four *Today* programme that the protest was a 'sign of free speech which is so much a part of the British tradition'. Rushdie complained that MacTaggart had failed to grasp the issue, which was essentially about the right of artists to express themselves. New Labour's equivocation on artistic freedom, he complained, contrasted sharply with the firm support from the state that he had received during the 'Rushdie Affair'.[56]

Sikh Responses

In enforcing the closure of *Behzti*, the Sikh community, at least in popular discourse, appeared to have reverted to type – as a militant, campaign tradition fixated on narrow communal objectives. Yet these simplistic characterisations overlooked the range of responses from Sikhs themselves, some of which, incidentally, were opposed to the cancellation.[57] First, there was a general tendency to deny that events depicted in *Behzti* occur in gurdwaras, which were described as open spaces that welcomed all.[58] Second, there was the argument of reasonableness; that the local Sikhs in Birmingham had gone to great lengths to seek a compromise that was denied by the theatre in the name of censorship. The experience of *Behzti* was contrasted with the filming of *Bend It Like Beckham* where, it was claimed, due consideration was given to Sikh religious sensitivities. Third, many took issue with 'double standards' – namely, that whereas there was a well-established tradition of banning, cancelling or withdrawing plays that offended the Christian and Judaic traditions, powerless religious minorities like the Sikhs had no recourse to legal action such as group libel that could achieve similar outcomes.[59] Consequently their only recourse was to act as 'primitive rebels' in the citadel of 'free expression'. Finally, there was an element of the post-colonial critique. 'We don't need lectures on freedom', declared Jasdev Singh Rai, director of Sikh Human Rights Group, because 'the Sikhs had freedom of speech long before the West and understand its limits'.[60] Citing Foucault and Derrida in defence of the subjectivity of rationalism, Rai likened the libertarian defence of Bhatti to neo-colonial sermonising that was now 'disguised as free speech', which, according to him, found its most 'xenophobic expression among liberals'. 'Offending the sacred', Rai concluded, 'wounds those whose hopes and cultures are orientated around the subjective inscrutability of sacred icons.'[61]

Perhaps because of the Rushdie Affair or perhaps because of the 'return of religion' to public affairs under New Labour and post-9/11, these Sikh responses failed to evoke the usual derision reserved for minority ethnic communities. At a juncture when Christian groups were protesting the BBC's plans to air *Jerry Springer: the Opera*, Sikh claims to be recognised by society as a group whose essential dignity is defined primarily by faith received sympathetic hearings in some quarters.[62] However, this demand has raised difficult issues – both for government and Sikhs – concerning how religious dissent expressed through art is to be balanced with pressure to declare group defamation an offence. Current government efforts to make incitement to religious hatred a criminal offence under the Racial and Religious Hatred Bill (2005) are unlikely to appease, either, for their aim is to protect 'people', not 'religious ideologies', from offence or ridicule. Given that the author of *Behzti* remains unrepentant and determined to restage the play,[63] the Sikh capacity for opting out of general rule making by lobbying will need to be supplemented by an auxiliary method – the occasional riot.

Local Multiculturalism

Historically, multiculturalism as a public policy in Britain has been heavily localised, often made voluntary, and linked essentially to issues of managing diversity in areas of migrant settlement.[64] The legislative frame-work on which this policy is based – for example, the Race Relations Acts (1965 and 1976) – recognised this contingency, giving additional resources to local authorities as well as new powers to better promote racial and ethnic equality. With these enabling powers, over the last forty years most local authorities with large minority ethnic community populations have transformed themselves from initially being the bastions of official racism to promoters of anti-racism and multicultural-ism, and in this change the strength of local ethnic community coalitions has played a pivotal role.

Sikhs and Local Governance
In the 1960s and 1970s, for Sikhs and other ethnic minorities the local state more often articulated strong resentment against new immigrants,

who appeared to threaten the post–1945 settlement that had institutionalised working-class interests. Hence there was open discrimination against ethnic minorities in the allocation of local services such as housing.[65] In some localities, such as Southall, migrant pupils were bussed to schools across the borough and surrounding areas to promote 'integration'. These polices were generally accompanied by systemic hostility within the Labour movement, with the Labour councillor who blamed immigrants for 'ruining my native Southall' being by no means an unusual figure up and down the country.[66]

Following the urban riots of the late 1970s and the early 1980s, however, radical labour councils came to power in areas with large non-white populations.[67] The riots in Southall (1979 and 1981) and Handsworth (1981 and 1985), for instance, gradually transformed the local politics of these authorities as they attempted to implement a more effective equality of opportunity that targeted service delivery, symbolic recognition of *difference* and, above all, more representative local authority employment at a time when unemployment was rising.[68] The thrust of much of this egalitarian multiculturalism was class-based anti-racism that remained wary of the politics of religion, as evidenced in the bitter struggles between religious and class constituencies in authorities like Ealing. Yet by the early 1990s the anti-racist coalition had collapsed, identity politics had become mainstream, and, after the 'Rushdie Affair', religion increasingly stalked the council chamber.[69]

Local multiculturalism, most notably in the 'Little Punjabs' like Southall, Slough and Handsworth, has enabled Sikh issues to be better recognised in the formation and implementation of local policy, as well as in more visible political representation. This, indeed, is a remarkable achievement because of the services and budgets controlled by local authorities. Nonetheless, the voluntarism built into British statecraft in managing ethnic diversity at the national level is replicated at the local government level: constant mobilisation is required if minority concerns are to be realised. For example, despite the legal exemption for the wearing of the *kirpan* by *amrit-dhari* pupils in schools, this matter continues to cause difficulties for local authorities, who more often than not delegate decision making to the headmaster.[70] Education, because it is locally managed, has frequently been the key battleground – over the teaching of Punjabi in schools, for example, or the desire to ensure the adequate representation of Sikhism in the local religious education curriculum. But, perhaps more important, the Sikh agenda for local government has focused on equality in employment, the recognition of Sikh difference and religious needs in service delivery – in social services, education, police administration and planning (especially for places of worship) – and the acceptance of Sikh institutions, particularly gurdwaras, as co-partners in contemporary local governance. More recently, urban regeneration programmes requiring that organised religions and the local state work as partners rather than as competitors have opened up new opportunities for political and social engagement that have been skilfully exploited.[71]

As well as the demand for equality within local government there has been a concerted drive for symbolic recognition. This has taken such forms as Sikh 'Lord Mayors' and the 'ethnification' of local public space. In the 'Little Punjabs', for instance, local authorities increasingly accommodate, celebrate and promote to wider audiences Sikh religious festivals such as *Vaisakhi* or the birthdays of Guru Nanak and Guru Gobind, which are often accompanied by traditional marches linking the main gurdwaras in the city. These festivals have become a regular feature of British urban life, providing new forms of pilgrimage and socialisation for the Sikh young. One of the consequences of this development is that a city like Leicester, which views itself a premier multicultural city in Europe, has been transformed into a 'city of festivals'.[72] Such efforts, moreover, extend to other areas: Sandwell is twinned with Amritsar (with a picture of the Golden Temple gracing the Council Hall), Ealing with Jalandhar. School, social services, police and business exchanges between localities in Britain and Punjab are becoming ever more frequent, and estates, roads and streets are occasionally being named after Punjabi and Sikh places and individuals.[73] Although these developments might be termed 'soft' or 'performative' multiculturalism, for Sikhs, who have always prided themselves on public recognition, they mark important inroads into previously excluded spaces.

Conclusion

For ideological multiculturalists, Sikhs are the pioneers of British multi-culturalism because through successive campaigns over the right to wear turbans, *kirpans* and beards, it is argued, they have clearly demonstrated that in a Western liberal democracy equality of opportunity cannot be a mere disembodied procedural process but needs to be very much *subject*-dependent. Achieving this has been slow and painful – at times, the labour of Sisyphus. It has, moreover, frequently required the community to draw on its Anglo-Sikh heritage, engage in systematic national and transnational lobbying and, more recently during the *Behzti* affair, resort to that most ancient of British traditions – the riot.

However these achievements have not hastened, as many multi-culturalists such as Parekh advocate, the emergence of a radically plural and diverse British democracy, a 'community of communities' where religions and cultures of New Commonwealth immigrants are accorded equal status or worth.[74] Far from it. The response of the British state to Sikh demands is to concede an opt-out from general rule making and this 'negative accommodation' remains poorly recognised in state structures and consciousness, resulting in *constant, competitive* and *reactive* mobilisations by Sikh groups against policy decisions and legislation from Parliament or the European Union. Perhaps this *modus operandi* might change as the new equalities legislation becomes the norm in everyday life. Such an optimistic reading, however, would seriously overlook two elements in British statecraft in managing ethnic diversity: its localisation and the implicit recognition of asymmetrical pluralism (between whites and non-whites).

Seven

Employment
and Education

The period since the Second World War has seen a dramatic transformation in the employment status of the ethnic minority population.
Whereas most post-war coloured immigrants entered the labour market
at the bottom of the employment hierarchy, as unskilled manual
labourers, over the last fifty years many of them have made remarkable
progress. Today, while some ethnic minorities continue to be poorly
represented in higher-status employment, others are outperforming the
white population in terms of both employment status and educational
qualifications.[1] Seen in this light, the British Sikhs are far from being
'ethnic high flyers'. Coming from a predominantly agrarian society, they
have adjusted well to the demands of an industrial and, increasingly, a
post-industrial, globalised economy. The ethic of hard work prescribed
by Guru Nanak for his followers has stood them in good stead as they
have moved up the employment ladder. But these changes have also had
profound consequences for the community's identity: the joint family as
an institution of collective production has been challenged by nuclear
patterns of employment, and the emergence of well-educated second,
third and fourth generations marks a significant break with the
proletarian culture that defined the initial Sikh settlers.

In this chapter we examine the general changes in the community's
employment structure since the Second World War. The chapter
reviews the patterns of initial employment that were closely related to
areas of settlement and examines issues of Sikh ethnicity at work. We
then explore the changes that have occurred since the mid-1970s by
focusing on self-employment and education. The chapter concludes by
reflecting on the current status of Sikhs within contemporary labour
markets.

From Peasants to Industrial Workers

Of the earliest Sikh settlers, the Bhatras created a niche for themselves as door-to-door tradesmen (peddlers). Although some worked in factories in industrial cities like Glasgow, Coventry and Birmingham, others sold clothing, mostly women's garments, by walking or cycling to remote villages in Scotland and Wales. By the late 1930s most had carved out a beat, often a set of villages, and would gather at their main base over weekends for fresh supplies and recreation. Old Sikhs still recall how in the 1930s a small colony of Sikh settlers had rented accommodation in the Balsall Heath area of Birmingham, parts of Glasgow and later Dundee.[2] However the introduction of postal shopping and link roads to remote areas reduced the demand for peddled goods and by the early 1950s peddling had become an in-between job for new Sikh migrants.

The overwhelming social profile of Sikh migrants from Punjab after 1945 was one of medium and small Jat peasants with a fair proportion of artisan castes (Ramgarhias, Ghumars, Julahas, Jhinwars, Nais) and landless labourers (Chamars and Chuhras). These groups had limited occupational skills or educational qualifications, even allowing for the Sikhs' wider exposure to the modern world during colonialism. In 1941, the Sikh literacy rate in Punjab was only 12 per cent and, though their ranks included many graduates, most migrants were without secondary education. Even in 1951 and 1961, the general literacy rate in Punjab averaged only 15 and 24 per cent respectively.[3] Consequently these immigrants found jobs in factories where there was a severe shortage of unskilled labour because of the post-war boom. Initially in some locations old imperial ties proved useful; occasionally, as in the Woolf Rubber Factory, Southall, where a manager had served in a Sikh regiment, employers or senior managers with past connections with Punjab were only too eager to welcome Sikh workers.[4] Nonetheless, the crucial help and assistance in securing the first job was normally provided by kith and kin who, by custom, were obliged to provide food and shelter and generally took the newly arrived migrant to local factories. The following example was typical of most Sikh arrivals:

> I came to Bedford with the help of my brother, but I was unable to find a job. Some friends told me about Gravesend, so I ventured there. Upon arrival I saw Bhuta Singh and immediately got a job on the Isle of Grain. He arranged everything for me … and I was at work the next day.[5]

Another Sikh recalled how, when he landed at Heathrow, he knew someone from his village who worked in Smethwick and I soon arrived at his door. Not only did he give me shelter, he also took me the very next morning to the nearby foundry and I was working where the melted iron was flowing like canal water in our Punjab farms. I was guided through everything for the next two months.[6]

Some localities and industries soon became magnets for incoming Sikhs. In west London the new Heathrow Airport (still one of the largest employers of Sikhs in the country) and the surrounding hub of light manufacturing (food and non-food) industries proved to be the great attraction. In due course this region would become *the* major centre of Sikh settlement in Britain. In the Medway towns of the South-East (Gravesend, Erith, Gillingham), it was the paper mills, cement, engineering and rubber works. In the East End of London, it was the rag trade, light manufacturing, London Transport and, later, the Ford Motor company's plant at Dagenham. In the East and East Midlands (Leicester, Derby, Nottingham and Bedford), it was light engineering, textiles, rubber, the food industry and the brick kilns. In the northern towns, it was the textiles, steel mills and heavy manufacturing. In West Yorkshire, the North-East and East Riding, it was clothing, heavy metals and steel. In Scotland, where there was a sizeable community dating from the pre-war period of Bhatras and Punjabi Muslims, Sikhs concentrated in Glasgow in the local metal industries. In the West Midlands (Birmingham, Wolverhampton, Coventry, Walsall, West Bromwich and Sandwell), it was iron foundries, light engineering and transport.

Apart from labour shortages, Duffield suggests that the reason for this concentration was weak unionisation in some of these industries.[7] Thus in Birmingham the first major concentration emerged in the Smethwick foundries, where the Midland Motor Cylinder Co Ltd, part of Birmid Industries, became the biggest employer of Sikh workers in the region. A few hundred Indian workers had been employed in the 1940s and in 1947 they constituted 20 per cent of the workforce.[8] The following year an undisclosed foundry in the same area also reported having employed '200 or so Indians' for several years.[9]

These early concentrations marked the beginning of Sikh communities that were often characterised by the presence of familiar signposts – the gurdwara, the factory, the public house and back-to-back terraced housing. Thus in the West Midlands, Birmid's four plants eventually employed more than two thousand Sikhs who purchased houses in the nearby localities of Cambridge Road, Whitehall Road and Oxford Road. As the demand for foundry workers was periodic, with a five-year cycle of boom and slump, Indian workers were circulated throughout the industry in the Midlands. In the mid-1950s, John Harper Qualcast also started recruiting Indian workers, a decision which triggered the large-scale settlement of Sikhs around Wolverhampton. Similarly, the openness of the Duport and Coneygre foundries in Tipton to new immigrant workers led to a substantial settlement of Sikhs in this area during the early 1960s. This pattern, moreover, was further reinforced by the tendency to separate the workforce into exclusive ethnic groups, which generally had a multiplier effect.

In the 1950s and 1960s the general profile of Sikh employment suggests that more than three-quarters of the community worked as manual, unskilled workers, often taking up employment that was either low-paid with irregular hours or marked by extremely difficult working conditions.[10] Night or shift work was the norm. Most Sikh workers were seen as 'hard-working'; they 'accepted jobs the English thought undignified, [and] employers liked to hire them'.[11] Although there were some graduates among the new migrants, they found the search for non-manual jobs difficult. Some subsequently qualified as teachers in the mid-1960s as recruitment of teachers was opened up to overcome shortages, but the pervasiveness of racial discrimination in the labour market often drove many professional Sikhs either to migrate to North America or to return to India. In the mid-1960s, however, the number of professional and skilled Sikhs increased significantly with the arrival of East African migrants.[12] Most of these Sikhs had enough capital or technical qualifications to avoid factory work, preferring instead white-collar and professional positions such as bank clerks, accountants, solicitors and teachers, though a significant proportion did enter the construction industry (see Chapter 6).

Ethnicity at Work

The first experience of mass industrial employment for Sikhs highlighted a number of distinct cultural practices. To overcome language difficulties managers relied on intermediaries, or *batoos,* 'by virtue of their command of English language'.[13] These 'middlemen' were generally drawn from the ranks of educated former school teachers, non-commissioned army officers or university students. Their presence was most evident in the West Midlands foundries, where they soon became indispensable to management as channels of communication, actively partaking in the regulation of the supply of labour – a process that included building supply networks stretching all the way back to Punjab, thereby circumventing both trade unions and the Labour Exchange.[14] Inevitably these middlemen, who in the factory had a favoured status, also doubled as local landlords and job brokers for the newly arrived migrants.[15]

A consequence of middlemen was the emergence of a 'bribery culture'. Until the mid-1960s many newcomers paid a bribe to an intermediary to obtain a job, the usual rate being between £2 and £5. In 1955 the managing director of John Tomkins Co. Ltd., Birmingham, claimed to have knowledge of six local companies where entry money was being demanded of Indians. The Stevens Enquiry also referred to this practice:

> at times the method of payment through more experienced coloured workers degenerates into what is sometimes called the 'uncle' system, whereby one coloured worker acts as a recruiting agent and receives a fee in return. In one case a weekly payment of £2 was mentioned, in another a single payment of £5.[16]

With the help of the trade unions a campaign was launched to eradicate the 'entry fee'.[17] As union officials became acquainted with such malpractices, they encouraged unionisation, and 'from being a segregated labour force in the hands of corrupt leaders, Indian foundry workers became a vanguard in the struggle for better pay and conditions'.[18]

The IWA's early activities focused on the eradication of corruption and efforts to unionise new workers.[19] The first industrial action by Indian workers in the Midlands arose from a case of bribery when, in 1959, a newly elected Indian Amalgamated Union of Engineering Workers' shop steward at Dartmouth Auto Castings Ltd., Smethwick, was dismissed after protesting that some Indians were offering the foreman money for 'favourable considerations'.[20] A stoppage by Indian workers brought his reinstatement. In 1965 a two-week strike by 500 Indian workers at Qualcast Ltd., Wolverhampton, also arose from the dismissal of a shop steward in similar circumstances. He, too, was reinstated and the bribery charge was placed in the hand of the police.[21]

Another practice common among early male migrants was to seek tax credits by falsifying the number of dependent children. This was a common practice at the time because it saved taxable income as well as providing justification for further inward migration at a later date. When the issue came into the public domain following a well-publicised scandal and newspaper allegations that the Treasury was losing over £30 million a year, desperate attempts were made to ensure appropriate documentation, often by bribing officials in India. Over a period of three years, in a wide-ranging enquiry, 648 people of Asian origin were asked for detailed proof of their progeny.[22]

Work Culture and Labourers' Songs

Where Sikhs concentrated in large numbers there soon emerged something akin to a distinctive work culture that was reflected in terms of strong masculinity, a competitiveness manifested in rivalry over the 'heaviest' job. Punjabi machismo came to co-exist alongside a deep sense of alienation in the unfamiliar and hostile environment. The industrial workplace generated a genre of poetry and popular folk songs that is still fondly remembered by the first generation of settlers. Retiring after a day's work to a nearby pub, some would talk melancholically about the Punjab left behind, contrasting the rigours of industrial life with the green fields of a home far away. Suitably inebriated, they composed folk songs, turning the old *qissa* genre into new songs. These songs became quite popular in a few pubs patronised exclusively by Punjabi workers.[23] The following are some illustrative examples:[24]

> The factory await us like sultry sister-in-law
> She does not allow flirting without paying for overtime
> Brothers, extra pay packet is just like a forbidden kiss

A bus conductor described his mechanical and alienating job as:

> Twirling like a sparrow
> Trooping up and down the wobbling double-decker bus
> Clocking the money
> Smiling mechanically at passengers
> What is all this logic of earning money
> Learning the language of money?

Night shift workers often became the butt of improvised songs:

> The wife complains,
> Alone I am at night
> For all you care is pounds,
> those white currency notes
> while I tremble at night alone
> during the freezing winter
> with my youth wasting away
> My man collects overtime wages
> Oh what a cruel fate in England!

In the case of old men who had married young women from Punjab, going out on a night shift offered additional hazards:

> The old man leaves his young bride
> for him pay packet is far dearer
> while the young men loiter around his house
> eyeing his lusty wife.

Racial Discrimination, Trade Unions and the IWAs

The hostility of established trade unions to migrant workers, popularly portrayed in Peter Sellers's movie *I'm All Right, Jack*, also enabled the IWAs to emerge as political organisations of the newly arrived migrants from Punjab (see Chapter 5) – and alternatives to the existing unions. The IWAs, with their hardened communist ideology, were exceptionally adept at organising the new workers. They campaigned against discrimination at work, the racialised polices of established trade unions, and anti-immigration laws. They were largely federal organisations that existed in most areas of Sikh settlement and most effectively in the West Midlands, Coventry and Southall. Their leaders frequently sought to become union officials so as to be able to exercise influence in the workplace and outside in the community. In the West Midlands in foundries like Birmid, elected shop stewards like Avtar Johal and Narinder Dosanjh held powerful portfolios, and on several occasions closed plants in prolonged strikes.[25] In Southall, the Woolf Rubber Company strike (30 November 1965 to 12 January 1966) became the site of a particularly bitter dispute in which the efforts of Sikh workers to establish a union were instigated by the local IWAs but received little support from the Transport and General Workers' Union and were openly opposed by the company. The strike lasted six weeks, involved almost 600 workers, and was undertaken without official union support. In the event, it ended in failure, a pattern that was to be repeated regularly throughout the 1960s and 1970s when the struggle against racism within the trade union movement was frequently deflected by a combination of employer intransigence and official trade union vacillation.[26]

Nor did the IWAs spare Asian or Sikh companies. In 1977, they lent strong support to Asian strikers at Grunwicks. Raindy and Raindy, another firm owned by two Sikh brothers in Birmingham with 200 employees, a majority of whom were women, was involved in a bitter strike in December 1982 for maternity leave, holiday pay and union recognition. Sympathy for the strikes split the local Sikh community, with the gurdwaras supplying *langar* (a community kitchen) for striking women while Sikh business leaders tried to dissuade women from pursuing their cause. For the IWA in Birmingham, however, the women's cause was one of clear exploitation that had to be pursued, even if, as was the case after a forty-day lockout, the company went bankrupt.[27]

The IWAs also brought into focus cases of racial discrimination, particularly around the right of Sikh workers to wear a turban (see Chapter 6).[28] In more recent years discrimination against turban wearing has focused on the construction industry which, according to some estimates, at one time employed about 40,000 Sikhs, many of whom were *kesh-dhari* of East African origin. In the early 1980s, following European Union directives, the mandatory wearing of hard safety hats on all construction sites posed a serious threat to Sikh employees. As a consequence, from 1983 to 1989 there was a major lobbying campaign of MPs, MEPs and the government to ensure rule exemption for Sikh workers, which resulted in the provision within the Employment Act (1989) sections 11 and 12 that exempts turban-wearing Sikhs from any requirement to wear hard hats on construction sites. However this exemption remained under something of a legal cloud following further proposed safety legislation emanating from the EU on health and safety. An additional round of campaigning and lobbying of the EU led to further guarantees from the Heath and Safety Executive in 1998 (see Chapter 6).

Despite these campaigns the turban continues to cause difficulties as a mode of dress, especially in high-profile posts that require the public to deal with customers – such as the railways, the airways, hotels, the catering trade and restaurants. Cases of discrimination appear with unsettling regularity in industrial tribunals. Even the efforts of the army to recruit more ethnic minorities remained insensitive to Sikhs' commitment to wearing a turban, provoking a community deputation to the Defence Minister that brought forth a negative response.[29] Although few turbaned Sikhs have sought employment in the armed forces, Sikh feelings were partly assuaged when Prince Andrew asked the army managers to encourage the recruitment of turbaned Sikhs.[30] In more recent times there have been efforts to market the turban as cosmopolitan 'designer chic', but this positive marketisation has received a noticeable setback post-9/11, as hate crimes have increased against turbaned, *kesh-dhari* Sikhs who are often mistaken for followers of bin Laden or Muslim extremists.

Women's Employment: Low Wages and Sweatshops
In the 1950s and 1960s, when families migrated together, the primary role of the mother was seen as a house builder. The strong patriarchal traditions of Punjab were reproduced and often strengthened by the initial dependence on the male household income and the need to establish a home. But gradually the cultural objections to women's employment gave way as families were reunited and the 'myth of return' was replaced by the needs of raising families in *Vilayet*. Notwithstanding the barriers of language, custom and tradition, by the mid-1960s many Sikh women were beginning to find employment in such sectors as the food, clothing and garments industries, which were heavily labour-

intensive and low-paid. Where these options were unavailable, they sometimes resorted to home work or part-time and casual employment in ethnic business, where hours were long and rates of pay exceptionally low, even by general standards. The position of most home workers resembled Victorian sweatshops with 30,000–35,000 in the West Midlands, it is claimed, working for less than £80 for a 40-hour week.[31]

As well as home working, women also found employment in low-paid jobs in ethnic business. By the 1960s ethnic entrepreneurs were beginning to enter the 'rag trade' in the West Midlands, East Midlands and the East End of London where low costs and low turnover were the norm and the labour force was recruited from the irregular labour market – older women, the culturally challenged, illegals, and unemployed men. For women such employment occasionally provided cultural security but little else. As Wilson noted at the time:

> Asian women are the worst of all British workers. They are at the bottom of the heap. They come unprepared, easy victims to unscrupulous employers. They don't know the language so their choice of jobs is limited to the worst and least skilled; they don't know their rights and so can be intimidated, they don't have much information about other, better-off workers so they can be paid poverty wages.... Neither their husbands and families, nor white trade unionists nor middle-class Asians are keen to help them.[32]

Such employment for Sikh women was both baffling and exciting. It was baffling in the sense that all was new and strange and they had to get used to new routines – clocking on, time keeping, strict piecework and the management of machinery, as well as interacting, where necessary, with male supervisory staff. But it was also exciting in that it provided many with an opportunity to earn an income, and a sense of space away from home. As a former Sikh sweatshop worker narrates:

> It used to be amazing at the end of the week to be paid, to have money in your hands for the work done. It was very little money really, but to me in those days it seemed like a lot.... At home (in Punjab), money meant food or perhaps, if one had saved a lot, more land, but here the shops were full of the most amazing commodities and getting money at the end of the week seemed to suggest that these things were within one's reach.[33]

These new opportunities, however limited, circumscribed or exploitative, strengthened Sikh women's autonomy and independence, fuelling a wry sense of male resentment that was recorded in folklore. As a popular song at the time noted:

ari ari ari
waiting at the bus stop for No. 207
awaits the woman whose name is Kartari
Say no word, brothers, for she is no ordinary woman
works at Heathrow
pockets a large pay packet
as she befriends the gaffa.[34]

These unsubtle efforts by male songwriters to patronise through humour sometimes backfired as workplace experience and new earning power bred militancy at work and home. Sikh women were at the forefront of a number of bitter strikes involving union recognition and demands for better conditions such as Chix bubble gum factory (Slough, 1979), Bursnall metal works (Birmingham, 1992), the Hillingdon hospital action against privatisation (1995), and the Lufthansa Skychief catering company strike (1998).[35] Most recently, Sikh women were significantly represented in the Gate Gourmet dispute with British Airways that virtually closed Heathrow Airport for several days in August 2005.[36]

Recession, Self-Employment and Education

By the mid-1960s quite a few of the labour brokers or middlemen had branched out into self-employment, beginning first with corner shops that provided Punjabi foods and clothes, but gradually expanding to other sectors such as estate agencies, travel, grocery stores and some professional services such as accountancy and law. Soon areas like Southall's Broadway, Birmingham's Soho Road, and Leicester's East Park and Narborough Roads became the new bazaars that resembled Doaba's 'model towns'. This shift into self-employment was a slow process. It would take three decades, and reflected the pattern of development of other British Asian communities. Above all, for Sikhs, it was hastened by the manufacturing slump of the 1970s and 1980s that all but destroyed the jobs of the early settlers. In Thatcherite Britain, with the unemployment total over 3 million, self-employment offered the only means of guaranteeing family security.

Rise of Self-Employment

To be sure, in cities like Nottingham and Leicester some families, like the Johals, had established a reputation as a close-knit entrepreneurial group, a foundation on which they were to thrive in the 1980s and 1990s. In the 1970s and 1980s many Sikhs took to market trading, often travelling several hundred miles to find new markets. Interviews with market traders indicate that because of the cost of established markets the search for new openings drove them all over the country, often as far as Cornwall, Scotland, and the remote towns of Wales.[37] Many worked long hours, living in vans or local bedsits to learn the new trading skills. For most, the move into self-employment usually came with the purchase of a shop when family savings were pooled, or more frequently, from the 1970s, as manufacturing redundancies loomed large. Loans were often sought from kith and kin because official institutions were reluctant to lend for the purchase of shops or because the applicants lacked a track record in such work. Nonetheless, rustic Sikhs who traditionally had a great deal of antipathy to shop work – normally associated in Punjab with *banyias* (traders) who historically had an exploitative relationship with farmers – readily took to selling. The first purchases often included newsagents, dairies, off-licences, cash-and-carrys, grocery stores, post offices, public houses, restaurants, food and clothes shops and travel agencies.

Although only East African or urban Sikhs from India had any meaningful prior business experience, those of rural background have adapted surprisingly well to the rigours of the commercial world. A part of this explanation, as Ballard has noted, probably lies in their innate 'peasant cunning',[38] a natural instinct to distrust institutions, individuals and officialdom while simultaneously having residual resources in case things go wrong. If the learning curve was steep, then it was helped by *dekhko dekhi* (looking around and imitating), the vibrant ethnic enclaves, and the diversification from shops into manufacturing, especially the cloth trade. In the West and East Midlands and the East End of London, small and much larger family-operated businesses have emerged, employing anything from a few to several hundred workers in the inner-city zones. In these semi-regulated zones the unofficial economy overlaps with lowest sectors of the labour market, providing cut-throat businesses that compete cheek-by-jowl in old industrial warehouses that resemble Victorian rather than twenty-first-century Britain. Especially during the 1980s many Sikhs, in common with Asian businesses, established very profitable enterprises built upon long hours, extensive family labour and minimal compliance with labour or tax regulations. In a neat reversal of fortune, the new proud businessmen/women became the owners of many inner-city sweatshops where their parents had often begun their industrial careers.

Since then Sikh businesses have diversified as well as expanded and adapted to changing market demands. Increasingly they have moved into mainstream areas and locations, with an emerging top-end sector that is well represented among the leading Asian businesses. Several factors have contributed to this development. First, there has been the continuous reinforcement and diversification of the original business idea. Second, family-based enterprises have benefited enormously from second- and third-generation family members, who have often undergone specialist higher education in fields such as business studies or computing. Sometimes they have foregone professional careers in such areas as pharmacy, dentistry, academia or computing, but they have brought to family businesses a degree of professionalism that previously did not exist. Third, like many Asian businesses, Sikh businesses are becoming better integrated with the wider economy while also simultaneously establishing complex networks in Europe, North America and India, particularly since the liberalisation of the economy in 1991. And finally, the dot.com and property booms of the late 1990s have added immeasurably to asset accumulation within the community, because the majority of the Sikhs live in the South and South East or the West Midlands, and have very high rates of household ownership. These factors combined have produced many business success stories that feature regularly in the Asian and non-Asian media. East End Foods in the West Midlands, for example, is typical. In 2000 it was estimated to have an annual turnover of over £25 million, with outlets in Canada and the US. Invited to a charity function organised by the company, former Tory cabinet minster Peter Walker praised it as a 'typical example of Asian family spirit and collective hard work. It is a remarkable contribution to the commercial life of this city and to that of the country.'[39]

The success of Sikh businesses can be seen by considering the top 200 Asian businesses listed by *Eastern Eye* annually. In 2000, 40 of these belonged to Sikhs. The richest Sikh in Britain is Tom Singh, the founder and director of New Look Plc – one of the UK's largest women's fashion retailers. He established the business in 1969, expanded it to a chain of 25 shops by 1986, and then successfully floated it on the London Stock Exchange. By 2000 the company was trading from over 500 stores with a turnover of £418 million.

Yet comparatively the British Sikh performance is remarkably undistinguished. Of the ethnic minorities of South Asian origin, Sikhs have some of the lowest levels of self-employment; they also remain significantly under-represented in the professions, with one survey recording only 0.5 per cent of the community (compared with 5 per cent for Hindus, 3.5 per cent for Jews and 2.9 per cent for Muslims) classified as medical practitioners.[40] This relatively modest achievement

Table 7.1 League of Sikh Businesses in Britain, 2004

Name	Business	Turnover ($ Millions)	Rank	Rank among Asians
Tom Singh	Fashion	330	1	3
Jasminder	Hotels	220	2	6
Gurchait/Gurnaik	Fashion	80	3	17
Dr Daljit Rana	Property/Hotels	49	4	40
Satinder Gulhati	Hotels	45	5	40
Paul Bassi	Property	42	6	42
Sukhdev Khebbal	IT	41	7	44
Jojar S. Dhinsa	Private Equity	40	8	46
Tej and Bobby Dhillon	Property/Hotels	40	9	46
R. S. Ranger	Shipping	38	10	54
M. Kholi	Distribution/Retail	35	11	60
Avtar Lit	Media	30	12	68
Gurbachan/ Sandy Chadha	Distribution	30	12	68
Amerjit Sandhu	Distribution	29	13	79
Karamjit Khera	Wholesale	29	13	79
Sukhpal Ahluwalia	Distribution	25	14	83
D. Singh and G. Kaur	Textiles	25	14	83
G. Bhalla	Pharmaceuticals	24	15	88

Source: *Eastern Eye* (2004).

is undoubtedly related to the community's moderate level of human capital.

Education

Table 7.2 ranks the highest level of educational qualifications for Sikhs identified in the labour force survey carried out between June 2003 and May 2004. Although a limited sample survey, it nonetheless provides an interesting national picture of the levels of educational attainment within the community. The most obvious fact is that Sikh achievement after nearly four generations of settlement in Britain remains *below* the national average on all major educational entry points into the labour markets, with a significant *under-representation* of females at these levels. The size of the community's population with no qualifications is also *disproportionately* large for both males and females, ranking second-

Table 7.2 Sikhs' Educational Qualifications by Sex, 2003/4

Qualification	Male	National average	Female	National average
Degree or equivalent	16.4	18.0	14.8	15.5
Higher education below degree	3.9	7.6	4.3	9.5
GCE A Level or equivalent	21.9	29.3	15.9	18.0
GSCE A–C or equivalent	17.0	17.5	16.4	26.5
Other qualifications	20.3	13.3	22.0	13.8
No qualifications	20.5	14.2	26.6	16.8

Source: Labour Force Survey, 2003/4 and Office of National Statistics.

highest after Muslims. In fact, over 40 per cent of all Sikhs have no qualifications or 'other qualifications' deemed to be sub-GCSE level. Indeed, overall educationally, the Sikh performance in this survey was only marginally better than British Muslims.[41]

However, these general figures do conceal some interesting variations. In the 16–30 age range, roughly covering the third or fourth generations, the performance of British-born Sikhs is generally *above* the national average – though significantly behind Jews, Hindus and Buddhists – with those with *no qualifications* at 6.8 per cent. For non-British-born Sikhs in this age group, in contrast, almost a *third* have no qualifications, while another third have 'other qualifications' deemed less than GCSE or equivalent. Taken as a whole, the Sikh population between 16 and 34 is generally just above or close to the national average at the key exit points in the education system, although a significant one-third of the 25–34 age group have no qualifications or qualifications below GCSE. In comparison, for the over-34s, the record of Sikh educational achievement is dismal, with those in the 35–44 age range almost co-equal with Muslims, and those in the 45–55 and 55–64 groups among the *least qualified of all religious groups*. In short, what is clearly evident from these statistics is that while the first and second generation of Sikhs entered the labour market with few qualifications, the third and fourth British-born generations of the community are beginning to perform close to or just above the national norm.

Given the long settlement of the British Sikh community, what factors can explain this relative under-achievement? Assuming the sample survey is a fair reflection of the community's national profile and that the first two generations had a poor educational background – a factor that was marginally qualified by East African Asians – there is a need to probe further the particular causes of underachievement. Punjabi peasants have generally placed a very instrumentalist value on education, and in the 1970s and 1980s, which saw the rise of a business culture and high unemployment, in some sections of the community higher education was frowned upon while new wealth encouraged a return to early female marriages and large business families. Equally noteworthy is the phenomenon of 'backward integration', of transnational marriage with partners from Punjab often with no qualifications or qualifications that remain unrecognised by British institutions. Even those with post-graduate degrees from Punjab have sometimes struggled to transform these into equivalent qualifications by undertaking new courses.[42] Space precludes a more extended discussion of 'backward integration' – the complex flows between British Sikhs and Punjab – but there is some reason for believing that the priorities of the first and second generations of settlers in Britain might well have had a delayed impact. From the 1950s to the late 1970s, Sikhs in Britain remitted large proportions of their disposable income to Punjab for the purposes of buying land and building new homes that would generally raise the social esteem or *izzat* of the family.[43] This outlook was a safe investment in family and community, but it was often at the expense of investment in children in Britain, who were also expected to accept partners from Punjab. It is only with the rise of the Khalistan movement in the 1980s and the chaos that it created that we see a discernible decline in British Sikh remittances to Punjab and, with it, some corresponding change in investment and educational strategies. Certainly the third and fourth generations of British Sikhs appear to be investing more heavily in education than their forefathers. A cursory survey of fee-paying schools in cities like Birmingham, Leicester and Coventry suggests that today Sikhs, like most Asians, are *disproportionately* represented in the independent sector.[44]

Similar trends can also be noticed in higher education. Sikh students are now entering British universities in greater numbers than ever before. This is partly because the expansion of higher education and the rise in Sikh student numbers, especially since the 1990s, coincides with their overwhelming concentration in the post-1992 'new' university sector, where entry is relatively less demanding. At the same time the proportion that goes to the 'old' universities is also on the rise, and, given current trends, is likely to increase substantially in the future.[45]

Sikh education in Britain is clearly in a transitional phase where the majority of those in the second, third and fourth generations, who are British-born, attach a greater value to education than their forefathers. This outlook, moreover, has generally avoided the 'communal option' –

a demand for separate Sikh schools – though two such schools exist in Hillingdon and Slough, with several others planned.[46] Instead, main-stream education, state or private, is preferred. These developments will certainly add significant value to the quality of Sikh educational experience, but to what extent they will also embrace the large segment of the community with 'no qualifications' or 'other qualifications', remains an issue for debate.

Current Employment Profile

A detailed breakdown of a recent sample survey of the Sikh community's occupational profile in Britain by industry is provided in Table 7.3. This table confirms the modest levels of achievement identified in our discussion of education. At the top end, Sikh representation in the service industries remains significantly below the national average, a fact underlined by the Sikhs' lowly representation in the professions.[47] Today, 72 per cent of the community's males and 55 per cent of females work in manufacturing, transport, hotels, restaurants and distribution. Although the male representation in manufacturing is now in line with the national average, in contrast females are grossly *over-represented* in this sector – perhaps reflecting the continued concentration of Sikh women's work in low-wage, inner-city factories, many of which are ethnically owned. In general the current Sikh employment profile is skewed towards non-tertiary industries, is significantly below the norm for *both* males and females in the service sector, and, especially with reference to female employment in this sector, lags seriously behind the performance of Hindus and Muslims. Sikh female employment rates tend to be high but they are high in sectors where incomes are low and hours of employment long.

One possible reason frequently cited for Sikhs' lowly employment status is the 'ethnic penalty' that the community members sometimes have to pay for racial discrimination. This, of course, is clearly the case for some individuals, as the turban issues have illustrated, but it does not explain why 'Indians', with a similar social profile to the Sikhs, have lower levels of *unemployment* or why they (both Hindu and Muslim) are able to secure more of the professional and service sector employment.[48] A more rigorous explanation would need to probe the nature of the community's 'human capital', age profile and geographical distribution, and the specific cultural and social factors that militate against the Sikhs' achievement. Certainly the low levels of educational qualifications of the

Table 7.3 Sikhs' Employment by Industry and Sex, 2003/4

Industry	Sikh males	All males	Sikh females	All females
Public administration, education & health	11.6	15.1	29.0	41.5
Banking, finance & insurance	10.6	16.1	13.1	15.0
Other services	3.4	5.4	2.6	7.1
Transport & communications	17.8	18.0	7.1	22.3
Distribution, hotels & restaurants	25.8	18.0	27.2	22.3
Construction	9.3	12.8	2.9	1.7
Manufacturing	19.6	19.6	17.7	7.8
Energy & water	1.9	1.5	0.5	0.4

Source: Labour Force Survey, 2003/4, Office of National Statistics.

first and second generations and their concentration in the manufacturing sector compounded these difficulties in the 1980s and 1990s, with one survey in 1994 noting that one in every four economically active Sikh was unemployed.[49] Since then the unemployment rates for Sikhs, in line with general trends, have come down, but they remain stubbornly above the national average for those above 49.[50] It is noticeable that many of the first generation who fall into this age category are geographically immobile and live in former manufacturing localities where regeneration, if it has taken place, has brought more demanding employment that requires new skills such as competence in information technology. That this group is struggling to remain in the labour markets is underscored by the fact that the average economic inactivity rate for Sikh men and women in the 50–64 age groups is 6.8 per cent above the national average.[51]

Although Sikhs, along with Muslims, may well suffer from the adverse 'religious effect' in the labour markets, the general employment profile of the community is more towards the middle or lower end of the British ethnic minority labour hierarchy, in which Chinese and Indians are clearly at the top with Muslims of Pakistani and Bangladeshi background at the bottom. This middle ranking parallels the middle-to-small-peasant background of the first settlers, notwithstanding the need to add the special qualification that Sikhs of East African background and parentage, who, according to community folklore, are *disproportionately* represented in the professions.

Sikh Social Groups

In contrast to the 1950s and 1960s, when Sikh migrants comfortably exchanged the egalitarianisms of rural Punjab for the promise of becoming a part of the advanced industrial proletariat, in today's highly flexible and globalised British economy a new social hierarchy has emerged within the community. This hierarchy is more pyramid-like and has business leaguers with assets over £20 million at its apex. These businessmen/women have become the icons of 'community successes' in an age in which achievement is largely measured in wealth. But this group remains highly fragmented, individualised and increasingly dominated by anglicised second and third generations who rarely see themselves as the community's custodians *à la* Rothschilds. Their desire for recognition in broader society generally impels them to pursue non-Sikh concerns. These 'big leaguers' are shown in Table 7.1.

Below the 'big leaguers' are the medium- to small-sized businessmen/women who have thrived in the 'Little Punjabs' to become the mainstay of the community. Many represent the familiar success story of transition in one or two generations from the family farm to the family business. This group retains most of the plebeian and rural Sikh values that prioritise individual rather than collective concerns, is deeply embedded in transnational kinship networks, and shows little indication of developing the classic consciousness of a bourgeoisie. If anything, its sense of 'community' continues to be defined by reference to local and village institutions, whether in Britain, Punjab or elsewhere.

On the next tier are the community's professionals – doctors, lawyers, accountants, academics and higher-level civil servants. The very poor representation of Sikhs in this category perhaps explains the shortcomings of a community leadership that generally has failed to develop the sense of intellectual autonomy professionals are capable of providing. Within mainstream British and Punjabi Sikh culture, moreover, professionals have suffered a special loss of status in recent decades because the esteem of being a *bharakoo* (educated one) has given way to the cult of *moti sami* (wealthy one, by whatever means) that accords a much higher premium to entrepreneurial skills. Consequently, professional high flyers tend to remain aloof from community concerns that often are mired in interminable factional politics.

Below the professionals are the managers, central and local government employees, and those employed in the light service industries such as IT, banking and insurance. The size of this group is increasing, especially as the better-educated third and fourth generations move through the labour markets. Within schools, the health service, and

Plate 8 Kartar Singh Sandhu, MBE, Chairperson of the Pensioners' Rights Campaign in Leicester, at a rally in London, 1998. (Reproduced with the permission of Leicester Mercury)

central and local government the politics of managing religious and ethnic diversity often requires the support of an ethnic/religious lobby for upward mobility. Not surprisingly, therefore, in recent years Sikhs have become extremely vocal in the state sector, where the community's own 'ethnic entrepreneurs' are to be found. Trapped in the local and national state sectors they have, over the last decade, sought to create organic links with the 'community' by championing community causes – such as ethnic monitoring for the Sikhs, mobilisation over the dress code, or the need to make New Labour's equalities legislation with its monitoring regimes 'work' for the community. They, above all, are the most outspoken champions of Sikh identity issues today, the frontline *nihangs* (traditional Sikh warriors) of today's politics of Sikh 'victimhood'.

Skilled and unskilled workers, who still constitute a substantial part of the community, are generally ranked below the salaried groups. Many play an active part in the community's political economy in which gurdwaras occupy a central place. This group also remains as the residual legacy of the industrial workers of the 1950s and 1960s, its ranks swelled by the successive waves of unqualified workers from Punjab over the decades. While some in this group remain loyal to the politics of the IWAs, since the 1980s a substantial majority, who are often identified as *Des Pardes* readers, became the youthful backbone of the Khalistan movement. Today, this group has become increasingly diverse, disorganised and fragmented, though it still remains most vulnerable to influences from developments in Punjab and Sikh politics. At the same time, as the Gate Gourmet dispute illustrated, this group has a residual legacy of class and industrial militancy that has not dissipated completely; under appropriate conditions, it has the potential to provide a constituency for rekindling the radical politics of the 1960s and 1970s.

Finally, the Sikh underclass, if so it can be termed, is comprised of 'illegals': as well as the *kabootars* ('pigeons' or asylum-seekers) there are others who are engaged in illegal activities. The size of this group is difficult to determine but its presence is widely acknowledged within the community, with one estimate suggesting that there is one *kabootar* for every four Sikh households (see Chapter 4). Like the early settlers, the Sikh underclass remains most prone to exploitation by its own brethren.

Conclusion

British Sikhs are often portrayed as the 'new Jews': a hardworking, deeply religious community. This picture generally overlooks the fact that British Sikh settlers came mainly from a preliterate, rural society and entered the labour market after the Second World War at its lowest level, as unskilled manual workers. As such, they have striven hard to match the national profile in education and employment, and after four generations still lag some way behind the national norms. Sikhs are clearly not Britain's 'ethnic high-flyers', but neither are they its 'ethnic underclass'. At best they are middle-level achievers whose profile is only now beginning to be transformed as the British-born third and fourth generations finish school and higher education. The changes in employment since the Second World War, moreover, have produced a more socially differentiated community that is segmented into sharply defined social groups and specialist labour markets marked by distinct generational differences. The solid core once provided by the proletarian culture and traditions of the early settlers has begun to erode, to be replaced by a more complex mosaic of social groups, identities and varied patterns of employment in which the rise of the business com-munity and increasing female employment have played a not inconsider-able part. As we shall see in the next chapter, the issue of gender equality has come to the fore within the community not only because of greater rates of participation in employment by Sikh women but also because of the need to adapt to changes within British society.

Eight

Family, Gender and Sexuality

For most non-Sikhs the familiar image of a Sikh family is one represented by the travails of Jess, the heroine of *Bend It Like Beckham*. Jess's struggle as a woman and as a footballer who is determined to succeed is seemingly frustrated at every point by her family, which is rooted in tradition, conservatism and unchanging values, if only to protect her against what are seen as the vicissitudes of life in a Western society. Although this portrayal is perhaps not far off the mark, it fails to appreciate the enormous changes to which the British Sikh family has been subjected and how it has adapted to British society. In this chapter we examine the impact of migration in the 1960s on family formation in Britain and the key changes that have taken place since. This is followed by an account of the debate within the community about changing gender roles and Sikh responses to emerging discourses on sexual identities.

Changing Nature of the Sikh Family

Most British Sikh migrants of the 1950s and 1960s came from family structures in rural Punjab similar to those described in Chapter 2, where joint and extended households were the norm. As immigration rules forbade the migration of joint families, the early years of settlement were taken up with re-establishing *biradari* connections that contributed to the concentration of Sikhs in areas like Southall and the West Midlands. East African Sikhs were especially predisposed to such extended networks because they were very useful in overcoming the initial difficulties of settlement. The folklore of early settlers is replete with heroic tales not only of how they negotiated everyday racism but also of how family and kinship support enabled them to establish a firm a footing. As one East African Southallian Sikh recollected:

> Our four families lived together in one household. We decided to pool our resources until successively every family was provided with a house. During this time we had one common kitchen and a common account book. Everybody's needs were met though, of course, looking back now, there were obvious tensions.[1]

After the Commonwealth Immigration Act (1962), a Sikh family was more likely to consist of a husband, wife and children – but also, where possible, husband's kin: his father, mother and, usually, unmarried younger brothers and sisters. Brothers and sisters were expected to set up an independent home well after their marriages; only then would they finally depart into separate homes. Sons were expected to retain their obligation towards parents, brothers and sisters. Parents normally resided with the eldest son, who was deemed to be responsible for them in old age as well as having to fulfil outstanding family obligations. The marriage of females was considered a collective family responsibility to which the entire household had to contribute.

Family unifications after 1962 re-established the household economy of Punjab in which wives and mothers reasserted control over the family income and reassumed the role of protectors of family *izzat*. Purchasing one's own home was often a priority that, as we have seen, became a major hallmark of social standing. Gradually, family reunions and the re-establishment of *biradari* networks recreated the familiar social and psychological norms of Sikh society in areas of heavy Sikh concentration such as Southall, the West Midlands and Gravesend. One of the enduring characteristics of this development was the social policing of young people, especially females.

Changing Households and Family Size

Since the 1960s the structure of the British Sikh family has undergone significant changes. In part this reflects the impact of the broader social changes that have taken place in British society, such as the increase in female employment, the rise in standards of living, increasing marital breakdown and the trend towards lone parenting. At the same time it reflects the adaptation of traditional Sikh norms and values to new challenges.

In 2001, the average size of a Sikh household was 3.6 persons, the second highest for religious communities after Muslims (3.8 persons).[2] Although household is an imperfect indicator of family size, as a general measure it is still indicative. As such it represents a noticeable decline in the size of the average Sikh household since the 1960s when 5–6 persons was often the norm. Further breakdown of these figures gives a more detailed picture of the variations within households: 45 per cent of the Sikh households have no dependent children, 19.4 per cent one dependent child, 21.9 per cent two, and 13.5 per cent three or more. The latter, notwithstanding the general decline in family size, is second highest after British Muslims (24.9 per cent). One explanation sometimes given for the large size of Sikh families is the 'preference' for male children. Couples with one or two sons tend to be satisfied with the norm of two children, whereas two girls are often accompanied by additional children until the arrival of a male offspring. Since the 1990s the ready availability of amniocentesis testing has provided a check against this trend, though it is sometimes claimed that the pattern is less common in Britain than Punjab, where sex selection has given rise to a serious debate about the emerging gender imbalance.[3]

Whereas the size of Sikh households is perhaps surprising, given that 56.1 per cent of Sikhs are now British-born, the types of Sikh households that exist indicate some interesting variations as well as the persistence of familiar patterns. In 2001, at one end of the spectrum were single or lone-parent households made up of a lone pensioner (3.5 per cent), 'other' (9.2 per cent), lone-parent families (9.2 per cent), unmarried cohabiting couples (2.3 per cent) and lone pensioners aged below the official retirement age (2.7). At the other end there were married-couple families (51.7 per cent) and households with more than one family (21.2 per cent).[4] The persistence of joint households may well represent a traditional norm in which there is a reluctance to divide families in Britain as well as ancestral property in Punjab. At the same time we need to note that the growth of self-employment among Sikhs has led to the rise of a business class that has encouraged traditional joint or multiple-family households, both as a means to economies of scale as well as a symbol of social status and prestige. Affluent suburbs in areas of Sikh settlement in Birmingham, Leicester, Slough, Coventry and Leeds are increasingly dotted with large dwellings occupied by joint or multiple families that are frequently run as 'communes', often to the amazement of the affluent local non-Sikh neighbours. Whatever the reasons for such cohabiting the joint family households have not disappeared and are likely to persist well into the foreseeable future because, among other things, Sikhs have the second highest rate of married-couple households (51.7 per cent after Hindus, 54.1 per cent).[5] Nevertheless, 27.1 per cent of all Sikh households today diverge from the community's traditional 'norm' of a joint, married or extended family household. In other words, the traditional family unit that for so long has been the mainstay of a Sikh family, underpinned as it was by a rural economy and the exigencies of migration, is increasingly fragmenting, with almost one-quarter of the British community now falling into this category.

Clash of Cultures

One of the recurring themes in the academic discourses on Sikh family life in the 1960s and 1970s is the 'clash of cultures'.[6] Working within the assimilationist paradigm of race relations, many sociologists and anthropologists argued that rural Sikh values and traditions clashed with the requirements of modern, secular industrial life, in which reproducing the traditional family was an uphill task, particularly given the state's pressure to assimilate and the all-pervasive racism. In the 1960s and 1970s, when community building was in its infancy, many voices were raised about the threats to the loss of Sikh heritage – of language, religion, and cultural traditions.[7] This concern was most apparent in the discussion about the challenges faced by Sikh children, whose socialisation was seen as a particularly onerous task since the competing pressures between home and school, and between work and family life, threatened to tear asunder the fabric of Sikh families. It was against the backdrop of these concerns that there emerged the movement to impart Punjabi in local gurdwaras or set up Sikh schools. Many parents even sent children to be educated in Punjab to counter the alleged vices of British culture. Young girls were considered to be especially 'vulnerable' because of the lure of 'freedom', 'self-expression' and the general 'permissiveness' of British society.

Whereas the first generation of Sikh males and females appear to have negotiated the 'clash of cultures' successfully, there was some evidence that for many young Sikhs the phenomenon was real. Studies of Sikh youths' attitudes confirmed that some Sikh youth were deeply divided by the requirements of family life that often required strict conformity to a dress code such as turban or *salwar kameez*, a 'modest' regime of behaviour, and even unfair treatment as between boys and girls.[8] For many young people in the 1960s and 1970s, rejecting Sikh tradition as stultifying was not uncommon; most – male and female – seem to have avoided the Sikh dress code.[9] In her study of second-generation Sikh girls in Nottingham, however, Drury found evidence of conservative compliance, an ambiguous acceptance of Sikh cultural boundaries but also strong evidence of liberal attitudes on socialising, dress and domestic responsibilities. She concluded that:

the majority of the second-generation respondents did maintain aspects of their ethnic culture especially within boundaries of the Sikh community. However it is important to note that whilst some were very happy to do so, and were in agreement with their parents, others were less dedicated and only deferred to pressures from their families and other members of the community, thereby containing or avoiding tensions.[10]

Drury's findings have been contested by Paur, who argues that the attitudes of Sikh girls to family, marriage, religion and language are far more complex than the 'clash of cultures' paradigm would allow. For her, Sikh girls are more likely to 'negotiate their identities' successfully within Sikh culture than to view the culture as a constraint on their freedom.[11]

These polarised interpretations of the challenges before Sikh youth have been somewhat undercut by the onset of globalisation, which has led to the fragmentation of social identities. Paradoxically after 1984 and Operation Blue Star, Sikh dress among the young became 'cool', an icon of 'militancy' and 'rebellion'. The development, moreover, of significant Sikh enclaves with a political economy locked into globalisation and forms of cultural and fashion industries such as *bhangra*, Bollywood and communications has created new social spaces and consumption-based social identities: the bipolar clash between Sikh values and British society is no longer as confrontational as it appeared in the past (see Chapter 9). Perhaps, more important, the 'clash of cultures' now faced by young Sikhs in Britain has more in common with Sikhs in other societies – including Punjab – beyond Britain.

Marriage

If the family is a key Sikh institution, then marriage is its necessary component. Of all the religious communities in Britain Sikhs have the second highest rate of marriage (59.2 per cent, after Hindus at 60.8 per cent) and the lowest percentage across all age groups of the single, the never-married (27.8 per cent).[12] A Sikh marriage is both a union between two individuals and an alliance of two families with complex *biradari* relations. Thus as a social institution marriage is an elaborate affair, often being the pinnacle of parents' lifetime commitment to their children: as such, it is the supreme institution for enhancing and maintaining *izzat*. In this carefully choreographed event little is left to chance, lest failure should bring loss of *izzat*. Consequently most Sikh marriages are caste-endogamous (*Khatri, Jat, Ramgarhia, Chamars*) and 'arranged' by parents or kith and kin. The concept of 'arranged' has changed remarkably from its rural Punjabi origins. Nowadays in most cases it means an introduction – not a forced marriage – with many 'love matches' being common. The role of introduction itself has changed but we need to remember that this has occurred in the context of developments since the 1960s.

In the late 1960s and 1970s, when men and women reached marriage-able age it was the parents who undertook the task of finding suitable partners. Because of the innate conservatism of new migrants, there was a tendency to marry at a very early age – a tradition still pervasive in a section of British Sikh society today. Marriage was invariably arranged through the kinship network in the Punjab; very few prospective brides and bridegrooms were married to local UK partners. The bride or bridegroom was selected by parents on a visit back, or by a relative, one to whom the other family's background would be known. Then visa papers were sent and brides or bridegrooms were summoned. Before marriage the new arrivals from Punjab would usually stay with a relative, or even with the middleman, until the official marriage ceremony in court followed by a traditional marriage in a gurdwara.

The stringent conditions attached to bringing a fiancé from South Asia in the 1970s, ensured that finding partners for women became an issue within the Sikh community. There was a sustained campaign to highlight the issue of our 'disappearing daughters' and appeals to parents to marry their sons in Britain so that Sikh daughters could find partners within the community.[13] William Whitelaw, Home Secretary during the Conservative government, was instrumental in passing a new law cracking down on what were called 'arranged marriages for sale' and 'marriages of convenience'. This law restricted the entry of bridegrooms-to-be to those wedding British-born girls; it also prescribed a probation-ary period for married partners of a year before the bridegroom would be given a permanent right to stay.

During these years, when there was something of a transition from 'hard' to 'soft' arranged marriage, it was not uncommon to come across stories of mismatch. While parents used many strategies to entice children into marriage, including the now famous melodramatic mother who regularly threatens suicide if her son or daughter marries a non-Sikh partner, children expressed disquiet at their incompatibility with the partners their parents had arranged.[14] A particular concern of young British Sikhs were partners from Punjab, sometimes dubbed *pendus* (rustic villagers) who, though they conformed to social norms, had difficulty in adjusting to the pace of Western society or imposed excessively restrict-ive social burdens. Many young Sikhs expressed their frustration at such marriages but felt powerless to challenge family or community norms. At the other extreme were young Sikhs eager to conform to the dominant community norms. As one young college Gravesendian in the late 1970s stated:

> I prefer a village girl who is a virgin and will obey me, love me, and look after me rather than an English girl who may flirt with other boys and may even divorce me at the slightest argument.[15]

By the 1990s, a combination of immigration controls and the emerging second — and in some case third and fourth generations — had turned the marriage market's focus to Britain. Although British Sikhs continue to marry partners from Punjab and elsewhere in the Sikh diaspora, it would be reasonable to say that most British-born Sikhs today seek partners in Britain or North America, a preference increasingly associated with a desire for joint income and a professional background in the prospective partner.[16] For many British Sikhs, Punjab still retains a powerful attraction when seeking marital partners, particularly if parents have resettled back in the province or there has been a divorce or separation, often viewed as an opportunity for a fresh start. But despite this appeal, Punjab is certainly no longer the primary marriage market.

Arranged marriage has also been modified by the emergence of marriage agencies, community newspaper advertisements and Internet sites. Sikhs of all age groups, castes or nationalities now have access to a world market. The range of contemporary Sikh marriage practices suggests that the conventional role of the family and extended kin is being eroded. Stories abound of couples who met at college or were introduced through the Internet. In the absence of serious research in this area, however, it is perhaps safe to assume that the majority of Sikh marriages still take place as a result of initial introductions by parents.[17]

These developments have also to be placed against a background in which Sikhs are now marrying at a much later age. In 2001, within the 16–24 age group the percentage of Sikhs who had married, remarried, separated or were divorced was 12.9 per cent. This figure was the second highest of all the religious communities after Muslims (23.6 per cent) and contrasted strongly with the Christian mainstream, where the comparable rate was 3.6 per cent. In the age group 25–34, however, the same figure rises to 73.3 per cent, and for the age group 45–54, it was 93.8 per cent.[18] Clearly the majority of Sikhs still recognise the force of marriage but are opting to tie the knot much later.

The Wedding
The centrepiece of the marriage ritual is, of course, the wedding. In the last forty years the Sikh wedding, like Asian weddings in general, has

been transformed from a rather austere affair conducted in makeshift gurdwaras with hospitality provided in a local pub or restaurant into the main driver of the ethnic economy. It is estimated that today the average Asian wedding in Britain costs about £25,000[19] and Sikh weddings are generally an elaborate affair, an opportunity to demonstrate achievement through conspicuous consumption in an intensely competitive social milieu. For most Sikh parents the wedding of their child, as well as being the high point of their lives, is a major financial burden, one which requires several years' saving and preparation. As the community has become more established the wedding ritual has become more complex, extended and structured. Nowadays an average wedding generally requires a year's preparation, if not longer. It involves relatives across the Sikh diaspora; the arrangement of the wedding day itself, with catering for several hundred guests; elaborate pre-wedding and post-wedding rituals; endless sorties for shopping, which may include a special trip to Punjab for the purchase of wedding clothes and jewellery; and the elaborate planning of the honeymoon. The contemporary Sikh wedding, indeed, is the theatre of modern Sikh life, a ritual of such complexity and confusion that its subtleties have eluded most anthropologists, Sikh or otherwise.[20]

A visit to an average British Sikh wedding today provides a salutary lesson.[21] As a result of pressure from gurdwaras the religious and social festivities involved with the wedding day are now delinked.[22] The marriage ceremony tends to take place in a gurdwara, typically located in the inner city close to areas of historic Sikh settlement, but the post-wedding party has become a site where diverging visions of the community clash. These parties are normally held in all-purpose marriage halls, community centres, local hotels, or, sometimes, country hotels with capacity for several hundred to over a thousand guests. Elaborate arrangements are made for food and drink, with an accompanying band or discothèque equipped with the latest audio-visual musical entertainment. The festivities normally begin after the entry into the hall of the newly married couple, which is carefully stage-managed for the benefit of the video production crew. After this the couple and their close family are seated along a high table at the centre of the event, framed and accoutred like a Bollywood film set. While the guests at this stage are plied with drinks and food – non-alcoholic weddings are rare – after a decent interval the couple, in a much-acclaimed 'innovation', 'cut the wedding cake' and proceed to the 'first dance', to the backdrop of popping corks, confetti and the latest Bollywood tunes. This is normally the cue for the ever-present DJ or the hired band to drown the hall in a cacophony of sound while the younger and more virile members of the party unleash themselves in wildly gyrating moves to the latest *bhangra* releases. At this point the party normally goes into free fall, dissolving into a discordant, anarchic social occasion peopled by different generations, most of whom rarely interact with each other beyond their own immediate families. Such dissonance is all too easily reflected in the pathos of most guests who, nowadays, if they can, try to limit their stay. The wedding party normally ends as the invited guests dwindle or 'disappear', exhausted by the heavy consumption of food and alcohol, the ear-splitting blasts of the music system and the mindless inanities of the DJ. Only close family and overseas guests are left to enact the remaining ceremony of the bride's departure from her familial home, traditionally one of the most poignant occasions of a Punjabi wedding ritual. Indeed, the bacchanalian climax to Jess's sister's wedding in *Bend It Like Beckham* is not too far from everyday reality.

Alongside the Westernisation of the Sikh wedding – 'cutting the cake', 'first dance', 'honeymoon', 'disco-fication', 'toasting the couple' and 'wedding lists' – some of the traditional practices have also survived. Of these perhaps the most interesting is contemporary dowry, which has undergone a significant inflation. Ratcheting the going rate up from its traditional base of a limited exchange, some affluent Sikh parents have set new scales in which a house, a sports car, a Mercedes or a BMW regularly feature. Generally this development has accompanied increasing community wealth. Women with a longer duration of employment before their marriages usually have more dowry as wages become part of the dowry, and items bought from this income are augmented by parental contribution.[23] There are some exceptions to this trend, the most prominent of these being the simple marriage ceremony preferred by the Namdhari sect, which neither accepts nor gives dowry and sometimes organises marriages *en masse* at which the sect's guru officiates. Despite this exception, the escalation of dowry has been a matter of constant discussion in the community. In the 1980s several meetings were held to emphasise the need for simple marriages, a development hastened by the rise of the Khalistan movement with its emphasis on Sikh puritanism.[24] These efforts have failed to eradicate the practice, however, and even members of the Sikh communist fraternity, often viewed as socially progressive, have succumbed to 'feudal practices'.[25]

Divorce and Out-Marriage

Historically, Sikhs have viewed marriage as a holy sacrament and not as a social contract. In Sikh tradition the marriage ceremony, *anand karaj*, is described as a ceremony of bliss signifying the union of two souls who become one, leading to the ultimate union with the Divine. As such the Sikh tradition has generally been hostile to divorce. The Anand Karaj Marriage Act (1909), which defined Sikh wedding practice during British colonial rule, *excluded* any provision for a divorce. In rural Punjabi society divorce as such was non-existent and its obvious symptoms were accommodated in long periods of separation or the all-too-frequent practice by males of taking a second wife.

For the early British Sikh settlers divorce became synonymous with the 'White Other': the inevitable outcome of shallow marriages founded on the principle of 'love' and selfish hedonism, without serious consideration of the long-term implications of a family. So strong was this idea, as we have seen, that parents went to extraordinary lengths to inculcate in their children notions of the degeneracy of British society. Even in *Bend It Like Beckham* there is disapproval of Jess's niece, who marries an English boy only to divorce three years later to the 'shame of her family'. This prejudice, however, has been more a parental strategy than based on sound evidence. In the last decade divorce rates among Sikhs have been rising, creating something of a moral panic within the community. This rise, moreover, is not a British phenomenon only, extending across the Sikh diaspora and in the homeland, Punjab.

In 2001, 8.3 per cent of all Sikhs were divorced, separated or re-married, a figure which was the second lowest after Hindus (6.3 per cent). But this overall total disguises significant variations across the age groups: within the 24–34 and 35–44 age groups the rates for the same categories are 10.7 per cent and 14.3 per cent, respectively. In other words, in the latter age group, one in seven marriages is prone to breakdown. These figures tail off significantly with the 45+ age group. Divorce on its own, on the other hand, within the 16–24 age group was the third highest (0.29 per cent) after Muslims (0.39 per cent) and the 'Other' category (0.43 per cent). This rate rises sharply among the 24–34 age group to 3.7 per cent and is the highest among the ethnic minorities of South Asia, a pattern sustained in the 35–44 age group with the exception of Buddhists (11.3 per cent). The rate then again dips for the 45+ age groups, presumably because most of the couples are still first-generation migrants.[26] In general, these figures indicate that while the overall divorce rate among Sikhs is still relatively low, when compared with the general norm it is higher than some other South Asian communities such as Hindus, and is significantly higher for the 16–45 age groups. There are no details about whether divorce for Sikh partners is higher if they marry non-Sikhs or about the gender breakdown of the primary mover in the process. A survey of matrimonial adverts in Punjabi newspapers indicates that there are many young Sikhs, both male and female, in this age group seeking remarriage.[27] Divorce therefore is no longer a taboo; it is becoming an accepted feature of British Sikh society.

There is no systematic research into the cause of marital breakdown. Among the reasons often cited in the community newspapers is the continuing tradition of incompatibility where couples marry under moral or, in some cases, actual duress. Second, many British-born Sikhs are no longer prepared to accept the long-term compromises which their parents were able to endure for the sake of family, to live in silence for the welfare of the family and the extended family unit. The culture of rights, it is sometimes claimed, has cut deep into the notion of a 'moral community', turning marriage into consumerism; divorce in this sense is seen as an extension of the marriage supermarket where there are often incentives if the divorcees then sponsor partners from India.[28]

In addition to divorce, the other great issue of concern within the community is the phenomenon of out-marriages. The common perception is that more and more young Sikhs are now opting for non-Sikh partners. Although there is no detailed research into this subject, it is not uncommon to come across Sikhs whose partners are 'white' (British, European, American), 'Asian' (non-South-Asian Asians), or from the many other minority ethnic communities. This pattern exists across the social groups in Sikh society and contrasts remarkably with the sense of social shame and ostracism associated by Sikh parents with out-marriage in the 1960s and 1970s. In those decades women who out-married were generally expelled from the family.[29] Some of these attitudes persist. In 2004, for example, a Sikh father was convicted of plotting to murder his estranged daughter, her elderly Jewish boyfriend and the boyfriend's father because he felt 'disgraced' by his daughter's actions.[30]

As well as out-marriages inter-caste marriages among Sikh sub-castes were considered taboo. Caste endogamy remains a constant feature of Sikh marriage alliance but occasionally these strict boundaries have been transgressed, creating testing situations for the socially conservative. In Walsall a *granthi* (Sikh preacher) refused to solemnise a marriage between a Jat Sikh boy and a Chimba Sikh woman; only when the issue was taken up by the Punjabi newspaper did he relent to perform the religious ceremony.[31] In another inter-caste marriage a Sikh woman was tortured by her parents; this eventually resulted in their prosecution.[32]

In the last decades social pressures against out-marriage and inter-caste alliances have begun to weaken. A number of factors have contributed to this development. First, Sikh males tend to marry late – perhaps because of rising rates of higher education – or sometime opt for a non-Punjabi bride or a bride from Punjab or elsewhere in the Sikh diaspora, thereby reducing the pool of potential Sikh bridegrooms. Second, many young Sikh professionals find the constraints of living and bringing up a traditional Sikh family too onerous for the contemporary lifestyle that requires constant change, travel and employment mobility. Intensively socialised into high achievement and successful careers, they feel that this goal can often be achieved only outside of a Sikh society that remains, by and large, essentially wedded to a rural Punjabi culture.[33] Third, the decline of the joint family – both in Britain and Punjab – has been accompanied by the decline of social pressures to conform as employ-ment, rising rates of participation in higher education, and a desire for self-autonomy have reinforced the idea of choice rather than predetermi-nation. Finally, the community's efforts to demonise out-marriages have probably been counter-productive: the rate of divorce in contemporary Sikh marriages has increased while the number of 'successful' marriages by Sikhs to non-Sikh partners has risen, defying the community myth that such alliances are doomed to divorce and despair.

Out-marriages, like British multiculturalism, are now introducing a rich diversity into British Sikh society that is likely to have significant long-term implications, perhaps not unlike the consequences historically suffered by British Jewry. If Sikhs are being 'lost' to non-Sikh partners, the latter are also, to some extent, being 'gained' for the community. Most non-Sikh partners often make extraordinary efforts to understand Sikhism, undergo the Sikh marriage ceremony, learn Punjabi and con-scientiously visit Punjab. This development is giving rise to the emergence of new Sikh hybridities reflected in new hyphenated names and interest in the *global* rather than an *ethnic* (Punjab-based) approach to Sikhism as a religious tradition. But, unlike in the United States, this hybridity has yet to reach a stage where *gora* (white) Sikhs can make up a sizeable element of the community.

Crime, Drugs and Alcohol Abuse

The successful reproduction of the Sikh family in Britain has also been accompanied by a rising trend in crime, drugs and alcohol abuse – the most serious issue vexing the community after divorce and out-marriage. There is growing evidence that more and more Sikh youth are becoming trapped in criminality, as demonstrated by the rise of the Sikh prison population and the links with inner-city crime.[34] The emergence of Sikh gangs in localities such as Southall and the West Midlands has given rise to allegations of widespread drug dealing as well as the control of extensive criminal networks spread across Asia.[35] At the same time there has been increasing professionalisation of crime. Tony Singh Hare of Leicester, for example, was described by the prosecution as a 'Mr Big' who ran a drug syndicate that at any one time was dealing in up to £3 million worth of drugs across the country. The 37-year-old from humble roots in Leicester's inner city built a multi-million empire, buying a farmhouse and a fleet of luxury cars and spending £10,000 on the hire of Leicester's main concert hall for the birthday of his son.[36] Hare was sentenced to 53 years in jail and described as someone 'who was seen as a role model by many young people'. Alongside drugs, smuggling immigrants from Punjab has frequently become a lucrative business; long-established, increasingly it has become professionalised, with some Sikh gangs offering 'club class' service.[37] Nor is this rising criminality a male preserve. Jasvinder Gill from West London, for instance, ran an elaborate marriage scam that is said to have netted her £1 million and involved a complex operation extending to South Asia.[38]

A particularly distinctive feature of British Sikh society today is the high rate of alcoholism among males. Consumption of alcohol has always been very high among Sikhs, with the *per capita* rate among Sikhs of Punjab among the highest in the world, but recent studies have shown a growing epidemic. Consumption rates are higher than in any other ethnic minority and in the white community; Sikhs from Punjab seem to be particularly prone to high levels of consumption; in one study 80 per cent of men of Asian origin who died from alcohol-related liver disease were judged to be of Sikh origin.[39] Alcohol-related problems are rarely discussed, as we shall see below, but are too evident in particular cases. For example, Gurdev Singh Mann, who was drunk at the time, stabbed his wife to death because he did 'not like the supper she had made for him'. As his son tried to disarm him, Mann rushed out to 'buy a can of beer'.[40] While such examples need to be placed in their proper context, community workers, Internet discussion forums and women's groups have increasingly highlighted the debilitating impact of alcoholism on the community.

Gender

Much of the debate within the Sikh community and in the academic discussion of British Sikh families has focused on the changing role of women in the transition from a patriarchal Sikh rural culture to a modern society. This change has been accentuated by the rise in Sikh female employment, increasing participation of females in secondary and higher education and, above all, engagement in a society where nowadays sexual equality is not only the norm but legally enforced. The intervention of state agencies into 'private life' – of social services, immigration authorities, police and education officers, for instance – has often exposed cultural practices that continue to legitimise the worst excesses of gender oppression. Indeed, since the 1970s there have been many *causes célèbres* involving violence, 'forced marriages' or 'honour killings' that have brought these issues into the public domain.[41] Such themes were dramatically highlighted by Gurpreet Kaur Bhatti's play *Behzti*, which was closed following violent Sikh protests in Birmingham (see Chapter 6). Its portrayal of physical and sexual abuse, which so riled the community, was uncomfortably close to reality. The case of Kiranjit Aluwalia provides an illustrative example.

> Kiranjit Aluwalia suffered violence and abuse for ten years, ever since the start of her marriage. The final straw came when she discovered that whilst her husband beat her day and night, he was also having an affair with another woman…. She felt humiliated and trapped. She made numerous attempts to end the relationship, often appealing to her family and his for help. She had sought court injunctions to restrain him from further violence but fell under the pressure to reconcile for the sake of maintaining family *izzat*. She attempted suicide.[42]

When Aluwalia's husband attacked her with a hot iron, she responded later by dousing him with petrol as he slept and then set him alight. Aluwalia was sentenced to life imprisonment but was eventually released upon appeal after a sustained campaign by the Southall Black Sisters group.[43]

The other side of this picture is one of successful achievement and adaptation as more and more Sikh parents recognise that the old certainties can no longer hold sway. The rise of enterprising Sikh women who have excelled in business, the professions and public affairs has begun to challenge the stereotypical view of Sikh women as obedient housewives. In fact, for third- and fourth-generation women, who now regularly combine the pressures of high-powered work with bringing up children, it is a common expectation that the husband will share in the house and non-house workload. And this sharing is expected across classes and education groups. The traditional Punjabi machismo, still so faithfully replicated in *bhangra* and Punjabi media, appears to be losing its hegemonic position as new expectations – and practical necessities – demand the recognition of equality.

The issue of gender and British Sikh society cannot be covered satisfactorily in this brief survey; instead, we highlight three particular discourses from within the community that throw an interesting light on how roles are changing and the processes of adaptation to conventional Sikh norms.

First there is the radical black feminist discourse represented by the Southall Black Sisters (SBS). Based in Southall the SBS group emerged at the end of the anti-racist campaigns in the 1970s and, in its own words, has become 'synonymous with black British feminism', campaigns against abuses suffered by women, religious fundamentalism, forced marriages, 'multiculturalism' and state responses to racialisation. SBS combines a strong emphasis on anti-racism with a pursuit of equality. As an SBS document states:

> … within the Asian community our priorities remain to challenge head-on practices of domestic violence, arranged marriages, the dowry system and sexual abuse in the family. If we do not confront these patriarchal structures and forces we will be guilty of colluding with them.[44]

This direct approach is seen as the only way. 'Our lives', as one of the SBS writes, 'will not be defined by community leaders. We will take up our rights to determine our own destines, not limited by religion, culture or nationality.'[45] Within Southall the SBS group has encountered determined opposition from traditionalists as 'home-breakers'. Piara Singh Khabra, Southall's first Sikh Labour MP, a former communist and IWA stalwart, tried to have the SBS closed down.[46] The IWA appealed to the local council to have the group's funding curtailed. Petitioning against the SBS and the Monitoring Group on domestic violence, the IWA claimed:

> We *on behalf of the community* would like to inform you that both these groups play a negative role through their activities in Southall … their *whole life style*, activity, and involvement is totally *alien* to the *customs, language, traditions and culture* of *the* black community.[47]

Despite these hostilities, the group has survived and has achieved international recognition, with growing recognition from official bodies such as the Home Office and the Foreign and Commonwealth Office of the value of its work.[48]

Second, revisionist (Sikh) feminist discourse has attempted to provide an alternative reading that challenges the conventional view of Sikh women as doomed to 'saris, samosas and arranged marriages'.[49] According to this perspective, the rise in employment among Sikh women since the 1960s has now coincided with new patterns of consumption, life-styles, identities and interests that are also distinctively intersected by regional variations (London and the South East, the Midlands and the North). Whereas most of the existing literature, it is argued, tends to focus on Sikh women's role as economic producers who are essential to the family unit, there is a real lack of understanding of 'women as cultural reproducers, individuals who actively manufacture their identi-ties'.[50] As Bhachu writes:

> There is little perception of Asian women as negotiators of cultural values that they choose to accept, and the lifestyles to which they subscribe, and of their roles as innovators and originators of new cultural forms, which take from their 'ethnic' traditions and which are continuously reformu-lated in the context of their class and local cultures. Their role as cultural entrepreneurs who are actively engaging with their cultural frameworks, whilst continuously transforming them, is one that is largely absent from the majority of the literature and from commonsense sensibilities.[51]

By focusing on the dynamics of the dowry system among British East African Sikhs, Bhachu has highlighted the changing nature of women's ability to redefine and adapt cultural norms in a context of increasing differentiation by class and geographical identities among British Sikhs. As Bhachu concludes:

> young Sikh women are influenced by and are responsive to class and regional trends, being products of particular consumption patterns which encode whole facets of their experience and locations and reflect lifestyles that shift continuously. All this applies equally to the identities negotiated and generated by Sikh women.[52]

While Bhachu's interpretation recognises the force of structural factors such as racism, patriarchy and cultural traditions that contribute to the image of Sikh women as victims, her analysis suggests that this vision has to be balanced with a more complex understanding involving class, ethnicity, and religious tradition, so that we do not overlook the 'self-determinative role of Punjabi Sikh women' as *active* agents who shape their own lives'.[53] Evidently, according to Bhachu, a sizeable pro-portion of Sikh women fall into this category.

Finally, there is a third discourse which lays claims to the feminist principle within Sikhism. For traditionalists, and some Sikh feminist revisionists, the frameworks of Western feminism are inadequate for understanding the radically progressive nature of Sikhism, its recognition of gender equality historically that can be dated from the time of the gurus. Sikhism as a revolutionary creed, it is argued, is distinguished by the designation of 'God' as gender-neutral and the teachings of the gurus who sought to eliminate many contemporary practices such as *sati* while providing positive equality for women, promoting anti-casteism and accepting the need to educate females. Theologically Sikh women, it is contended, were recognised as co-equal with men, empowered to hold all major positions, a possibility strengthened by the absence of a priestly class within the faith. Thus both theologically and practically, it is often argued, gender equality is embedded within Sikhism; and if there has been a deviation from these ideals, this is the result of accretions of history or the colonial 'reconstruction' of the Sikh female subject within the familiar paradigm of (Western) social hierarchy.[54]

Whereas the traditional Sikh feminist discourse has occupied a 'respectable' position within global and British Sikh society, occasionally coming into prominence at times of crisis such as gurdwara management disputes, or in response to new demands from the national or local state, in the last decade neo-orthodox Sikh feminists have attempted to re-interpret it as the basis of a wholesale critique of contemporary Sikh practices as they apply to women. The Sikh Nari Manch (UK), for example, through its well-publicised campaign sought to ensure that women at the Golden Temple have equal rights to participate in the *seva* (service). By combining a normative critique of theological practices with the language of gender discrimination, this discourse provides an unsettling threat to established authorities within Sikhism while creating a new space for Sikh feminists disenchanted by the conventional radicalism of Western feminist thought. Perhaps, more important, it also provides a critical agenda within the discourse of Sikhism for women to contest established structures of power.[55]

These three discourses – radical, revisionist and traditionalist – provide useful ideal types around which to recognise the evolving debate about Sikhism and gender in contemporary British society. Each one makes the claim to hegemonic status but in reality there are many overlapping spheres in the lives of Sikh women, who make tactical as well as strategic choices. As the character of Jess in *Bend It Like Beckham* demonstrated, Sikh women, whose lives appear to be regulated and controlled, can also be capable of negotiating freedom and recognition.

Sexuality

If the issue of gender has caused difficulties for the British Sikh community, it pales into insignificance when compared with the emerging debate on Sikh sexualities. Since the 1980s the 'sexual revolution' in Western liberal democracies has resulted in greater public recognition of different sexual orientations. This has led, in cases such as Canada's, to the recognition of same-sex marriages, and created a major challenge for religious communities like the Sikhs. As states in the West move towards a public culture of recognising sexual difference – for example, through a European Union equal opportunities directive to outlaw discrimination based on sexual orientation (2000) and to legitimise such recognition of difference in systems of public education – the Sikh community's main institutions have come out vehemently against these developments. Struggling to be heard against them is a small minority of Sikh gay, bisexual, lesbian and libertarian voices.

Historically Sikh society has been hyper-masculine, reflecting the character of rural Punjab, which evolved as a frontier zone. This masculinity has also been present within Sikhism in an iconography, namely the male dress code, that projects the symbolism of the aggressive male.[56] But underlying such powerful representations of masculinity are serious ambiguities about sexuality – the patterns of male bondage, historically the easy tolerance of homosexuality and bisexuality in rural Punjab, and the nurturing of sisterhood. Certainly the colonial state sought to reinforce hyper-masculinity through the stereotyping of Sikhs as a martial race, a reification of the Sikh subject that highlighted the equally ambiguous sexualities of the colonial masters.[57] These traits are all too evident in colonial art, literature and history. In this respect *Behzti* and the furore it aroused touched a raw nerve in the Sikh psyche, one that was pricked by thematic aspects that ranged beyond the setting of the play in a gurdwara.

The subject of Sikh sexualities remains largely under-researched but, broadly speaking, the debate spurred by the developments highlighted above has created three camps: Sikh traditionalists, pragmatists and radicals. For Sikh traditionalists, problematising the accepted notion of Sikh sexuality is a total anathema, a 'modern Western disease' that is 'anti-Sikh, anti-family and anti-God'. It is, in short, the product of a politically correct culture in which the views of a tiny minority are being imposed on a moral majority.[58] The issue was forced by the decision of the ruling Liberal Party in Canada to introduce a Same Sex Marriage Bill in the Canadian parliament at the end of January 2005. Gurdwaras in Canada publicly opposed the bill and lobbied the Akal Takht and the SGPC to condemn the proposal. The latter quickly declared that 'such marriages were against *gurmat* (Guru's teaching) and Sikh code of conduct [and] because of this reason the SGPC was against such marriages'.[59] The Akal

Takht in a follow-up statement issued an ordinance against the proposal, noting that:

> the rising trend of same-sex marriages in Western countries was a matter of concern. The move of certain countries to give legal accordance to such marriages had already initiated a worldwide debate. The Sikh code of conduct did not allow such marriages.[60]

The head of the Akal Takht, Joginder Singh Vedanti, claimed that such proposals originated from 'sick minds' and that such 'anti-human tendencies' had to be stopped. This hostile response was blamed for the cancellation of Canadian Prime Minister Paul Martin's visit to the Golden Temple. Given that British gurdwaras normally follow the lead of these apex institutions, it is safe to assume that this declaration defines the formal outlook of the Sikh leadership in Britain.

For Sikh pragmatists the traditionalist position is too absolute and ignores the complexities of the modern condition. This perspective has been articulated clearly by Navdeep Singh Bains, an MP in the Canadian Liberal Party, who supported the proposed legislation. For him the measure is another move in the recognition of minority rights in a country which is 'a land of minorities'. According to Bains, the legislation did not 'violate any religious sanctity, faith or belief' as it was to be a civil right and as no court would require religious institutions to ordain such marriages. The Sikh clergy, in Bains's view, had acted in haste and, as one of his spokesmen further elaborated, the 'human rights of minorities cannot be suppressed'.[61]

For radicals, the issue of Sikh sexualities goes beyond the debate begun by the same-sex legislation: it is, first and foremost, about the need for *recognition* of sexualities of *difference*. Very few Sikhs have openly 'come out' as gay, bisexual or lesbian, and those who have raised the issue in Britain have mostly been students. Jasbir Singh, studying in London, has noted how 'gay Sikhs [feel] isolated from both the gay and Asian communities'. There is, he claims, a desperate need to recognise the *fact* of Sikh gays. This is a minimal condition if repression and unhappiness are to be avoided: it must be recognized that 'gay Sikhs exist and it is now time to acknowledge their presence in the Sikh community'. To further this effort, Singh first founded Masala for bisexual and gay men from the South Asian community and later established Darshan, an organisation for Sikh gays with chapters in many university societies.[62]

Sikh gays justify their case by appealing to arguments for equality derived from the contemporary Western discourses that they wish to ground within the Sikh tradition and Punjabi cultural history. Jasbir Singh claims that Sikh spirituality impelled him to 'create an organisation for gay Sikhs' because he could not conceive of himself as gay and *not* Sikh'. Writing on a prominent Sikh website, Jasbir Singh made his case by appealing to the egalitarian message of the tenth guru and the rich tradition of the Sikh community in fighting for the rights of others. This heritage, he adds, has also to be placed alongside the culture of rural Punjab where historically sexualities were far more plural and diverse than is admitted, with the last Sikh Maharaja, Ranjit Singh, running a male concubine.[63]

Although Sikh gays, bisexuals and lesbians currently make up a small minority of the community, the assertion of their rights has raised uncomfortable questions for the community as a whole. These questions, furthermore, have arisen at a time of rapid change in biotechnologies, and stem cell research, and when new equalities legislation is under-cutting the community leadership's traditional pro-life outlook. On all these critical issues, the dominant discourse has been that of Sikh tradi-tionalists, but, as with traditionalists within other faiths, it would be premature to conclude that they have won the argument or succeeded in winning the hearts and minds of 'misguided youth' – who, if anything, remain on course to question and further problematise Sikh sexualities.

Conclusion

Since the middle of the twentieth century the average British Sikh family has undergone a tremendous transformation from an economic and social unit transplanted from rural Punjab to one that has begun to come to terms with a post-industrial and globalised society. It retains some of its distinctive characteristics: high family size, joint households, high marriage rates, and an emphasis on extended *biradari* networks. How-ever, adaptation has also exposed it to familiar trends within mainstream British society – a rising divorce rate, late marriage and increasing out-marriages. Change has been most dramatic in the status of women and children. For some Sikh women education and employment have enabled them to overcome, or better negotiate, the traditional patri-archal culture, while for others it has led to a radical reassessment of their selfhood through feminist discourses or critiques located within Sikhism itself. At the same time, Sikh children are no longer polarised 'between two cultures', with a range of identities and options to choose from in a 'cool Britannia' where diversity and difference are now increasingly embedded in social life and legally recognised. As a result, all aspects of 'traditional' Sikh family life have been put under the microscope, including Sikh sexualities, a theme that resonated in the opposition to the play *Behzti*. If within British Sikh families today there are sharp cleavages, then these cleavages arise not as the result of a 'clash of cultures' between the young and the old, between Sikh familial values and British society, but because of an ongoing contestation within the Western Sikh diaspora between traditionalists who view themselves as the repositories of the dominant community discourse, on the one hand, and the moderates and radicals for whom adaptation and change are a necessity, on the other.

Nine

Punjabi, *Bhangra* and
Youth Identities

In 2003 Punjabi MC, a pop group based in Coventry, had a Europe-wide smash hit with the release of their single *Mundian tu bach ke rahin* (Be careful of the boys). Sung in the style of a rustic Punjabi folksong against a high-tempo backing, its success surprised most observers of the music scene, already familiar with efforts at cross-over and fusion that had characterised much of the output of the *bhangra* industry over the previous decade. The song became at once a statement of the vibrancy of Punjabi culture, an iconic representation of Punjabi youth in Britain and a demonstration that Punjabi as a language has a future. For Sikhs, Punjabi is not only a language; it is a *sacred* language written in the Gurmukhi script – literally, words from the guru's mouth. Accordingly, its maintenance among the new generations has been one of the foremost preoccupations of community leaders, Sikh spokespersons and parents.

In this chapter we examine how the development of Punjabi has been sustained by efforts to institutionalise its teaching to new generations and the growth of a Punjabi market in newspapers, journals and literature. Against the efforts of the dominant discourse of Sikh identity, which has sought to bind itself to Punjabi, we also examine the rise of *bhangra* as a medium for fusion, cross-over and hybridities where Sikh identities are often contested. Finally, the chapter reflects on Sikh youth culture and the question of heritage transmission.

Punjabi Language

First-generation Sikh parents were very much vexed by the need to maintain their heritage, in which Punjabi always occupied pride of place. As the community grew from the mid-1960s, the issue of how

Punjabi was to be transmitted to children soon came to the fore, a concern heightened by the initial emphasis on learning English. The Intensive English programmes for new immigrant pupils stoked fears of decline in competence in the mother tongue, and though initially some parents were reluctant to complain, and others even insisted that children at home spoke only English in order to facilitate assimilation and language competence,[1] the stress on English created a moral panic within the community that was aired in the Punjabi press in the debates about linguistic muddle in the school playgrounds, a novel mix and code-switching between Punjabi and English to produce a new hybrid described as 'Punglish' or 'Southalli'.[2] Naturally it was the gurdwaras that responded to parent demand for Punjabi teaching. In Smethwick the Guru Nanak Gurdwara established one of the earliest Punjabi schools (1965). In 1967 the International Sikh Brotherhood commenced Punjabi classes at a welfare centre in Balsall Heath. A number of former teachers from Punjab played a prominent role in organising a Punjabi school, as well as encouraging the import of written materials from Punjab.

These voluntary attempts were aided by the emergence of an institutionalised system of support for minority languages. Under Section 11 of the Local Government Act (1966) national government made available support to local authorities to enable pupils of minority ethnic communities to receive additional English teaching as a second language. Subsequently, some local authorities began to make provision for minority languages, a development facilitated further by the Bullock Report (1975), the European Directives on the Education of Children of Migrant Workers (1977 and 1981) and the Swann Report (1985). The latter marked something of a watershed in the official discourse on multiculturalism.[3] While it recognised the need for the teaching of minority languages in school where there was sufficient demand, in general it viewed the concern for mother tongue maintenance as best achieved within the communities themselves.[4] Nonetheless this recommendation was drawn upon by some local authorities and was further underpinned by the introduction of the National Curriculum in 1988, in which the modern language syllabi were revised to include Asian languages. Punjabi was thus put on a par with German and French for GCSEs and A Levels, but making this choice available in school remained at the discretion of the local head teacher.

Current Provision
From the mid-1970s a few examination boards framed syllabi for South Asian languages in response to demand from Punjabi, Urdu and Gujarati

Table 9.1 Number of Students for Punjabi GCSE, AS and A Level
Examinations, 1985–2004

Year	GCSE	AS	A
1985	....		28
1986	....		36
1987	....		56
1988	....		74
1989	....		....
1990	1,220		88
1991	1,281		123
1992	1,440		160
1993	1,509		166
1994	1,479		159
1995	1,732		185
1996	1,880		269
1997	1,938		259
1998	1,670		268
1999	1,611		176
2000	1,651		233
2001	1,581	90	226
2002	1,484	132	250
2003	1,458	182	300
2004	1,452	154	277

Source: NEAB, JMB, MEG, ULECA, AQA.

students. In 1988 as part of the new National Curriculum old syllabi were standardised, with greater emphasis on communication. Currently the Assessment and Qualifications Alliance (AQA) offers Punjabi both at General Certificate in Secondary Education (GCSE) and Advanced (A) levels. The net result of these efforts is that Punjabi teaching has witnessed a gradual increase in the number of candidates appearing at GCSE and A level examinations, as indicated in Table 9.1.

The figures for Punjabi are significantly lower than those for Urdu but similar to those for Gujarati.[5] A few universities, among them Warwick and Birmingham, have given Punjabi A-level recognition within their admissions procedure, but among students a suspicion remains that it is less valued than other subjects. At university level the School of Oriental and African Studies provides the most comprehensive provision, offering its undergraduates a Punjabi option and postgraduate research. This has arisen mainly as a result of the efforts of Professor Christopher Shackle, a distinguished linguist with interests in Punjabi grammar, literature and Sikh Studies. The University of York's Department of Linguistics also provides specialist research degrees in Punjabi.

Despite these developments, the general picture remains gloomy. There is a strong perception within the Sikh community, notably among its elders and the first generation, that competence in the mother tongue among second-, third- and fourth-generation Sikhs is firmly on the decline. Although confidence in spoken Punjabi remains high, and many more students attend regular or irregular Punjabi classes than those who progress to the examination stage, this is not matched by an ability to write or communicate fluently. Even the ease of regular links with Punjab and the growth of the Punjabi media (see below) have failed to add new vigour to the learning of the mother tongue. In fact, the opposite has happened. Since the decline of militancy in Punjab and economic liberalisation, Punjabi has increasingly given way to English as the preferred examination language in the Sikhs' home province.[6] Moreover, among the younger generations in the diaspora who use Punjabi there is a growing preference for Romanisation rather than Gurmukhi script, a trend hastened by new software and information technologies.[7] For British Sikhs Punjabi remains the language of first-generation migrants, while second, third and fourth generations are increasingly bilingual and code-switch between Punjabi and English, depending upon the situation and contexts.[8]

Punjabi Broadcasting

As well as efforts to institutionalise Punjabi, Sikhs have consistently campaigned to obtain a better share of public broadcasting for Punjabi. A Punjabi lobby was established in 1972 when a committee sought a BBC programme in Punjabi to replace or supplement *Apna hi ghar samjhie* on Sundays.[9] In 1998 a committee led by Kashmir Singh from Wolverhampton sought more time for Punjabi programmes on BBC radio programming. Kashmir Singh claimed that Punjabi was the largest common language understood by South Asian speakers and, quoting census figures and the BBC's own surveys of its listeners, he argued that the Punjabi language was significantly underrepresented in proportion to Hindi and Urdu programming.[10] However, an independent audit conducted for the BBC Asian Network found that these claims were unsubstantiated. The output of the programmes reviewed, it noted, 'has a significant Punjabi content and in some of these programmes this is nearly fifty per cent, and in most never less than about thirty per cent. The Punjabi content in programming is overrepresented.'[11] Despite this assessment, opposition persisted, and since then the growth of the BBC Asian Network, with its specialised output for British South Asians, has been able to accommodate the demand for Punjabi-language and religious programming.

The major fillip to Punjabi broadcasting has come from the arrival of commercial radio and satellite television channels. Sunrise Radio, based in Southall, has capitalised on the growth of the Asian economy and the *bhangra* industry by offering a range of broadcasting for all generations: a mixture of chat shows, discussions and recycled favourites for the older generation, who are largely house-bound. This formula has produced many imitators in other localities such as Birmingham, Leicester and Leeds. There are now many stations that broadcast a mixture of Punjabi folksongs, *Gurbani* (sayings from the *Guru Granth Sahib*) and chat shows: Raj Radio, Punjab Radio, Desi Radio, Amrit Bani and Akash Radio. Some of these have arrangements with local gurdwaras to broadcast special programmes on a daily basis. However, it is the unprecedented growth in satellite broadcasting through channels such as Zee TV, Star TV, Alpha TV and Punjabi TV that has captured the domestic entertainment market. By combining a popular mixture of Bollywood, *bhangra* and South Asian soaps, these channels have both fuelled the growth of transnational markets in commodities and cultural products and – in real time – linked Punjab and Punjabis in Britain. All the Sikh festivals and anniversaries are telecast from Punjab, with the daily recital of *Gurbani* from the Golden Temple in Amritsar. The depth of these links is likely to intensify further, but so far the global commercialisation and commodification of Punjabi culture has failed to produce a corresponding interest in the use of the Punjabi language.

The British Punjabi Press

Until the 1990s the main mode of communication for the community was the Punjabi press, a distinctive ethnic industry.[12] This industry emerged in the mid-1960s, only to divide along factional and ideological lines. Nevertheless it has become the focus of community concerns as well as the medium through which its own internal dramas are debated and given space for discussion. As such the history of the Punjabi press is the history of the Sikh community in Britain.

Ekta, a monthly founded by Vishnu Dutt Sharma, an IWA activist in Southall, was the first paper to be launched, in January 1964. It was

Table 9.2 British Punjabi Press, 1964–2005

Title	Year	Editor/Proprietor	Location	Orientation
Ekta	1964–5	Vishnu Dutt Sharma	Southall	IWA (CPI)
Des Pardes	1965–	Tarsem. S. Purewal/Gurbax Virk	Southall	Independent
Punjab Weekly	1965	Gurnam Singh Sahni	Southall	Pro-IOC
Punjab Times	1966–	Gurnam Singh Sahni/Purewal	Southall/Derby	Independent
Mamta	1966–7	Gurdial Singh Rai	East London	Independent
Awaz	1967	Manjit Rana	Southall	Independent
Kirnan	1967	Kesar Singh Mand	Southall	Independent
Punjabi Patrika	1969–70	Giani Bakhshish Singh	Leamington	pro–Akali
Nawan Sandesh	1969–70	Gurdial Singh Rai	East London	Independent
Sikh Times	1970	Amolak Singh	Southall	Akali
Sher-e-Punjab	1971	Giani Ajaib Singh	Southall	Panthic/Pro–India
Sandesh	1972–7	Avtar Jandialvi	Southall	Pro–IOC
Sandesh Intl	1973	Avinash Azad	Southall	Pro–IOC
Punjabi Post	1979–86	Gurdial Singh Rai	Birmingham	Independent
India Times	1980–7	Ranjit Kanwar	Southall	Pro–IOC
Asian Post	1981–3	Gurdial Singh Rai	Birmingham	Independent
Sikh Tribune	1983–5	Collective	Southall	Khalistani
Punjabi Jarnail	1984–5	B. Singh	Birmingham	Khalistani
Punjabi Darpan	1985–9	Ram Kaushal	Southall	Pro–India
Awaz-e-Quam	1986–	ISYF	Southall	Khalistani
Punjabi Guardian	1987–2000	Sujinder Singh Sangha	Birmingham	Independent
Shere-Punjab	1987–90	Balwant S. Kapoor	Southall	Pro–India
Sikh Times	2002–	Jaspal Singh Bains	Birmingham	Independent
Ajit	2003–	Dalvir Summan	London/Canada	Commercial/free
Man-Jit	2005–	Karm Singh Karm	Darlaston	Commercial/free

Notes: All titles were published in Punjabi except the following bilingual papers: *Sikh Tribune, Punjabi Guardian, Sikh Times, Ajit, Man-Jit.*

Table 9.3 Punjabi Magazines, 1962–2005

Title	Year	Editor/Proprietor	Location	Orientation
		Religious		
Amrit	1962	Ratan Singh Reehal	Wolverhampton	Religious
Prabhoo Nere Hai	1978–85	Collective	Birmingham	Christian Punjabi
Gagan Damama	1980–5	Collective/Akhand Kirtani Jatha	Birmingham	Sikhism
Sangat Samachar	1981–3	Collective	Cardiff	Bhatra Sikhs
Sangat Bhatra Samprda	1985–90 ?	Collective	east London	Bhatra Sikhs
Sikh Pariwar	1987–92	Ranjti Singh Rana	Birmingham	Sikhism
Sewadar	1999–2001	Collective (Ramgarhia Gurdwara)	Southall	Religion
		Literary Pursuits		
Basera	1961	H. Atwal	Erith	Literary
Ujala	1964	Ratan Singh Reehal	Wolverhampton	Literary
Pardesi	1964	S. Dhariwal	Slough	Literary
Parkash	1966	Ranjit Kanwar	Southall	Literary
Savera	1967–8	Gurcharan Sagoo	east London	Literary
Poorab te Pacham	1967–8	Gurdial Singh Rai	east London	Literary
Kiran	1967	Raghbir Virdee	Bradford	Literary
Punjabi Sahit	1969	H. Singh	London	Literary
Jagmag	1969	R. Singh	Leicester	Literary
Lakeer	1970–80	Surjit Hans/Prem Parkash	Southall/Jalandhar	Literary
Nilgiri	1970–2	Tarsem Nilgiri	Jalandhar//Southall	Literary
Quami Bahar	1971	P. Singh	Coventry	Literary
Pardesi	1974	R. S. Reehal/ Hunjan	Wolverhampton	Literary
Rachna	1981–90?	Gursharna Singh Ajeeb	east London	Literary
Sahib	2002–	Ranjit Singh Rana	Birmingham	Literary
Shabad	2002–	Harjit Atwal	London/Jalandhar	Literary
Parvachan	2003–	Swaran Chandan	Wolverhampton	Literary
Hun	2005–	Avtar Jandialvi	London/Mohali	Literary

Table 9.3 continued....

Political: IWAs/Akalis/Khalistani

Nawan Chanan	1963–7	Avtar Johal	Birmingham	IWA–CPI(M)
Lalkar	1967–	Avtar Johal/Harcharan Brar	Southall	IWA(ML)
Hind Mazdoor Lahir	1970–5	Collective	Southall	CPI(ML)
Sanghrash	1971	Harbaksh Maksoodpuri	Derby	Socialist
Lok Yudh	1972	Kesar Singh Rampuri	Nottingham	Independent
Sangram	1972–3	Collective	Bradford	IWA–CPI(M)
Ekta	1972	Vishnu Dutt Sharma	Southall	IWA–CPI
Lok Shakti	1979–83	Collective: Avtar Sadiq	Nottingham	IWA–CPI(M)
Khalistan Times	1977–85	Davinder Singh Parmar	London	Khalistani
Charcha	1984–5	Vishnu Dutt Sharma	Southall	IWA–CPI
Lokta	1983–7?	Avtar Sadiq	Leicester	IWA–CPI(M)
Sooraj	1983–6?	Swaran Chandan	Southall	Politics/Literary
Khalistan News	1984	Collective	London	Khalistani
Poorab te Pacham	1987	Harbhajan Singh Virk	Coventry	CPI(M)
Charcha	2002	Darshan Singh Dhillon	Bhatinda/London	Current Affairs

Special Interests: Films, Women and Children

Roopvati International	1968–75	Kailsh Puri	Liverpool/Delhi	Women
Nari Sansar	1969	Malkiat S. Takhar	Bradford	Women
Matwala	1969–77	Gurnam Singh Singh	Southall	Film/Porn
Pardesi Balak	1972–3	Surjit Singh Kalra	Birmingham	Children
Rustam	1973–5	Balbir Singh Kanwal	East London	Wrestling
Pardesan	1981–	H. S. Bedi and Kaur	Southall	Women
Meri Boli Mera Dharam	1993–2000	Gurbachan Singh Bhui	Telford	*Bhangra*/Youth

Table 9.4 English-Language Periodicals on British Sikhs, 1960–2005

Title	Year	Editor/Proprietor	Location	Orientation
Sikhism				
Sikh Courier	1960–	Sukhbir S. Kapoor	London	Sikh Religion
Sikh Messenger	1984–	Indarjit Singh	London	Sikh Affairs
Sikh Reformer	1991–6	Arvindpal Singh	Coventry	Sikh Affairs
Lions and Princesses	1994–5	Harjinder Singh	Birmingham	Sikh Students
Current Affairs				
Shakti	1981–3	Amarjit Chandan	Southall	Current Affairs
Politics	1981–4	Nirpal Singh Shergill	Southall	Current Affairs
Sikh Youth International	1985–97	Rajinder Singh	Nottingham	Current Affairs
Asian Chronicle	1987–96	Gurnam Singh Sahni	Southall	Current affairs
Unity	1985–97	Jaswant Singh	London	Politics/India
Koh-i-Noor	1985–1999	R. S. Chaudhry	London	Nostalgia/India
Sikh/Punjab Academic Studies				
Sikh Bulletin	1984 –	Owen Cole & E. Nesbitt	Coventry	Sikh Studies
International Journal of Punjab Studies	1994 –	Association for Punjab Studies	Coventry	Academic
Sikh Formations: Religion, Culture and Theory	2005–	Pal Ahaluwalia, Gurharpal Singh Arvind-pal Singh Mandair	Oxford	Academic
Bhangra/Youth				
Spice	1997–8	Parminder Singh	Birmingham	*Bhangra/* Youth
Tan	1994–5	–	Birmingham	*Bhangra/*Youth

Note: There has been a proliferation of titles on *bhangra*. For a sample see *Gazal, Beat* and *Desi Express*.

followed a year later by *Punjab Times* and *Des Pardes*, reflecting respectively the urban-rural cleavage in Sikh society. Both papers have
remained afloat since, with *Des Pardes* becoming popular with a circula-
tion of over 10,000 and a readership spread across Europe, North
America and the Far East. Its founding editor, Tarsem Singh Purewal,
had an uncanny knack for exploiting the Punjabi idiom and was
singularly responsible for the paper's success. His untimely death in 1995
deprived the publication of its main dynamism.[13]

In addition to the weeklies there has been a proliferation of monthlies
and occasional journals, in both Punjabi and English, which cover very
broad fields.

These are noted in Table 9.3 and are distinguished by their extremely
short shelf life: most struggle to survive. Among the few that have
survived are the *Sikh Courier* and *Lalkar*, the latter being the mouthpiece
of the Naxalite section of the Punjabi communist movement.

British Punjabi Literature
British Punjabi literature has a long lineage beginning with accounts by
Sikh sojourners, including observations on British life at the turn of the
twentieth century by Kahan Singh, a Sikh scholar and colleague of
Macauliffe. In the early 1960s the first poetry symposiums were held in
Southall by a newly formed literary association, Punjabi Sahit Sabha.[14] Its
first annual conference on 30 October 1964 was attended by several
hundred people with a *kavi darbar,* a late evening poetry symposium.
Ishwar Chitarkar, a self-exiled poet and dramatist from Delhi, was among
the newly elected office bearers of this association. In the late 1960s
another literary association, the national Progressive Punjabi Writers'
Association, was also established.[15] The emerging writers found outlets
in the popular Punjabi weeklies such as *Des Pardes*, though some gurdwaras also encouraged *kavi darbars*, especially after 1984.[16] However the
grand occasions for Punjabi writers are the meetings of 'literary associations' such as the International Punjabi Literary Society of East London,
a Punjabi Arts Council based in Birmingham and the Progressive
Writers' Association of Wolverhampton.

The world of Punjabi writers is comparable to those of other migrants
for whom sensibilities of home cultures determine their responses to the
new world. Given that the majority were of small- and middle-peasant
background, their determination and resilience seem remarkable, yet
understandable because the majority had come under the influence of
the communist movement in Punjab and retained this loyalty once in
Britain.[17] In the early 1970s, the IWAs attempted to set up literary

associations in every town where they had a significant following, but these had to be dissolved as political and personal factionalism quickly came to the fore. Instead of official party publications it was the burgeoning Punjabi media, especially the Punjabi weeklies, that played a crucial role in establishing literary reputations. While some writers have branched out to establish literary journals, in recent times the growth of the *bhangra* industry and, much more broadly, the Punjabi media, has given major encouragement to writers of lyrics, plays, TV scripts and radio programmes.

The quality and range of Punjabi literature are too extensive to be summarised here: suffice it to highlight some of the common themes.[18] At one level there is a linear development, with initial responses to life and racism in industrial post-war Britain. At another there are the recurring themes of settlement, homeland and the dilemmas of staying on, most lucidly expressed in poetic offerings like this one from Avtar:

> Mother, promise me to wait till I return
> To shower you, with magnificent gifts as I return
> When you will behold me again.
> Father, promise to stay alive till I return
> With the wealth I gather from the far shore
> To buy you more land to till
> A proud new turban to don on your head
> To make our adversaries look upon our household
> With greed and envy.[19]

Jagtar Dhaw, another poet, recognises the inevitability of seeking 'roots within these walls' and even 'if we cry, cry we must, [because] Thames would caress our remains, nay even of our children'.[20] Or in the words of Baldev Bawa, the return to the native land is becoming a chimera:

> The day I shall return seems still far away
> It never arrives, prolonged
> Still the hope smoulders on
> As doubts gather and linger.[21]

After 1984 Baldev Bawa's reflection on Punjab was typical of many of the offerings:

> Punjab, oh my country, is forlorn among nations
> Let me write thy name, on the vast canvas of the sky
> Let the beautiful moon encircle my homeland.
> Let Punjab shine among the studded stars.[22]

These few excerpts highlight the fact that Punjabi literature is very much an *ethnic* product, which, by and large, has failed to appeal to the much broader constituency of black or post-colonial writers in Britain. Little of this output has been translated into English; Amarjit Chandan is one of the few poets who has crossed this boundary and established a reputation in some Western literary circles for his Punjabi translations.[23] His poem 'Peacock in Walpole Park, Ealing' has found a way to resonate for some English readers:

> The heart sinks when the peacock screams
> The night bleeds pierced with its cries
> The heart sinks when the peacock screams
> It yearns for mango flowers lost long ago.[24]

Nonetheless most Punjabi writers in Britain seek recognition and status in Punjab, India and within the Punjabi diaspora. The Languages Department of the Punjab government awards literary prizes to overseas Punjabi writers and several from Britain have been recipients of such awards.[25] There is also active exchange among the diaspora writers, with British Punjabi writers regularly participating in these events. Since the 1980s several international gatherings have taken place, the first of which was held in London in 1980, with follow-up conferences in Singapore, Toronto, Vancouver, and locations throughout the USA.

British Sikhs in English Literature

A more noticeable development has been the emergence of creative literature by Sikhs and non-Sikhs on British Sikhs. One of the earliest such novels was *The Immigrants* (1973)[26] by Reginald Massey and Jamila Massey. Its central character, Iqbal Singh, is a Sikh villager uprooted by partition who migrates to Britain and there experiences disillusionment, racism and romance. Almost a decade later Len Webster's *The Turban-wallah* (1984) explored the subjects of caste, racism and arranged marriages.[27] It narrates the story of how Rupinder Singh, nicknamed Ruby ('turban-wallah'), falls in love with Tara, a Gujarati Hindu girl whose parents disapprove of the relationship, and highlights key issues in the development of the Smethwick Sikh community. *Pig* (1994) sensitively depicts a teenager's understanding of racism and street relations through Danny, an English boy, who is involved with Surinder, a Sikh girl. It explores the racial stereotypes and beliefs held by some working-class English families about Sikhs and Asians.[28]

Although the British Sikh community has so far failed to produced a Zadie Smith or a Monica Ali – Gurinder Chadda's script for *Bend It Like*

Beckham perhaps comes the closest – there is now a generation of British-born and -educated writers of Sikh background who are beginning to explore the familiar themes within the community's narrative of development in Britain from their own perspective of living and growing up in multicultural Britain. Bali Rai's *(Un)arranged Marriage* (2001) explores sensitively the dilemmas of a Sikh boy growing up in Leicester whose 'deviant excesses' his parents seek to correct through an arranged marriage in Punjab. The novel speaks directly to the young against the backdrop of 'forced marriages'. Its lead character, Manjit, after deftly extricating himself from his difficult predicament, re-evaluates the Jat Punjabi culture of his parents. He concludes:

> I've been reading up on on it [Sikhism] lately and I've found that Sikhism preaches tolerance and equality towards everything…. Men, women, Black, White. All the same. The problem is that people like my old dad tie all these old traditions to the religion – arranged marriages, all the racist shit [against blacks], the caste system stuff, things which have nothing to do with religion and more to do with culture and politics and social norms.[29]

In *(Un)arranged Marriage* there is no anxiety about the loss of a Punjabi heritage; instead, the major concern is how Sikh tradition, as interpreted by some parents of the first generation in a globalised, multicultural Britain, fetters communal and personal development.

An equally refreshing assessment is offered by Bally Kaur Mahal of Derby in her debut novel *The Pocket Guide to Being an Indian Girl* (2004).[30] In this semi-autobiographical account the central character, Susham, struggles as a teenager to negotiate the worlds of a Punjabi home and English society. Instead of rebelling as Manjit does in *(Un)arranged Marriage,* Susham provides guidelines for Indian girls to negotiate the imponderables, thereby rejecting the idea of the 'clash of cultures' or the more stylised versions of British Asian society represented by Bollywood and the cable media. Hailed as a refreshingly realistic account,[31] *The Pocket Guide to Being an Indian Girl* gained favourable reviews from literary and non-literary critics alike; one commented a trifle glibly that Susham was neither a 'complete coconut (pro-assimilation) nor a complete *pendu* (rustic villager)'.[32]

Bhangra

If Punjabi has largely failed to function as the key medium of cultural transmission for successive generations of British Sikhs, then its role as

Plate 9 A bhangra club organised by the Indian Workers' Association in Leicester, 1965.
(Source Gurharpal Singh)

the social glue that binds the younger and older generations has been usurped by the 'reinvention' of *bhangra* – a traditional Punjabi folk music. Since the early 1980s *bhangra* has become the emblem of British Punjabis, coinciding with the emergence of an identifiable youth culture and the new information entertainment technologies. Emerging from the highly charged conditions of the multi-race inner cities of the 1970s and 1980s, the growth of the *bhangra* industry, and its global impact, has been hailed as the precursor of social hybridities, cross-over and multiple identities, changes that explode the myth in dominant discourses of ethnic and religious identity among Britain's minority populations. For Sikhs, however, the success of *bhangra* is fraught with tensions that arise from the possibilities of mainstreaming, on the one hand, and impulses towards communal cohesion on the other. Like the Punjabi poetry of the early Sikh settlers, *bhangra* harbours deep anxieties as well as possible futures, especially for the young.

Bhangra's origins in Britain can be traced to wedding celebrations in the late 1960s and early 1970s when local and Punjabi singers and groups, like Golden Star, became a regular feature of post-ceremony entertainment. Rapid growth in wedding expenditure encouraged new entrants into the field who often began their careers as weekend entertainers at student concerts and special occasions such as *Diwali*. At this juncture the distinctive *bhangra* beat grew out of 'cooperation of musicians from Punjab versed in traditional *bhangra* songs and music, and producers from East Africa who contributed their technical skills and business acumen'.[33] By the early 1980s, a vibrant mix was bringing new British-based groups – DCS, Holle Holle, Alaap, Suraj, Chirag Pehchan, Heera, Culture Shock, Apache Indian, Bally Sagoo, Golden Star and Koma – into contact with those from Punjab who had established a well-trodden circuit at leading venues in Southall, Birmingham, Glasgow, Coventry, Nottingham and Leicester. The new British-based bands quickly attracted a significant following among the Asian youth – Sikh and non-Sikh – thus helping to create an infrastructure of production, distribution and competing charts for a sizeable alternative music industry. Some organised daytime concerts to cater for the restricted social hours of Asian youngsters, with venues such as the London Hippodrome, the Birmingham Dome, and the Hammersmith Palais attracting anything up to 3,000 spectators. This mass following was quickly translated into burgeoning record sales in Britain and abroad, with artists like Malkit Singh and Apache Indian, who fronted a band from Birmingham, becoming global best sellers, while Bally Sagoo's 'Dil Cheez' topped many unofficial charts and reached number 12 on Top of the Pops on 18 October 1996.

Taken from Sagoo's album *Rising from the East*, it was the first Asian-language track to have broken into the mainstream music market, justifying his manager's comment that it was 'brilliant news for Bally and for Asians in general'.[34] In 1998 high-profile achievers included Talvin Singh, Cornershop, Asian Dub Foundation, Nitin Sawhney and a 19-year-old Punjabi singer, Amar.

Bhangra's success was the result of several simultaneous developments. In the late 1980s and early 1990s leading artists like Madonna began to rediscover – Kalra and Hutnyk prefer the term 're-appropriate'[35] – ethnic music, a trend first popularised by the Beatles. At the same time 'Asian Kool's' market appeal was recognised not only by the burgeoning sales in the unofficial charts and the rise of Asian specialist labels such as Multitone, but also by the desire of leading record companies to exploit the new niche market. Thus Sony signed Bally Sagoo for a million-pound record deal, heralding what was claimed as 'the emergence of a new genre of dance music'.[36] Concurrently the explosion of info-entertainment technologies and the emergence of Asian media in Britain and India modelled on channels like MTV – Apache Indian had presented a reggae and travel series for MTV – created a new space in which the music and the media provided a mutually reinforcing dynamism. Commercial channels like Zee-TV gave extensive programming space to *bhangra*, thereby helping to promote new output and new market rivals. Even official media channels such as the BBC were compelled to accommodate the new demand through the reorganisation of the BBC Asian Network with its specialist music output. But perhaps the biggest boost to *bhangra* has come not from mainstreaming but from the 'Bhangrafication' of Bollywood from the mid-1990s. As Bollywood has restructured itself post-1991 (with the economic liberalisation of India) to become a global player in the entertainment industry, *bhangra* artists from Britain and Punjab have transformed the tempo of Bolly-wood films dramatically and in the process have created the largest creative industry in Punjab, with a vast transnational global network engaged in writing, producing, performing and organising the regular concert circuits. This 'reverse integration' has not gone without criticism. For Kalra for, example, it smacks of old-style colonialism, when artists like Bally Sagoo are shunted off to Bombay while multinational record companies like Sony sell '"homeboy" music back to Asian youth, simultaneously denying while appropriating the music of "Asia"'.[37]

The success of the *bhangra* industry remains a largely undocumented affair thus far, but a more interesting issue has arisen with reference to its impact on Punjab/Sikh identity. If *bhangra* is a more potent social glue between Sikh generations, what has been its impact on identity/cultural transmission?

At one end of the spectrum there is the commonsense interpretation that *bhangra* is reinventing Punjabi tradition in a modernised form. For most parents *bhangra*'s unexpected success represents a renewal of the cultural heritage, enduring testimony to the permanent exuberance of Punjabi character, those cherished values of cultural particularity that distinguish Punjabis from 'other' Indians. An anthropologist interpreting the phenomenon in late 1980s west London was effusive in his recognition of the cultural importance of the music. For him, the texts of *bhangra* songs are

> celebratory in tone, and can focus on the beauties of the harvest season, on natural and human beauty, and the range of, usually male, sentiments about attraction, companionship, friendship and love.[38]

This reinvention was the outcome of multiple influences from Punjab, East Africa and Afro-Caribbean musicians in the inner city, resulting in different styles such as the '*bhangra* beat', 'rock *bhangra*', 'house *bhangra*' and 'ragga *bhangra*'. Underpinning the music, however, was a form of lyrical realism firmly rooted in the Punjabi heritage. Taken in this vein, according to Baumann, *bhangra*, far from marking a radical departure, actually *reinforced* many of the pre-existing traits of Punjabi/ Sikh identity. This point is borne out in most of the lyrics and songs. As Malkit Singh, the lead singer of Golden Star, laments in one of his most popular works:

> I dreamed of my homeland, my Punjab, last night
> Of its fields, the rivers
> My friends there and my love for all of them
> In this strange land, happiness eludes me
> Cos' I miss my Punjab,
> The land, that is surely mine.[39]

At the other extreme are those for whom the complex influences on contemporary *bangra* are emblematic of a deep social hybridity that has been melding within the inner city and has been accentuated by globalisation. In direct contradiction of the dominant discourse on Sikh identity pervading the narratives of Sikh settlement in Britain, *bhangra*'s hybridity has been highlighted because it transcends the former's narrow and particularistic boundaries, inscribed as they are by caste, language, gender and community. Many *bhangra* bands have sought to overcome these limits with their lyrics 'presenting a forceful critique of issues such as drugs, AIDS and the dowry system'.[40] The free flow of Punjabi and English lyrics, and of different musical styles, it is argued, marks a distinctive turn in social hybridity. Back offers this comment on the collaboration of reggae singer Maxi Priest with Apache Indian on a tune that successfully entered the mainstream charts:

> The tune constituted an extraordinary historic moment because not only did Apache Indian perform in his combination style but Maxi Priest sang part of the lyrics in Punjabi, taking the motif of cultural translation to new heights.[41]

For Back this 'cultural translation' is a symptom of wider evidence of hybrid social identities manifested in everyday patterns of consumption, leisure and entertainment. Considered in this way, Punjabi/Sikh identity is as prone to social fragmentation and reinvention as other identities.

Back's optimistic reading, however, is not shared by Kalra, who detects through a realist reading of *bhangra* lyrics an 'ethnicisation' project in which particularism and continuation of tradition are all too evident in the output of contemporary artists. Kalra recognises that these lyrics express 'the motions and nuances of diaspora', but for him they can also 'work to inspire political change' and draw attention to the 'marginalisation of women's voices'.[42] The output *reflects* rather than *reinvents* the existing dimensions of Punjabi/Sikh social identity, drawing attention to the sense of loss and memory of the homeland as well as highlighting, for example, a political radicalism that links Punjabis to the anti-colonial struggle (through iconic reference points such as Udham Singh Shahid). Women are conspicuous by their absence, and effectively *giddha*, the female equivalent of *banghra,* has been marginalised. Indeed:

> In conventional Bhangra texts, women tend to appear as fit and fashionable temptresses to be watched, teased, commented upon and owned; e.g. *goriye* (fair one), *soniye* (pretty one), *ni zara nach kurye* (do a little dance, girlie), *shakeenan* (fashionable women), *disco wichari, fashion di maari* (fashion-obsessed disco queen). This is quite different from the whore/wife dichotomies some might find in Black rap, for instance, but inevitably is similar in that the representation of women is stereotypical and of limited focus.[43]

Such representations of women are common. The only exception seems to be Mohinder Kaur Bhamra, a female singer who has consistently presented a woman's viewpoint on a range of issues. In one such song she advises:

Don't come to *vilayet*, girlfriend
Working on the shifts has stripped my good looks
There's no one to give me any consolation
I wash my face with tears, who should I cry to?
[the man] who married me and brought me here on a lie
Don't come to England, girlfriend.[44]

In general, perhaps, the most complex cultural studies' explanations of *bhangra* overlook the most obvious: that it is merely the adaptation of traditional folk music to new mediums of communication. As such, *bhangra*'s limitations – all too obvious in the inane banality of most of the lyrics – need to be contrasted with its achievements as representing a radically new musical genre. Like new patterns of consumption, music might well provide the basis of new social identities, but it is necessary to question further how young British Sikhs themselves define their social identification.

Youth Culture

The debate around the significance of *bhangra* clearly intersects with a broader understanding of Sikh youth culture. Current scholarship has gone beyond the narrow fixation with Sikh youth being 'trapped between two cultures', but the existences of multiple identities between the 'home' and the 'world', defined by other things such as consumption and lifestyles, has raised the issue of whether religious identity is still paramount and where, if at all, it is located in the self-identification of Sikh youth.[45]

In one example the tensions within Sikh/Punjabi identity found a familiar expression in the emergence of a gang culture in Southall and elsewhere. In the mid-1980s, against the background of anti-racism and the rise of the Khalistani movement, Southall witnessed the emergence of two gangs: the Holy Smokes and Tuti Nangs. These gangs achieved considerable national notoriety when a Channel Four documentary accused them of being engaged in international criminal organisations, rapes, drug dealing, petty crimes and 'protection rackets'.[46] The documentary claimed that Southall was held in a 'grip of fear' by these two gangs, who recruited among local school pupils, some of them as young as 11 or 12. Although the gangs were very much an expression of juvenile delinquency, what distinguished them was that they were divided along *caste* lines. The Holy Smokes were mainly Jat-dominated and identified with the militant Khalistan movement that had a substantial following in Southall. The Tuti Nangs, on the other hand, were far more mixed, perhaps reflecting the local caste and ethnic diversity. Religious identification was important in the imagery of the gangs; caste divisions, however, were pre-eminent as markers of militancy.[47]

Studies of Sikh school pupils have also highlighted how Sikh children engage in daily acts of cultural translation by appropriating the 'multiple (situational) identities' in their own ways to better negotiate contradictions between 'home' and 'world'.[48] Gillespie, in her detailed research on media consumption among Sikh youth in Southall, noted how family viewing, especially of popular soaps and Indian media, both challenged and reaffirmed parental ideas of tradition in the eyes of their children. Whereas parents often encouraged the consumption of Indian media in the belief that it would reinforce traditional values, Sikh children were inclined to deconstruct popular genres to meet their own needs of living in a multicultural society and a racist locality.[49]

For Hall, Sikh youth 'participate in a number of cultural fields in which they "act Indian" or "act English"'.[50] These cultural fields include those that are 'highly regulated' (the gurdwaras, home, family life), where expectations of normative behaviour prevail, and those that are 'relatively unregulated' (school, work, consumption) where the youth have the opportunities to "act English". What emerges from this insight into the 'consciousness of the young people' is how skilfully they negotiate these different fields, often being very 'performative' in the highly regulated cultural fields. The boundaries between 'Indian' and 'English' are, indeed, difficult to cross, but according to Hall these are mediated by class, gender and geography. Sikh teenagers who were most associated with hybrid identities tended to identify themselves as 'working-class', particularly with working-class Afro-Caribbeans, or imagine their futures as being 'English'. British Sikh teenagers, in Hall's summary,

> live their lives between two ideological forces, two invented status communities. But these teenagers possess desires and imaginings and encounter social relations and cultural influences through which they consciously and practically apprehend a world filled with a broader range of possibilities. As they acquire additional life experiences, they deepen their sense of self-awareness and develop forms of self-expression associated with imagined future lives. For those who are choosing the route of social mobility, their journeys are forging a variety of distinctive life paths. On their journeys, they come to know intimately what is gained and what is sacrificed along the road to success.[51]

Indeed, as we have noted elsewhere (see Chapter 8), technological and social change has also mediated the earlier 'clash of cultures'. The new Asian media, with specialist programmes for the young, and the Internet have provided opportunities for Sikh youth to negotiate these dilemmas as well as accessing Sikh tradition outside the definitions of parents and the local gurdwaras. There is a proliferation of discussion groups catering for young Sikhs, with well-organised groups such as the British Organisation of Sikh Students (BOSS) and *ad hoc* forums and chatrooms where the vexed issues of tradition, Sikhism, gender, marriage and freedom are hotly debated.[52] These discussion groups, moreover, tend to be global, to share common concerns and to encourage issue-based activism. The general impact of cyber-socialisation on young Sikhs remains to be fully explored, but we can assume that increasing introspection focused on Sikh identity and the dilemmas facing young Sikhs in developed societies is both consolidating and differentiating pre-existing divisions within the Sikh tradition.

In summarising the fragmentary research reviewed above, it would be reasonable to say that for young British Sikhs, despite the advent of 'multiple (situation) identities', religion remains the important marker of cultural distinction.[53] Among this group religion is viewed as the main differentiator of ethnic identity in Britain today, a development no doubt reinforced by 9/11 and 7/7. Yet if there is a feeling among the older Sikh generations that there is pronounced reluctance among the young to assert Sikh identity positively through such practices as wearing the turban, competence in Punjabi, attendance at gurdwaras and in-marriage, there is equally a feeling among the young that Sikh identity as such does not warrant an outright rejection. This ambivalence in a way reflects the process whereby British Sikh youth are creating their own religio-cultural space and adaptation, an outlook that is open to greater possibilities than were available to their parents. It is also less hidebound by traditions of caste, gender and the dominant discourse of Sikh identity, even when young Sikhs go on to make conservative life choices. There is, as in the case of Manjit in *(Un)arranged Marriage,* a great desire to overcome the limited meaning of the world of their parents so that their lives are more meaningful in a diverse, modern and plural society.

Conclusion

The dominant discourse of Sikh identity in Britain has faced its most difficult challenge in the transmission of community values to younger generations. While the gurdwara movement, as we saw in Chapter 4, has institutionalised this discourse, efforts to extend it more widely, for instance through the development of Punjabi language teaching, have only been partly successful; and though a great deal of effort and energy has been expended in formalising the teaching of Punjabi to the young, this endeavour has had to struggle against the lack of institutional support and declining enthusiasm for the language among young Sikhs themselves, a process hastened by the global rise of English and the expansion of new media and communications technologies catering for the community. Thus while competence in oral Punjabi seems high among British Sikhs, its usage disguises the tremendous changes that have taken place.

The emergence of a Sikh youth culture around the *bhangra* industry illustrates how language and tradition have melded together in a new context to provide a distinctive cultural space for the young. *Bhangra* appears to provide a bridge between the 'old' and the 'young', between Britain and Punjab and between British Sikhs and non-Sikhs. However it is also the inevitable result of the late commodification of Punjabi culture and, in leading this development, British Sikh youth have imposed their own distinctive imprint on a music genre that has global appeal.

Finally, Sikh youth today clearly continue to identify with the religious tradition but this identification is also far more complex and ambiguous than hitherto, vitiated as it is by 'negotiation', searches for other spaces, and sometimes, as we have seen in Chapter 8, a desire to interrogate the dominant discourse of Sikh identity so that contemporary dilemmas, such as the debates over Sikh sexualities, can be satisfactorily addressed. In the absence of more detailed, systematic and comprehensive research in this extremely important area, all conclusions must remain tentative. The culture of young British Sikhs today remains an area of darkness for the community and a testing ground for its uncertain futures.

Conclusion

At the beginning of the twenty-first century Britain is faced with the renewed challenge of managing religious and ethnic diversity, a challenge ever-present in the settlement of minority ethnic communities from the New Commonwealth after 1945 that has assumed a new importance with the onset of globalisation and the aftermath of the tragic events of 9/11 and 7/7. The current backlash against the Muslim community has called into question the gradual evolution of ideological multiculturalism within the public domain, a debate that is generally conducted by employing the language of a 'clash of civilisations' *within* the nation or, more recently within the British establishment, by posing the question, 'Who are we?'[1] The various policy initiatives now planned by the Labour government seem destined to undermine the multicultural settlement precisely at a juncture when, arguably, it stands in need of further consolidation.[2]

In this policy environment it is important to reflect on lessons that can be learnt from the development of non-Muslim communities like the Sikhs. At the height of the domestic opposition to coloured immigration in the 1960s there were two typical responses to the settlement of Sikhs in large numbers. The first, using language not too dissimilar from the current discourses on British Muslims, questioned the possibility of Sikhs ever being able to integrate fully into British society. Writing about the initial Sikh settlement in Gravesend, Selwyn Gummer and John Gummer argued that

> the situation in Gravesend shows quite clearly that the Sikh community is law-abiding only in a restricted sense. Their dealings with outsiders are certainly regulated according to law but within the community house

purchase, rent money lending, women's rights and the punishment of crimes are regulated much more by their own internal rules imposed by the strongest or derived from custom brought over from homeland ... they are strangers in a strange land and they are intellectually and educationally ill-equipped to deal with the complexities of a modern civilisation.[3]

John Gummer subsequently became a close confidant of Margaret Thatcher, a cabinet minister and Chairman of the Conservative Party.

The second response reflected the concerns of the seriously engaged policy analysts commissioned to identify the degree of racial discrimination and policies to combat it. Following a detailed survey, Rose *et al.* were more optimistic about the future development of Sikhs in Britain, notwithstanding the pressures against community building in a very hostile environment. As they noted:

> With so many forces playing upon traditional Sikhism, the way in which these communities will develop is still very open; the direction they will take depends to a large extent on the attitudes and the policies of the British. Positive efforts by the government and by local authorities will be needed to help adolescents to remain within their own culture while feeling at home in the culture of their adopted country.[4]

This analysis eventually informed the policy formation process on 'race relations' of the then Labour government. One of its leading figures, the Home Secretary Roy Jenkins, is credited with formulating the credo of British multiculturalism as not 'a flattening process of uniformity but cultural diversity coupled with equal opportunity in an atmosphere of mutual tolerance'.[5] In retrospect Jenkins's view became the axiomatic statement of the British state's intent to accommodate cultural diversity through an emphasis on equality of opportunity and political integration in the public domain while promoting mutual tolerance as a necessary condition of coexistence where minority cultures could flourish in the private sphere.[6]

In the forty years since Jenkins outlined his vision, the Sikh community has tested, if not expanded, the limits of this framework. As we saw in Chapter 6, successive campaigns over the right to wear turbans, *kirpans* and beards have generated intense debates about the limits of public accommodation of Sikh religious demands; and while conservative opinion has generally been reluctant to make any concessions to such demands, a combination of persistent campaigns and appeals to the Anglo-Sikh heritage has secured for the community a mode of 'negative accommodation', what Barry has called an opt-out from general rule making (see Chapter 6). This 'opt-out' may well reflect the status of Sikhs as a 'favoured community', or their concentration in a number of crucial parliamentary constituencies, but as the recent furore over the play *Behzti* has demonstrated, such an arrangement is unlikely to suffice in the future, with sections of the community calling for 'deep multiculturalism' that goes beyond mere recognition. In this respect, Sikhs have played a crucial role as a bridgehead community which has 'pioneered' British multiculturalism, but in so doing have also expanded its remit to include greater public recognition of the cultures and traditions of other minority ethnic communities.

The history of the community, furthermore, suggests that radical politics is the natural response of most victimised and racialised immigrant groups in the West. For British Sikhs this was marked from the earliest period of their political and social organisations in the inter-war years; it has remained a distinctive feature of the community with the rise of the Communist-led IWAs and their supersession by pro-Khalistan and neo-Khalistan groups. Class has given way to the politics of identity but its substantive element is the same: to make claims on Britishness through forms of identity mobilisation and 'victimhood'. The more radical and anti-British that Sikh organisations have been over the last sixty years, the more they have articulated the genuine grievances of the community. Sikh organisations therefore share the common traits of other minority ethnic organisations that have naturally gravitated towards radical, anti- and post-colonial movements.

The third key lesson that has to be noted is that community development over time is marked not only by community consolidation: core values are not only reaffirmed in a new environment, but also change as they are reinterpreted and adapted to new circumstances. As a relatively small community, British Sikhs have shown a remarkable capacity for adaptation as reflected in changes in the gurdwara, the family and the workplace, and at the interface with wider social and economic currents. To be sure, these changes (as we shall see below) have introduced sharp disjunctions within British Sikh society. Yet what is distinctive is the nature of these changes, the relative ease with which Sikh identities have been accommodated and coexist in a British society increasingly marked by hyper-diversity. Although the state has doubtless played a critical role in *making* the community by, among other things, giving recognition to the dominant discourse of Sikhism as it did in the *Mandla v. Dowell Lee* judgement, this intervention has not undermined a religiously plural and socially diverse community, a condition further reinforced by the autonomous development of Sikh subgroups. In other words, the recognition of religious identity by the state is no guarantee of communal cohesion.

In fact in some circumstances it may well accentuate existing schisms and sectarianism.

There are, of course, a number of major differences in how British Sikhs and Muslims and other minority ethnic communities are perceived, and these differences will continue to influence the future fortunes of the community. Perhaps the most important of these is that since the demise of the Khalistan movement, which provided a critical moment in the evolution of the self-consciousness of the community in Britain, there is no longer a major source of conflict between the British state and Sikhs. As we saw in Chapter 5, from 1984 to the mid-1990s the rise of the Khalistan movement led to an uncomfortable period in Anglo-Sikh relations when the organised Sikh lobby sought to influence British foreign policy against India while domestically challenging the writ of the government in anti-terrorist cases and human rights appeals. A residual element of this movement survives, but its influence is greatly diminished, despite its efforts to mobilise support around new modes of 'victimhood' emanating from anti-terrorist policies since 9/11 and 7/7. The neo-Khalistan movement retains a potential for revival, particularly if another 'critical event' like the storming of the Golden Temple in 1984 overtakes the community. Barring such an eventuality, however, the political interests of the Sikh community are unlikely to be seriously at variance with the interests of the British state and may actually intersect with these in the near future.

India's economic development and the peace process with Pakistan, for instance, are beginning to create a new architecture for peace in South Asia, and in this development, overseen by the Sikh prime minister of India, Dr Manmohan Singh, both the global Sikh diaspora and Indian Sikhs face new opportunities and challenges that require a broader vision than narrow territorial nationalism. This process is also likely to be hastened by the rapidly increasing Anglo-Indian trade, which is already offering opportunities for British Sikhs (along with other non-resident Indians) to exploit the emerging markets as well as acting as brokers for the British economy. As the broad Sikh diaspora increasingly comes to reflect concerns similar to those of non-resident Indians, there are reasonable prospects that it will become a part of the virtuous cycle of growth involving British trade and development in India.[7] To what extent the British element of this diaspora will fulfil this role will be determined primarily by the policies of the Indian government, especially in Punjab where the state government has lagged well behind in framing an environment to attract non-resident Indian investment.[8]

Plate 10 Her Majesty Queen Elizabeth II during a visit to the Guru Nanak Gurdwara, Holy Bones, Leicester, August 2002. (Reproduced with permission of Leicester Mercury.)

Another crucial difference between British Muslims and Sikhs is that the latter are sometimes viewed as the 'favoured community'. This understanding has been implied by non-Sikh ethnic minorities,[9] and it has more than a grain of truth in it. The link with the British monarchy dating from Duleep Singh's entry into Queen Victoria's court is an enduring symbolic bond. It assumed a renewed vigour from the early 1990s when it was popularly revived to commemorate the centenary of Duleep Singh's death with the establishment of a trust dedicated to promoting the Anglo-Sikh heritage. This revival coincided with a serious strain in Indo-British relations (caused by the Khalistan movement) and the enthusiastic welcome given to the Queen by Sikhs during her visit to the Golden Temple in 1997 to mark the fiftieth anniversary of the partition of India. The sense that there is a 'special relationship' between the monarchy and the Sikhs is today best articulated in the concern and interest in the community's fortunes shown by Prince Charles in recent years. He has patronised Sikh institutions and even floated the idea of the establishment of a Sikh regiment in the British Army.[10] This rekindling of royal interest in Sikh tradition and culture could well be interpreted as the modern-day manifestation of the

Victorian interest in the 'model colonised community', now reflected as the 'model multicultural community'. Such a simplistic misreading, however, would seriously overlook how new loyalties and identities are being re-imagined and refashioned in contemporary Britain.

Beyond the monarchy the Sikhs have always been able to count on a sympathetic hearing within the military establishment. This link proved critical in support of many of the turban campaigns, and has been assiduously nurtured by associations of retired Sikh veterans who fought in the two World Wars. In the last decade it has been further strengthened by participation in the annual Remembrance Day parade, the establishment of a memorial dedicated to Indian soldiers, and a more reflective assessment of Britain's imperial army. This most demonstrable act of 'loyalty' has doubtless contributed over the years to enhancing the community's social capital with the British state, but whether this relationship will endure depends mainly on how it is re-imagined and reinvented beyond the lifetimes of existing veterans.

Finally, perhaps because of its earlier settlement, the Sikh community seems to have achieved a greater degree of social integration into wider British society than Muslims. One of the reasons for this is that the initial leadership of the IWAs from the 1950s onwards actively encouraged integration into working-class life as part of the general mission of building a class movement. Although as we saw in Chapter 7 such efforts were not welcomed very enthusiastically by the institutions of the Labour movement, Sikhs readily adopted many of the popular habits. As Sandhu, the chief protagonist in *Behzti*, observes,

> since its arrival, spanning the last forty years, the Sikh community has played an important role.... Our principles of hard work, humility, family values, coupled with our integrationalist attitude ... for example going down the pub ... have stood us in good stead.[11]

Indeed, in the 1950s and 1960s the pub became the quintessential icon of Sikh British culture, a legacy that is still symbolised in Southall's 'Glassy Junction' which combines the ambience of rural Punjab with a traditional public house.[12] This kind of melding between popular British culture and Sikh culture has been further highlighted by films such as *Bend It Like Beckham*, television series such as *Goodness Gracious Me!* and *Meet the Magoons*, and the unprecedented growth of *bhangra* music. It is also reflected in the Sikh love of sports, best epitomised by Fujja Singh, the 93-year-old marathon runner who has become an international celebrity. At a more serious level a reflective approach to British identity since the early 1990s, together with the emergence of the inter-faith movement, has provided creative spaces for individuals like Indarjit Singh, editor of the *Sikh Messenger*, to establish a wider understanding of Sikhs and Sikhism within the British establishment. Indarjit Singh's soft-spoken contributions to BBC Radio Four's 'Thought for the Day' have greatly enhanced the idiomatic translation of Sikhism for British and international audiences. His consistent emphasis on the modernism of Sikh values of equality, democracy and respect for others has struck a responsive chord within British public culture, to a point where prime ministers and princes feel comfortable in appropriating Sikh values as British values.[13]

These distinctive characteristics are further underpinned by secular trends within the community itself: 56.1 per cent of Sikhs are now British-born, with the proportion of those from India in rapid decline. British-born Sikhs, as we saw in Chapter 8, are better educated than non-British-born, show a higher degree of association with British identity, and have been at the forefront of representation within political and social institutions. They are also far more comfortable with contemporary social values that embrace gender and sexual equality as well as the need to be more self-reflective about one's own tradition. They, more than any other group within the community, appear to have fulfilled Khushwant Singh's hope, expressed in the late 1970s, that the time has come when a Sikh can say with pride, 'I'm a Sikh; I am an Englishman.'[14]

Although British-born Sikhs are likely to be the main drivers of the community's fortunes in the future, the extent to which they will shape a vision different from one defined by the early Punjab settlers remains to be seen. Deculturalisation, assimilation and denaturing provide no certainties that the Anglo-Sikh relationship will avoid turbulent phases in the future, and in this respect the life of Duleep Singh in the nineteenth century still provides a haunting reminder that the strongest professions of loyalty remain tempered with an acute awareness of the community's own interest. Citing a statement that has become the defining principle of the Sikh place in Britain, many contemporary Sikhs point to the rejection by Duleep Singh of an offer by Queen Victoria of peerages for his sons, Victor Albert and Frederick. He gave the following reason for his refusal:

> I thank Her Majesty most heartily and humbly and convey to her my esteem, affection and admiration. Beyond that I cannot go. I claim myself to be royal; I am not English, and neither I nor my children will ever become so. Such titles – though kindly offered – we do not need and

cannot assume. We love the English and especially their monarch, *but we must remain Sikhs*.[15]

Duleep Singh's reply, and subsequent rebellion against the *raj*, it is argued, demonstrate that British Sikh loyalty to the state and the monarchy is very much contingent upon the community's ideals and values not being transgressed or, as in the case of Operation Blue Star in 1984 and the play *Behzti*, compromised in the greater interests of the state and ideals such as freedom of expression. The roots of potential dissent are therefore implicit in the existence of British Sikhs as a moral and religious community; any serious violation of these ideals could easily give rise to a political Sikhism in the style of the Khalistan movement, whatever the degree of integration.

While the possibilities of such a development in the immediate future run against the grain of the changes noted above, it is necessary to remember that there is a large section of the community that does not share in the achievements of the British-born. This section, as we saw in Chapter 8, struggles to perform in the education and labour markets, is concentrated in the 'Little Punjabs', and suffers from the kind of socio-economic disadvantage identified with large sections of the Muslim community. Made up of residual members of the old industrial working class and new migrants from Punjab, it also has a political and social outlook best typified by the readers of *Des Pardes*, with its mixture of Sikh nationalism, industrial militancy (recently highlighted by the Gate Gourmet strike) and opposition to immigration policies that restrict exchanges with Punjab. Intimately interwoven into the Sikh cultural and religious economy in the inner cities, the *Des Pardes* wallahs have traditionally provided the community's leadership and remain exceptionally sensitive to developments in Punjab. Their institutional control of gurdwaras, moreover, gives them access to exceptional resources to continually replenish these ideals while perpetuating what Ballard has called a form of 'backward integration'.[16] They remain, in Axel's words, '"primitive peoples" positioned within modernity'[17] whose ideals and values have changed little, if at all, from the mid-twentieth-century Punjabi village, thereby placing them at odds both with Punjabi society in India itself and with the emerging culture of young British Sikhs.

It is the dominance of the first generation of Punjabi settlers in the leadership of the community that is generally seen as the cause of the serious failure to establish enduring institutions that could have articulated its interests better, if not replicated the trajectory of other communities such as the British Jews. Apart from the gurdwara movement and the political and social organisations tied to this central hub, British Sikhs have evolved few national institutions that command legitimacy, and most of these have been undermined regularly by factionalism, internecine conflicts and leadership struggles. Recent efforts to establish a British Sikh Consultative Forum illustrate the difficulties of cooperation among Sikh organisations like the Network of Sikh Organisations, Sikh Human Rights Group, Guru Nanak Nishkam Sewak Jatha and the Sikh Federation (UK) that have some degree of support beyond their immediate locality but cannot command broader legitimacy within the community. Intense rivalry between these organisations for 'who represents the Sikhs' militates against the establishment of an institutional hierarchy and enables the British state to produce policy outcomes that are consonant with what it sees as the demands of governance and the interests of the community. Thus an innate pluralism within the Sikh community tends to buttress pragmatic British statecraft that seeks to 'manage' it by encouraging the evolution of a 'moderate' leadership, the marginalisation of radicals (like the Sikh Federation (UK)), and the production of policy outcomes desired by the state.

British Sikh responses to the failures of institution building by the community itself take three forms. The first is that the Sikhs are largely a 'self-fulfilled', decentralised, 'republican' community, which, with the exception of a few dress code issues, has adapted well to the British way of life.[18] As such they do not need to extend beyond their immediate and local concerns, which are largely satisfied by the community's own local institutions. It is only when issues of honour and interest arise – for example, over turbans, *kirpans* and 1984 – that there is a need for a national response, and this can best be met by single-issue mobilisation, which has been perfected into an art form. The idea of an autonomous, 'self-fulfilled' community chimes both with the historical mode of federal Sikh organisations as *misls* and its inherent pluralism, which is reflected in the gurdwara movement, subgroups and castes.

The second response is more sociological and argues that the main Jat middle- and poor-peasant Doabian profile of the community has shackled its imagination. In the late 1960s, Pettigrew reported how visions of general community development among the newly arrived immigrants from Punjab were mainly confined to immediate concerns.[19] This social profile preserved the community's values, enabling it to generate a reactive response to 1984 in the form of the Khalistan movement, as a modern-day jacquerie against the Indian state, with support for the movement repackaged as a form of 'social remittance'. However, it was unable to go beyond those norms and values rooted in rural Punjab that were also, paradoxically, antithetical to the idea of a Sikh homeland itself.[20] Only with the arrival of non-Jat Sikhs from East Africa and South East Asia and the active mobilisation of urban British Sikhs, who traditionally have been the custodians of the community's fortunes, has some meaningful progress been made in building structures and institutions. The British Sikh community thus lags well behind its professionalised brethren in the United States, and the prospects of its assuming the leadership of the Sikh diaspora remain bleak.[21]

The third response, which is now articulated by the young British-educated Sikhs, draws heavily on critical theory in re-evaluating the post-Khalistan, post-9/11 and post-7/7 worlds.[22] Arising from radical introspection into the Sikh condition both in Britain and Punjab, it argues that conventional accounts of the failure of institution building provide an unhelpful guide to contemporary dilemmas. Sikhs, it is contended, are 'deconstructionists' by instinct and practice, and such Western-styled institutions and hierarchy cannot be imposed on them nor expected of them. Accordingly, in Britain they have built the institutions 'they know' and 'can control' because previous institution-building efforts were undermined by IWA secularists and assimilationist leaders. While some leaders, it is claimed, have responded to the pressures of the dominant discourse of the church, hierarchy and state institutions by attempting to project a form of 'Anglo-Sikhism' that is suitably 'idiomatic', 'reformed', or 'universally insightful' for contemporary concerns, this development does not probe the 'unconscious translation' of the Sikh tradition into the dominant discourse which has been ongoing *since* the colonial encounter and the Singh Sabha movement. Today this process has run its course with the ethnocidal politics of the Khalistan movement and the guidance it provides to the post-modern, post-colonial and globalised condition in which the community finds itself is too inflexible to generate meaningful responses to issues such as sexualities, bio-ethics and the Sikhs' place in the post-nationalist world. Consequently, there are three options before the community: to reassert the dominant discourse of Sikh identity; to adopt a neo-modern form of 'Anglo-Sikhism', with its Western definitions of Sikh institutions and culture; or to revert to a contextual Sikhism where an understanding of Sikh scriptures as a guide is mediated by values more approximate to the teaching of the gurus. Only the latter offers any serious hope for the spiritual revival of Sikhism; it may also enable the British Sikhs to spearhead the Sikh diaspora by cutting, once and for all, the intellectual umbilical cord with the British colonial heritage.

Which option the British Sikh community will take in the future will be determined mainly by the outcome of the struggle within it between the British-born and non-British-born generations. The former have long-term trends on their side and are more able and at ease with British institutions. For them Punjab increasingly resembles a 'distant holy land' (of religious places) 'pleasure' (holidays, marriages and *bhangra*) and 'pain' (of extended and family obligations), but not a 'homeland' that can command their futures. Their vision of future society has been nurtured on cultural and religious diversity in contemporary Britain, where they, like many other minority ethnic communities, appear to belong nowhere but actually belong everywhere. Yet this vision runs across the stubborn and unyielding outlook of the Punjab-born Sikhs who still control the political and religious economy of the community and show little sign of divesting themselves of these powers or of moving away from neo-orthodoxy. The growing dissonance within the community between the young and the old, the British-born and the Punjab-born, the educated and the uneducated, might well give birth to a new reform movement to realign British Sikh institutions to the needs of new generations. There are some signs that these processes are already in motion at the margins. Neo-orthodoxy might well be in power, but it is increasingly disengaged from the daily lives of most Sikhs.[23]

In one sense, however, this struggle is unlikely to be simply an inter-generational one. It will be structured against the broader background of Sikhs as a global community with global concerns. As a small religious community Sikhs in Britain and elsewhere are always prone to the effects of a 'critical event' like 1984, a periodic tsunami that restructures the political and social outlook of the community. Such a reoccurrence cannot be ruled out. At the same time, diaspora Sikh communities like the British Sikhs are now far more able to deal with such potential 'waves' than ever before. They have also, through their own upheavals, educated the British state to be far more sensitive than hitherto to their transnational needs.

Almost a century and a half after Duleep Singh first appeared at Queen Victoria's court, a British Sikh community has come into being. It is a community that has been self-consciously made by the choices of Sikh migrants themselves and their interaction with wider British society since the Second World War. Despite being so long at the heart of the 'motherland', it has taken time to mature, to establish a distinctive autonomy from its 'colonialised self'. Of all the Sikhs in the diaspora, it is the British who have gone through the most intimate process of self-discovery as post-colonial people. Today they are faced with a stark choice between a historical, imperial and neo-modern past and plural, cosmopolitan futures.[24] The choice they make will have profound consequences for Sikhs all over the globe.

Notes

Introduction

1 *Times*, 3 April 2004.
2 *Guardian*, 5 August 2005.
3 National Statistics Online, accessed 4 September 2005.
4 Tiryakian makes a useful distinction between demographic and ideological multiculturalism. Whereas the former is an empirical condition to be found in most societies, the latter refers to public policies designed to overcome 'institutional arrangements of the public sphere that are seen as injuring or depriving a cultural minority of its rights'. Edward A. Tiryakian, 'Assessing Multiculturalism Theoretically: *E Pluribus Unum, Sic et Non'*, in John Rex and Gurharpal Singh, eds., *Governance in Multicultural Societies* (Aldershot: Ashgate, 2003), 9.
5 Runnymede Trust, *The Future of Multi-Ethnic Britain: the Parekh Report* (London: Profile Books, 2000), 9.
6 See Samuel P. Huntington, *The Clash of Civilisations and the Remaking of World Order* (London: Simon and Schuster, 1997).
7 See contributors to a new journal, *Sikh Formations*, 1: 1 (2005), 1–154, and Christopher Shackle, Gurharpal Singh and Arvind-pal S. Mandair eds., *Sikh Religion, Culture and Ethnicity* (Richmond: Curzon, 2001).
8 For a survey of this literature see Darshan S. Tatla and Eleanor M. Nesbitt, *Sikhs in Britain: an Annotated Bibliography* (University of Warwick: Centre for Research in Ethnic Relations, second edition,1994).
9 Among these are Arthur W. Helweg, *Sikhs in England* (Delhi: Oxford University Press, 1986, second edition) which is a study of Sikhs in Gravesend; Sewa Singh Kalsi, *The Evolution of a Sikh Community in Britain* (Leeds: University of Leeds, 1992), which has as its subtitle 'Religious and Social Change among Sikhs of Leeds and Bradford'; Raminder Singh, *Sikhs and Sikhism in Britain – Fifty Years On: the Bradford Perspective* (Bradford: Bradford Arts, Museums and Library Service, 2000).
10 Only now, as many of the first-generation migrants pass away, is the oral history of Britain's non-white communities being taken seriously. We have drawn on

several local projects – Leicester, Coventry and Manchester – as well as our own extensive links with the community.

11   For further insights into some of the methodological issues involved see Bhikhu Parekh, Gurharpal Singh and Steven Vertovec, eds., *Cultural and Economy in the Indian Diaspora* (London: Routledge, 2003).

12   See Shackle *et al.*, *Sikh Religion, Culture and Ethnicity* and Pal Aluwhalia, Arvind-Pal S. Mandair and Gurharpal Singh, 'The *Subject* of Sikh Studies', *Sikh Formations*, 1: 1 (2005), 1–11.

13   The Punjab Research Group was founded by some of us as a response to the on-going 'Punjab Crisis' in the early 1980s. It functioned regularly until the late 1990s and produced over 100 discussion papers as well serving as a forum for young and established scholars on Punjab Studies.

14   The *International Journal of Punjab Studies* was published by Sage. It is now the in-house publication of the Centre for Punjab and Sikh Studies at the University of California, Santa Barbara.

15   See Darshan S. Tatla, *The Sikh Diaspora: the Search for Statehood* (London: UCL Press, 1999).

16   See Shackle *et al.*, *Sikh Religion, Culture and Ethnicity*.

17   Many of the founders of the Punjab Research Group and the *International Journal of Punjab Studies* are now the driving force of the new journal.

Chapter 1

1   See Darshan Singh Tatla, *The Sikh Diaspora: the Search for Statehood* (London: UCL Press, 1999).

2   Joyce Pettigrew, *Robber Noblemen: a Study of the Political System of Sikh Jats* (London: Routledge and Keegan Paul, 1975), 32.

3   Joyce Pettigrew, 'Take not Arms Against thy Sovereign: the Present Punjab Crisis and the Storming of the Golden Temple', *South Asia Research*, 4: 2 (1984), 102.

4   Danzil Ibbetson, *Punjab Castes* (Delhi: BR Publishing Corporation, 1974), 14.

5   See Richard C. Temple, *Legends of the Punjab* (London: Tribner, 1983).

6   For a discussion of this see W. H. McLeod, *Guru Nanak and the Sikh Religion* (Oxford: Oxford University Press, 1968).

7   Christopher Shackle, *The Sikhs* (London: Minority Rights Group Report, 1985, No. 65), 3.

8   Gurharpal Singh, 'Sikhism', *Encarta* (2002).

9   Singh, 'Sikhism'.

10   See W. H. McLeod, *The Sikhs: History, Religion and Society* (New York: Columbia University Press), Chapter 3.

11   McLeod, *Sikhs*, Chapter 3.

12   J. S. Grewal, *The Sikhs of Punjab* (Cambridge: Cambridge University Press, 1990), 93.

13   Grewal, *Sikhs,* 113.

14   Grewal, *Sikh*, 114–15.

15   Grewal, *Sikhs*, 118.

16   Kushwant Singh, *A History of the Sikhs, Vol. 2: 1839–1988* (Delhi: Oxford University Press, 1991), 119, 160.

17   See Richard Fox, *The Lions of Punjab: Culture in the Making* (Berkeley: University of California Press, 1985), 10.

18   See Imran Ali, *The Punjab under Imperialism, 1885–1947* (Princeton: Princeton University Press, 1988).

19   See McLeod, *The Sikh,* Chapter 3; Harjot Oberoi, *The Construction of Religious Boundaries: Culture, Identity and Diversity within the Sikh Tradition* (Delhi: Oxford University Press, 1994); Christopher Shackle, 'Sikhism', in Linda Woodhead, *et al., Religions in the Modern World: Tradition and Transformations* (London: Routledge, 2002), 70–85.

20   For a further discussion of this see McLeod, *The Sikhs*, chapters 3 and 5; and Oberoi, *Construction.*

21   Gerwal, *Sikhs,* 162.

22   See P. Wallace, 'Religious and Secular Politics in Punjab: The Sikh Dilemma in Competing Political Systems', in Paul Wallace and Surendra Chopra, eds., *Political Dynamics of Punjab* (Amritsar: Guru Nanak Dev University Press, 1983), 1–32.

23   McLeod, *The Sikhs,* 79. For clarity and standardisation this section has drawn upon the categories employed by Gerwal and McLeod. The latter's point about *patit Sikh* as a more appropriate designation for *mona-Singhs* is acknowledged, but for sociological reasons it is necessary to recognise that the *mona-Singhs*, especially those in the diaspora, are closer to the Sikh mainstream than traditional *sahaj-dharis*.

24   Baldev Raj Nayar, *Minority Politics in the Punjab* (New Jersey: Princeton University Press, 1966), 86

25   Gurharpal Singh, 'The Communist Party of India and the Demand for a Sikh Homeland, 1942–1947', *Indo-British Review,* (April 1994), 89–95.

26   Quoted in Singh, *A History,* Vol. 2, 291.

27   Gerwal, *Sikhs,* 180.

28   *Economic Survey, 1988–89* (Chandigarh: Economic Adviser to Punjab Government), 59.

29   *Economic Survey,* 3.

30   See Robin Jeffrey, *What's Happening to India? Punjab, Ethnic Conflict, Mrs Gandhi's Death and the Test for Federalism* (Basingstoke: Macmillan, 1986), 8.

31   See Jeffery, *What's Happening.*

32   Gurharpal Singh, *Ethnic Conflict in India: a Case Study of Punjab* (Basingstoke: Macmillan, 2000), 96.

33   Singh, *Ethnic Conflict,* chapters 8–10.

34   Paul R. Brass, *Language, Religion and Politics in North India* (Cambridge: Cambridge University Press, 1974), 277.

Chapter 2

1   See Joyce J. M. Chaudhri (née Pettigrew), *The Emigration of Sikh Jats from the Punjab to England* (SSRC Project HR331/1, Final Report, 1971). On a lighter

note, see Bali Rai, *(Un)arranged Marriage* (London: Corgi Books, 2001).

2   The issue of caste in Sikh society is a source of intense disagreement among scholars. For some, 'the Sikh community officially and in its system of official beliefs repudiates the concept of caste [and] shows no recognition of the concept of hierarchy as such' (Joyce Pettigrew, *Robber Noblemen: a Study of the Political System of Sikh Jats* (London: Routledge & Kegan Paul, 1975), 45). For Ethne K. Marenco (*The Transformation of Sikh Society*, Portland: Hapi Press, 1976), the Sikh caste hierarchy is significantly at variance with the classic Hindu varna system. W. H. McLeod (*The Sikhs: History, Religion and Society*, New York: Columbia University Press, 1989) suggests that a clear distinction between the normative injunction against caste in the Sikh tradition and actual practice has to be balanced with the possibility that the Sikh gurus' teaching was aimed primarily at the *discriminatory* attributes of caste. See Chapter 5.

3   See Pettigrew, *Robber Noblemen* for a classic study of Jats.

4   Arthur W. Helweg, *Sikhs in England* (Delhi: Oxford University Press, second edition 1986), 7.

5   See Parminder Bhachu, *Twice Migrants: East African Sikh Settlers in Britain* (London: Tavistock, 1985).

6   See Mark Juergensmeyer, 'Political Origins of a Punjabi Lower Caste Religion', *Punjab Journal of Politics*, 5:1 (1981),157–78 and *Religious Rebels in the Punjab: the Social Vision of Untouchables* (Delhi: Ajanta, 1988); S. L. Malhotra, 'Hindu Politics and Untouchability in Punjab, 1900–35', *The Social Science Research Journal*, 1: 1 (1976), 74-88; Surinder S. Jodhka, 'Caste Tensions in Punjab: Talhan and Beyond', *Economic and Political Weekly* (12 July 2003), 2923–6 and 'Prejudice without Pollution? Scheduled Castes in Contemporary Punjab', *Journal of Indian School of Political Economy*, 12: 3–4, 381–402; and Ronki Ram, 'Untouchability, Dalit Consciousness, and the Ad Dharm Movement in Punjab', *Contributions to Indian Sociology* 38: 3 (2004), 323-49.

7   Pettigrew, *Robber Noblemen*, 58–9; P. Hershman, *Punjabi Kinship and Marriage* (Delhi: Hindustan Publishing Corporation, 1981).

8   See A. Alavi, 'Kinship in West Punjab Villages', *Contributions to Indian Sociology*, 6 (1972), 57-89; Roger Ballard, 'South Asian Families: Structure and Process', in R N. Rapport, M. P. Fogarty and R. Rapport, eds., *Families in Britain* (London: Routledge, 1982), 174-204; and Tom G. Kessinger, *Vilayatpur, 1848–1968: Social and Economic Change in a North Indian Village* (Berkeley: University of California Press, 1974).

9   Helweg, *Sikhs in England*, Chapter 2.

10   Pettigrew, *Robber Noblemen*, 19.

11   Gurharpal Singh, *Communism in Punjab: a Study of the Movement up to 1967* (Delhi: Ajanta, 1994).

12   This is discussed in detail in chapters 4 and 5.

13   In the pre-1947 period most villages had Sikhs, Muslims and Hindus living side by side. For a picture of pre-1947 rural social life see Prakash Tandon, *Punjabi Century: 1857–1947* (Berkeley: University of California Press, 1968).

14   Pettigrew, *Robber Nobleman*, 24

15   Nahar Singh, *Malve de Lok Geet* (Patiala: Punjabi University Press, 1987–89), 3

vols. There is a rich tradition of folksongs relating to migration. Many revolve
around the theme of separation of a husband who is going to be away for
employment and his lamenting wife. Employment during colonial times was
usually in the form of recruitment into the army. Thus the song starts with a
wife's lament:

je toon turiyon noukr (if you are going away for employment)
mainv thaan vasangi kehrhe (where will I stay?)
Noukra ve main thaan vasan gi kehrhe (Tell me, o government's servant, what place will
be my home?)
To this lament the husband replies:
If there was enough work at home, why would I leave you
Be brave, I will send you money to build a double-storey house for you to dwell in.

16   W. H. McLeod, *Punjabis in New Zealand* (Amritsar: Guru Nanak University
      Press, 1986); Kernial Singh Sandhu, *Indians in Malaya* (Cambridge University
      Press, 1969).

17   For a comprehensive history of Indian migration, see Hugh Tinker, *A New
      System of Slavery: the Export of Indian Labour Overseas, 1830–1920* (London:
      Oxford University Press, 1974), *Separate and Unequal* (London: Hurst, 1976)
      and *The Banyan Tree: Overseas Emigration from India, Pakistan and Bangladesh*
      (London: Oxford University Press, 1977).

18   For East Africa, see M. F. Hill, *Permanent Way: the Story of Kenya and Uganda
      Railway* (Nairobi: East African Literatures Bureau, 1949); J. S. Mangat, *A
      History of Asians in East Africa* (Oxford University Press, 1969); M. S. Sidhu,
      Sikhs in Kenya (Chandigarh: Punjab University Press, n.d.); and Bhachu, *Twice
      Migrants*.

19   'Sikhs', writes Hugh Tinker , 'were an unusual group in the India migration:
      they were prepared to fight for their rights. The mass of the poor labourers
      mainly from Madras, and the traders and shopkeepers from Gujarat, who
      formed the bulk of the emigrants were not prepared or organised for struggle',
      Separate and Unequal, 29.

20   Bruce La Brack, *The Sikhs of California, 1904–1986* (New York: AMS Press,
      1988). Hugh Johnston, *The Voyage of Komagata Maru: the Sikh Challenge to
      Canada's Colour Bar* (Delhi: Oxford University Press, 1979). Both Canada and
      the United States reversed their earlier restrictive policies on Asian immigration
      in the 1940s. In the US, the Lucy-Cellar Bill (Public Law 483) removed Asian
      Indians from its 'Barred Zone' in 1946 and allocated a quota of 100 immigrants
      per year. This quota was sharply increased in subsequent years. Similarly
      Canada repealed its restrictive laws and started accepting fresh Asian
      immigration in the 1950s and emerged as the single most popular destination
      for Sikh migrants from the 1970s.

21   E. J. B. Rose *et al.*, *Colour and Citizenship: a Report on Race Relations* (Oxford
      University Press, 1969); John Solomos, *Race and Racism in Contemporary Britain*
      (London: Macmillan, 1989).

22   Helweg, *Sikhs in England*, chapters 4 and 5.

23   For the US the precise figures for Sikh population are elusive because Sikhs are
      counted as Asian Indians. The 2000 Census puts Asian Indians at 1,678,765.

Estimates of the Sikh population vary between 200,000 and 250,000, with several thousand 'illegals' and 'refugees'.

24   Prakash C. Jain, 'Culture and Economy in the "Incipient" Diaspora', in Bhikhu Parekh, Gurharpal Singh and Steve Vertovec, eds., *Culture and Economy in the Indian Diaspora* (London: Routledge 2003), 102–22.

25   See M. S. Randhawa, *Out of Ashes: an Account of the Rehabilitation of Refugees from West Pakistan in Rural Areas of East Punjab* (Chandigarh: Public Relations Department, Government of Punjab, 1954); *International Journal of Punjab Studies* 4:1 (1997), Special Issue on Partition of Punjab; Ian Talbot and Gurharpal Singh, eds., *Region and Partition: Bengal, Punjab and the Partition of the Indian Subcontinent* (Karachi: Oxford University Press, 1999).

26   Charles Wardle's answer to a written question. House of Commons, 23 October 1992.

27   In general, officials in most countries were sceptical of Sikhs' claims for asylum, calling even genuine claimants 'economic migrants'. See Medical Foundation for the Care of Victims of Torture, *Lives under Threat: a Study of Sikhs Coming to the UK from the Punjab* (London: 1999, second edition). To ascertain Sikh applicants' claims, Denmark, Sweden and Canada sent their own missions to investigate the situation in Punjab.

28   Kessinger, *Vilayatpur*, 92–93. W. H. McLeod, 'The First Forty Years of Sikh Migration: Problems and Some Possible Solutions,' in Norman. G. Barrier and Verne Dusenbery eds., *The Sikh Diaspora: Migration and Experience Beyond Punjab* (Delhi: Chanakya, 1989), 29-48.

29   *Census of India, 1951.* vol.viii, *Punjab-PEPSU, Himachal Pradesh and Delhi, pt.1-A, ptII-B, ptII-A.*

30   See the World Bank, *Restoring Punjab's Prosperity: the Opportunities and Challenges Ahead* (Washington: World Bank, 2004); Surinder S. Jodhka, 'Beyond Crisis: Rethinking Contemporary Punjab Agriculture', unpublished paper, 2004.

31   Carmen Voigt-Graf, 'Indians at Home in the Antipodes: Migrating with PhDs, Bytes or *Kava* in their Bags', in Bhikhu Parekh, Gurharpal Singh and S. Vertovec, eds., *Culture and Economy in the Indian Diaspora* (London: Routledge, 2003), 142–66.

32   Jalandhar, as Doaba's main city, is the base of more than a hundred immigration service operators.

33   In October 2004 we visited several travel agencies in the city, who, for obvious reasons, would like to remain anonymous.

34   Most recently Britain and Canada have introduced visa processing facilities in Jalandhar and Chandigarh. There are also plans afoot to expand the international airport at Amritsar and build a new international airport at Ludihana.

35   Kessinger, *Vilayatpu*, 90-3; Archana B. Verma, *The Making of Little Punjab in Canada: Patterns of Migration* (Delhi: Sage Publications, 2002).

36   See Helweg, *Sikhs in England.*

37   See Gurharpal Singh, *Religious Transnationalism and Philanthropy in Punjab* (forthcoming). This research is part of a project on religion and development funded by the Department for International Development at the University of Birmingham, 2006–2010.

38 Bruce LeBrack, 'The New Patrons', in Norman G. Barrier and Verne Dusen-
    berry, *The Sikh Diaspora: Migration and Experience Beyond the Punjab* (Columbia,
    Missouri: South Asia Books, 1989), 289.
39 *Punjab Statistical Abstract* (Chandigarh: 2004).

Chapter 3

1   Roger Ballard, 'The South Asian Presence in Britain and its Transnational
    Connections', in Bhikhu Parekh, Gurharpal Singh and Steve Vertovec, eds.,
    Culture and Economy in the Indian Diaspora (London: Routledge, 2003), 197–8.
2   Rozina Visram, *Ayahs, Lascars and Princes* (London: Pluto Press, 1986) and
    Asians in Britain: 400 Hundred Years of History (London: Zed Books, 2000).
3   On the history of Koh-i-noor, see Stephen Howarth, *The Koh-i-noor Diamond*
    (London: 1986) and Iradj Amini, *The Koh-i-noor Diamond* (Delhi: Roli Books,
    2001). Whether the diamond was a gift or a prize of conquest has been debated
    ever since. For a fascinating account of an encounter between Duleep Singh
    and Queen Victoria over the Koh-i-noor, see E. Dalhousie Login, *Lady Login's
    Recollections: Court Life, and Camp Life, 1820–1904* (London: John Murray
    1906), 123–6. However the diamond's ownership has been contested by the
    Sikhs, the governments of Pakistan, India and Iran. With a replica made
    recently of the original, the Koh-i-noor lies in the Tower of London. It was
    embedded in the Coronation Crown in 1937 and placed atop the Queen
    Mother's coffin during her funeral in April 2002 which caused a fresh contro-
    versy, see *Guardian* 27 April 2002.
4   See Michael Alexander and Suhila Anand, *Queen Victoria's Maharajah: Duleep
    Singh, 1838–1893* (London: Weidenfeld and Nicolson).
5   Queen Victoria noted in her journal, '[he is] extremely handsome and speaks
    English perfectly, and has a pretty, graceful and dignified manner'. Royal
    Archives, *Queen Victoria's Journal,* 6 July 1854.
6   *Times*, 28 August 1882 carried a long letter from Duleep Singh. His case was
    also published by a friend, Evans Bell, *The Annexation of Punjab and the
    Maharajah Duleep Singh* (London: Trubner, 1882).
7   Ganda Singh, *Maharaja Duleep Singh's Correspondence.* (Patiala: Punjabi
    University, 1980). British Library: India Office Records, IOR: L/P&S/
    18D/17, Minute to Dalhousie, 15 February 1856; IOR: L/P&S/18D/19-25;
    IOR: L/P&S/18D/18 pt iv, GOI, 17 August 1883; IOR: R/I/I/44, demi-
    official, 22 July 1886; IOR: L/P&S/18/D/105 concerning the family of the
    late Maharajah Duleep Singh; IOR: MSS EUR E 377/4-8/10.Also see Christy
    Campbell, *The Maharajah's Box: an Imperial Story of Conspiracy, Love and a
    Guru's Prophecy* (London: HarperCollins, 2000). Lady Login, *Sir John Login and
    Duleep Singh* (London: W. H. Allen, 1890).
8   Peter Bance, *The Duleep Singhs: the Photograph Album of Queen Victoria's
    Maharaja* (Gloucestershire: Sutton Publishers, 2004).
9   Campbell, *The Mahrajah's Box*, 442.
10 See Brian Keith Axel, *The Nation's Tortured Body: Violence, Representation and the
    Formation of the Sikh 'Diaspora'* (Duke: Duke University Press, 2001); Tony

Ballantyne, 'Maharajah Dalip Singh, History and the Negotiation of Sikh Identity', in Pashaura Singh and N. G. Barrier, eds., *Sikhism and History* (Delhi: Oxford University Press, 2004), 151–75.

11 On Punjab princely states and their maharajahs see Lepel H. Griffin, *The Rajas of Punjab: Being the History of the Principal States in the Punjab and their Political Relations with the British Government* (published in 1873, reprint 1970, Patiala: Languages Department) and *Chiefs and Families of Punjab* (Lahore: Superintendent, Government Printing, 1940, 2 vols).

12 One notable variation on the 'soldiers' theme was Ram Singh, a Sikh architect from Lahore and vice-principal of the Mayo Arts College. He was especially invited by the Queen Victoria to design the Durbar Hall at Osborne House in 1890.

13 M. S. Leigh, *Punjab and the War* (Patiala: Language Department, 1970 reprint of 1920); S. S. Thorburn, *The Punjab in Peace and War* (Patiala: Punjab Language Department, 1970).

14 For details of Hardit Singh Malik's life see *Nishaan*, 3 (2002), 16–28.

15 British Library: India Office Records, Censor's report: IOR: L/MIL/5/825-828 and 828 pt 1; IOR: MSS EUR F 143/84/91/ 93; 84 is Censor's Report prepared by Mr Howell, 91 relates to 24 February 1916 letter from a Sikh soldier. Also see David Omissi, *The Sepoy and the Raj: the Indian Army, 1860–1940* (London: Macmillan, 1994) and David Omissi, ed. *Indian Voices of the Great War: Soldiers' Letters, 1914–18* (Basingstoke, Macmillan, 1999).

16 Joyce, Collins, *Dr Brighton's Indian Patients: December 1914 – January 1916.* (Brighton Books Publishing, 1997)

17 Mahinder Singh Pujji saw action in Europe, North Africa and Burma, see *Guardian*, 6 November 2002.

18 Of this marriage, a daughter was born, Amrita Sher-Gil (1913–1941) who became a famous painter of Punjabi life. N. Iqbal Singh, *Amrita Sher-Gil: a Biography* (Delhi: Vikas, 1984).

19 Rachpal Kaur, ed., *Bhai Kahan Singh de Aprkashat Safrname* (Nabha: Virjesh Parkashan, 1983).

20 Teja Singh, *Jivan Kahani Raj Yog: Sant Atar Singh ji Maharaj de Varosae Sant Teja Singh ji di Aplni Kalm ton Likhi hoi* (Baru Sahib: Kalgidhar Trust, 1989).

21 See Lal Singh Kamla, *Mera Vilayeti Safarnama* (Lahore: Lahore Bookshop, 1931) and Gyani Sher Singh, who completed a doctoral dissertation on Sikhism in 1938 at the University of London and published his letters to his wife as *Vilayeti Chithian* (Ludhiana: 1939).

22 Kushwant Singh, *Life, Love and Little Malice* (Delhi: Penguin, 2001), 53–86.

23 PRO/MEPO 2/5064. Thus at Limehouse Station in Reading district, records of peddler certificates relate to some Sikhs. One entry reads: 'Gurbachen Singh with certificate no. 432, passport no. 73591 issued at Bombay arrived via France at Dieppe on 5/3/32.' Others mentioned are: Kabul Singh, Surian Singh, Gurdas, Ganga Khana, Kartar Singh, Guggar Singh, Surbaran Pratap Singh, Arjan Singh, Kishan Singh, Babu Kishan Singh and Kartar Singh. The police inspector's note says, 'They were all issued passports at Lahore, but none of their passports had stamps of place of landing.'

24 E. W. Macfarland, 'Clyde Opinion on an Old Controversy: Indian and Chinese Seafarers in Glasgow', *Ethnic and Racial Studies*, 14: 4 (1991), 493–515. Anne Dunlop, 'Lascars and Labourers: Reaction to the Indian Presence in the West of Scotland during the 1920s and 1930s', *Scottish Labour History Society Journal* 25 (1991), 40–57.

25 Kitty Fitzgerald, *Speaking for Ourselves: Sikh Oral History* (Manchester Sikh History Project, 1986), 42.

26 *Manchester Evening News*, 20 August 1997.

27 Bashir Maan, *The New Scots: the Story of Asians in Scotland* (Edinburgh: J. Donald, 1992), Chapter 4.

28 Interview with Bawa Singh Dhesi , Bradford, 6 July 2002. Also see Darshan S. Tatla, 'This is My Home Now: Reminiscences of a Punjabi in Coventry', *Oral History*, 21:1 (1993), 68–74. Personal communication from Sujinder Singh Sangha, whose grandfather arrived in Britain in the 1930s and eventually settled in Newcastle.

29 IOR L/P&J/12/646 IPI Indian Activities in the UK, 8 March 1944. Indian Organisations in the UK: a Review 1942-46. IOR L/P&J/12/645 IPI note on IWA 14 April 1942: History Sheets of Kartar Singh Nagra LCMM, September 1936. Also see Julius Silverman, 'The India League in the Freedom Movement', *Indo-British Review*, 16:2 (1989), 47–56.

30 Public Records Office: CRIM 1/1177; British Library: India Office Records, IOR: L/P&J/7/3610, 3882; IOR: L/P&J/11/2/354 For passport; IOR: L/P&J/12/500; IOR: MEPO 3/1743. See also Navtej Singh and Avtar Singh Johal, eds., *Emergence of the Image: Redact Documents of Udham Singh* (Delhi: National Book Organisation, 2002).

31 John Solomos, *Race and Racism in Britain* (Basingstoke, Macmillan, 1989), 40-4.

32 Arthur W. Helweg, *Sikhs in England* (New Delhi: Oxford University Press, 1986, second edition), 29.

33 Interview with Chanan Singh 'Chitti', Jalandhar, 30 November 2003. As a travel agent from Jalandhar with a large network of agents in Doaba, Chitti claimed to have sent almost half of the Doabian emigrants to Britain during the 1960s. For individual experiences of settlement, see East Midlands Oral History Archives Collection, Leicester (University of Leicester). Particularly, Singh, C. India to Leicester, English, 740 LO/108/059; Sandhu. Punjab to England London 1962, then Leicester English, 962, LO/317/268.

34 Interview, 'Chitti'.

35 E. J. B. Rose, *et al.*, *Colour and Citizenship: a Report on British Race Relations* (London: Oxford University Press, 1969), 70.

36 The Indian Workers' Association in Southall started showing Indian films at the Dominion Cinema, which soon became a popular weekend pastime for newly arrived families.

37 Darshan S. Tatla, 'A Passage to England: Oral Tradition and Popular Culture among Early Punjabi Settlers in Britain', *Oral History*, 30: 2 (2002), 61-72.

38 M. Dalton and J. M. Seaman, 'The Distribution of New Commonwealth Immigrants in the London Borough of Ealing, 1961–66', *Institute of Geographers* (1973), 21–36.

39 Solomos, *Race and Racism in Britain,* 54.

40 See Parminder Bhachu, *Twice Migrants: East African Sikh Settlers in Britain* (London: Tavistock, 1985).

41 Like globalised Islam, the formation of the Sikh diaspora since the 1980s is also contributing to the emergence of a globalised Sikhism in which British Sikhs have played a crucial part. This theme is discussed in more detail in the Conclusion.

42 Darshan S. Tatla, *The Sikh Diaspora: the Search for Statehood* (London: UCL Press, 1999), 85–99.

43 The case of Vijay and Parveen Saini, two young brothers aged 19 and 20, who travelled in the undercarriage of a British Airways flight from Delhi to London in October 1996, was reported widely. Vijay was dead on arrival, but Parveen miraculously survived 10 hours of sub-polar temperatures. As he walked through customs, immigration staff were 'horrified'. Received by his uncle, Tarsem Singh Bola in Southall, Saini's application for asylum was rejected by the adjudicator, but he was allowed to stay by the Home Secretary under 'exceptional' circumstances. *Daily Telegraph,* 13 March 1997. Joginder Singh recalled his journey in 1959 with over a hundred other illegal Sikh migrants from Germany by a specially chartered aeroplane to a remote airport in England; from there, to everyone's 'surprise', they were all taken to their friends' or relatives' homes (Interview, Wolverhampton, 10 August 2004). News relating to travel agencies that have duped Sikh migrants appears regularly in the British Punjabi press and Punjab's news media. See *Tribune,* 9 and 20 February 2005, for a report on Punjabi youth in Pakistan jails who have been returned by various governments from Europe. Earlier in 2004 two of Punjab's pop singers were arrested for smuggling people abroad. *Tribune,* 29 December 2005.

44 Interviews with community leaders in Southall, Birmingham and Leicester, August 2005. For obvious reasons these individuals wish to remain anonymous.

45 Colin Brown, *Black and White Britain: the Third PSI Survey* (London: Heinemann, 1984); Shamit Saggar, 'The 1983 Labour Force Survey and Britain's "Asian" Population: a Research Note', *New Community,* 12:3 (1985), 418–39.

46 The higher figure was normally cited by Sikh organisations.

47 Private communication from Professor Ceri Peach, University of Oxford.

48 Email discussion with Ram Lokha, Coventry, 12 July 2005.

49 Anecdotal evidence suggests that one in four Sikh families seem to 'know' an 'illegal' or 'asylum seeker'. We are grateful to a number of people for providing this information.

50 Home Office, *Citizenship Survey 2001* (London: Home Office, 2003).

51 Labour Force Survey, 2003/4, Office of National Statistics.

52 Census 2001, Office of National Statistics.

Chapter 4

1 Dr Parminder Singh Garcha, spokesman for the Gurdwara. http://news.bbc. co.uk/1/hi/england/2898761.stm. Prince Charles visited the gurdwara on 13 June 2003 and was welcomed by several hundred Sikhs. During his speech he

remarked, 'The Sikh community is a vital part in the modern multicultural life of this country.' Interview with Himmat Singh Sohi, Southall, 13 August 2003.

2   The term is Ceri Peach's, 'New Cathedrals of Muslims, Hindus and Sikhs: the Cultural Landscape of South Asian Religions in England and Wales', (unpublished), 1–22. Also see Ceri Peach and Richard Gale, 'Muslims, Hindus and Sikhs in the New Religious Landscape of England', *The Geographical Review*, 93:4 (2003), 469–90.

3   See Gurharpal Singh, *Ethnic Conflict in India: a Case Study of Punjab* (Basingstoke: Macmillan, 2000), Chapter 6.

4   Darshan S. Tatla, '*Khalsa Samachar* as a Source for the Study of Sikh Diaspora', *Journal of Sikh Studies*, 12:2 (2004), 47–55.

5   Darshan S. Tatla, *Sant Teja Singh: a Short Biography* (Jalandhar: Punjab Centre for Migration Studies, 2004).

6   Joyce Collins, *Dr Brighton's Indian Patients* (Brighton: Brighton Publishing, 1997), 7.

7   Southall Singh Sabha Gurdwara, *Vaisakhi Brochure* (1991). This provides a short history of earlier efforts at building a gurdwara.

8   Interview with Durga Dutt Shukla and Amrik Singh Sihota, Birmingham, 19 August 2003. Both Shukla and Sihota's father were involved in raising funds for the gurdwara. Shukla became the gurdwara's treasurer for the first four years.

9   Details from a letter from the President, Gurdwara Management Committee.

10   Ramgarhia Sikh Temple, Graham Street, Handsworth and Ramgarhia Gurdwara at Waverley Road.

11   Sri Guru Dasmesh Gurdwara, Wheelar Street.

12   Gurharpal Singh, *Leicester: the Making of a Multicultural City* (Bristol: Polity Press, forthcoming).

13   Darshan S. Tatla, 'Nurturing the Faithful: The Role of the Sants among Britain's Sikhs', *Religion*, 22(1992), 348-74.

14   Puran Singh died on 5 June 1983 and was succeeded by Naraung Singh, a Malaysian Sikh, who died on 3 July 1995. The current head is Mohinder Singh, an engineer by profession, from Zambia.

15   Peach and Gale, 'Muslims, Hindus and Sikhs', 479

16   Paul Weller, ed., *Religions in the UK: a Multi-faith Directory, 2001* (Derby: The Multi-Faith Centre, University of Derby in association with the Inter Faith Network for the United Kingdom, 2003).

17   The role of local planning departments in restricting the development of places of worship by minority ethnic communities in the 1960s and 1970s was a significant factor limiting their growth. The 1980s saw the rise of more liberal planning regimes: see Richard Gale and S. Naylor, 'Religion, Planning and the City: the Spatial Politics of Ethnic Minority Expression in British Cities and Towns', *Ethnicities* 2:3 (2002), 387–409.

18   Roger Ballard, 'Differentiation and Disjunction among the Sikhs', in Roger Ballard, ed., *Desh Pardesh: the South Asian Presence in Britain* (London: Hurst and Co. 1994), 88–116 ; Eleanor Nesbitt, 'Religion and Identity: The Valmiki Community in Coventry', *New Community*, 16: 2 (1990), 261–74; and Sewa Singh Kalsi, *The Evolution of a Sikh Community in Britain: Religious and Social*

Change among the Sikhs of Leeds and Bradford (Leeds: Department of Theology and Religious Studies, University of Leeds, 1992).

19   This data were compiled by recognising self-identification in these publications and supplemented by interviews and telephone conversations with gurdwara officials where necessary. Such an exercise is, of course, necessarily incomplete because not all gurdwaras publicly proclaim their caste identity. However, on the other hand it must be recognised that Ramgarhia and Bhatra gurdwaras do in fact assert such recognition. The claim of marginal Sikh groups to be recognised as Sikhs, or their places of worship to be recognised as gurdwaras, is more contested. See below.

20   It has been pointed out that some of these gurdwaras used *indirect* practices to keep non-Jats at bay. I am grateful to Verinder Kalra for pointing this out.

21   Parminder Bhachu, *Twice Migrants: East African Sikh Settlers in Britain* (London: Tavistock, 1985), 50–1.

22   Ballard, *Desh Pardesh*, 111.

23   Ballard, *Desh Pardesh*.

24   P. A. S. Ghuman, 'Bhatra Sikhs in Cardiff: Family and Kinship Organisation', *New Community* 8:3 (1980), 308–16; Eleanor Nesbitt, 'A Note on Bhatra Sikhs,' *New Community* 9: 1 (1981), 70–2.

25   Where castes ends and sects begin is a difficult distinction to draw in the case of Sikhs and, indeed, one that potentially carries normative implications for a community such as the Sikhs with one dominant caste group. Our aim here is to group together similar movements while recognising the distinctions between them and 'mainstream' Sikhism. The adjective 'lower-caste' is used with reference to the position of those traditionally seen as outside the classical Hindu caste system.

26   For a detailed discussion see Kalsi, *The Evolution of a Sikh Community in Britain*, 125–47.

27   A. D. W. Leivesley, 'Ravidasias of the West Midlands', *Sikh Bulletin* 3 (1986), 37.

28   Of the 100 Ravidasis asked to identify their religion, 97 replies gave the following classification: Hindus 5, Ad-Dharmis 70, Ravidasi 21, and Radhasoami 1. None identified themselves as Sikhs. See A. D. W. Leivesley, 'Problems of the Ravidasi Community in India and West Midlands' (unpublished M.Phil. thesis, University of Aston, 1985). Kalsi's argument (*The Evolution of a Sikh Community in Britain*, 125-47), that Ravidasis are a form of caste identity politics *within Sikhism* is not substantiated by this group's self-identification.

29   Eleanor Nesbitt, 'Valmikis in Coventry: the Settlement and Reconstruction of a Community', in Ballard, *Desh Pradesh*, 130–1. Also see Julia Leslie, *Authority and Meaning in Indian Religions: Hinduism and the Case of Valmiki* (Aldershot: Ashgate, 2003).

30   Beant Kaur, *The Namdhari Sikhs* (London: Namdhari Sikhs Historical Museum, 1999).

31   Darshan S. Tatla, 'A Note on Namdhari Sikhs in Britain', *Khera: a Journal of Religious Understanding*, 10: 1 (1991), 50–7.

32   Following a violent clash between Nirankaris and some Sikhs in Amritsar in
     April 1978, the Jathedar of Akal Takht issued a *hukamnama* (a religious
     indictment) forbidding Sikhs to have dealings with Nirankaris. The bitterness
     that followed ultimately claimed the life of Nirankari chief Gurbachan Singh,
     who was killed in 1979. His widow visited Nirankari followers in the West
     Midlands in 1989.

33   Mark Juergensmeyer, *Radhasoami Reality: the Logic of a Modern Faith* (Princeton:
     Princeton University Press, 1991).

34   This is calculated on the basis of average values varying between £500,000 and
     £1,000,000 for about 250 institutions. Given that most of these properties are
     in the South, South East and the Midlands, and often command additional
     premises such as a sports hall and welfare centre, the real value at current prices
     is probably much higher.

35   See Kalsi, *The Evolution of a Sikh Community in Britain*, Chapter 5.

36   One of the earliest examples of such a manoeuvre was a resolution passed at a
     Slough gurdwara at the instance of Pamela Wylam, a Sikh convert, for the
     removal of *mona*-Sikhs from the management committee. She subsequently
     became an editor of the *Sikh Courier*.

37   This is discussed in more detail in Chapter 6.

38   *Illaqa* rivalries were also found to be prominent in the politics of the IWAs; see
     John DeWitt, *Indian Workers' Associations in Britain* (London: Oxford University
     Press, 1969), 48–52.

39   For an extensive discussion of caste conflict in the management of gurdwaras in
     Leeds and Bradford see Kalsi, *The Evolution of a Sikh Community in Britain*.

40   The Charity Commission does not require the elections of officers, but the
     majority of gurdwaras' constitutions stipulates an elected management com-
     mittee. Gurdwaras managed by sants usually have no provision for elections.

41   Interview, member of the management committee, 16 June 2003.

42   In this case the communist parties backed the Giani Amolak Singh faction.

43   *Coventry Evening Telegraph,* 29 May 2001.

44   *Coventry Evening Telegraph,* 25 February 1984.

45   *Leicester Mercury,* 18 July 2005.

46   Such cases are too numerous to cite but the adjudication of the Charity
     Commissioners in disputes is an interesting subject for further research. For
     further insights into the subject see Eleanor M. Nesbitt, 'Gurdwaras in the
     British Sikh Press' (unpublished, n.d), 1–17.

47   See   <http://www.charity-commission.gov.uk/investigation/inquiryreports/
     guru. p.2>. Emphasis added.

48   *Des Pardes,* 20 December 1970, 26 March and 30 April 1976.

49   See Charity Commission's report, <http://www.charity-commission.gov.uk/
     investigations/inquiryreports/cgurd.asp>.

50   The Singh Sabha Gurdwara, Hounslow, lists its range of activities as follows:
     computer training for beginners, English classes for adults, *Harmonium* and *Tabla*
     classes, induction courses for police and local authority personnel, inter-faith
     liaison, *Kirtan* classes for young and adults, outdoors summer *Gurmat* camps for
     the young, Punjabi classes to GCSE and 'A' levels, citizens' advice bureau, third

party reporting on racial abuse and crime, Member of Parliament surgery, disability network Hounslow monthly meeting, sponsored walk, coach trips for senior citizens, distribution of hot drinks for the homeless, document attestation service, funeral service, nursing home residents' visits, matrimonial service, visit to detention centres, martial arts and football team. And this excludes the *normal* functions related to religious service. See <http://www.sgss.org/>

51 Information posted at the gurdwara's noticeboard.

52 See <http://www.charitiesdirect.com/CharityDetail.asp?orgid=17415>. Accessed 11 October 2005.

53 <http://www.befordgurdwara.org.uk/gncharity.htm>, accessed 30 January 2005.

54 <http://www.charity-commission.gov.uk/registeredcharities/showcharity.asp?chyno+10...>, accessed 30 January 2005.

55 <http://www.charity-commission.gov.uk/investigations/inquiryreports/guru.asp>

56 There is very little detailed analysis of how these changes have impacted on minority ethnic community religious institutions. The intersections between these developments are explored further in Singh, *Leicester*.

57 See Gurharpal Singh, 'Multiculturalism in Contemporary Britain: Community, Cohesion, Urban Riots and the "Leicester Model"', in John Rex and Gurharpal Singh, eds., *Governance in Multicultural Societies* (Aldershot: Ashgate, 2003), 56.

58 For further insights into these developments see Home Office, *Working Together: Co-operation between Government and Faith Communities* (2003), <http://www.homeoffice.gov.uk/docs3/workingtog_faith040329.pdf>; Home Office Community and Race Unit, <http://www.homeoffice.gov.uk/comrace/faith/>, Robert Farnell *et al.* *"Faith" in Urban Regeneration? Engaging Faith Communities in Urban Regeneration.* (Bristol: Policy Press, 2003).

59 Council of Sikh Gurdwaras in Birmingham Annual Report, available on <http://www.sikhcouncil.org/pdf/report2001.pdf>.

60 See Hansard, 19 January 2005.

61 These observations are based on several meetings attended by the authors at which efforts were made to establish a British Sikh Consultative Forum, from April 2003 onwards.

62 The constant competitive lobbying of the Home Office by Sikh groups on issues of policy, for example, provides an instructive case study of the innate rivalry between these bodies. The promotion of the 'Sikh interest' often barely conceals the efforts to outmanoeuvre rival organisations.

63 See <http://www.bbc.co.uk/religion/religions/sikhism/sikh_worshipgrd.shtml>.

64 Recently a new English version of *Guru Granth Sahib* has become available.

65 Owen Cole, 'The Settlement of Sikhs in the U.K.', *Panjab Past and Present,* 16–17: 2 (1982), 417–24; Verne Dusenbery, 'The Word as Guru: Sikh Scripture and the Translation Controversy', *History of Religions* 31: 4 (1992), 385–40, however, argues that such an innovation would negate the core essence of Sikh scriptures.

66 See Cynthia Mahmood and Stacy Brady, *The Guru's Gift: an Ethnography*

Exploring Gender Equality with North American Sikh Women (New York: McGraw-Hill, 1999).

67   See, for example, debate by members of the Sikh diaspora group provided by Yahoo.com.

68   See *Daily Telegraph*, 23 July 2004. The Home Office issued new regulations on 31 August 2004 requiring ministers of religion to be competent in English up to IELTS certificate level, with further imminent changes.

69   Many gurdwaras in the past have sponsored *ragis*, *dhadis* and other functionaries who have subsequently settled in Britain. While the numbers are probably very small, they do provide an important source of patronage.

70   Thus the Guru Nanak Nishkam Sewak Jatha runs its gurdwaras with strict adherence to discipline and is valued by the Sikh sanagat for its 'simplicity'.

71   For example, at the Guru Nanak Gursikh Gurdwara at Foleshill, Coventry, run by the Nanksar sants, a small notice prohibits discussion of politics within the gurdwara.

72   *Des Pardes*, 31 August 1984; *Sandesh International* August/September 1984; *Independent*, 13 November 1987.

73   Thakur Singh, head of Damdami Taksal, visited Britain during 2001 and again in 2004.

74   See *Nishaan*, IV (2002),17–19. It also contains the text of a petition presented to Akal Takht, Amritsar demanding recognition for women's right to equally participate in *seva* at Harmandir. See www.VoicesforFreedom.com

Chapter 5

1   John Rex, *Ethnic Identity and Ethnic Mobilisation* (Coventry: Centre for Research in Ethnic Relations, 1991).

2   See Brian Keith Axel, *The Nation's Tortured Body: Violence, Representation and the Formation of a Sikh 'Diaspora'* (Duke: Duke University Press, 2001); Darshan S. Tatla, *The Sikh Diaspora: The Search for Statehood* (London: UCL Press 1999); Gurharpal Singh, 'A Victim Diaspora? The Case of the Sikhs', *Diaspora* 8:3, 293–307; Laurent Gayer, 'The Globalisation of Identity Politics: The Sikh Experience', *International Journal of Punjab Studies* 7: 2, 224– 62.

3   Rozine Visram *Asians in Britain:400 Years of History* (London: Pluto Press, 2002), 271–3; Darshan S. Tatla, 'This is My Home Now: Reminiscences of a Punjabi in Coventry', *Oral History*, 21 (1993), 68–74. Bashir Maan, *The New Scots: The Story of Asians in Scotland* (Edinburgh: J. Donald, 1991); IOR: L/P&J/12/646, IOR: L/P/&J/12/645; L/P&J/12/646, L/P&J/12/646, IPI, L/P&J/646.

4   John DeWitt, *Indian Workers' Associations in Britain*, (London: Oxford University Press, 1969), 45.

5   The Indian Workers' Association was set up on 3 March 1957 in Southall. The founders of the new IWA were Ratan Singh, Amar Singh Takhar, Ajit Singh Rai, Harbans Singh Ruprah, Jaswant Singh Dhami. Takhar became its first President while Rai was Secretary. An office was acquired at 16–18

Featherstone Road, Southall, and in 1966, it purchased a nearby Odeon cinema for screening Indian films. For a brief history of IWAs see *Des Pardes*, 14 May 1982; *Punjabi Darpan*, 11 July 1986; Sasha Josephides, *Towards a History of Indian Workers Associations* (Coventry: Centre for Research in Ethnic Relations, University of Warwick, 1991).

6   See Gurharpal Singh: *Communism in Punjab: a Study of the Movement up to 1967* (Delhi: Ajanta, 1994).

7   Ajit Singh Rai, interview, Southall, 14 May 1982.

8   De Witt, *Indian Workers*, 47.

9   Some other activists included Teja Singh Sahota, Manchanda Kumari Ranjana and Harpal Singh Brar. For details of resignations and allegations, see *Des Pardes*, 11 September 1968.

10 For the relation between CARD and the IWA, see Sasha Josephides, *Toward a History*.

11 *Des Pardes*, 16 July 1976.

12 Such essays were published throughout 1972. See *Des Pardes*, 20 February; 5, 12, 19, 26 March; 4, 11, 18, 25 June, 29 October, 5 November of 1972.

13 *Des Pardes*, 13 August 1972.

14 Ajit Rai's associates were Jaspal Singh Khangura, Harbhajan Singh, Gurnam Singh Gill, Parminder Singh Bal, Jarnail Singh Brar, Kewal Singh Takhar; Gurbux Singh; Sumiter Singh Uppal. The faction led by Vishnu Sharma lost the case. See *Des Pardes*, 15 October 1972.

15 *Des Pardes* 20 and, 22 July 1977.

16 *Des Pardes*, 20 July 1977.

17 Gurdip Singh Chaggar's funeral turned into a protest march. His body, wrapped in full Sikh dress, was routed from Ramgarhia Gurdwara at Oswald Road to his home in Florence Road then onwards to Singh Sabha Gurdwara, Havelock Road. *Des Pardes*, 11 July 1976 reported that some members of Southall Youth Movement tried to set the Dominion Cinema on fire.

18 *Des Pardes*, 11 July 1976.

19 Harkishan Singh Surjeet, the veteran Indian communist leader, presided over the newly reorganised IWA; new office bearers included Prem Singh as President, Avtar Johal as Secretary, Avtar Sadiq as Deputy Secretary and Makhan Johal as Vice-President.

20 He visited the Shepherd's Bush gurdwaras and made a trip to Coventry.

21 *Des Pardes*, 18 September 1966.

22 Institute of Race Relations, *Newsletter* (March 1967), 107.

23 Those elected were Joginder Singh Sandhu as President, Hazara Singh as Vice-President, Kashmira Singh Gill as General Secretary, Piara Singh Sandhu as Joint Secretary, Mihrban Singh as Secretary, Mota Singh of Leamington Spa as Chief Organiser, Pritam Singh Dalewal as Propaganda Secretary and Professor Harbhajan Singh as Joint Secretary, with the following members elected to the Executive Committee: Giani Amolak Singh, Sohan Singh, Makhan Singh Mirgind; Charan Singh (of Gravesend); Madan Singh (of Birmingham), Mohinder Singh (of Leicester); Sajan Singh (Grewal); Chanan Singh Sandhu (Slough), Master Nirmal Singh (Leamington Spa) and Joginder Singh Minhas.

24   *New York Times*, 12 October 1971.

25   *Des Pardes*, 30 July 1972.

26   *Des Pardes*, 12 December 1971.

27   *Des Pardes*, June 1972.

28   *Des Pardes*, 3 December 1972.

29   *Des Pardes*, November 1979.

30   The Corporation was led by Gurbachan Singh Gill, a London businessman.

31   See Tatla, *The Sikh Diaspora*, Chapter 5.

32   Khushwant Singh, *My Bleeding Punjab* (Delhi: UPSBD, 1992), a noted journalist and historian from Delhi, debated the issue of a Sikh homeland with Ganga Singh Dhillon. Writing against Dhillon he noted: 'in your articles you make a large number of assertions which are totally at variance with my reading of Sikh history ... the demand for Khalistan is based on erroneous interpretation of the word "nation" which has an entirely different connotation when used by the historians you quoted and acquired a sinister innuendo after the Muslim League demand for Pakistan. The demand is manifestly mischievous and goes against the interests of the Sikhs. It is wrong of you to dismiss the strong opposition to this demand among the Sikhs themselves as being born out of fear of the government or the Hindu majority. Nor do for that matter people like me oppose it to seek any favour from the government. ... [W]e have the interests of the Khalsa at heart as much you and your supporters in the States and Canada. Only we happen to be, as it were, on the scene, and you, despite your emotional attachment to your ancestral faith, live in comfort in a foreign country. For you this may be an academic exercise; for us it is hard reality' , 41–2.

33   *Des Pardes*, 14 January 1983. Sant Jarnail Singh Bhindranwale in a letter to Dr. Chohan praised his services to the *panth* in publicising its cause among the international community but took exception to Chohan's lax faith.

34   For the full text see, Tatla, *The Sikh Diaspora*, 214–15.

35   Bachittar Singh, an Akali activist from Southall, joined the campaign and spent much of 1983 in a Punjab jail.

36   *Globe and Mail* (Tronto), 19 April 1984.

37   See *Times*, 6, 11, 18 June 1984, *Sunday Times,* 10 June 1984.

38   A Hindu temple in Southall was damaged slightly in June 1984.

39   A North London gurdwara placed an advertisement in a national newspaper seeking an enquiry into Delhi's anti-Sikh riots. See also *New Statesman*, 16 November 1984, 12 April 1985.

40   *Sikh Messenger*, Summer 1987. Indrajit Singh sought query about Indian army news sheet, *Baatcheet* 153, July 1984.

41   This was especially the case in West Bromwich.

42   *Times*, 1 November 1984.

43   People's Union of Democratic Rights and Peoples' Union for Civil Liberties, 'Who are the Guilty?' Report of a Joint Inquiry into the Causes and Impact of the Riots in Delhi from 31 October to 10 November 1984.

44   *Evening Mail* (Birmingham), 6 November 1984. A Birmingham gurdwara donated £2,000 to Delhi's distressed Sikhs.

45   See Gurharpal Singh, *Ethnic Conflict in India: a Case-Study of Punjab* (Basingstoke: Macmillan, 2000).

46   *Des Pardes*, 29 June 1984.

47   For a few months, Radio Caroline, a pirate station outside British territorial waters, broadcasted a half-hour programme of Sikh religious and cultural affairs.

48   *Observer*, 5 May 1985.

49   Since his return to Punjab Chohan has continued his campaign for a Sikh state by holding conventions and flamboyant acts of defiance such as the burning of the Indian national flag. See *The Tribune,* 18 January, 4 February 2005.

50   International Sikh Youth Federation, *Draft Policy Programme and the Constitution* (September 1984).

51   *Guardian*, 7 January 1985. Rode was detained at London airport on return from Dubai, refused entry and flown to Dubai and then to Manila where a special Indian plane took him to a Delhi jail. *The Tribune,* 17 April 1985. *The Times,* 11 February 1986.

52   *Guardian*, 7 June 1986.

53   See *Wangar* (monthly) for 1991.

54   See *Wangar,* October 1991.

55   Gurdeep Singh's much-publicised surrender at Chandigarh on 12 August 1992 coincided with the killing of Sukhdev Singh, the chief of Babbar Khalsa. His confessional statement was widely discussed in the Punjabi media. After spending two years in a Punjab jail he was provided with police protection on his return to Britain.

56   *Des Pardes,* 29 September 1981.

57   Jaswant Singh Thekedar, *Nanakvad* (Southall, 1983). Thekedar was granted asylum in July 1993.

58   A Punjabi writer, Harinder Singh Mehboob, was honoured with the Bhai Kahan Singh Nabha award in 1990. Mehboob was also given the Indian Sahit Academy award in 1991 for his collection *Jhans di Raat*, with its two poems praising Beant Singh, the assassin of Indian prime minister Indira Gandhi.

59   *Coventry Evening Telegraph*, 2 August 1984, *Des Pardes*, April 1993.

60   *Sunday Times*, 17 May 1987, *Erith and Crayford Times*, 13 August 1987.

61   See Chapter Four.

62   *Des Pardes*, 23 September 1988.

63   At a meeting on 22 July 1984 attended by leading Ramgarhias, among them Prem Singh, Baldev Ubhi, H. S. Gahir and Mohan Singh, a resolution was moved by Sardul Marwaha. At this meeting Chohan offered an apology for past misunderstanding between Ramgarhias and Jats, and praised the former as the Sikh community's 'cream'. He asked, amidst laughter and applause, 'how can Khalistan be governed without the Ramgarhias' expertise?'

64   From 1983 onwards Indian Congress leaders and ministers had to address the Sikhs through Ravidasi or other platforms as most gurdwaras refused to entertain them.

65   In January 1985 a Ramgarhia gurdwara in Birmingham donated £3,500 for orphans and widows of the Delhi riots.

66   While Bhatra gurdwaras offered venues for Khalistani organisations, Ravidasis

showed no interest in the Sikh predicament. Indeed, Mr Badhan, a Ravidasi and member of the Indian Overseas Congress, issued a statement that 'extremist Sikhs have threatened him'. *Solihull Daily Times*, 29 January 1986.

67   During the February 1992 elections in Punjab he urged Sikh voters to boycott the polls.

68   International Sikh Youth Federation, *Annual Report* (Walsall: September 1986).

69   *Guardian*, 31 March 1995. Raghbir Singh was arrested on 29 March 1995 in connection with the murder of Tarsem Singh Purewal, the editor-proprietor of the Punjabi weekly *Des Pardes*. Detained under the National Security Act, he was served with a deportation order on grounds of 'national security'. However, following a campaign by ISYF, several MPs, human rights activists and members of the National Union of Journalists, he was finally released on 6 December 1996.

70   Such as Labh Singh, Avtar Singh Brahma, Anokh Singh, Shubeg Singh and many others. Also see Joyce Pettigrew, 'Songs of the Sikh Resistance Movement,' *Asian Music* (1991/2), 85–118.

71   Balhar Singh Randhawa, *Sada Masiah* (1985), Baldev Bawa, *Punjabnama* (Amritsar: Ravi Parkashan, 1994), Gurcharan Singh Lote, *Khuni Churasi* (Birmingham: self-published, 1985).

72   The Khalistan Council, press release, Slough, 30 April 1990.

73   Sangtar Singh Sandhu, the only Sikh leader to publicly welcome the Indian Prime Minister, was shot and suffered injuries.

74   *The Times*, 18 October 1985, *Sunday Observer*, 13 October 1985. The case was decided at Birmingham High Court on 28 December 1986. Of the three Sikhs, Sukhwindar Singh Gill and Jarnail Singh were found guilty and jailed for 14 and 20 years respectively while Parmatma Singh was freed.

75   The Punjab police chief K. P. S. Gill was met by a large demonstration on 23 June 1994. His press conference was cancelled.

76   *Nottingham Chronicle and Echo,* 15 August 1997, *Bristol Evening Post*, 22 August 1997.

77   *India Abroad*, 26 August 1994.

78   Jasbir Singh Ghuman and Jagrup Singh Batth, two Babbar Khalsa activists, were arrested in London and accused of conspiracy to murder Sumedh Saini, Deputy Inspector-General of Punjab police, while on a visit to London in August 1997. Another British Sikh, Gurnam Singh, was arrested in Punjab after a tip-off by the British police. See *Asian Age,* 11 November 1997.

79   She visited Britain in April 1991 after a trip to North America.

80   Michael Foot, the veteran Labour leader, paid a warm tribute to Indira Gandhi following her death in November 1984. The Labour Party, while responsive to demands from Khalistanis and Kashmiris for actions against human rights abuses, has remained steadfast in its opposition to the demands for self-determination by Kashmiri and Khalistani nationalists.

81   Green Party, *Policy Statement: Punjab* (September 1988) and Green Party, *Background Papers on Punjab* (September 1988).

82   Letter to Jagdish Singh, 21 February 1990. Similarly the Plaid Cymru leader, Gwynor Evans, wrote, 'we are in full support of Sikh national freedom.... India

is an empire just as the USSR was'. Letter, 7 June 1994.

83   *Guardian*, 20 August 1986.

84   See Amnesty International, *India. Human Rights Violations in Punjab. Use and Abuse of Law* (London: May 1991).

85   *Guardian*, 2 and 18 September 1995. Karamjit Singh Chahal was arrested on 16 August 1990 and threatened with deportation to India 'for reasons of national security and reasons of political nature'. After the Court of Appeal rejected Chahal's plea for asylum, the case was taken to the European Court of Human Rights. This case became highly contested with many Sikh organisations campaigning for Chahal's release. Max Madden MP sought Chahal's bail, supported by 83 cross-party MPs. *The Independent*, 4 August 1992 reported that the 'Indian government has put intense pressure on Britain to send Chahal to India'. After six years in custody Chahal was released on 15 November 1996. This landmark case has recently come to prominence following the announcements of the current Labour government that it will deport 'foreign terrorists' in the light of the suicide bombing in London in July 2005. For a discussion of the case's contemporary implications see *Daily Telegraph*, 8 September 2005.

86   Khalsa Human Rights, *Report* (Leicester: 1994).

87   This meeting was arranged by Sikh Human Rights (Southall) and Keith Vaz MP on 25 July 1989. D. S. Gill from Punjab read out summaries of human rights abuses in Punjab.

88   On 1 July 1992, the ISYF, Dal Khalsa, Shromani Akali Dal, the Khalistan Liberation Front, the Sikh Information Centre and the Sikh Refugee Association jointly presented their case to MPs, with Buta Singh Rai leading this delegation.

89   For instance, the ISYF sent £7,500 to Thakur Singh of Taksal Jatha for distribution among Sikh widows and distressed families.

90   *Des Pardes*, 20 February 1989.

91   *Guardian*, 6 February 1986.

92   A journal, *Unity*, was launched to 'unite overseas Indians'.

93   Its sub-editor, Kartar Singh, was killed in an arson attack on *Sandesh*'s office in July 1984, while the weekly's proprietor, Ajit Sat Bhamra, was jailed for heroin smuggling. See Tatla, *Sikh Diaspora*, 153–4.

94   *Des Pardes*, 31 August 1984.

95   *Independent*, 13 November, 1987. *Des Pardes*, 20 November 1987. Darshan Das was shot dead on 11 November 1987 along with two other followers, Joga Singh and Satwant Singh Panesar. Rajinder Singh Batth and Manjit Singh Sandher, both members of the ISYF, were sentenced to life imprisonment.

96   See *Lokta,* July 1987.

97   *Express and Star*, 8 July 1986. At the IWA[ML] meeting at Summerfield School, several people were hurt as the ISYF activists disturbed the meeting. Another similar incident occurred in July 1987.

98   Among the leading communists killed by Khalistanis in Punjab were Chanan Singh Dhoot, Deepak Dhavan, and Darshan Singh 'Canadian'.

99   Government of India, *White Paper on the Punjab Agitation* (New Delhi: 1984).

100   *India Today*, July 1985.

101 Air India 182 flight from Canada on way to London and Delhi crashed into the Irish Sea, killing all of its 326 passengers, on 20 June 1985. See Zuhair Kashmeri and Brian McAndrew, *Soft Target: How the Indian Intelligence Services Penetrated Canada* (Toronto: Lorimar, 1989).

102 See K. N. Malik and Peter Robb, eds., *India and Britain: Recent Past and Present Challenges* (Delhi: Allied, 1994).

103 *Hindustan Times,* 3 August 1984. *Times of India,* 21, 25 September. Chohan's speech, broadcast by the BBC, drew strong protest from the Indian government, which termed it an 'incitement to violence'.

104 *Guardian,* 7 June 1986.

105 *Sunday Times,* 23 December 1984.

106 *Times,* 15 April 1985.

107 House of Commons, Debates, vol. 140 (11 November 1988), 724

108 V. S. Mani, 'Indo-British Treaty', *International Studies,* 32:2, 139–50.

109 House of Commons, Debates, vol. 229 (22 July 1993), 461–3.

110 *India Today,* 15 October 1992.

111 House of Commons, Debates, vol. 140 (11 November 1988), 718–26.

112 House of Common, Debates, vol. 140 (11 November 1988), 724.

113 House of Commons, Debates, vol. 169 (22 March 1990), 1330–40.

114 House of Commons, Debates, vol. 201 (13 January 1992), 463–4.

115 House of Commons, Debates, vol. 199 (29 November 1991), 1241.

116 House of Commons, Debates, vol. 199 (29 November 1991), 1248.

117 House of Commons, Debates, vol. 239 (17 March 1994), 1054.

118 House of Commons, Debates, vol. 259 (9 May 1995), 651–9.

119 *Observer,* 5 October 1997.

120 *Observer,* 19 October 1997,

121 *Awaze-Qaum,* October 1997.

122 *Sunday Timer,* 19 October 1997.

123 See Kashmir Singh's letter in *Asian Times,* October 1997.

124 Singh, *Ethnic Conflict in India,* Chapter 11.

125 Sikhs are now seen as the premier exponents of 'messy politics' – an outgrowth of globalisation and transnationalism. For an insightful account see Giorgio Shani, 'Globalisation and Identity: Sikh Nationalism, Diaspora and International Relations' (School of Oriental and African Studies, unpublished PhD thesis, 2005).

126 See, for example, the Human Rights Advisory Group of the Punjabis in Britain All-Parliamentary Group, 'Self-Determination as a Human Right and its Application to the Sikhs' (March 2005).

127 Quoted in House of Commons, Debates, vol. 388 (3 July 2002), 73WH.

128 John McDonnell MP, House of Commons, Debates, vol. 388 (3 July 2002), 74WH.

129 Kasmir Singh, British Sikh Federation, 'Memorandum Submitted by the British Sikh Federation to House of Commons Select Committee on Works and Pensions' (dated 18 July 2003).

130 Fiona Mactaggart, Home Office Minister, Hansard, (2 February 2005), http://www.publications.parliament.uk/pa/cm200405/cmhansrd/cm050202/

debtext/50202-41.htm.

131 *Guardian,* 1 March 2001.

132 House of Commons, Hansard Debates, vol. 338 (3 July 2002), 69WH-91WH.

133 See <http://forums.waheguru.com/index.php?showtopic=11448>.

134 See BBC News, 13 September, 2003, <http://www.bbc.co.uk/1/hi/uk/3104948.stm>.

135 SF http://www.sikhfederation.com/aboutus.htm

136 BBC News, 13 September 2005.

Chapter 6

1   Brian Barry, *Culture and Equality: an Egalitarian Critique* (Cambridge: Polity Press, 1999), 39.

2   In particular see the contributions by Susan Mendus, David Miller and Bhikhu Parekh in Paul Kelly, ed., *Multiculturalism Reconsidered: Culture and Equality and its Critics* (Cambridge: Polity Press, 2002).

3   This point is discussed at some length in Darshan S. Tatla, 'Sikhs in Multicultural Societies', in John Rex and Gurharpal Singh, eds., *Governance in Multicultural Societies* (Aldershot: Ashgate, 2003), 199–213.

4   *Manchester Evening News,* 22 June 1959.

5   *Daily Telegraph,* 5 October 1966.

6   See G. S. S. Sagar, *Sikhs and Turbans* (Manchester: Turban Committee, Manchester Sikh Temples, 1966).

7   See David Beetham, *Transport and Turbans: a Study in Local Politics* (London: Oxford University Press, 1970). A Transport Department spokesman described Sandhu's action as 'to have dismissed himself by failing to comply with long-standing conditions of employment', *Express and Star,* 24 August 1967.

8   Whereas the divisions between Powellites (supporters of Enoch Powell, an anti-immigration Member of Parliament from Wolverhampton) and the Labour Party ran along the local and national axes of British politics, those between the IWA and SAD supporters reflected the cleavages in British and Punjab Sikh politics and were frequently extended transnationally. See Frank Reeves, *Race and Borough Politics* (Aldershot: Avebury, 1989) and Wolverhampton's evening paper, *Express and Star* from May 1967 to April 1969.

9   *Express* and *Star,* 28 August 1967.

10 *Express and Star,* 29 November 1967.

11 *Des Pardes,* 22 September 1968.

12 *Times,* 7 April 1969.

13 Beetham, *Transport and Turban,* 63

14 Charan Singh Panchi was the chief campaigner in the dispute. Subsequently he became a convinced supporter of Dr Jagjit Singh Chohan, who floated the idea of an independent Sikh homeland. According to Panchi, 'he had seen through Indian ambassador's lip-service to the Sikhs' legitimate demand and felt unless the community had a sovereign government with its own diplomats, overseas Sikhs would always remain vulnerable'. Interview, Birmingham, 13 August 2003.

15   Sebastian Poulter, *Ethnicity, Law and Human Rights: the English Experience* (Oxford: Clarendon, 1998), 293.

16   Poulter, *Ethnicity, Law and Human Rights,* 293.

17   Poulter, *Ethnicity, Law and Human Rights,* 324.

18   See in particular Susan Medus, 'Choice, Chance and Multiculturalism', in Kelly ed., *Multiculturalism Reconsidered,* 31-44.

19   Poulter, *Ethnicity, Law and Human Rights,* 293–7.

20   Poulter, *Ethnicity, Law and Human Rights,* 297.

21   Poulter, *Ethnicity, Law and Human Rights,* 295–6.

22   *Des Pardes,* 22 July 1983.

23   *Motor Cycle Weekly,* 16 April 1983.

24   Gerd Baumann, *Contesting Culture: Discourses of Identity in Multi-ethnic London* (Cambridge: Cambridge University Press, 1996), 74.

25   *All England Law Reports,* Vol. 3 (London: Butterworth and Co. 1982), 1120.

26   *Guardian,* 31 July 1982; *Sunday Times,* 1 August 1982; *New Statesman,* 6 August 1982.

27   *New Society,* 5 August 1982.

28   *Daily Telegraph,* 18 August 1982.

29   *Guardian,* 16 October 1982.

30   All England Law Report, vol.1 (House of Lords) (London: Butterworth and Co. 1983), 1062.

31   Poulter, *Ethnicity, Law and Human Rights,* 304.

32   See *Des Pardes* and *Punjab Times* (1979–80), which covered this issue extensively. The British Sikh Federation campaigned consistently on this issue.

33   Poulter, *Ethnicity, Law and Human Rights,* 320.

34   Poulter, *Ethnicity, Law and Human Rights,* 315–9.

35   House of Lords, Debates, vol. 511 (16 October 1989), 738.

36   House of Commons Debates, vol. 259 (11 May 1995), 900.

37   House of Commons Debates, vol. 259 (11 May 1995), 900. Today the matter stands between statutory exemption, in the United Kingdom and the unchanged EU directive on public health and safety for the construction industry.

38   In some gurdwara disputes traditional *kirpans* have been used; see *Leicester Mercury,* 18 July 2005.

39   On 29 September 1981 an Indian Airlines Boeing 737 scheduled for Srinagar was hijacked with 117 persons on board and forced to proceed to Lahore. Gajinder Singh, one of the hijackers, became head of the Dal Khalsa, an organisation later banned by the Government of India.

40   See a general circular from the Department of Education and Science. <www.dfes.gov.uk/school security/dwtannexf.shtml>.

41   <http://www.sikhmediawatch.org/pubs/SMART_Kirpan_Memorandum.PDF>, 6 January 1998.

42   See House of Commons Debates, vol. 338 (3 July 2002), 78WH; <http://cfrterrorism.org/policy/hatecrimes.html>.

43   *The Tribune,* (online) 5 December 2002.

44   *Scotsman* (online), 29 July 2002.

45   R. Jones and W. Gnanapala, *Ethnic Minorities in English Law* (Trentham Books, 2000): 228
46   *Times*, 6 August 1985.
47   Poulter, *English Law and Ethnic Minority Customs* (London: Butterworths, 1986), 260.
48   Poulter, *English Law*, 187–8.
49   My comment (Gurharpal Singh) in *Guardian*, 21 December 2004.
50   Gurpreet Kaur Bhatti, *Behzti* (London: Oberon Books, 2004).
51   BBC News (online), 19 December 2004.
52   *The Hindu* (online), 31 December 2004.
53   *Guardian*, 21 December 2004.
54   See Gurharpal Singh, 'Sikhs are Real Losers from *Behzti*', *Guardian*, 24 December 2004.
55   *Daily Mail*, 21 December 2004. See also the *Guardian*, 22 December 2004, *Independent*, 21 December 2004, and the *Sunday Times*, 20 December 2004.
56   *Telegraph*, 26 December 2004.
57   In response to my article in the *Guardian* (Gurharpal Singh), I had nearly 110 emails of which 78 (mostly from Sikhs) were supportive of Bhatti's right to stage the play.
58   This argument, however, was soon undermined by the 'discovery' of other cases of abuse and in particular by the comment of Simranjit Singh Mann, a leading Sikh politician from the Punjab, that 'abuse does sometimes occur in gurdwaras'.
59   This point was made by Sewa Singh Mandla, University of Birmingham, 15 February 2005.
60   *Observer*, 26 December 2004.
61   *Guardian*, 17 January 2005.
62   For example, see comments of Birmingham's Catholic Archbishop, BBC News (online), 20 December 2004.
63   *Guardian*, 13 January 2005.
64   See Rex and Singh, *Governance in Multicultural Societies*, Chapter 5.
65   See Wendy Ball and John Solomos, eds., *Race and Local Politics* (London: Macmillan, 1990).
66   Campaign Against Racism and Fascism. Southall Rights, *Southall: the Birth of a Black Community* (London: Institute of Race Relations, 1981), 25.
67   See Ball and Solomos, *Race and Politics*.
68   John Solomos and Gurharpal Singh, 'Racial Equality, Housing and the Local State', in Ball and Solomos, *Race and Politics*, 95–114.
69   See K. Malik, 'Born in Bradford', *Prospect* (October 2005), 54–6.
70   Several Local Educational Authorities (LEAs) have issued guidelines regarding the wearing of turbans and *kirpans* in schools. Such initiatives usually arise as Sikh pupils start coming to school wearing a turban or *kirpan*, thus forcing a particular school to seek guidance from the local LEA. This was the case in Walsall, Wolverhampton, Strathclyde, South Tyneside and Birmingham. In the past the Department of Education has also provided guidelines to LEAs on the possible impact of the Race Relations Act (1976) and the *Mandla v Dowell Lee* judgement.

71 See Gurharpal Singh, *Leicester: the Making of a Multicultural City* (Bristol: Polity Press, forthcoming).

72 Gurharpal Singh, 'Multiculturalism in Contemporary Britain: Community Cohesion, Urban Riots and the "Leicester Model"', in Rex and Singh, eds., *Governance in Multicultural Societies*, 55–69. Also John Martin and Gurharpal Singh, *Asian Leicester* (Stroud: Sutton Publishing, 2002).

73 Examples include a few signposts in Punjabi to gurdwaras in Southall, a road leading to an Erith gurdwara and, in Smethwick, an inconspicuous end-road estate named 'Punjab Gardens'.

74 Runneymede Trust, *The Future of Multi-Ethnic Britain: the Parekh Report* (London: Profile Books, 2002).

Chapter 7

1 See in particular Cabinet Office (Strategy Unit), *Ethnic Minorities and the Labour Markets. Final Report* (London: Cabinet Office, 2003).

2 Interview with Bir Singh, Birmingham, 9 July 1992.

3 Gurharpal Singh, *Communism in Punjab: A Study of the Movement up to 1967* (Delhi: Ajanta Publications, 1994), 26.

4 Peter Marsh, *Anatomy of a Strike: Employers and Punjabi Workers in a Southall Factory* (London: Institute for Race Relations, 1967).

5 Arthur W. Helweg, *Sikhs in England* (Delhi: Oxford University Press, second edition, 1986), 45.

6 Interview with Sarwan Singh, Birmingham, 13 March 1998.

7 See Mark Duffield, *Black Radicalism and the Politics of De-industrialisation: the Hidden History of Indian Foundry Workers* (Aldershot: Avebury, 1988).

8 Duffield, *Black Radicalism*, 99.

9 Duffield, *Black Radicalism*, 105.

10 E. J. B. Rose *et al.*, *Colour and Citizenship: a Report on British Race Relations* (Oxford University Press, 1969), 183.

11 Helweg, *Sikhs in England*, 44.

12 Parminder Bhachu, *Twice Migrants: East African Sikh Settlers in Britain* (London: Tavistock, 1985).

13 P. L. Wright, *The Coloured Worker in British Industry* (Oxford University Press, 1968), 36.

14 See Dennis Brooks and Karmjit Singh, 'Pivots and Presents: Asian Brokers in British Foundries', in Sandra Wallman, ed., *Ethnicity at Work*, (London: Macmillan, 1979), 99–112.

15 Interview with Avtar Johal, Birmingham, 20 June 2000.

16 Duffield, *Black Radicalism*, 44.

17 Sujinder Singh Sangha, 'Employment and Trade Union Participation among Punjabis,' *The Asian*, (October/November 1980).

18 Duffield, *Black Radicalism*, 124.

19 Sangha, 'Employment and TU Participation among Punjabis'.

20 Duffield, *Black Radicalism*, 122.

21 Duffield, *Black Radicalism*, 123.

22   *Des Pardes,* 18 August 1968.

23   Joginder Shamsher, *The Overtime People* (Jalandhar, ABS Publishers, 1989); Darshan. S. Tatla, 'A Passage to England: Oral Tradition and Popular Culture among Early Punjab Settlers in Britain', *Oral History,* 30:2 (2002), 61–72.

24   See Tatla, 'A Passage to England', 61–72.

25   Sasha Josephides, *Towards a History of the Indian Workers' Association* (Coventry: University of Warwick, Centre for Research in Ethnic Relations, 1991).

26   John DeWitt, *Indian Workers' Associations in Britain* (London: Oxford University Press, 1969), 137–50.

27   See Sujinder Singh Sangha, 'Struggle of Punjabi Women for Trade Union Recognition' (Wolverhampton: Industrial Language Unit, Bilston Community College, 1983, unpublished paper) and Surinder Guru, 'Struggle and Resistance: Punjabi Women in Birmingham' (University of Keele, PhD thesis, 1987).

28   David Beetham, *Transport and Turbans: Aa Comparative Study in Local Politics.* (Oxford University Press for Institute for Race Relations, 1970).

29   *Independent,* 23 June 2001.

30   *Sunday Telegraph,* 21 September 1997. Asifa Hussain and Mohammed Ishaq, 'British Sikhs' Identification with the Armed Forces', *Defense and Security Analysis,* 18: 2 (2002), 171–83. A Sikh deputation met Prince Andrew to appraise the problems faced by Sikhs who wish to enlist in the forces. The Duke of York, as Colonel-in-Chief of the Staffordshire Regiment, told Sikh delegates attending a Maharajah Duleep Singh Centenary Trust function that to bar Sikhs from the army was 'to ignore one of the world's finest fighting nations and one of Britain's best friends'. Major Robert Anderson, who had served in the Royal Ludhiana Sikhs between 1936 and 1948, endorsed the prince's views and in Parliament had supported the Bill that exempted Sikhs from wearing crash helmets. The army has only 6 Sikh officers and 18 other ranks among its 105,000 personnel.

31   See a report issued by the National Union of Tailors and Garment Workers which claimed 'some 30,000-35,000 Asian women working in sweatshops, underpaid, without overtime rates and their employers paying no tax contributions or social security benefits', *Des Pardes,* 17 January 1986.

32   Amrit Wilson, *Finding a Voice: Asian Women in Britain* (London: Virago Press, 1978), 48.

33   Wilson, *Finding a Voice,* 50.

34   Tatla, 'A Passage to England', 64.

35   See *Guardian,* 27 August 2005. Burnsall was a metal finishing firm in Smethwick supplying Jaguar, Rover and Ford, employing 29 workers with a majority of Sikh women. With conditions of work appalling and an average wage of £2 an hour, workers went on strike led by Nirmal Kaur and Surinder Bassi through the cold winter of 1992/3, without support from their union. See Sarbjit Johal, *The Burnsall Strike* (*Inqilab,* South Asia Solidarity Group Magazine, 1993).

36   See *Guardian,* 27 August 2005

37   Interview with Grewal Brothers, Wolverhampton, 28 June 2005.

38   See two articles by Roger Ballard, 'The Socio-economic Educational

Achievements of Britain's Visible Minorities', <http://www.art.man.ac.uk/casas/pdfpapers/mobility.pdf>, 1999 and 'Progress? But on Whose Terms and at What Cost? The Paradoxical Consequences of Successful Transnational Entrepreneurship' <http://www.art.man.ac.uk/casas/pdfpapers/progress.pdf>, 2001.

39 Interview with Tarlok Singh, *Punjabi Guardian Supplement* (1998).

40 Labour Force Survey and Office of National Statistics 2003/4.

41 Labour Force Survey.

42 This is particularly the case with female Sikhs from Punjab, who often endure immense difficulties in getting recognition of their qualifications from British institutions while adjusting to their new life in Britain, which often involves immediate pressures to build families.

43 See Helwig, *Sikhs in England*, 203–6.

44 Interviews with staff at independent schools in Leicester, Coventry and Birmingham, January 2003.

45 For a general discussion of racial discrimination and higher education see Tariq Madood and Tony Acland, eds., *Race and Higher Education: Experiences, Challenges and Policy Implications* (Policy Studies Institute: University of Westminister, 1998).

46 The Guru Nanak Sikh School for boys and girls in Hayes, Middlesex was opened as an independent 4-18 school in 1993. It was granted state support in 1999. A primary Sikh school was established in Slough in 2005.

47 Cabinet Office, *Ethnic Minorities*, notes that 'Sikhs, Pakistani and Bangladeshi Muslims experience particular under-representation in professional employment, with this area showing higher concentration of Hindus and Indian Muslims', 32.

48 See C. Brown, *Black and White Britain: the Third PSI Survey* (London: Policy Studies Institute/Heinemann 1984).

49 M. S. Brown, 'Religion and Economic Activity in the South Asian Population', *Ethnic and Racial Studies*, 23: 6 (2000),1035–6.

50 The rate of unemployment for Sikhs (male and female) above 49 in 2001 was 6.5 per cent compared with the national average of 3.9 per cent for the same category. Census 2001, Office of National Statistics.

51 Labour Force Survey, 2003/4. Office of National Statistics.

Chapter 8

1 Interview with an East African Sikh (who wished to remain anonymous) at the World Parliament of Religions, Barcelona, 11 July 2004.

2 These and subsequent data are derived from *Religion in Britain*, Census April 2001, Office of National Statistics, 2004 available on http://www.statistics.gov.uk/focuson/religion/, henceforth (Census 2001).

3 For a discussion of this issue see C. Christine Fair, 'Female Foeticide among Vancouver Sikhs: Re-contextualising Sex Selection in the North American Diaspora', *International Journal of Punjab Studies*, 3:1 (1996), 1–44.

4 Census 2001. Households Section.

5 Census 2001. Households Section.

6   See Mark Thompson, 'The Second Generation: Punjabi or English?', *New Community*, 3 (1974), 242–8; Beatrice Drury, 'Sikh Girls and the Maintenance of an Ethnic Culture', *New Community* 17: 3 (1991), 387–99; Roger Ballard and Catharine Ballard, 'The Sikhs: the Development of South Asian Settlement in Britain', in J. L. Watson ed., *Between Two Cultures* (Oxford: Blackwell, 1977), 21–56.

7   See Arthur W. Helweg, *Sikhs in England* (Delhi: Oxford University Press, 1986 second edition), 98–115.

8   See Marie Gillespie, *Television, Ethnicity and Cultural Change* (London: Routledge, 1995).

9   Drury, 'Sikh Girls'; Jasbir K. Puar, 'Resituating Discourses of "Whiteness" and "Asianness" in Northern England: Second Generation Sikh Women and Constructions of Identity', *Socialist Review*, 24: 1-2 (1995), 21–53; Parminder Bhachu, 'Culture, Ethnicity and Class among Punjabi Women in 1990s Britain', *New Community* 17: 3 (1991), 401–12.

10   Drury, 'Sikh Girls', 391.

11   Puar, 'Resituating Discourses', 45.

12   Census 2001, Marriage Patterns.

13   In 1974 the Labour government introduced immigration rules that a woman, whether a British citizen or not, was entitled to bring a husband or fiancé from overseas. In 1979 the Conservative government changed this rule so that women had 'no automatic right' to bring their fiancé or husband. However under pressure from cases pending before the European Commission on Human Rights, this rule was amended whereby women could bring a fiancé subject to a number of qualifications, including passing the 'primary purpose rule'. See *Daily Telegraph,* 26 October 1982.

14   See *Sunday Telegraph*, 12 December 1982; *Times*, 15 December 1982.

15   Helweg, *Sikhs in England*, 127.

16   The desire for such matches can be found in the matrimonial advertisements in the Punjabi press (see Chapter 9) and, increasingly, Internet sites.

17   See Jagbir Jhutti-Johal, 'A Study of Change in Marriage Practices among Sikhs in Britain', (University of Oxford: D.Phil thesis, 1998).

18   Census 2001, Marriage Patterns.

19   This is an estimate by a website, 'Your Dream Shadi', which offers insurance 'should the worst happen', <http://www.yourdreamshaadi.co.uk/Articles/WeddingInsurance1.htm>

20   Limited coverage is provided by Parminder Bhachu's *Twice Migrants: East African Sikh Settlers in Britain* (London: Tavistock, 1985).

21   The comments that follow are based on attendance by the authors at over 100 Sikh weddings since 1980.

22   This delinking has not been accepted by all and as a result in recent years has led to a 'Respect for the *Guru Granth Sahib* Campaign', which has attempted to forcibly remove the *Guru Granth Sahib* from wedding ceremonies scheduled in the same location as the wedding party. For an interesting case in which these protesters disrupted the wedding of Anton Gazizov and Ranjit Virk scheduled at Woburn Abbey see *Cambridge Evening News*, 16 September 2005.

23   A traditional *daaj* (dowry) varied from 11 to 21 clothing items in Punjab. In Britain this has become standardised at 21 items. The dowry items now include several silk suits with a whole range of accompanying accessories and prestigious household items, china sets, electronic music instruments, exclusive linen, fridges, washing machines, bedding and sofas, and increasingly a car. On 9 July 1995 the *Independent* reported that in London and the Home Counties businesses servicing Asian weddings have a total turnover of more than £25 million. The average middle-class Asian family will spend £80,000 on a wedding with all the cultural trimmings, while the less well-off can manage on £30,000. Many rich Sikhs' marriages now introduce novelties such as hiring an elephant for the bridegroom or a horse-drawn buggy for the arrival of the bride at the gurdwara, while in the case of one Sikh businessman a German chef was flown in to make his daughter's table-sized wedding cake at a cost of £30,000.

24   During the rise of the militant movement in Punjab ostentatious expenditure on weddings was drastically cut, but this 'reform movement' had little impact on British Sikhs.

25   *Des Pardes,* 9 December 1973 reported the wedding of a leading IWA activist with a large amount of dowry and gold items.

26   Census 2001, Marriage Patterns.

27   During a two-month period from March to April 2005, of the matrimonial advertisements appearing in *Des Pardes,* 52 per cent were from parents seeking a bridegroom for the daughter, 20 per cent from parents seeking brides for their sons, 14 per cent from male visitors and 6 per cent from female visitors. Divorced partners seeking re-marriage accounted for 8 per cent of each sex.

28   See BBC News (online), 30 January 2004.

29   *Guardian,* 11 March 1986.

30   BBC News (online), 15 December 2004.

31   *Des Pardes,* 3 November 1968.

32   *Des Pardes*, 8 September 1968. The father, brother, mother and sister were prosecuted in this case.

33   These themes are well portrayed in Gurpreet Kaur Bhatti's controversial play *Behzti* (Dishonour) (London: Oberon Modern Plays, 2004), 17–8.

34   The prison population of Sikhs in England and Wales has risen from 307 in 1991 to 394 in 1998. See also James A. Beckford, 'Ethnic and Religious Diversity among Prisoners: the Politics of Prison Chaplaincy,' *Social Compass*, 45: 2 (1998), 265–77.

35   *Evening Standard,* 22 May 1997.

36   *Leicester Mercury* 29 August 2003.

37   *Guardian,* 29 May 2004.

38   BBC News (online), 25 April 2005.

39   J. I. Orford, M. Johnson and B. Purser, 'Drinking in Second Generation Black and Asian Communities in the English Midlands', *Addiction, Research and Theory*, 12: 1 (2004), 11–30; Raymond Cochrane and Sukhwant Bal, 'The Drinking Habits of Sikh, Hindu, Muslim and White Men in the West Midlands: a Community Survey', *British Journal of Addiction*, 85:6 (1990), 759– 69.

40   *Leicester Mercury,* 26 June 2003. A more comprehensive survey of problems is in

Arpinder Kaur Sekhon, 'Understanding Family Coping with Alcohol Problems in the Sikh Community' (University of Birmingham, PhD thesis, 2000).

41   See BBC News (online), 7 December 2004; Foreign and Commonwealth Office, *Community Perceptions of Forced Marriages* (London: Community Liaison Unit); Rahila Gupta, ed., *From Homebreakers to Jailbreakers: Southall Black Sisters* (London: Zed Books, 2003).

42   Pargan Patel, 'Shifting Terrains: Old Struggles for New', in Gupta *From Homebreakers*, 237.

43   Kiranjit Ahluwalia, 'Why I Burned My Husband Alive', *Asian Woman and Bride* (Spring 2000), 91: 5. Kiranjit Ahluwalia, *Circle of Light* (London: HarperCollins, 1997).

44   Gerd Baumann, *Contesting Culture: Discourses of Identity in Multi-ethnic Britain* (Cambridge: Cambridge University Press, 1996), 159.

45   Gita Sahgal, 'Fundamentalism and the Multicultural Fallacy', in *Against the Grain: a Celebration of Survival and Struggle* (Southall: Southall Black Sisters Collective, 1990), 24.

46   Gupta, *From Homebreakers*, 22.

47   Baumann, *Contesting Culture*, 159. Emphasis in the original.

48   Gupta, *From Homebreakers*.

49   Bhachu, 'Culture, Ethnicity and Class', 401.

50   Bhachu, 'Culture, Ethnicity and Class', 403.

51   Bhachu, 'Culture, Ethnicity and Class', 403.

52   Bhachu, 'Culture, Ethnicity and Class', 408.

53   Bhachu, 'Culture, Ethnicity and Class', 412.

54   See Nikky Guninder Kaur Singh, *The Feminine Principle in the Sikh Vision of the Transcendent* (Cambridge University Press, 1993); Doris R. Jakabosh, *Relocating Gender in Sikh History* (Delhi: Oxford University Press, 2003).

55   Two British Sikh women, Manjinderpal Kaur, a London solicitor, and Lakhbir Kaur, were involved in the campaign for equality at the Golden Temple. See www.VoicesFor Freedom.com; *Sikh Women's Network* (2000); *Sikhnet*, 2 July 2003.

56   See Brian Keith Axel, *The Nation's Tortured Body: Violence, Representation and the Formation of a Sikh 'Diaspora'* (Durham: Duke University Press, 2001).

57   See Navdeep Mandir, '[En]gendered Sikhism', *Sikh Formations: Religion, Culture, Theory* 1: 1 (June 2005), 39–55.

58   See the comments of Amrik S. Kang, *Punjabi Manch*, 2 September 2004.

59   *The Tribune*, 13 January 2005.

60   *The Tribune*, 17 January 2005.

61   *The Tribune*, 25 January 2005.

62   See www.sikhi.com. The first British Sikh gay website was put up in 2001 and it asked members to organise locally.

63   Jasbir Singh, 'Homosexuality and Sikhism', <www.*sikhe.com*/gsdno/articles/ essay/07232001homosexualityandsikhism.htm>.

Chapter 9

1   Interview with Shivcharan Gill, A school teacher, creative writer and author of Punjabi teaching materials, Southall, 9 June 2004.

2   Darshan S. Tatla, *Bartania vich Panjabi Bhasha* (Patiala: Punjabi University Press, 1996). Professor Suzanne Romaine, then at the University of Birmingham, coined the term Punglish while researching bilingualism among second generation Punjabis in the city.

3   Verity Saifullah Khan, Euan Reid and Xavier Couillaud, *The Mother Tongue Teaching Directory Survey of the Linguistic Minorities Project*. (London: Linguistic Minorities Project, 1984); Michael Stubbs, ed., *The Other Languages of England* (London: Routledge, 1986); *Education for All (Swann Report): the Report of the Committee of Inquiry into the Education of Children from Ethnic Minority Groups* (London: HMSO, Cmnd. 9453, 1985).

4   *Swann Report*, 406.

5   For the year 2003 the number of Urdu candidates for GCSE was 3,498.

6   In 1999 the SAD government in Punjab made English a compulsory subject at primary level, thereby, according to its critics, abandoning its post-Independence campaign for Punjabi. See Pritam Singh ed., *Punjab, Punjabi and Panjabiat* (Amritsar: Singh Brothers, 2000).

7   Word-processing for Punjabi language and learners' packages has been developed in Britain and North America as well as by Punjabi University, Patiala.

8   See D. Martin, R. Krishnamurthy, M. Bhardwaj and R. Charles, 'Language Change in Young Punjabi/English Children: Implications for Bilingual Assessment', *Child Language Teaching and Therapy*, 19: 3, 245–65; Ben Rampton, R. Harris, C. Leung, 'Education in England and Speakers of Languages other than English' (Working Papers in Urban Language and Literacies, King's College, London 2001); D. Martin, 'Punjabi and English of Young Bilinguals' (Leverhulme Research Fellowship final report, F&G/11040, 1999).

9   Its members included, Jarnail Haer, Sohan Cheema, Giani Bakhshish Singh, Zorawar Singh, Kewal Krishan Sharma, Ajit Singh Rai, Sujinder Singh Sangha, Sohan Singh and A. S. Shatar. See also *Des Pardes*, 27 September 1970.

10 Exchange of letters between BBC Asian Radio, Birmingham and several listeners including a lobbying group led by Dr Kashmir Singh.

11 BBC Asian Service, 'Asian Language Audit of BBC Asian Network' (unpublished, 10 December 2000).

12 Darshan S. Tatla and Gurharpal Singh, 'The Punjabi Press', *New Community*, 15: 2 (1989), 171–84.

13 Tarsem Singh Purewal was murdered on the evening of 17 January 1995 as he left his newspaper's office; *Sunday Telegraph,* 29 January 1995. Although the police pursued the case – arresting Raghbir Singh, the editor of *Awaz-e-Quam*, a Punjabi weekly from Birmingham, and questioning several International Sikh Youth Federation activists – investigation led to no charges. See Brian. K. Axel, 'National Interruption: Diaspora Theory and Multiculturalism in the UK', *Cultural Dynamics*, 14: 3 (2002), 235–56.

14 For a history of Punjabi literary activities in London see *Des Pardes*, 15 August 1985.

15   Harbhajan Singh Virk, *England Vasda Punjab* (Coventry, 1985).

16   See Joyce Pettigrew, 'Songs of the Sikh Resistance Movement,' *Asian Music,* Fall/Winter (1992), 85–118.

17   For an insight into the origins of the Progressive Writers' Associations, see Gurharpal Singh, *Communism in Punjab: a Study of the Movement up to 1967* (New Delhi: Ajanta, 1994).

18   Darshan S. Tatla , 'A Chorus of Hushed Voices: An Introduction to Punjabi Literature in Britain', *Indo-British Review,* XXI: 1 (1994), 111–18; Joginder Shamsher, *The Overtime People* (Jalandhar, ABS Publishers, 1989); Ralph Russell and Joginder Shamsher, 'The Punjabi Short Story in Britain', *New Community,* 7: 2 (1978), 233–46 and 'Punjabi Poetry in Britain', *New Community,* 7: 3 (1978), 291–305.

19   Avtar Jandialvi, *Mere prt aon tk* (Delhi: Navyug Publishers, 1983).

20   Jagtar Dhaw, *Guache ghar di talash* (Delhi: Navyug, 1981).

21   Baldev Bawa, *Ik khat* (Amritsar: Ravi Parkashan, 1992).

22   Baldev Bawa, *Punjabnama* (Amritsar: Ravi Parkashan, 1994).

23   Amarjit Chandan, *Being Here* (London: The Many Press, 1993). Chandan's poems have appeared in *Poetry Review* and he was invited by the Poet Laureate, Andrew Motion, to a poetry session arranged by the BBC at the British Library, London, 2001. However, there is little recognition of British Punjabi literature outside the community circles or Punjab's universities. Thus Debjani Chatterjee ed., *The Redbeck Anthology of British South Asian Poetry* (Bradford: Redbeck: 2000) in the *Made in Britain* series carries a solitary poem by Niranjan Singh Noor.

24   Chandan, *Being Here,* 9.

25   The British Punjabi writers who have received such awards include Kailsh Puri, Amarjit Chandan, Swaran Chandan, Avtar Jandialvi and Darshan Dhir.

26   Reginald Massey and Jamila Massey, *The Immigrants* (Bombay: Hind Pocket Books, 1973).

27   Len Webster, *The Turban-wallah: A Tale of Little India* (London: Oxford University Press, 1984). Harjeet Kaur Tatla, 'The Formation of Identity in Meera Syal's *Anita and Me* and Len Webster's *The Turban-wallah*' (University of Birmingham, BA Hons. dissertation, 2004).

28   Andrew Cowan, *Pig* (London: Penguin, 1994).

29   Bali Rai, *(Un)arranged Marriage* (London; Corgi Books, 2001), 270.

30   Bally Kaur Mahal, *The Pocket Guide to Being an Indian Girl* (London: Black Amber Books, 2004).

31   *Daily Telegraph,* 7 July 2004.

32   See a review of *The Pocket Guide to Being an Indian Girl* on the Amazon.co.uk listing of the volume.

33   Marie Gillespie, *Television, Ethnicity and Cultural Change* (London: Routledge, 1995), 46.

34   Bally Sagoo, 'Interview' in Sanjay Sharma, John Hutnyk and A. Sharma, eds., *Disorienting Rhythms: the Politics of the New Asian Dance Music* (London: Zed Books, 1996), 81–104.

35   Virinder S. Kalra and John Hutnyk, 'Brimful of Agitation, Authenticity and

Appropriation: Madonna's "Asian Cool'", *Postcolonial Studies* 1: 3 (1998), 339–55.

36   Kalra and Hutnyk, 'Brimful of Agitation', 342.

37   Kalra and Hutnyk, 'Brimful of Agitation', 343.

38   Baumann, 'The Re-invention of *Bhangra*', 90.

39   G. Gopinath, 'Bombay, UK Yuba City: Bhangra Music and the Engendering of Diaspora', *Diaspora*, 4: 3 (1995), 303–21.

40   Gillespie, *Television, Ethnicity and Cultural Change,* 46.

41   Les Back, *New Ethnicities and Urban Culture: Racism and Multiculturalism in Young Lives* (London: University College London Press, 1996), 222–3.

42   Virinder S. Kalra, 'Vilayeti Rhythms: Beyond Bhangra's Emblematic Status to a Translation of Lyrical Text', *Theory, Culture and Society* 17: 3 (2000), 80.

43   Raminder Kaur and Virinder S. Kalra, 'Xi Amount of Bhangra and Ragga' (unpublished paper presented at the 'Margins within Margins' workshop, SOAS, 1996), 5.

44   Kalra, 'Vilayeti Rhythms', 95.

45   See Gillespie, *Television, Ethnicity and Cultural Change.*

46   Channel 4, *Bandung File*, 1989. See Also *Express and Star,* 20 April 1988.

47   Gillespie, *Television, Ethnicity and Cultural Change*, 45.

48   Kathleen D. Hall, *Lives in Translation: Sikh Youth as British Citizens* (Philadelphia: University of Pennsylvania Press, 2002).

49   Gillespie, *Television, Ethnicity and Cultural Change*, 205–9.

50   Hall, *Lives in Translation*, 171.

51   Hall, *Lives in Translation*, 192–3.

52   For an insight into these groups, search websites under 'Sikhs', 'Punjabis' and 'Sikh Youth'.

53   Gillespie, *Television, Ethnicity and Cultural Change*, 30.

Conclusion

1   See, for example, Martin Wolf, 'When Multiculturalism is Nonsense', *Financial Times*, 31 August 2005. The allusion, of course, is to the American debate launched by Samuel P. Huntington's *Who Are We? America's Great Debate* (London: Free Press, 2005).

2   See in particular such an argument made by Tariq Madood, *Multicultural Politics: Racism, Ethnicity and Muslims in Britain* (Edinburgh: Edinburgh University Press, 2005) and 'Remaking Multiculturalism After 7/7', *openDemocracy* (29 September 2005), http://www.opendemocracy.net/debates/article.jsp?id=2&debateId=124&articleId=2879.

3   Selwyn Gummer and John Gummer, *When the Coloured People Came* (London: Oldbourne Books Co. 1966), 115.

4   E. J. B. Rose, *et al. Colour and Citizenship: a Report on British Race Relations* (London: Oxford University Press, 1969), 468.

5   John Rex and Gurharpal Singh eds., *Governance in Multicultural Societies* (Aldershot: Ashgate, 2003), 39.

6   See John Rex, 'Multiculturalism and Political Integration in the Modern

Nation-State', in Rex and Singh, *Governance*, 36–55.

7 For the role of the Indian diaspora see Bhikhu Parekh, Gurharpal Singh and Steve Vertovec eds., *Culture and Economy in the Indian Diaspora* (London: Routledge, 2003).

8 See in particular World Bank, 2004, *Resuming Punjab's Prosperity: the Opportunities and Challenges Ahead*. New Delhi: World Bank, available on http://siteresources.worldbank.org/INTINDIA/Resources/PunjabReport.pdf

9 See Madood, *Multicultural Politics*, Chapter 6.

10 Interview with Indarjit Singh, Wimbledon, 9 December 2005.

11 Gurpreet Kaur Bhatti, *Behzti (Dishonour)* (London: Oberon Books, 2004), 131.

12 See Brian Keith Axel, *The Nation's Tortured Body: Violence, Representation and the Formation of a Sikh 'Diaspora'* (London: Duke University Press, 2001), Chapter 4.

13 In April 1999, during a visit to Birmingham, Prime Minister Tony Blair chose to dwell on the NATO campaign in Kosovo. This campaign, asserted Blair, vindicated a key element of the Sikh faith: namely, that when all modes of redressing injustice have failed, it was right and just to take up the sword. See, Gurharpal Singh, 'Sikhism and Just War', in Paul Robinson ed., *Just War in Comparative Perspective* (Aldershot: Ashgate, 2003), 126–37.

14 Quoted in BBC Open University programme, 'Punjab to Britain', E354, *Ethnic Minorities and Community Relations* (Milton Keynes: Open University, 1981).

15 *Vanity Fair,* 26 June 1878. Emphasis added.

16 Ballard makes this point with reference to the Mirpuri community, but it is equally valid in the case of Sikhs. See Roger Ballard, 'South Asian Presence in Britain and its Transnational Connections', in Bhikhu Parekh, Gurharpal Singh and Steve Vertovec, eds., *Culture and Economy in the Indian Diaspora* (London: Routledge, 2003), 197–222.

17 Axel, *The Nation's Tortured Body*, 7.

18 Interview with Indrajit Singh, Wimbledon, 9 December 2005.

19 Joyce Pettigrew, *The Emigration of Sikh Jats from Punjab to England* (London: Social Science Research Council, 1971), HR331/1.

20 See Joyce Pettigrew, *The Sikhs of Punjab: Unheard Voices of State and Guerrilla Violence* (London: Zed Books, 1995); Gurharpal Singh, 'What is Happing to the Political Science of Ethnic Conflict? (II)', *International Journal of Punjab Studies* 3: 2 (June–December 1996), 229–241.

21 Interview with Indarjit Singh, Wimbledon, 9 December 2005.

22 This section is based on an interview with Jasdev Singh Rai, Director of the Sikh Human Rights Group (UK), Leicester, 20 August 2005 and the input of many young Sikh scholars into the journal *Sikh Formations: Religion, Culture and Theory* over the last few years.

23 This point is made by both Indarjit Singh and Jasdev Singh Rai.

24 For an interesting argument suggesting that the Labour government has chosen to promote cosmopolitanism rather than multiculturalism, see Derek McGhee, *Intolerant Britain? Hate, Citizenship and Difference* (Berkshire: Open University Press, 2005).

Bibliographical Note
and Select Bibliography

All sources are cited fully in the notes, but because this volume has gone through several different incarnations we have decided to include a note clarifying the sources and detailing where these are located.

For the pre-1945 period, the main collections of materials on Sikhs are found at the Oriental and India Office Collection (IOR) at the British Library, the Royal Archives, Windsor, the National Army Museum, Chelsea, and the Public Record Office (PRO), Kew. Of these the IOR collection is the most significant. It holds the records for Duleep Singh and his family, of Sikh soldiers' correspondence during the First World War, and of the British Sikh associations before 1947. Some material on Udham Singh is also to be found at the PRO. In addition, there is emerging material in oral archives (see below) on Sikh settlement in Britain during the inter-war period, especially in cities such as Coventry, Nottingham, Leicester, Birmingham, Glasgow and Manchester. Although there is a rich collection of sources on Sikhs before 1945, these sources remain to be integrated into a meaningful narrative. A comprehensive history of Sikhs in Britain before 1945 is badly needed and, if undertaken, would need to take account of the different social classes – the princes, students, soldiers, workers and itinerants – and the extremely fragmented nature of the fledgling community.

In the last decade there has been a substantial growth in local oral archives. Partly because of race equality legislation and partly because of the increasing interest in multiculturalism, local authorities have encouraged oral history projects on particular local communities. In the case of the Sikhs, the Birmingham City Council, Bradford Metropolitan Council, Leeds City Council, Liverpool City Council, Manchester Metropolitan Council, Coventry City Council, Leicester City Council,

Nottingham City Council and the London Museum have all sponsored oral research. In Leicester this work has become part of the East Midland Oral History Archives Collection (housed at the University of Leicester) which works in collaboration with the Sikh museum at the Guru Nanak Gurdwara, Holy Bones. These local efforts have been further supplemented by Heritage Lottery funding for projects such as the Sikh Cyber Museum and the Anglo-Sikh Heritage Trail.

A good survey of the published literature is to found in Tatla and Nesbitt's *Sikhs in Britain: An Annotated Bibliography*, but it is badly dated and tends to focus on the materials published from the 1950s to the 1970s. Tatla's *The Sikh Diaspora: The Search for Statehood* has a valuable bibliography that updates some of the earlier material.

Another useful source is the theses and dissertations on Sikhs in Britain. The increase in the number of Sikh students in universities has been accompanied by interest in the community's development. Most of the doctoral dissertations are listed in *Abstract of Thesis*, but the master's or graduate theses can be more difficult to locate. For specialist work on Punjab and Sikhs, see Tatla's *Theses on Punjab* which provides an exhaustive listing of master's and doctoral dissertations in the United Kingdom and Europe between 1900 and 1995.

A particularly invaluable source for understanding the community's development is the Punjabi press, magazines and English-language periodicals on British Sikhs (see Chapter 9 for a full listing). Of these *Des Pardes* and *Punjab Times* are the two oldest weeklies that have published continuously since the mid-1960s. *Des Pardes* based in Southall is an essential resource for historians interested in the community's fortunes since the mid-1960s. Few Sikh institutions keep back copies of *Des Pardes*, and for detailed research a visit to its Southall office is an essential prerequisite. British Punjabi newspapers and magazines can be very fruitful if they are utilised alongside local English newspapers (for example, *Evening Post*, Birmingham, *Coventry Evening Telegraph* and *Leicester Mercury*) and newspapers from Punjab (for example, *The Tribune,* Chandigarh).

In addition to Punjabi newspapers and magazines, publications in Punjabi are especially relevant for providing an 'insider's' account. Sikh activists within the IWAs and the Khalistan organisations tended to publish prolifically in Punjabi. These publications are normally available from individuals and organisations concerned. Most gurdwaras also tend to be very active in producing brochures that narrate their history, though these are increasingly giving way to websites. Some gurdwaras also produce publications for special occasions such as *Vaisakhi*, which can be quite informative.

Today there is no national centre in Britain which acts as home for documentation on the community. The Modern Record Centre at the University of Warwick and the Birmingham City Library hold collections on the Punjab Communist Party and the IWAs; and while many gurdwaras have 'libraries', these tend to be poorly resourced, filled with volumes from Punjab and have limited references on the published material on Sikhs in Britain.

Finally, the *International Journal of Punjab Studies* (1994–2003) and *Sikh Formations: Religion, Culture and Theory* (2005–) provide the main academic outlet for publications on Sikhs and Sikhism in the diaspora. As such they are an appropriate starting point for further reading. Below we provide a select bibliography for further reading.

Select Bibliography

Alexander, Michael and Sushila Anand. 1979. *Queen Victoria's Maharajah Duleep Singh, 1838–1839* (London: Weidenfeld and Nicolson).

Axel, Brian Keith. 2001. *The Nation's Tortured Body: Violence, Representation and the Formation of the Sikh 'Diaspora'* (Durham: Duke University Press).

Ballard, Roger. 1994. 'Differentiation and Disjunction among the Sikhs in Britain', in Roger Ballard (ed.), *Desh Pardesh: The South Asian Presence in Britain* (London: Hurst), 88–116.

—— and Catharine Ballard, 1977. 'The Sikhs: the Development of South Asian Settlements in Britain', in W. L. Watson (ed.), *Between Two Cultures* (Oxford: Blackwell), 21–56.

Bance, Peter. 2004. *The Duleep Singhs: the Photograph Albums of Queen Victoria's Maharajah* (Stroud: Sutton).

Barrier, N.G. and Verne Dusenbury (eds). 1989. *The Sikh Diaspora: Migration and the Experience Beyond Punjab* (Delhi: Chanakya).

Barry, Brian. 1999. *Culture and Equality: an Egalitarian Critique of Multiculturalism* (Cambridge: Polity Press).

Baumann, Gerd. 1996. *Contesting Culture: Discourses of Identity in Multi-ethnic London* (Cambridge: Cambridge University Press).

Beetham, David. 1970. *Transport and Turbans: a Comparative Study in Local Politics* (London: Oxford University Press).

Bhachu, Parminder. 1989. 'Culture, Ethnicity and Class among Punjabi Sikh Women in 1990s Britain', *New Community* 17: 3, 401–12.

—— 1985. *Twice Migrants: East African Sikh Settlers in Britain* (London: Tavistock).

Bhatti, Gurpreet Kaur. 2004. *Behzti* (Dishonour) (London: Oberon Books).

Brown, Colin. 1984. *Black and White Britain: the Third PSI Survey* (London: Heinemann).

Brown, M. S. 2000. 'Religion and Economic Activity in the South Asian Population', *Ethnic and Racial Studies* 23: 6, 1035–61.

Brass, Paul R. 1974. *Language, Religion and Politics in North India* (Cambridge: Cambridge University Press).

Campbell, Christy. 2000. *The Maharajah's Box: an Imperial Story of Conspiracy, Love and a Guru's Prophecy* (London: HarperCollins).

Chandan, Amarjit. 1993. *Being Here* (London: The Many Press).

DeWitt, John. 1969. *Indian Workers' Associations in Britain* (London: Oxford University Press).

Drury, Beatrice. 1991. 'Sikh Girls and the Maintenance of Ethnic Culture', *New Community*, 17: 3, 387–99.

Duffield, Mark. 1988. *Black Radicalism and the Politics of De-industrialisation* (Aldershot: Avebury).

Gillespie, Marie. 1995. *Television, Ethnicity and Cultural Change* (London: Routledge).

Grewal, J. S. 1990. *The Sikhs of Punjab* (Cambridge: Cambridge University Press).

Guhamn, P. A. S. 1980. 'Bhatra Sikhs in Cardiff: Family and Kinship Organisation', *New Community* 8: 3, 308–16.

Gupta, Rahila, (ed.), 2003. *From Homebreakers to Jailbreakers: Southall Black Sisters* (London: Zed Books).

Hall, Kathleen, D. 2002. *Lives in Translation: Sikh Youth as British Citizens* (Philadelphia: University of Pennsylvania Press).

Helweg, Arthur, W. 1986. *Sikhs in England* (Delhi: Oxford University Press, 2nd edn).

Huntington, Samuel P. 1997. *The Clash of Civilisations and the Remaking of World Order* (London: Simon and Schuster).

—— 2005. *Who are We? America's Great Debate* (London: Free Press).

Jakabosh, Doris, R. 2003. *Relocating Gender in Sikh History* (Delhi: Oxford University Press).

Jurgensmeyer, Mark. 1991. *Radhaswami Reality: the Logic of a Modern Faith* (Princeton: Princeton University Press).

Kalra, Virinder S. and John Hutnyk. 1998. 'Brimful of Agitation, Authenticity and Appropriation: Madonna's "Asian Cool"', *Postcolonial Studies* 1: 3, 339–55.

Kalsi, Sewa Singh. 1992. *The Evolution of a Sikh Community in Britain: Religious and Social Change among Sikhs of Leeds and Bradford* (Leeds: The Department of Theology and Religious Studies, University of Leeds).

Kelly, Paul, (ed.) 2002. *Multiculturalism Reconsidered: Culture and Equality and its Critics* (Cambridge: Polity Press).

La Brack, Bruce. 1988. *The Sikhs of California, 1904–1986* (New York: AMS Press).

Login, E. Dalhousie. 1906. *Lady Login's Recollections: Court Life and Camp Life* (London: John Murray).

McLeod, W. H. 1989. *The Sikhs: History, Religion and Society* (New York: Columbia University Press).

Maan, Bashir. 1992. *The New Scots: the Story of Asians in Scotland* (Edinburgh: J. Donald).

Madood, Tariq. 2005. *Multicultural Politics: Racism, Ethnicity and Muslims in Britain* (Edinburgh: Edinburgh University Press).

National Statistics On-line. 2004. *Focus on Religion*, <http://www.statistics.gov.uk/focuson/religion/>

Nesbitt, Eleanor. 2005. *Sikhism: a Very Short Introduction* (Oxford: Oxford University Press).

—— and Tatla, Darshan S. 1994. *Sikhs in Britain: an Annotated Bibilography* (Coventry: Centre for Research in Ethnic Relations, 2nd edn).

Parekh Bhikhu, Gurharpal Singh and Steve Vertovec (eds). 2003. *Culture and Economy in the Indian Diaspora* (London: Routledge).

Pettigrew, Joyce. 1995. *The Sikhs of Punjab: Unheard Voices of State and Guerrilla Violence* (London: Zed Books).

—— 1975. *Robber Noblemen: a Study of the Political System of Sikh Jats* (Routledge and

Keegan Paul).

Poulter, Sebastian. 1998. *Ethnicity, Law and Human Rights: the English Experience* (Oxford: Clarendon Press).

Oberoi, Harjot. 1994. *The Construction of Religious Boundaries: Culture, Identity and Diversity within the Sikh Tradition* (New Delhi: Oxford University Press).

Rai, Bali. 2001. *(Un) arranged Marriage* (London: Corgi Books).

Rex, John and Gurharpal Singh (eds). 2003. *Governance in Multicultural Societies* (Aldershot: Ashgate).

Rose, E. J. B. and Associates. 1969. *Colour and Citizenship: a Report on British Race Relations* (London: Oxford University Press).

Runnymede Trust. *The Future of Multi-Ethnic Britain: The Parekh Report* (London: Profile Books).

Shackle, Christopher, Gurharpal Singh and Arvind-pal S. Mandair (eds). 2001. *Sikh Religion, Culture and Ethnicity* (Richmond: Curzon Press).

—— 1985. *The Sikhs* (London: Minority Rights Group), no. 65.

Sharma, Sanjay, John Hutnyk and A. Sharma (eds). 1996. *Dis-orienting Rhythms: the Politics of the New Asian Dance Music* (London: Zed Books).

Singh, Gurharpal. 2005. 'British Multiculturalism and Sikhs', *Sikh Formations* 1: 2 (December), 157–73.

—— 2004. 'Sikhs are the Real Losers from *Behzti'*, *Guardian* 23 December.

—— 2003. 'Sikhism and Just War', in Paul Robinson (ed.), *Just War in Comparative Perspective* (Aldershot: Ashgate), 126–36.

—— 2003. 'Multiculturalism in Contemporary Britain: Community Cohesion, Urban Riots and the "Leicester Model"', in *International Journal on Multicultural Societies* 5: 1, (September), <http://portal.unesco.org/shs/en/ev.php-URL_ID=2552&URL_DO=DO_TOPIC&URL_SECTION=-465.html>

—— 2000. *Ethnic Conflict in India: A Case-Study of Punjab* (Basingstoke: Macmillan).

—— 1999. 'A Victim Diaspora? The Case of the Sikhs', *Diaspora* 8: 3 (Winter), 293–307.

—— 1996. 'What is Happening to the Political Science of Ethnic Conflict?' (II) *International Journal of Punjab Studies* 3: 2 (December), 229–41.

—— 1994. *Communism in Punjab: A Study of the Movement up to 1967* (Delhi: Ajanta).

Singh, Nikky-Guninder Kaur. 1993. *The Feminine Principle in the Sikh Vision of the Transcendent* (Cambridge: Cambridge University Press).

Singh, Kushwant. 1991. *A History of the Sikhs. Vol 1: 1469–1839 and Vol 2: 1939–1988* (Oxford: Oxford University Press).

Solomos, John. 1989. *Race and Racism in Contemporary Britain* (Basingstoke: Macmillan).

Tatla, Darshan S. 1999. *The Sikh Diaspora: the Search for Statehood* (London: UCL Press).

—— 1996. *Theses on Punjab Vol. 1: UK and Europe, 1900–1995* (Coventry: Association for Punjab Studies).

—— 1993. 'This is our Home Now: Reminiscences of a Punjabi in Coventry', *Oral History*, 21, 68–74.

—— 1992. 'Nurturing the Faithful: the Role of Sants among Britain's Sikhs', *Religion*, 22, 349–74.

—— and Ian Talbot. 1995. *Punjab* (World Bibliographical Series no. 180) (Oxford: Clio).

—— and Gurharpal Singh. 1989. 'The Punjabi Press', *New Community* 15: 2, 171–84.

Visram, Rozina. 2002. *Asians in Britain: 400 Years of History* (London: Pluto).

Wilson, Amrit. 1978. *Finding a Voice: Asian Women in Britain* (London: Virago).

Index

Afghanistan 10, 13-14, 32, 37
Africa 9, 33, 54, 58; East 2, 27-8, 33, 37, 42,
   46, 53-4, 58-9, 74-5,77, 82, 127, 129,
   148, 152, 159, 161, 165-6, 180, 202,
   316; North 47
Africanisation 53,77
Afro-Caribbean music 202
agriculture 10, 15-16, 23-5, 36-8, 41
Ahaluwalia, Pal 194
Ahluwalia, Sukhpal 157
Ajeeb, Gursharna Singh 192
Ajit 191
Akali, Sohan Singh 72
Akash Radio 190
Akhand, Kirtani Jatha 106, 108
Alaap 200
alcoholism 177
Ali, Monica 197
Alpha TV 190
Aluwalia, Kiranjit 178
Amalgamated Union of Engineering
   Workers 149
Amar 201
Ambala 20
Amrit Bani 190
Amritsar 13, 71, 81, 88-9, 104-5, 117, 143,
   190
Anand, Balwant Singh 47
Anand, Mulk Raj 47
Andrew, Prince 152
Apache Indian 200-1, 203
Argentina 32-3
Arjan, Guru 13
Arnold, Jacques 117

Arya Samaj 17
Asia, 58, 177; Central 33; South 2, 32-3, 43,
   177, 187; South East 316
Asian Dub Foundation 201
Asian Post 191
Atwal, Harjit 192
Auckland 32
Aujala, Dr. A. K. S. 103
Australia 32-3, 56
Awaz 191
Awaz-e-Quam 110, 191
Azad, Avinash 191

Babbar Khalsa (BK) 106-7, 109-11, 120
Baghapurana, Gurmel Singh 91
Bahrain 32
Bains, Jaspal Singh 191
Bains, Navdeep Singh 183
Balsall Heath 73, 146, 189
Bangladesh 161
Barcelona 32
Barking 51
Bassi, Paul 157
batoos (labour recruitment middlemen) 148-
   9, 154-5, 170
Bawa, Baldev 196
Bedford 40-1, 51, 80, 147
Behzti 2, 6, 126, 138-41, 143, 178, 182, 185,
   210, 213, 215
Belfast 63
Belgium 32, 46, 55
Bend It Like Beckham 63, 140, 165, 173-4,
   181, 197-8
Bhaini 48

Bhaji on the Beach 63
Bhalla, G. 157
Bhamra, Mohinder Kaur 203-4
bhangra 2, 7, 67, 169, 178, 186, 190, 193-4, 196, 198-204, 207
Bharatiya Janata Party (BJP) 25
Bhatinda 193
Bhatras 48, 72-3, 77-9, 110, 146-7
Bhatti, Gurpreet Kaur 139-41, 178
Bhindranwale, Sant Jarnail Singh 24, 92, 103-8, 112
Bidwell, Sidney 130
Bihar 38
Bilga 48
Bilga, Surjit Singh 72
Bindman, Geoffrey 132
Birmid Industries 147, 151
Birmingham 51, 63-4, 73-5, 78-80, 85-9, 91, 97, 102, 105-7, 109, 111, 114, 123, 132, 146-7, 149, 151, 154, 167, 178, 190-5, 200
Birmingham Repertory Theatre 6, 139
Blair, Tony 1, 120, 136
Boyle, Sir Edward 100
Bradford 41, 51, 63, 80, 91, 97-8, 116, 121-2, 192-3
Brar, Harcharan 193
Brar, Harpal 123
Brighton 46, 72
Bristol 79, 105
British Airways, 135, 156
British Broadcasting Corporation (BBC) 89, 114, 140-1, 189, 201, 214; Asian Network 189, 201
British Columbia 32
British Organisation of Sikh Students (BOSS) 206
British Sikh Consultation Forum 88, 216
British Sikh Federation 119
Buddhism 1, 174
Budhiraja, Arjan Singh 99
Bundala 48
Burma 32
Bursnall metal works strike 156
Burundi, Amar Singh 91

Cabinet Mission (1946) 19-20
California 32
Cambridge University 45, 47, 70-1, 96
Campaign against Racial Discrimination (CARD) 97
Canada 32-5, 37, 39-40, 56, 58, 71, 75, 103,

105, 108, 114, 135, 156, 171, 182-3, 191, 195
Cape Province (South Africa) 33
Cardiff 79, 192
Caribbean *see* West Indies, Jamaica, Trinidad
Carlton Club 44
caste, artisan castes 28, 146; Bhanghi (cleaners) 28; *bhangra* and 202-2; Bhatras 72-3, 77-9, 110, 146-7, 192; Brahmins (priests) 10, 27; Chamars (labourers) 28, 146; Chimbas 175; Chuhras 146; and endogamy 175; and gangs 204-5; Ghumars (potters) 74, 146; and gurdwara movement 69, 81; Guru Nanak and 13; INC's broad appeal to 100-1; as inerasable cleavage and pluralism in Sikh society 27, 216; irregular caste pattern in Punjab 10; Jalahas 146; Jats 10, 27-8, 30-1, 41-2, 60,77, 109, 146, 175, 198, 204, 216-17; Jhinwars 146; Kashatriaya (warriors) 10; Khatris 77; labouring/ service castes (Ad-Dharms or Dalits) 28, 40-1, 60; and landholding 27-9; literary treatment of 197; Mazbis (sweepers) 28, 60; and migration 28, 41-2; Nais 146; Namdharis 79-81, 91, 110, 173; Nirankaris 79-80; and patron–client rela- tionships 27; and political parties 40; and pollution 27; Radhaswamis 79-80; Ramgarhias (carpenters) 28, 54, 74, 77-9, 109-10, 134, 146, 192; Ravidasis 74, 79- 80, 110; Scheduled Castes 28, 80, 101; and social mobility 28, 78; Sudra (service caste) 10; Valmikis 79-80; in village society 27; Visyya (traders) 10; and youth culture 206
Castle Menzies 44
Chadda, Gurinder 197
Chadha, Gurbachan and Sandy 157
Chaggar, Gurdip 98
Chahal, Balder Singh 129
Chahal, Karamjit Singh 112
Chandan, Amarjit 194, 197
Chandan, Swaran 192
Chandigarh 21, 91, 104
Channel Four 204
Charan Singh Panchi 102-3; *see also* Khalistani Movement
Charcha 114, 193
Charity Commission 83, 85, 89
Charles, Prince 45, 69, 71, 89, 212
Chaudhry, R. S. 194

Chief Khalsa Divan (CKD) 71
Chinese 161
Chirag Pehchan 200
Chitarkar, Ishwar 195
Chix bubble gum strike 154
Chohan, Dr Jaggit Singh 102-4, 106-7, 110,
    114
Christianity 17, 44, 140-1, 171
class 5, 94, 96-102, 121, 123-4, 142, 162-3,
    210, 213
Cole, Owen 194
Colombo 32
Colville, Lord 44
Commission for Racial Equality (CRE) 1,
    132-3
Commission on the Future of Multi-Ethnic
    Britain 1
Communist Party (Great Britain) 96
Communist Party of India (CPI) 30-1, 39,
    82-3, 96-7, 102-4, 109-10, 193, 195
Communist Party of India (Marxist) (CPI
    (M)) 74, 82, 97, 104, 193
Communist Party of India (Marxist-Leninist
    Great Britain) (CPI (MLGB)) 97, 104,
    193, 195
community 26, 29-30; bhangra and 202-3;
    building 52, 69, 81, 126, 128-9, 137,
    168, 209-10; bus services 63; community
    cohesion87, 117, 119-24, 200, 210-11;
    factions in 81-2; gurdwaras 69, 81;
    illegals in 60; izzat and other regulating
    concepts 29-30; leadership 82; 'moral
    community' 175; in new social hierarchy
    162; services (seva) 13, 86-8; support for
    strikers 151; typical Sikh 'signposts' 147;
    vision of 216-17
Coneygre foundry 148
Conservative Party 112, 115-16, 120, 122,
    170
Cook, Robin, 109
Copenhagen 32
Cornershop 201
Cornwall 155
Council of European Communities 134
Council of Khalistan (COK) 106-7, 109-10,
    112-13, 116
Coventry 49, 51, 63-4, 75, 80, 85, 88, 91,
    96-7, 105, 109, 121-2, 131, 146-7, 151,
    167, 186, 192-4, 200
crime 176-7, 204
Cripps mission 19
Culture Shock 200

culture, bhangra 2, 7, 67, 169, 178, 186, 190,
    193-4, 196, 198-204, 207; Bollywood
    169, 190, 201; and broadcast media 189-
    90, 196, 205-6; clash of cultures 168-9,
    184-5, 198, 204-5; of consumption 175,
    179-80, 203-5; culture of rights 175;
    dhadis (folk singers) 110; epics 10;
    festivals 12; folklore 10; folksongs 12;
    gang culture 204; giddha 203; and
    heritage transmission 186, 202; hybridity
    186, 200, 202, 205; and Internet 206; of
    Jata 198; machismo 150, 178, 182;
    Punglish/Southalli language 187; qissa
    genre 150; and religion 206; translation
    of 205; worksongs 150-1; youth culture
    186, 204-6
Curzon, Lord, Viceroy of India 46
Cyprus 32

Daddriwale, Ranjit Singh 91
Dagenham 147
Dal Khalsa (DK) 106, 108-10
Danda, Parmjit 121
Darlaston 191
Dartmouth Auto Castings Ltd 149
Das, Darbari 91
Das, Darshan 113, 116
Das, Garib 91
Daska Tahsil 48
Dawan, Shanti Sarup 128
DCS 200
Delhi 10, 20, 32, 36, 50, 53, 91, 101-2, 106,
    114, 193, 195
Denmark 32, 36
Denning, Lord 132, 138
Derby 51, 62, 80, 97, 109, 147, 191, 193,
    198
Derrida, Jacques 140
Des Pardes 100, 163, 191, 195, 215
Desi Radio 190
Dhadi, Pritam Singh 72
Dhand, Raghbir 97
Dhanjal v British Steel (2003) 137
Dhaw, Jagtar 196
Dhillon, Ganga Singh 104
Dhillon, Tej and Bobby 157
Dhinsa, Jojar S. 157
diaspora 2, 6, 9, 18, 25, 36, 38-9, 41, 54-5,
    57, 62, 75-6, 90, 94, 104, 185, 197; con-
    structed 94
Dicks, Terry 115-17
difference 138, 142, 182-4

Doaba region 5, 37-41, 48, 73, 83, 96, 101, 154, 216
Domeliwale 75
Domeliwale, Harbans Singh 91
Dominion Cinema 52, 98-9
Dosanj, Narinder 151
Dowell Lee, A. G. 132; see also *Mandla v Dowell Lee*
drugs 176-7, 203-4
Dubai 32
Dundee 146
Duport foundry 148
Dwyer, Sir Michael 49, 96

Ealing 100, 121-3, 129, 142-3
East End Foods 156
East Ham 40, 51
East India Company 2, 15, 44
East Midlands 62, 72, 76-8, 96, 153, 155
Edgbaston 64, 132
Edinburgh 79, 117
Edmonton (Canada) 91
education 39-40, 47, 70, 133, 142-3, 145-6, 157-64, 168, 176, 178, 181, 184, 187
Egypt 46
Ekta 190-1
Elizabeth, Queen 117
Elveden Hall 44-5
employment 66, 67, 99, 119, 134, 142, 145-64, 166, 173, 178-80, 184
Ennals, David 100, 128
equality 13, 15, 26-7, 30, 80, 138, 141-3, 162, 178-9, 181, 183-4, 214
Erith 40, 147, 192
ethnic cleansing 20, 36
Eton School 45
Europe 9, 32, 36, 47, 58, 90, 156, 195; Eastern 50
European Commission on Human Rights 138
European Convention on Human Rights 129
European Union 60,87, 118-21, 138, 144, 152, 182

factionalism 27, 30-1, 74-6, 81-6, 95, 98, 100, 162, 196, 216
family, change in 210; clash of cultures and 168-9, 184-5; divorce and 174-5, 184; dowry system and 173, 179-80, 203; and dress code 168; education and 168; employment and 166; extended structure of 166; home ownership and 166; *izzat* (honour) 29-30, 83, 127, 166, 169, 178, 216; kinship (*biradari*) connections and 29-30, 51, 55, 82, 86, 100, 146, 155, 162, 165-6, 170, 184; loyalty 29; male children prioritised 167; marriage 55, 159, 166, 169-76, 178, 184, 197-9, 203, 206; migration and 165; between moral community and consumerism 175; out-marriages and 175, 184; professionals and 176; self-employment and 167; size of 166-7, 184; social policing of young in 166;traditional joint households 167-8, 184; unifications (geographical) and 166; weddings as drivers of economy 171-3; wives' and mothers' role 166
Far East 2, 9, 27, 32-3, 37, 53, 195
Faridkot 91
Ferozepore 91
Festival of India (1982) 104
Fiji 33-4, 54
First World War 15, 46, 72
Foley, Maurice 99
Ford Motor Company 146
Forest Gate 51
Foucault, Michel 140
France 32, 46, 55, 127
Frankfurt 32
freedom of expression 138, 215
Futtaghar 44

Gandhi, Indira 24, 98, 100, 104, 106, 111, 132
Gandhi, Mohandas K. 19
Gandhi, Rajiv 24, 111, 115-16
Garel-Jones, Tristan 116
Garshankar village 40
Gate Gourmet strike 156, 163, 215
gender, and alcoholism 177; *bhangra* and 202-3; British-born Sikhs and 214; and caste 181; changing relations of 6; colonialism and 181; and consumption 179-80; and crime 177; and domestic violence 178; and dowry system 173, 179-80; and education 157, 181, 184; and employment 152-4, 178-80, 184; equality 164, 178-9, 181, 214; and forced marriages 178-9; in gurdwaras 84-5, 92, 109; and honour (*izzat*) 29-30, 166, 169, 178; and Indian/English cultural fields 205; kinship and 165-6; male children prioritised 167; and modernity 177-8;

and multiculturalism 179; and patriarchy 30, 177-80, 184; and racism 179-80; radical black feminist discourse on 179, 184; *sati* 181; and sexual abuse 179; Sikh feminist discourse on 179-80, 184; Sikh traditionalist discourse on 180-1; youth culture and 206

Germany 32, 36, 55

Gian Singh Surjeet (folksong group) 110

Gill, Balwant Singh 73

Gill, Jasvinder 177

Gill, K. P. S. 111

Gill, Nina 121

Gill, Parmjit Singh 122

Gill, Sardul Singh 96

Gillingham 147

Glasgow 40, 48, 51, 63, 79-80, 96, 146-7, 200

globalisation 4, 28, 34, 38, 41, 56, 68, 94, 162, 169, 184, 202, 206, 208, 217-18

Gobind, Guru 13-14, 143

Golden Star 200, 202

Golden Temple 6, 13, 20, 24, 100, 105, 113-16, 117-18, 143, 181, 183, 190, 211

Goodness Gracious Me! 63

Gravesend 40, 51, 63, 80, 121, 146-7, 166, 171, 208

Greece 2, 46

Green Party 111, 122

Greenwich 121

Grunwicks 151

Gujarat 57

Gujarati language 187, 197

Gujral, Inder Kumar 117

Gulf states 34-5

Gulhati, Satinder 157

Gummer, John 208-9

Gummer, Selwyn 208

gurdwaras, and Akal Takht 183; attendance of religious services in 89; *Behzti* set in 139; Bhatras and 72-3, 77; Canadian 182; and caste 41, 83; changing role of 210; and clash of cultures 168; and communities 69, 81, 147; Council of Sikh Gurdwaras in Birmingham (CSGB) 87-8, 139; cyber gurdwaras 90; *Des Pardes* readers and 215; and education 86; elections in 83-4; factional disputes in 81-6; and festivals 98, 143; fundraising for 40; gender representation in 84-5, 92, 109; and Ghumar Sikhs (potters) 74; as guardians of values 69; Gurdwara Act

(1925) 17; gurdwara movement 5, 72, 207, 216; Guru Amar Das Gurdwara (Leicester) 74; Guru Nanak Gurdwara (Bedford) 86; Guru Nanak Gurdwara (Leicester) 74, 84, 86, 212; Guru Nanak Gurdwara (Smethwick) 73-4, 83, 85-6, 187; Guru Nanak Parkash Gurdwara (GNPG) (Coventry) 85, 109; Guru Nanak Singh Sabha 73; Guru Tegh Bahadur Gurdwara (Leicester) 74, 85; *illaqa* (local) rivalries in 74, 83; and the inner city 2, 69, 72,87, 92; Kensington/Chelsea Gurdwara 72; and Khalistani movement 103-11, 118, 124; and *langar* 151; literary evenings in 195; and localised multiculturalism 141-4; and the local state 88; management of 81-4; and matrimonial matchmaking 86; and new social hierarchy 163; and patriarchy 152; and political organisations 81-2, 100, 102-5; Punjabi language teaching in 187; radio broadcasts 190; Ramgarhia Board Gurdwara (Leicester) 74; Ramgarhia Sikh Gurdwara (Slough) 86; and Ramgarhias 74, 77; and Ravidasis 74, 80; *sants* and 75; and service provision 86-8; Shepherd's Bush Gurdwara 46, 49, 71-2, 85, 92, 103; and 'Sikh political system' 69-70; Singh Sabha, Southall 72; Singh Sabhas movement and 17; Southall Cultural Society 72-3; Sri Dasmesh Gurdwara 74; Sri Guru Ravidass Bhawan 74; Sri Guru Singh Sabha Gurdwara, Southall (SGSSGS) 64, 69-71, 73, 84, 92, 109; Sri Ravidas Gurdwara (Leicester) 74; and strikes 151; transparency and democracy in 92; in UK landscape 43; violent disputes in 84-5; and weddings 171-2; welfare role 86, 87-8; young people and 89-90, 205-6

Guru Granth Sahib 13

Guru Nanak Nishkam Sewak Jatha (GNNSJ) 75, 92, 133, 216

gurus 9-15, 25, 28, 180, 182, 184, 186, 217

Handsworth 41, 63, 75, 113, 142

Hans, Surjit 192

Hare, Tony Singh 177

Hargobind, Guru 13

Haripur village 48

Harrow School 46

Haryana State 21, 32

Hattersley, Roy 133
Hayes 137
Heathrow Airport 73, 97, 99, 135-6, 146-7, 154, 156
Heera 200
Heidelberg 32
Heseltine, Michael 114
Highfields 74
Hillingdon 63, 123, 154, 160
Himachal Pradesh 20
Himalayas 10
Hind Mazoor Lahir 104
Hindi language 189
Hindus/Hinduism 1-2, 12, 15-17, 19-21, 31, 36, 49, 57-9, 80, 96-7, 100-1, 113, 157, 160, 167, 169, 174, 197
Holle Holle 200
Holy Smokes gang 204
home ownership 67, 156, 166
Hong Kong 34, 37, 54
honour (*izzat*) 29-30, 83, 127, 166, 169, 178, 216
Hoshiarpur 37, 40, 91
Hounslow 63, 75, 80, 123, 136
household size 67-8
Howe, Sir Geoffrey 115
Huddersfield 51, 63, 80, 109
human rights 112, 115-17, 129, 183, 211, 216
Humberside 62, 76
Huntington, Samuel P. 1

illegal immigration 35, 51, 53, 55-6, 60, 163
indentured labour 33; 'neo-indenture' 35
India, and anti-Sikh riots (1984) 106; British expansion in 14-15; Dalit movemenmt in 80; East India Company 15; economic liberalisation in 38, 211; High Commission in UK 101-6, 111, 114-15, 128; and Khalistani movement in UK 102-8, 114-17; labour recruitment from 33-4; and *Mandla v Dowell Lee* 132; migration from 34-5; Mogul rule 12-14; partition in 16, 19-20, 31, 34, 36, 50, 197; peace process with Pakistan 211; political organisations in 82; post-colonial 20-5; Scheduled Castes in 28, 60; and Sikh separatism 104, 132; Sikh population in 32; State of Emergency (1975–7) 98; Terrorist and Disruptive Act 117; trade future with UK 211
India House 71

India League 47, 49
India Times 191
Indian Airlines 108, 114, 135
Indian Army 3, 6, 13, 15, 20, 24, 33, 39, 41, 46, 51, 100, 105
Indian Chamber of Princes 46
Indian Civil Service 47
Indian Mutiny 15
Indian National Congress (INC) 12, 19-21, 23-5, 80, 82, 98, 102, 109-11
Indian National Front 102
Indian Overseas Congress (IOC) 94-5, 100-2, 109-10, 113
Indian Workers' Association (IWA) 49, 67, 94-101, 109, 113-14, 121, 123, 128, 149-52, 163, 179, 190, 193, 195, 210, 213, 217; Indian Workers' Association (CPI (M)) 98; Indian Workers' Association (CPI (MLGB)) 97-8, 193
Indonesia 32
Indus river 10
information technology (IT) 161
International Golden Temple Corporation 103
International Punjabi Literary Society (east London) 195
International Sikh Brotherhood 187
International Sikh Youth Federation (ISYF) 106-14, 117, 120; International Sikh Youth Federation (ISYF) (DT) 108
Internet 171, 177, 206
Islam 1-2, 31, 36, 49, 57-8, 92, 96, 120, 152, 174; *see also* Muslim League; Pakistan; Punjab and UK, Muslims in
Italy 32, 36, 47

Jacob, Stephen 100
Jago Wale (folksong group) 110
Jahangir, Emperor 13
Jalandhar 20, 37-40, 53, 91, 143, 192
Jallianwala Bagh massacre (1920) 49, 117
Jamaica 33
Jamuna river 10
Jandialvi, Avtar 191-2, 196
Jandialvis 83
Jasminder 157
Jatha, Akhand Kirtani 192
Jats 10, 13, 27-8, 30-1, 41-2, 60, 109, 146, 175, 198, 204, 216-17
Jenkins, Roy 209
Jerry Springer: the Opera 141
Jews 1, 157, 164

Jinnah, Muhammad Ali 19
Johal family 154
Johal, Avtar 97, 151, 193
Johal, Makhan 97
John Tomkins Company 149
Jolly, Sohan Singh 128
Joshi, Jagmohan 97
July 7 (2015) attack (7/7) 1, 3, 5, 88, 90, 93, 96, 120, 206, 208, 211, 217

Kabul 32
Kailay, Karam Singh 72
Kambliwale, Gurbachan Singh 91
Kanshal, Ram 191
Kanwar, Ranjit 191
Kapoor, Balwant Singh 191
Kapoor, Sukhbir Singh 194
Karichowale, Sant Puran Singh 75, 91, 105, 133
Karm, Karm Singh 191
Karnana, Bakhshish Singh 102
Karpurthala 37, 40
Karpurthala, Maharaja of 46
Kashmir 14, 24, 105, 110, 117
Kashmiri Liberation Front 105, 110
Kaur, Basant 111
Kaur, Bibi Gurdial 73
Kaur, Chatur 47
Kaur, G. 157
Kaur, Rani Jindan 44
Kenya 34, 75, 129
Kericho (Kenya) 75, 91
Khabra, Piara Singh 99, 115, 121, 123, 179
Khalistan News 110
Khalistani Movement 2, 6, 14, 19-21, 24-5, 60, 82, 84, 92, 94-124, 128, 132-3, 159, 163, 173, 191, 193, 204, 210-11, 215, 216-17; neo-Khalistani movement 124, 210-11
Khalsa Human Rights
Khalsa Jatha of the British Isles (KJBI) 70-1, 96
Khalsa Samachar 71
Khebbal, Sukhdev 157
Khera, Karamjit 157
Khiali's Dhadi Jatha (folksong group) 110
Kholi, M. 157
King, Tarsem 121
Kingston 64
kinship (*biradari*) connections 29-30, 51, 55, 82, 86, 100, 146, 155, 162, 165-6, 170, 184

Kiri 48
Kirnan 191
Koh-i-Noor diamond 14, 44
Koma 200
Kot Bakal Khan village 48
Kuala Lumpur 32
Kuldip Singh v British Rail (1985) 137

Labour Party 87-8, 111, 115-16, 120-4, 124, 128-30, 140-2, 209
Lahore 14, 32, 44, 108
Lahsa 14
Lalkar 97, 123, 193, 195
Lamme, Bhag Singh 91
landholding 27-9, 39, 67
Langowal, Sant Harchand Singh 104
Leamington Spa 40, 191
Leeds 51, 54, 63, 75, 78, 91, 97, 167, 190
Leicester 40, 51, 54, 62, 64, 74-5, 83, 85, 88-9, 97, 109, 111-12, 115, 121-2, 131, 143, 147, 154, 163, 167, 177, 190, 192-3, 198-9
Liberal Democratic Party 120, 122
Libya 107
Lidder, Sohan Singh 113
Lit, Avtar 157
Liverpool 79, 193
Login, Dr 44
London 32, 44, 47, 51-4, 62-4, 70-2, 76, 78, 91, 96, 105-6, 111, 121, 133, 147, 153, 155, 163, 180, 191-4, 197,
Londonderry 63
Lozells 74
Ludhiana 53, 91
Lufthansa Skychief strike 154
Lund 32
Luton 109, 113
Luxemburg 32

Macauliffe, M. A. 47, 195
MacTaggart, Fiona 140
Madden, Max 115-16
Madonna 201
Mahal, Bally Kaur 198
Maharaja Duleep Singh Centenary Trust 45
Maharashtra 32
Majaha region 73
Majithia, Sir Sundar Singh 47
Malaysia 32-3, 54, 73
Malik, Hardit Singh 46
Malsian 48
Malwa region 73

Mamta 191
Manchester 51, 79, 91, 100, 127-8
Mand, Kesar Singh 73, 191
Mandair, Arvind-pal Singh 194
Mandla v Dowell Lee (1983) 130-3, 138, 210
Mandla, Gurinder Singh 132, 139
Manila 32
Man-Jit 191
Mann, Gurdev Singh 177
Marks, Kenneth 130
Martin, Paul 183
matriarchy 29
Mauritius 33
Mazbis 28, 60
McDonnell, John 120
Mehatpur 48
Menon, Krishna 49
Mexico 32-3
Middle East 32, 34-5, 41, 47
middlemen *see batoos*
Midland Motor Cylinder Co. Ltd 147
Midlands 48, 91, 96-8, 114, 133, 180
migration, areas of origin 26; asylum/refugee
    settlement 35-7, 55, 60; of Bhatras 48;
    and caste 28, 41-2; chain migration 34,
    39-40, 48, 51; colonial modernity and
    26; of Dalits 40-1, 60; cultural factors in
    38, 42; economic migration 55; and
    education 187; and the family 51, 165;
    first wave (1860s–1890s) 33, 39; of
    graduates 38; to Gulf states 34; illegal 51,
    53, 55, 60; of indentured (and 'neo-
    indentured') workers 33, 35; Indian
    Army as mechanism of 33, 39, 41; IWA
    and 101; labour demand as pull factor 34,
    41, 50; land shortage as push factor 29;
    liberal immigration policies as pull factor
    34; of local groups *en bloc* 39-40, 51;
    migration industry 38-9; New
    Commonwealth migrants 31, 34, 43, 50,
    144, 208; oil boom (1970s) and 35;
    political dislocation and 41, 50; post-
    1945 2-3, 34-6, 43, 50, 208; post-1972
    54-5; pre-1945 31-4; of princes 44-6; as
    Punjabi/Sikh tradition 26, 31, 56;
    push/pull factors 34-8; as safety valve 38;
    second wave (1880s–1940s) 33-4; Sikhs
    knowledgeable about 36; of soldiers 46-
    7; of students 47; 'twice migrants' 53-4,
    77; unemployment as push factor 38;
    waves of 9;
modernity 3, 23, 25-6, 146, 177-8, 183, 215

Mohali 192
Mohammed, Fateh 48
Mohammed, Nathoo 48
Moranwalians 83
Mosley 64
MTV 201
Muller, Bamba 44
multiculturalism, and 9/11, 7/7 1, 93, 208;
    and asymmetric pluralism 144; and *Behzti*
    affair 126, 138-41, in Canada 35; and
    'clash of civilisations' debate 1, 208; as
    'community of communities' 144; and
    festivals 143; as first formulated by Roy
    Jenkins 209; gurdwaras as 'cathedrals' of
    multicultural inner city 2, 69, 72, 87, 92;
    ideological 1; Labour Party and minori-
    ties linked through 87-8; literature and
    198; as localised policy 6, 141-4; and
    media 205; and 'negative accommoda-
    tion' 144, 209; post 9/11 and 7/7 93; and
    racism 141; and radical black feminism
    179; and Sikh dress code 126-38; Sikhs as
    'favoured community' 212; Sikh history
    and 9; Sikhs as pioneers of British multi-
    culturalism 2, 6, 143, 210; Sikh rule
    exemption in 6, 126, 137, 141, 144, 209-
    10; 'soft'/performative 143; and Swann
    Report (1985) 187; and urban riots
    (1970s–1980s) 142; and youth culture
    205
Multitone 201
Muslim League 12, 19-20

Nabha, Maharaja of 46-7
Nagas 105, 110
Nakodar village/sub-district 40, 48
Namaksarias 75
Namdharis 79-81, 91, 110, 173
Nanak, Guru 12-13, 49, 71, 100, 143, 145
Nanaksar sants 75
Nangal 48
Natal (South Africa) 33
National Front (UK) 98
nationalism 12, 19-21, 25
Nawan Sandesh 191
Nawanshahar 40
Nehru, Jawaharlal 20-1, 46, 101
Nesbitt, E. 194
Nestlé 137
Netherlands 36, 55
Network of Sikh Organisations 88, 136, 216
New Commonwealth immigrants 31, 34,

43, 50, 144
New Look plc 156
New York 32, 38
New Zealand 32-3
Nicholas, Brian 130
Nigeria 54
Nilgiri, Tarsem 192
Nirankaris 91, 104
Noor, Niranjan Singh 97
Norfolk 44
North America 9
Northern Ireland 62-3, 76-9
Notting Hill riots 52
Nottingham 51, 62, 97, 109, 147, 154, 193-4, 200

Oadby 64
oil boom (1970s) 35
Oldbury 91
Oman 32
Ontario 32
Operation Blue Star 6, 13, 20, 24, 36, 55, 95-6, 100, 105-6, 114, 124, 135, 169, 211, 215
Osama bin Laden 152
Oxford 80, 194
Oxford University 45, 57

Paban village 48
Pakistan, birth of 12, 16, 19-21; Indian border 21; labour recruitment from 34; migration from 34-5, 161; peace process with India 211; Sikh population in 32
Palestine 46
Panama 33
Pandori Khas 48
Panesar 137
Panthic Committee 113
Paris 32, 45, 47
Parkash, Prem 192
Patiala and East Punjab States Union (PEPSU) 20
Patiala, Maharaja of 73; and see Singh, Bhupendra
patriarchy 29-30
Peach, Blair 98
Penang 32
Pensioners' Rights campaign 163
Perthshire 44
Peterborough 79
Phagwara village 40
Philippines 32

Phillips, Trevor 1
Pindori 48
Plaid Cymru Party 120
Powell, Enoch 128
Priest, Maxi 203
Progressive Punjabi Writers' Association 195
Progressive Writers Association (Wolverhampton) 195
Pujji, Mohinder Singh 47
Punjab All-Party Parliamentary Group 120
Punjab Human Rights Organisation 112
Punjab Radio 190
Punjab Times 100, 191, 195
Punjab Unity Forum 113
Punjab Weekly 191
Punjab, agriculture in 10, 15-16, 23-5, 36-8, 41; Anandpur Sahib Resolution (ASR) 24-5; annexation by East India Company (1849) 2, 15, 44, 46; *bhangra* industry in 201-2; 'Canal Colonies' 16, 23, 36, 39; and *Des Pardes* readers in UK 215; *dharm yud morcha* 24, 100, 104; emigration push factors 34; employment in 159; exile literature and 195-7; family in 165; as frontier society 31-3, 182; gender relations in 167; 'Green Revolution' in 23, 37-8; Haryana State created 21; identity politics in 133; 'internal colonialism' charge 23; literacy in 146; marriage in 169-75, media in 105; modernity and 3, 23, 25; Muslims in 147; myth of return to 152-3; and 'Naxalite' communists 97; and new Indian economy 211; origin of name 10; partition of 16, 19-21, 31, 34, 36, 50; patron–client politics in 94-5, 100; political organisations in 82; princely states of 43, 46; Punjab Reorganisation Act (1966) 21; Punjab–UK exchange schemes 143; Punjabi-speaking province (Punjabi Suba) campaigns 21-3, 38, 99; Radhaswamis in 81; Rajiv–Longowal Accord 24; Ravidasis in 80; remains the Sikh homeland 9, 40, 196, 202-3; 'remembered villages' in 5, 31, 42, 83; as remittance economy 35; return migration to 56-7; SAD leads autonomy movement in 133; SAD in power in 100, 118; satellite TV link to UK 190; sectarian clashes in (1980s-2000s) 81; separate Sikh state ('Khalistan')

campaigns 2, 6, 14, 19-21, 24-5, 60, 82, 84, 92, 94-124, 128, 132-3, 159, 163, 173, 191, 193, 204, 210-11, 215, 216-17; sexual diversity in 184; and Sikh organisations overseas 94-5; Sikh population in 32; social consequences of colonialism in 3, 17, 146, 181-2, 201; as transitional (Hindu–Muslim) zone 10; travel agents in 39, 55; urban–rural distinctions in 27, 36; village society in 27, 29-30, 40-2
Punjabi Arts Council (Birmingham) 195
Punjabi broadcasting 189-90
Punjabi Darpan 191
Punjabi Guardian 191
Punjabi Jarnail 191
Punjabi language 6-7, 10, 12, 89, 142, 168, 186-207
Punjabi MC 186
Punjabi Patrika 191
Punjabi Post 191
Punjabi Sahit Sabha 195
Punjabi TV 190
Purewal, Balraj 98
Purewal, Tarsem Singh 191, 195
Putney 71

Qualcast 148-9

racism 3, 97-9, 118-19, 121, 129, 141, 144, 148, 151-2, 160, 165, 179-81, 196-7, 204-5
Radhaswamis 91
Rai, Ajit Singh 96, 98
Rai, Bali 198, 206
Rai, E. N. Mangat 47
Rai, Gurdial Singh 191-2
Rai, Jasdev Singh 88, 112, 140
Rai, Sulakhan Singh 113
Rai, Zorawar Singh 103
Raindy and Raindy 151
Raison, Timothy 135
Raj Radio 190
Rajasthan 32
Ram, Mansa 48
Ramgarhia Panthic Convention
Ramgarhia, Jassa Singh 28
Ramgarhias 28, 54, 74, 77-9, 109-11, 134
Rana, Dr Daljit 157
Rana, Dilip Singh 123
Rana, Manjit 191
Rana, Ranjit Singh 108-10, 192
Ranger, R. S. 157

Rangoon 32
Rao, (Prime Minister) Narsimha 111
Rarewala, Ishar Singh 91
Rarewalas 75
Rarewale, Mann Singh 91
Rathore Mohinder Singh 108
Ravidas (Sant religious leader) 29
Ravidasis 28, 60, 74, 79-80 110
Redbridge 63-4, 123
Reehal, Ratan Singh 192
Richmond, Duke of 44
Rode, Jasbir Singh 107-8
Rooker, Jeff 117
Royal Air Force (RAF) 47
Rurka Kalan 48
Rushdie, Salman 138, 140-2
Russia 45

Sachkhand Nanak Dham 113
Sadarpura 48
Sadiq, Avtar 97
Sagar, G. S. S. 127-8
Sagoo, Bally 200-1
Sagoo, Gurcharam 192
Sahib Bhaini 91
Sahni, Gurnam Sungh 191, 194
Salimpura 48
Sanderson, Neville 133
Sandesh 191
Sandesh International 113
Sandhu, Amerjit 157
Sandhu, Harmander Singh 113
Sandhu, Joginder Singh 100, 103
Sandhu, Kartar Singh 163
Sandhu, Tarsem Singh 128
Sandwell 63, 74, 88, 121-2, 143, 147
Sanga, Sujinder Singh 191
Sanghera, Gurnam Singh 98
Sant (religious) tradition 12, 19, 29
Sawhney, Nitin 201
School of African and Oriental Studies (SOAS) 188-9
Scotland 43-4, 48, 62-3, 72, 76-9, 146-7, 155
Scottish National Party 112, 120
Scunthorpe 51
Seattle 38
Second World War 2, 31, 33-4, 43, 47, 68, 72, 92, 96, 124, 137, 145, 164, 218
September 11 (2011) attack (9/11) 1, 3, 5, 88, 90, 93, 96, 118, 120, 124, 136, 138, 141, 152, 206, 208, 211, 217

service 26, 30

Sewak, Avtar Singh 72

sexuality, bisexuals 182-4; changing nature of 6; as difference 182-4; and equality 178-9, 183-4, 214; gays 182-4; and identity 207; lesbians 182-4; machismo and 182; and post-colonial Sikh dilemmas 217; 'pragmatic' view of 183; 'radical' view of 183-4; sexual abuse 179; sexual revolution 181; Sikh/colonial sexual ambiguity 182; traditional standpoint on 182-3; young people and 184

Shackle, Christopher 189

Shankar 48

Sharma, Vishnu Dutt 96-8, 114, 190-1

Shastri, Lal Bahadur 101-2

Shere-Punjab 103, 191

Sher-e-Punjab 191

Shergill, Nirpal Singh 194

Shiromani Akali Dal (SAD) 17, 20-5, 38, 69, 74, 82, 94-5, 99-100, 102-4, 106, 111, 128, 133

Shiromani Gurdwara Parbandhak Committee (SGPC) 17, 69, 82, 88-9, 93, 182

Shukla, Durga Dutt 73

Sialkot 48, 79

Siarhwale, Mihan Singh 91

Sidhwan 48

Sikh Agenda 120

Sikh Courier 193

Sikh Federation (UK) 88, 119-23, 216

Sikh Forum 113

Sikh global networks 34

Sikh Homeland Front 102-3

Sikh Human Rights Group 88, 112, 119, 136, 140, 216

Sikh Nari Manch (UK) 181

Sikh Political Party (UK) 94

Sikh population 32

Sikh Religious Symbols Action Committee 135

Sikh Secretariat 120, 136

Sikh soldiers 15

Sikh Times 191

Sikh Tribune 191

Sikhism, Ad-Dharm movement and 19; agrarian roots of 26, 145-6, 161; Akal Takht 13, 81, 88-9, 105, 107, 111, 113, 120, 182-3; Akalis 17, 19-20, 24, 69, 83, 98-100, 102-3, 109, 111; and alcoholism 177; *amrit-dhari* Khalsa 17-18, 82, 127, 135, 137, 142; Anglo-Sikh heritage 3, 6,

45, 116, 130, 134, 143, 209, 212, 217; beliefs 12-13; British-born vs non-British-born 216-18; and class 5, 94, 96-100, 142, 210, 213; and difference 138, 142; diversity of 77; dress code 2, 6, 9, 78, 99, 126-38, 142, 168-9, 182, 206, 209, 216; ethnicisation of 203; ethnicity and religion 74, 81, 87-8, 119, 132-3, 138; family 145; as 'favoured community' 3, 212; festivals 12, 71, 86, 98, 104, 143, 190; founding of 12; five Ks 13, 18, 89, 127; *Guru Granth Sahib* 12-13, 28, 73, 89, 113, 190; 'heroic age' (rise of) 13-14; identity 2-7, 13, 17, 51, 65-68, 69, 94, 96, 107, 118-26, 127, 132-3, 138, 142-3, 145, 169, 179-80, 184, 186, 200, 202-7, 210, 213; ideological 54; institution building, failure of 95; Internet-based Sikh organisations 95; and Jats 27; Kaurs 13, 17-18; *kesh-dhari* Khalsa 18, 82, 121, 127, 152; Khalsas (the pure) 13-15, 17-19, 77, 79; *kirpan*-carrying issues and campaigns 6, 135-8, 142, 209, 216; labour recruitment network 148-9; literacy 146; and marriage 55, 159, 169-76, 178, 184; *misls* (warrior organisations) 14, 28, 88, 216; and modernity 3, 146, 177-8, 183, 215; *mona*-Sikhs 18, 82, 96; and multiculturalism 1, 126-43; as 'new Jews' 164; *panth* (Sikh community) 13, 15, 28, 60, 73, 77, 80, 104, 109; patriarchy 177-9, 184; pluralism of 216; and political organisations 41, 94-5; post-colonial dilemmas of 198, 217, 218; professionals 2, 42, 90, 157, 160, 162, 176; puritanism 173; and racism 3, 118-19, 121, 129, 141-2, 144, 148, 151-2, 160, 165, 179-80, 196-7, 204-5, 210; Radhaswami movement and 19; *Rahit Maryada* (code of conduct) 17; reassimilation by Hinduism 17, 19; *sahaj-dharis* 18-19; and sants 75-7, 88, 90-2, 103, 109, 113; Sant Nirankar movement and 19; shedding of the turban 51; Shiromani Akali Dal (SAD) 17, 20-5, 38, 69, 74, 82, 94-5, 99-100, 102-4, 106, 111, 128, 133; Shiromani Gurdwara Parbandhak Committee (SGPC) 17, 69, 82, 88-9, 93, 182; 'Sikh political system' 17, 25, 69; Singh Sabha movement 17, 217; Singhs 13-15, 17-18; social vision of 216-17; spirituality and the sublime in

90, 92; as transnational group 2-3, 9, 40-
1, 56, 75-7, 89, 93, 108, 117-19, 124,
143, 159, 162, 169, 190, 201; turban-
wearing issues and campaigns 6, 51, 99-
100, 102, 126-38, 152, 209, 213, 216;
values (incorrectly) conflated with
ethnicity 26; and Vaisakhi festival 71, 86,
143; veteran Sikh soldiers 213; and vic-
timhood politics 118, 120-4, 180, 210-
11; wanderlust 26, 31, 56; *see also*
equality, gurdwaras, honour, Punjab,
service
Sikhs in England 119
Simla Conference (1945) 19-20
Singapore 32, 54, 73, 75, 197
Singh, Amolak 191
Singh, Amrik 106, 117
Singh, Ajmer Matharu 131
Singh, Arvindpal 194
Singh, Baba Joginder 108
Singh, Baba Thakur 92
Singh, Bachittar 117
Singh, Basant 47
Singh, Beant 111
Singh, Bhupendra 46, 71
Singh, Bhuta 146
Singh, Buta 73
Singh, Charan 91
Singh, D. 157
Singh, Darshan 111
Singh, Duleep 2, 14, 44-6, 212, 214
Singh, Fujja 213
Singh, G. B. 47
Singh, Gajinder 108
Singh, Gian 91
Singh, Giani Ajaib 191
Singh, Giani Amolak 106
Singh, Giani Bakhshish 103, 191
Singh, Giani Sher 47
Singh, Gurbachan 81, 91
Singh, Gurbax 123
Singh, Gurdev 91
Singh, Gurharpal 194
Singh, Gurmej 106-8
Singh, Guru Gobind 71, 73, 99
Singh, Hardev 91
Singh, Harjinder 194
Singh, Harmander 106
Singh, Harnek 91
Singh, Harpal 107
Singh, Indarjit 88-9, 194, 214
Singh, Jagjit 91

Singh, Jasbir 112, 183-4
Singh, Jaswant 194
Singh, Kahan 47, 195
Singh, Kapur 47
Singh, Karamjit 106-7, 123
Singh, Kashmir 119, 189
Singh, Khem 91
Singh, Khushwant 47, 214
Singh, Kirpal 91
Singh, Lachman 73
Singh, Malkit 200, 202
Singh, Manjit 111
Singh, Manmohan (Prime Minister of India)
47, 102, 108, 211
Singh, Mann 91
Singh, Marsha 121-2
Singh, Master Tara 20, 99
Singh, Mihan 75
Singh, Mohinder 91
Singh, Nahar 91
Singh, Narain 48
Singh, Naurang 91
Singh, Niranjan 91
Singh, Dr Pargat 107
Singh, Parminder 194
Singh, Patwant 47
Singh, Prem 97
Singh, Prince Ripduman 47
Singh, Pritam 122
Singh, Puran 75
Singh, Raghbir 110, 112
Singh, Rajinder 194
Singh, Rajit 14
Singh, Ranjit 81, 184
Singh, Sadhu 91
Singh, Sant Amar 75
Singh, Sant Fateh 99
Singh, Sant Mann 69
Singh, Sarup 91
Singh, Satinder 47
Singh, Sewa 106
Singh, Shahbeg 105
Singh, Shivdev 47
Singh, Swaran 113
Singh, Talvin 201
Singh, Tarlok 47
Singh, Teja 47, 70-1, 91, 96
Singh, Thakur 48
Singh, Tom 156, 157
Singh, Udham 49, 96, 203
Singh, Umaro 47
Singh, Zail 110

Singhvi, L. M. 115
single parents 166-7
Slough 51, 63, 123, 140, 142, 154, 160, 167,
    192
Smethwick 40, 63, 73-4, 83-4, 91, 109, 147,
    149, 187, 197
Smith, Zadie 197
Socialist Labour Party 123
Solihull 64
Sony 201
South Africa 37, 46, 54
Southall 51, 53-4, 63, 72, 74, 78, 80, 83, 89,
    91-2, 96-9, 106-7, 109, 111-15, 123,
    127, 129-30, 136, 142, 146, 151, 165-6,
    176, 178-9, 187, 190-5, 200, 204
Southall Black Sisters (SBS) group 178-9
Southall Youth Movement (SYM) 98
Spain 32
Spellar, John 117
Sri Lanka 32-3, 48
Star TV 190
Stevens Enquiry 149
Stratford 91
Strathclyde, Lord 134
Stychill 64
Sudan 46
Suffolk 44
Summan, Dalvir 191
Sunrise Radio 190
Suraj 200
Sweden 32
Switzerland 32, 36
Sydney 32, 38

Talwan village 48
Talwandi 48
Tanzania 53
Telford 193
Templeman, Lord 133
terrorism 2, 9, 114-15, 211; see also 9/11,
    7/7
Thailand 32
Thatcher, Margaret 4, 35, 54, 114, 135, 154,
    209
Thekedar, Jaswant Singh 108
Thetford 45
Tibet 14
Tihara 48
Tipton 148
Toor, Tarsem Singh 113, 116
Toronto 75, 197
trade unions 41, 121, 123, 147, 149-50

Transvaal (South Africa) 33
travel agents 39, 55
Trinidad 33
Tur, Mohan Singh 99
Turkey 46
Tuti Nangs gang 204

Uganda 33-4, 53-4, 131
Ukraine 32
United Akali Dal (UAD) 108
United Kingdom (UK), anti-immigration
    policies 35, 151; Anti-Terrorism, Crime
    and Security Act (2001) 138; army
    recruitment in 152; asylum-seeking
    immigration to 35-6, 55, 60; banning of
    organisations in 120; Bhatras (peddlers) in
    48, 72-3, 77-8, 146-7; British
    Nationality Act (1914) 34; British
    Nationality Act (1948) 50; British
    Nationality Act (1981) 55; Bullock
    Report (1975) 181; business culture in
    159; class in 5, 94, 96-102, 162-3, 213;
    'colonisation from below' 43, 68;
    Commonwealth Immigrants Act (1962)
    35, 50, 52-3, 166; cornershops in 154;
    Criminal Justice Act (1988) 135; depen-
    dants as immigrants to 53-5, 59; dharm
    yud morcha (1982) in 100; dot.com boom
    in 35, 156; Duleep Singh as emblem of
    Sikh experience in 45; East African Sikhs
    in 53-4, 82; economic migration to 55;
    education in 70, 133, 142-3, 145-64,
    168, 176, 178, 181, 184; Employment
    Act (1989) 134, 152; employment of
    Sikhs in 6, 66, 67, 99, 119, 134, 142,
    145-6, 166, 173, 178-80, 184; entry
    into 33-6; ethnic business in 151-6, 160,
    167, 172; ethnic organisation of
    workforce in 148-9; ethnicity and
    religion in 74, 81, 87-8, 119, 132-3, 138;
    and European Directives on the
    Education of Children of Migrant
    Workers 187; 'flexible' economy in 162;
    Health and Safety Act (1974) 137; history
    of South Asian people in 43; housing in
    142; Human Rights Act (2008) 138;
    illegal immigrants in 51, 53, 55-6, 60;
    Immigration Act (1971) 54; Indo-British
    Extradition Treaty (2002) 55, 115; indus-
    trial identity of Sikhs in 51; industrial
    tribunals in 137-8, 152; informal controls

on immigration 34, 50; informal economy 155; Khalistani movement in 6, 82, 84, 92, 94-124, 128, 132, 159, 163, 173, 191, 193, 204, 210-11, 215, 217; *kirpan*-carrying issues campaigns in 6, 135-8, 142, 209; labour needs of 50, 146; language programme for immigrants 187; leader and faction organisational form in 95, 100, 162; liberal immigration regime in 34-5, 41; litigation by Sikh rivals 98; 'Little Punjabs' in 2, 43, 60, 63-4, 121, 142-3, 162, 215; Local Government Act (1966) 187; local state in 141-3; managerial intermediary class 162-3; manufacturing economy in 35; market trading in 155; militant Sikh leadership (1984-97) 106; Motor-Cycle Crash Helmets (Religious Exemption) Act (1976) 130; Muslims in 1-2, 147, 157-8, 160-1, 166, 171, 174, 208, 211-15; National Act (1948) 34; National Curriculum (1988) 187-8; National Front in 53; national organisation for Sikhs unlikely 88-9; Naxalite campaigns in 97, 100; new social hierarchy in 162-3; out-migration from 56; overstayers in 56, 60; Powellism in 53; premier symbol of Sikh presence 69; professional Sikhs in 90; property boom in 156; Punjabi literature in 195-6; and Punjabi migration industry 39; Punjabi press in 190-5; Race Relations Act (1965, 1968, 1976) 129, 132-3, 137-8, 141; Race Relations Amendment Act (2000) 119, 138; Racial and Religious Hatred Bill (2005) 141; racism in 3, 50, 97-9, 118-19, 121, 129, 141, 144, 148, 151-2, 160, 165, 179-80, 196-7, 204-5, 210; Road Traffic Act (1972, 1988) 130; sectarian violence in 81; self-employment in 6, 154-5, 167; service provision in 142-3; Shiromani Akali Dal UK (SAD (UK)) 99-100, 103, 128, 133; Shiromani Khalsa Dal (UK) 100; Sikh family in 165-85; Sikh identity in UK 51, 65-68, 127, 132-3, 138, 142-3; Sikh middlemen and bribery culture in 148-9; Sikh political organisation in 94-124; Sikhs as 'ornaments of Empire' in 43-4, 68; Sikh population in 32-3, 36, 41, 43, 51, 57-68; Sikh princes in 44-6; Sikh settlement pattern in 2, 43-68; Sikh soldiers in 46-7;

Sikh students in 47, 56; Sikh village associations in 40-1; single-issue politics in 2, 95, 124, 126, 129, 216; social wefare system in 87, 119; Swann Report (1985) 187; sweatshops in 152-4; Terrorism Act (2000) 120; Thatcherism in 35, 54; turban-wearing issues/campaigns in 6, 99-100, 102, 126-38, 152, 209, 213, 216; UK–Punjab exchanges 143; underclass in 163; urban riots in (1970s–1980s) 1, 142; women employees in 151-4, 157, 160

United Nations 118, 120; World Conference on Racism (Durban, 2001) 118

United States (US) 32-5, 37, 40, 56, 58, 71, 75, 90, 105, 156, 171, 195, 217

University of Birmingham 188

University of Warwick 188

University of York 189

Urdu language 187, 189

Vancouver 38, 75, 197

Vedanti, Joginder Singh 120, 136

Velan, Nihal Singh Harian 91

Victoria, Queen 14, 44-5, 212, 214

violence, *Behzti* affair 138-41, 143, 178; at cricket match 123; in defence of religious sensibilities 2; domestic 178; in gurdwaras 84-5, 109; hijacking 135; and 'Khalistan' 20, 24, 94-124; *kirpan* misused 135; and poetry 12; Operation Blue Star and aftermath 105-6, 108; in Punjab history 10; sectarian 81

Virdee, Raghbir 192

Virk, Gurbax 191

Waldegrave, William 115-16

Wales 48, 62-3, 76-9, 146, 155

Walker, Peter 156

Walsall 40-1, 51, 107, 147, 175

Walsingham, Lord 44

Wangar 108, 110

war on terrorism 96, 120, 137, 211

welfare state 87

West Bromwich 75, 91, 147

West Indies 33-4, 37, 54

West Midlands 2, 32, 51-2, 62, 72, 76-8, 88-9, 96, 121, 147, 151, 153, 155-6, 165-6, 176

Whitelaw, William 170

Widgery, Lord 129

Wigston 64

Wolverhampton 51, 63, 75, 80, 91, 99, 103,

120, 123, 128, 147-8, 189, 192, 195
Woolagoogla 32
Woolf Rubber Factory 146, 151
World Sikh Festival (1982) 104

Yorkshire 62, 76-8, 147
youth 186-207

Zambia 54, 91
Zee-TV 190, 201